Probate Practitioner's Handbook

Fourth Edition

PROBATE PRACTITIONER'S HANDBOOK

Fourth Edition

General Editor:

Lesley King *Solicitor*
Principal Lecturer at The College of Law

The Law Society

First published 1991
2nd edition 1995
3rd edition 1999
This 4th edition 2003

ISBN 1 85328 831 4

The Solicitors' (Non-Contentious Business) Remuneration Order 1994
reproduced in Chapter 2 is Crown copyright.

Published by the Law Society
113 Chancery Lane, London WC2A 1PL
Typeset by J&L Composition, Filey, North Yorkshire
Printed by TJ International Ltd, Padstow, Cornwall

Contents

Preface

This is the fourth edition of the Handbook. I hope that it will be as useful to the profession as the previous ones. Practice in general is changing with frightening speed and probate practice particularly so. Practitioners need to be aware of recent developments in law, tax, practice and client care. At the same time they have to be able to market themselves and their firms effectively. It is a daunting task and I hope that this Handbook will assist by gathering together the different areas into one book.

I am very grateful for all the help I have received from the Law Society and from the contributors who have been so generous with their time.

Professor Lesley King
College of Law and Member of the Law Society's Wills and Equity Committee

Abbreviations

ACTAPS	Association of Contentious Trusts and Probate Practitioners
AEA 1925	Administration of Estates Act 1925
AIDA	attention, interest, desire, action
AIEDPO 1986	Administration of Insolvent Estates of Deceased Persons Order 1986, SI 1986/1999
AJA 1982	Administration of Justice Act 1982
BMA	British Medical Association
CGT	capital gains tax
CPR	Civil Procedure Rules 1998, SI 1998/3132
CRM	client relationship management
CTO	Capital Taxes Office
DPB	designated professional body
ECA 2000	Electronic Communication Act 2000
EPA	enduring power of attorney
FILEX	Fellow of the Institute of Legal Executives
FOS	Financial Services Ombudsman
FSA	Financial Services Authority
FSMA 2000	Financial Services and Markets Act 2000
IHT	inheritance tax
IHTA 1984	Inheritance Tax Act 1984
IIP	Investors in People
IT	information technology
ITT	invitation to tender
IPFDA 1975	Inheritance (Provision for Family and Dependants) Act 1975
IPS	inadequate professional services
LSC	Legal Services Commission
NCPR 1987	Non-Contentious Probate Rules 1987, SI 1987/2024
OSS	Office for the Supervision of Solicitors
PESTE	political, economic, sociological, technological, environmental
PMS	Practice Management Standards

PR	personal representative
RAO 2000	Financial Services and Markets Act 2000 (Regulated Activities) Order 2000, SI 2000/544
ROI	return on investment
RSC	Rules of the Supreme Court 1965, SI 1965/1776
SDV	superior delivered value
SIF	Solicitors' Indemnity Fund
SMART	specific, measurable, achievable, realistic, timed
STEP	Society of Trust and Estate Practitioners
SWOT	strengths, weaknesses, opportunities, threats
TCGA 1992	Taxation of Chargeable Gains Act 1992
TLATA 1996	Trusts of Land and Appointment of Trustees Act 1996
TMA 1970	Taxes Management Act 1970
WPS	written professional standards

Notes on contributors

Meg Andrews is Senior Partner at Hartley & Worstenholme Solicitors, West Yorkshire.

Richard Bark-Jones is Partner at Morecroft Urquhart Solicitors, Liverpool.

Peter Camp runs his own training consultancy, Educational and Professional Services and is a visiting Professor of Ethics at the College of Law.

Charles Christian is Editor of the *Legal Technology Insider* newsletter and the Law Society's annual *Software Solutions Guide*.

Helen Clarke is Partner at Beviss and Beckingsale Solicitors, Somerset.

Gillian E. Cockburn runs her own practice, Cockburns, Guildford.

Steven Fennell is Partner at Dibb Lupton Allsop (DLA), Sheffield.

Mike Frith is Consultant, Client Care and Practice Standards based at the Law's Society's Office for the Supervision of Solicitors.

Henry Frydenson is Partner at Berwin Leighton Paisner, London.

Dawn Goodman is Partner at Withers LLP, London.

David Hodson is Partner at The Family Law Consortium (www.tflc.co.uk).

Peter Johnson is former Head of Client Care and Compliance at the Law Society's Office for the Supervision of Solicitors.

Lesley King is a solicitor and Principal Lecturer at the College of Law.

Sue Medder is a solicitor at Withers LLP, London.

Gill Steel is a solicitor and Director of LawSkills Ltd, Consultants and Trainers.

Kim Tasso is a marketing consultant and freelance journalist specialising in marketing the professions.

David Wright is Customer Services Manager at Inland Revenue (Capital Taxes), Nottingham.

PART I

Probate and the Professional Rules

This Part covers the interaction of the professional rules with probate and estate administration work and deals particularly with some of the aspects of those rules which have caused difficulty to practitioners in the past.

The Professional Ethics Division of the Law Society (see Appendix 6) may be able to help you with difficult matters. You can write or phone and help is confidential.

Please note that in this Handbook references are made to *The Guide to the Professional Conduct of Solicitors 1999*. Updates to the Guide are available on the Law Society website at **www.guide-on-line.lawsociety.org.uk**.

CHAPTER 1

Solicitors and instructions

Richard Bark-Jones

1.1 WHO IS MY CLIENT?

1.1.1 Personal representatives (PRs)

In probate and estate administration, the solicitor's clients are the personal representatives (PRs) and not the beneficiaries or friends and family of the PR. Problems can arise if a PR is elderly and a son or daughter offers to act for him or her. Here, as in other legal work, a solicitor's instructions should come directly from the client – otherwise the PR should consider renunciation or the appointment of an attorney. A PR may be replaced under Administration of Justice Act 1985, s.50 or passed over under Supreme Court Act 1981, s.116.

As an alternative to renunciation, one of two or more executors may choose to have power reserved to him or her which gives the option to get involved later (the power reserved process is simpler than that for renunciation). Renunciation or the reservation of power might also be considered by prospective PRs who plan to be away for long periods of time, or who clearly do not wish to be involved in the administration. If this is suggested, the pros and cons should be clearly pointed out to those concerned. (A useful article on this by Philip Rossdale appeared in [1995] *Solicitors Journal*, 13 January.)

Other problems can arise if, for example, two PRs instruct one firm and later one of the PRs fails to respond to letters. If possible, grasp the nettle and clarify matters as soon as possible. There may be a clash of interests where one PR is also a beneficiary and may need to seek separate advice. Some assistance with the resulting difficulty over costs may be available (see 15.8 below; see also requests from clients at 15.11 below).

1.1.2 Beneficiaries

Some recent cases may point the way to an extension of the liability of professionals to third parties. (Aspects of liability are considered in Chapter 6.) However, in general, beneficiaries' rights in estate administration are limited. They have the right to have the estate properly administered, but are not entitled, unless they are also PRs, to make decisions about the conduct of the administration, or to be involved in the day-to-day business of administering the estate. (Residuary beneficiaries have the right to obtain remuneration certificates in certain cases, see Chapter 2.)

Beneficiaries who are not PRs are not clients of the solicitor acting for the PRs, so it is not up to them to instruct those solicitors, but rather the PRs. Where appropriate, of course, beneficiaries' wishes, and particularly those of residuary beneficiaries, can be taken into account. This may be of particular relevance if the beneficiary is a charity and can, for example, reclaim income tax paid or avoid capital gains tax where assets are sold on behalf of the charity as bare trustee. (Charitable beneficiaries are considered further at 16.8 below.)

Bear in mind that most beneficiaries will have no idea of how much needs to be done to complete the winding up of an estate and how long it can take to do it. They may expect payment of their legacies or to be able to take possession of their gifts within, at most, a few weeks of the death. This, together with their lack of involvement in the administration, can mean worry and uncertainty for them and may possibly result in expression of unjustified dissatisfaction with the firm involved. Accordingly, obtaining the PRs' consent to telling the beneficiaries briefly of the expected timescale for completing the administration, or how long an unexpected hold-up may take to resolve, is likely to be beneficial all round. It is a good idea, when establishing the terms of your retainer with the PRs, to agree how often you will communicate with beneficiaries and the kind of information you will divulge.

It is the usual practice of many firms to notify all beneficiaries of their entitlements or legacies at an early stage. (See [1995] *New Law Journal*, Probate Supplement, 29 September for an interesting discussion of the cases by James Sunnucks.) Legatees may simply be informed or sent a copy of the relevant part of the will and residuary beneficiaries may be sent a copy of the whole will. Taking this action, and including an indication of the realistic likely date of payment, may put the beneficiaries' minds at rest and lower unrealistic expectations, as well as save time and costs in unnecessary correspondence. If your anticipated timetable changes you will need to update people who are still working to the original dates.

Solicitors approached for information by beneficiaries during the administration may wish to agree with and advise the PRs on the information to be given. This will depend on factors such as the beneficiaries' status and relationship to the PRs (and the deceased), the nature of the questions and the costs which would be involved in dealing with them. Although beneficiaries are not clients, the Office for the Supervision of Solicitors (OSS) would expect replies to letters of enquiry to be reasonably informative and to be sent reasonably promptly.

More information about trustees and beneficiaries, and the information which beneficiaries are entitled to have, is available in works such as Underhill and Hayton, *Law Relating to Trusts and Trustees* (see Appendix 5).

1.2   INSTRUCTIONS

1.2.1   General reminders

Generally, see *The Guide to the Professional Conduct of Solicitors 1999*, published by the Law Society ('the Guide'), ch. 13 on client care.

You need to be sure that the person purporting to instruct you has authority to do so (are the next of kin to be administrators or might there be an as yet untraced will appointing others as executors?) and that you know what they want you to do (agree precisely what is possible and what your firm can do). Making a summary of your instructions for the front of the file can be a useful reminder of the extent of your original retainer, particularly if more than one person is likely to be working on the file. Extensions or alterations to the retainer can be dealt with in the same way, together with the date. As a matter of routine, instructions and alterations should, of course, be confirmed in writing as soon as possible. See the Guide, ch. 13 on client care.

The case of *Cancer Research Campaign* v. *Ernest Brown & Co* [1997] STC 1425 illustrates the importance of identifying the scope of the retainer.

At this stage also consider what information the client needs from you. This Handbook contains some specimen materials which solicitors in private practice may adapt or adopt for the purpose set out on page iv but not for any other purpose. They are intended to cover certain basic points relating to succession and estate administration work.

Other materials for clients can be obtained from the Law Society (see Appendix 6). Appendix 5 contains details of what is available.

1.2.2   Difficulty with instructions

Light may be shed upon some difficulties by going back to the beginning and finding exact answers to the questions:

- Who is my client? (usually, but not always, the same as Who will pay my bill?)
- What have I been instructed to do?
- What is my role – professional, legal, practical?

The answer to the first question will help disentangle conflicts in areas where these might arise; contradictory or unacceptable instructions can be revealed by the answer to question two; and the answer to the third question can pinpoint where the difficulty lies.

Some other problems which can arise in the course of estate administration are dealt with in Chapter 15.

1.3   CONFLICTS AND DISPUTES

Conflicts sometimes arise for clients between their roles as beneficiary and PR. It is preferable for a PR to renounce before taking the grant if there are reasons to suspect a conflict. Another problem, particularly where an intestacy and a step-relationship are involved, is that one PR may feel left out or that the other is being favoured, especially if the firm acting is the other PR's usual solicitor. Both PRs should be involved in the decision-taking and it may be helpful, in these sensitive situations, to ensure that the content of conversations and correspondence with one PR is fully and promptly reported to the other.

Disputes can, of course, arise on any number of grounds – because a will is challenged, through disappointment on the part of the family about the disposition of the estate, or about the identity of the PRs. It may be appropriate to advise the client what steps the other side may take, whether seeking an opinion from counsel or a specialist solicitor or even commencing litigation, and about the costs and time implications. Clear preliminary instructions need to be obtained and confirmed in writing. Family companies can be a fertile source of difficulty. Firms who have acted for the founder and members of his or her family personally and on behalf of the business may find that the various parties are at loggerheads after the death. This may mean the firm having to cease to act for some or all of those involved.

The Guide deals extensively with conflicts of interest, principally in ch. 15.

1.3.1   Independent advice

From time to time, beneficiaries or PRs may seek independent advice about their position, perhaps because they think a lay or co-PR is mishandling an administration, or because they consider a solicitors' firm is working too slowly. Such a move creates some practical difficulties. The main one usually relates to costs. The opinion set out at 15.8 below, although it relates to PRs seeking independent advice only, may be of interest in this connection. In any event, you may wish to discuss the costs issue with those involved early on. It may also be appropriate to discuss the implications for the administration of what has happened.

Another difficulty may relate to access to papers, particularly if the disagreement centres on dissatisfaction with the firm of solicitors handling the administration. The solution to these problems is difficult, but dealing with the following questions may shed some light on the matter:

- Who is the original client of the firm?
- Has the retainer been terminated? By whom?
- To whom will duties, such as the duty of confidentiality, be owed?
- To whom should reports be made?

- If a conflict appears to have arisen, is there a conflict for the firm, in fact a conflict for the PR?

The Guide deals with termination of retainers in ch. 12.

You may have to advise a client to seek independent advice if you have made a mistake or there is concern that a mistake may have been made by you: see at 15.16 below. Remember that you must comply with the terms of your insurance contract in informing them of possible claims against you.

1.3.2   Solicitors giving evidence as to circumstances in which will was made

Solicitors may be drawn into disputes about a will after a death, for example if it is questioned whether the testator or testatrix had capacity.

Some years ago the Council of the Law Society obtained the opinion of leading counsel as a result of *Larke* v. *Nugus* on the duty of a solicitor who had acted for a testator in drawing up his will which, after the death, had been the subject of a dispute.

It was decided that a solicitor should make available a statement of his or her evidence regarding the execution of the will and circumstances surrounding it, to a person who is either a party to probate proceedings or whom the solicitor believes to have a reasonable claim under the will but who is not yet a party to any proceedings, whether or not the solicitor acted for those propounding the will. Further guidance on the position of a solicitor who may be a material witness can be found in the Guide, Principle 21.12. (Also see Chapter 11 on contentious probate.) While the facts of each matter will differ, the principle that the available information should be made accessible impartially to both sides is likely to be of value.

The advice of Professional Ethics (see Appendix 6) on all such points may be sought.

1.4   EXECUTORS IN THE OFFICE

1.4.1   Retired and non-practising solicitors

Many solicitors take up executorships during retirement or during a period in which they are consultants to their previous firms. As far as charging clauses are concerned, these will need to be interpreted to see whether they are wide enough to cover charging by a person not involved in any business. A person may not act as a solicitor, of course, unless he or she holds a current practising certificate. Solicitors merely on the Roll, i.e. non-practising and retired solicitors not holding practising certificates, may not describe themselves as solicitors or act as such, by, for example, making an application for the grant of representation as a solicitor.

1.4.2   Fee-earners about to retire or move firms

When a fee-earner leaves your firm, you may wish to resolve the question of their appointment as executor or executrix. What is to happen? Was the appointment of the individual personally (so that the testator or testatrix will probably want the fee-earner to continue to act after going to the new firm) or in effect of the firm (so that someone else in your firm should now be appointed)? Ideally the client's instructions should be obtained. Making contact in this way can also usefully remind the client that other aspects of the will may need review and revision. You should, from a marketing point of view, include an invitation to make an appointment for this; why not send a copy of the firm's brochure too? (For more on marketing, see Chapter 21.)

1.4.3   Supervision of employee PRs

The following (updated) guidance was first issued in 1991 by the Property and Commercial Services and the Standards and Guidance Committees of the Council of the Law Society:

Solicitor's clerk appointed executor of a clients will: duty of supervision

The Solicitors Complaints Bureau [as it then was] has recently had to deal with a case involving the misappropriation of trust funds by an unqualified employee of a solicitor who drafted a will for a client and was appointed under that will as sole executor. The clerk in that case administered the estate through the firm by which he was employed but the monies were held outside the firm. The Standards and Guidance Committee, in conjunction with the Property and Commercial Services Committee and the Wills and Equity Committee wish to remind solicitors of their obligation to supervise both their admitted and unadmitted staff. Principle 3.01 of the Guide states, 'A solicitor is responsible for exercising proper supervision over both admitted and unadmitted staff'.

Further, Principle 3.13 of the Guide states that, 'As a matter of conduct a partner is prima facie responsible for the acts or omissions of the firm and this extends to the acts or omissions of staff'. In particular a solicitor should take special care when exercising these functions in circumstances where a clerk is an executor or executrix whether alone or with a lay person and is administering the estate through the firm, but the money involved is being paid into an account which is outside the Accounts Rules.

Firms may wish to consider whether it would be appropriate to prohibit unqualified staff from being appointed executor or executrix for clients of the firm by inserting appropriate clauses into the contracts of employment of those staff. However, the solicitor's duty to act in the best interest of the client may mean that such a blanket prohibition would be inappropriate. Therefore consideration should be given to clauses restricting unqualified staff from being named as executor or executrix unless prior approval of a partner is obtained. Any such restrictions must not prejudice the interest of the firm's client. The contract could also provide that where an unqualified member of staff became executor or executrix on the death of a client, all estate monies should be paid into the firm's client account.

Similar points should be borne in mind where an unqualified member of staff is appointed attorney or enduring attorney for a client.

It is worth noting that the Solicitors' Accounts Rules 1998 impose some record-keeping requirements where money is held outside a firm's client bank account (e.g. where a client's own bank account is operated). See Chapter 5 for a fuller discussion.

CHAPTER 2

Costs and charging

Richard Bark-Jones

2.1 SOURCES OF INFORMATION

More information about costs and charging can be found in *The Guide to the Professional Conduct of Solicitors 1999*, published by the Law Society ('the Guide') and publications produced from time to time by the Law Society.

Textbooks such as *Cordery on Solicitors* and works on practice management may also be of interest in this connection (Appendix 5 includes details of a number of general works).

In probates the client is the lay executor. Problems may arise where the solicitor is the executor. Residuary beneficiaries have a right to obtain a remuneration certificate in certain circumstances. Details of the Solicitors' (Non-Contentions Business) Remuneration Order 1994, SI 1994/2616 (L.16) are given at 2.4 below.

In December 1998, the Council of the Law Society made the Solicitors' Costs Information and Client Care Code which is incorporated into the Solicitors' Practice (Costs Information and Client Care) Amendment Rule. The existing Rule 15 was deleted and replaced. The Code and new Rule took effect as from 3 September 1999 (see para.3.1 for full text).

The Code replaces the existing written professional standards on costs information to be provided to the client and seeks to be more specific as to what is meant by giving the best information possible on costs as well as dealing with other information that must be given to clients at the commencement of a retainer. It also details requirements concerning complaints handling and the necessity of firms having a written complaints handling procedure in place.

2.2 COSTS AND THE CLIENT

The Law Society wants openness about costs. The final charge for the administration of an estate may be difficult to predict at the outset, but most clients will not understand why and are likely to interpret vagueness and uncertainty about costs as a signal that they will be enormous or that the firm is not being frank. Either way, it is in the firm's interests (as well as in accordance with the obligations imposed by the Law Society) to give clients the facts as far as is possible. If you cannot give an idea of the cost for the whole administration, you can tell the client why, as well as what work you will have to do before you can estimate the total costs and how much it will cost the client for you to reach that point. If nothing else, clients can be told the hourly charging rate of the person handling their work, and given an idea of the number of hours involved, plus details of any known disbursements.

Such evidence as is available indicates that most clients feel they get good value from solicitors. So do not shrink from discussing fees and do include everything the client is likely to have to pay for, including disbursements. Plain speaking about costs is in everyone's interests. (See at 2.7 below and also Chapter 3 on client care.)

Solicitors should always remember Practice Rule 1 when it comes to billing. Solicitors should never put their own interests before those of the client. This is particularly important in a contentious probate when a client is proposing to spend a lot of money on legal work when there may be very little at stake.

2.3   CHARGING FOR WILLS

Although this Handbook is primarily about estate administration, will drafting is, of course, closely related. A number of general points about wills are included in Chapter 12. As with estate administration, there is a need to be open with clients and potential clients about the cost involved. However, it is often feasible to quote a definite fee for drafting a will.

Many firms offer will preparation at a price similar to the commercial will-selling services; making this known will encourage clients to consult solicitors. If your firm's charges are higher, be open about the cost and explain the good value your service offers. Explain all the reasons why seeing a solicitor is worth the extra amount. Where clients have a Legal Help contract some clients can still get help with will drafting under the Legal Help Scheme. Eligibility is the same as that which applied to the Green Form Scheme.

2.4   SOLICITORS' (NON-CONTENTIOUS BUSINESS) REMUNERATION ORDER 1994

(This section is based on an article which originally appeared in [1994] *Gazette*, 28 September, 31.)

The main text of the Order is set out below. An article-by-article commentary starts at 2.5 below. A specimen of the information you must give entitled persons is given at para. 2.6. A statement entitled 'Relevant factors when giving costs information for non-contentious work' appears at para. 2.7 and draws together and updates existing guidance about giving costs information to clients.

SOLICITORS (NON-CONTENTIOUS BUSINESS) REMUNERATION ORDER 1994, SI 1994/2616 (L. 16)

The Lord Chancellor, the Lord Chief Justice, the Master of the Rolls, the President of the Law Society, the president of Holborn law society and the Chief Land Registrar (in respect of business done under the Land Registration Act 1925 [1925 c.21], together constituting the committee authorised to make orders under section 56 of the Solicitors Act 1974 [1974 c.47, as modified by the Administration of Justice Act 1985 (c.61), Schedule 2, paragraphs 22 and 23], in exercise of the powers conferred on them by that section and having complied with the requirements of section 56(3), hereby make the following Order:

Citation, commencement and revocation

1. – (1)   This Order may be cited as the Solicitors' (Non-Contentious Business) Remuneration Order 1994.
   (2)   This Order shall come into force on 1st November 1994 and shall apply to all non-contentious business for which bills are delivered on or after that date.
   (3)   The Solicitors' Remuneration Order 1972 [SI 1972/1139] is hereby revoked except in its application to business for which bills are delivered before this Order comes into force.

Interpretation

2.   In this Order:
   'client' means the client of a solicitor;
   'costs' means the amount charged in a solicitor's bill, exclusive of disbursements and value added tax, in respect of non-contentious business or common form probate business;
   'entitled person' means a client or an entitled third party;
   'entitled third party' means a residuary beneficiary absolutely and immediately (and not contingently) entitled to an inheritance, where a solicitor has charged the estate for his professional costs for acting in the administration of the estate, and either

   (a)   the only personal representatives are solicitors (whether or not acting in a professional capacity); or
   (b)   the only personal representatives are solicitors acting jointly with partners or employees in a professional capacity;

   'paid disbursements' means disbursements already paid by the solicitor;
   'recognised body' means a body corporate recognised by the Council under section 9 of the Administration of Justice Act 1985 [1985, c.61];
   'remuneration certificate' means a certificate issued by the Council pursuant to this Order;

'residuary beneficiary' includes a person entitled to all or part of the residue of an intestate estate;

'solicitor' includes a recognised body;

'the Council' means the Council of the Law Society.

Solicitors' costs

3.   A solicitor's costs shall be such sum as may be fair and reasonable to both solicitor and entitled person, having regard to all the circumstances of the case and in particular to:

(a)   the complexity of the matter or the difficulty or novelty of the questions raised;

(b)   the skill, labour, specialised knowledge and responsibility involved;

(c)   the time spent on the business;

(d)   the number and importance of the documents prepared or perused, without regard to length;

(e)   the place where and the circumstances in which the business or any part thereof is transacted;

(f)   the amount or value of any money or property involved;

(g)   whether any land involved is registered land;

(h)   the importance of the matter to the client; and

(i)   the approval (express or implied) of the entitled person or the express approval of the testator to:

   (i)   the solicitor undertaking all or any part of the work giving rise to the costs or

   (ii)   the amount of the costs.

Right to certification

4. – (1)   Without prejudice to the provisions of sections 70, 71 and 72 of the Solicitors Act 1974 (which relate to taxation of costs), an entitled person may, subject to the provisions of this Order, require a solicitor to obtain a remuneration certificate from the Council in respect of a bill which has been delivered where the costs are not more than £50,000.

(2)   The remuneration certificate must state what sum, in the opinion of the Council, would be a fair and reasonable charge for the business covered by the bill (whether it be the sum charged or a lesser sum). In the absence of taxation the sum payable in respect of such costs is the sum stated in the remuneration certificate.

Disciplinary and other measures

5. – (1)   If on a taxation the taxing officer allows less than one half of the costs, he must bring the facts of the case to the attention of the Council.

(2)   The provisions of this Order are without prejudice to the general powers of the Council under the Solicitors Act 1974.

Commencement of proceedings against a client

6. –   Before a solicitor brings proceedings to recover costs against a client on a bill for non-contentious business he must inform the client in writing of the matters specified in article 8, except where the bill has been taxed.

Costs paid by deduction

7. – (1) If a solicitor deducts his costs from monies held for or on behalf of a client or of an estate in satisfaction of a bill and an entitled person objects in writing to the amount of the bill within the prescribed time, the solicitor must immediately inform the entitled person in writing of the matters specified in article 8, unless he has already done so.

(2) In this article and in article 10, 'the prescribed time' means:

(a) in respect of a client, three months after delivery of the relevant bill, or a lesser time (which may not be less than one month) specified in writing to the client at the time of delivery of the bill, or

(b) in respect of an entitled third party, three months after delivery of notification to the entitled party of the amount of the costs, or a lesser time (which may not be less than one month) specified in writing to the entitled third party at the time of such notification.

Information to be given in writing to entitled person

8. When required by articles 6 or 7, a solicitor shall inform an entitled person in writing of the following matters:

(a) where article 4(1) applies:

(i) that the entitled person may, within one month of receiving from the solicitor the information specified in this article or (if later) of delivery of the bill or notification of the amount of the costs, require the solicitor to obtain a remuneration certificate; and

(ii) that (unless the solicitor has agreed to do so) the Council may waive the requirements of article 11(1), if satisfied from the client's written application that exceptional circumstances exist to justify granting a waiver;

(b) that sections 70, 71 and 72 of the Solicitors Act 1974 set out the entitled person's rights in relation to taxation;

(c) that (where the whole of the bill has not been paid, by deduction or otherwise) the solicitor may charge interest on the outstanding amount of the bill in accordance with article 14.

Loss by client of right to certification

9. A client may not require a solicitor to obtain a remuneration certificate:

(a) after a bill has been delivered and paid by the client, other than by deduction;

(b) where a bill has been delivered, after the expiry of one month from the date on which the client was informed in writing of the matters specified in article 8 or from delivery of the bill if later;

(c) after the solicitor and client have entered into a non-contentious business agreement in accordance with the provisions of section 57 of the Solicitors Act 1974;

(d) after a court has ordered the bill to be taxed;

(e) if article 11(2) applies.

Loss by entitled third party of right to certification

10. – An entitled third party may not require a solicitor to obtain a remuneration certificate:

    (a) after the prescribed time (within the meaning of article 7(2)(b)) has elapsed without any objection being received to the amount of the costs;

    (b) after the expiry of one month from the date on which the entitled third party was (in compliance with article 7) informed in writing of the matters specified in article 8 or from notification of the costs if later;

    (c) after a court has ordered the bill to be taxed.

Requirement to pay a sum towards the costs

11. – (1) On requiring a solicitor to obtain a remuneration certificate a client must pay to the solicitor the paid disbursements and value added tax comprised in the bill together with 50% of the costs unless:

    (a) the client has already paid the amount required under this article, by deduction from monies held or otherwise; or

    (b) the solicitor or (if the solicitor refuses) the Council has agreed in writing to waive all or part of this requirement.

    (2) The Council shall be under no obligation to provide a remuneration certificate, and the solicitor may take steps to obtain payment of his bill if the client, having been informed of his right to seek a waiver of the requirements of paragraph (1), has not:

    (a) within one month of receipt of the information specified in article 8, either paid in accordance with paragraph (1) or applied to the Council in writing for a waiver of the requirements of paragraph (1); or

    (b) made payment in accordance with the requirements of paragraph (1) within one month of written notification that he has been refused a waiver of those requirements by the Council.

Miscellaneous provisions

12. – (1) After an application has been made by a solicitor for a remuneration certificate the client may pay the bill in full without invalidating the application.

    (2) A solicitor and entitled person may agree in writing to waive the provisions of sub-paragraphs (a) or (b) of articles 9 or 10.

    (3) A solicitor may take from his client security for the payment of any costs, including the amount of any interest to which the solicitor may become entitled under article 14.

Refunds by solicitor

13. – (1) If a solicitor has received payment of all or part of his costs and a remuneration certificate is issued for less than the sum already paid, the solicitor must immediately pay to the entitled person any refund which may be due (after taking into account any other sums which may properly be payable to the solicitor whether for costs, paid disbursements, value added tax or otherwise) unless the solicitor has

applied for an order for taxation within one month of receipt by him of the remuneration certificate.

(2) Where a solicitor applies for taxation, his liability to pay any refund under paragraph (1) shall be suspended for so long as the taxation is still pending.

(3) The obligation of the solicitor to repay costs under paragraph (1) is without prejudice to any liability of the solicitor to pay interest on the repayment by virtue of any enactment, rule of law or professional rule.

Interest

14. –(1) After the information specified in article 8 has been given to an entitled person in compliance with articles 6 or 7, a solicitor may charge interest on the unpaid amount of his costs plus any paid disbursements and value added tax, subject to paragraphs (2) and (3) below.

(2) Where an entitlement to interest arises under paragraph (1), and subject to any agreement made between a solicitor and client, the period for which interest may be charged may run from one month after the date of delivery of a bill, unless the solicitor fails to lodge an application within one month of receipt of a request for a remuneration certificate under article 4, in which case no interest is payable in respect of the period between one month after receiving the request and the actual date on which the application is lodged.

(3) Subject to any agreement made between a solicitor and client, the rate of interest must not exceed the rate for the time being payable on judgment debts.

(4) Interest charged under this article must be calculated, where applicable, by reference to the following:

(a) if a solicitor is required to obtain a remuneration certificate, the total amount of the costs certified by the Council to be fair and reasonable plus paid disbursements and value added tax;

(b) if an application is made for the bill to be taxed, the amount ascertained on taxation;

(c) if an application is made for the bill to be taxed or a solicitor is required to obtain a remuneration certificate and for any reason the taxation or application for a remuneration certificate does not proceed, the unpaid amount of the costs shown in the bill or such lesser sum as may be agreed between the solicitor and the client, plus paid disbursements and value added tax.

Application by solicitor

15. A solicitor, when making an application for a remuneration certificate in accordance with the provisions of this Order, must deliver to the Council the complete relevant file and working papers, and any other information or documentation which the Council may require for the purpose of providing a remuneration certificate.

Explanatory Note

(This note is not part of the Order)

Section 56 of the Solicitors Act 1974 establishes a Committee with power to make general orders regulating the remuneration of solicitors in respect of non-contentious business. Paragraph 22(2) of Schedule 2 to the Administration of Justice Act 1985 modifies the section so that references to solicitors include references to recognised bodies (solicitors' incorporated practices recognised under section 9 of the Administration of Justice Act 1985). This Order sets out the rights of solicitors' clients and residuary beneficiaries of certain estates to require the solicitor charging the client or estate to obtain a certificate from the Law Society as to the reasonableness of his costs. The Order prescribes requirements in relation to information to be given in writing to clients and beneficiaries who are entitled to require a solicitor to obtain a certificate, and lays certain obligations on clients, beneficiaries and solicitors.

2.5 LAW SOCIETY'S COMMENTARY ON THE 1994 ORDER

2.5.1 Article 1: citation, commencement and revocation

The Order came into force on 1 November 1994. It applies only to matters for which bills are delivered on or after 1 November 1994; the Solicitors' Remuneration Order 1972 applies to bills delivered previously. The Solicitors' Remuneration Order 1972 is revoked from 1 November 1994 in respect of all bills delivered on or after that date.

2.5.2 Article 2: Interpretation

Although it is not stated, the Interpretation Act 1978 applies in the new Order where article 2 is silent. 'Client', 'paid disbursements', 'recognised body', 'remuneration certificate', 'solicitor' and 'the Council' are defined. 'Costs' is defined as the amount charged exclusive of VAT and disbursements. 'Residuary beneficiary' is defined as including a person entitled to all or part of the residue of an intestate estate.

'Entitled third party' is defined as a residuary beneficiary who is entitled to ask the solicitor to obtain a remuneration certificate. The definition has the following effect:

- A residuary beneficiary of an estate where there is at least one lay executor or executrix is *not* an entitled third party.
- A residuary beneficiary of an estate in which all the personal representatives are solicitors *would* be able to ask the solicitor billing the estate to obtain a remuneration certificate, even if the bill is from another solicitor (not a personal representative) instructed by the personal representatives to do the work.

- A residuary beneficiary who will become entitled only upon the happening of some event – for example a person entitled subject to a life interest, or a minor entitled only on majority – is *not* an entitled third party.

'Entitled person' is defined as a person entitled to a remuneration certificate – a client or an entitled third party.

2.5.3 Article 3: matters taken into account 'in particular'

Note the importance of an entitled person's express or implied approval, or a testator's or testatrix's express approval, of the amount of the costs or any particular work giving rise to the costs. If, for example, the file shows compliance with the written professional standards, recorded discussions with the client authorising unusual work, or an express provision in a will or in a document referred to in a will, it could operate in a solicitor's favour in assessing the reasonableness of the costs.

2.5.4 Article 4: right to certification

Note the £50,000 limit.

2.5.5 Article 5: disciplinary and other measures

Note the reference to the general disciplinary powers of the Law Society.

2.5.6 Article 6: obligation to give information before suing on a bill

Note the information required to be given. (See the specimen 'Notice of Rights' at 2.6 below.)

2.5.7 Article 7: obligation to give information when costs have been taken by deduction

Note there is no *automatic* obligation in deduction cases to send out the information which a solicitor must send to a client before suing on an unpaid bill. There is an obligation, where costs have been taken by deduction from money held by the solicitor on behalf of a client or on behalf of an estate, and an entitled person (client or residuary beneficiary) raises written objections to the amount of the costs within three months, that information must be given 'immediately' to the person raising the objections.

The normal time which must be allowed for the entitled person to raise objections is three months. The solicitor may, however, stipulate a shorter time when sending the bill or notification of costs. The shorter time must not be less than one month.

2.5.8   Article 8: information to be given to the entitled person

If required to do so under article 6 or 7 the solicitor must inform the entitled person:

- of the right to ask for a remuneration certificate;
- that the entitled person must ask for a remuneration certificate within one month of receipt of the information about their rights, or within one month of receipt of the bill or notification of the costs if later;
- that the client may apply to the Society for a waiver of the requirement to pay half the amount of the bill, VAT and paid disbursements, when requesting a remuneration certificate, if exceptional circumstances apply. (The solicitor can, of course, waive the advance payment. This may reduce delay in obtaining the certificate and eventual payment of costs);
- of the entitled person's rights in connection with taxation of the bill; and
- of the solicitor's right to charge interest on the outstanding bill.

2.5.9   Article 9: loss by client of the right to a remuneration certificate

Note the situations in which a client loses this right and, in particular:

- where there is a non-contentious business agreement; and
- where the client has not paid half the costs in advance of the application as required by article 11, and has not obtained or applied in writing for a waiver.

2.5.10   Article 10: loss by entitled third party of the right to a remuneration certificate

The provisions of this article are, with the appropriate modifications, the same as those applying in respect of clients, except that there is no mention of the bill being delivered and paid, or of the requirement that half the costs be paid, as costs will have been taken by deduction from the estate. There is no mention of a non-contentious business agreement; normally there could be no such agreement as a person cannot enter into a contract with himself or herself.

2.5.11   Article 11: requirement to pay a sum towards the costs

As a prerequisite to obtaining a remuneration certificate a client who has not already done so must pay half the costs and all the VAT and paid disbursements before the solicitor is obliged to apply for a remuneration certificate. The requirement may be waived by the solicitor or by the Law Society on application by the client if the solicitor has refused to do so, providing exceptional circumstances exist to justify waiving the requirement. The Law Society will have regard to the fact that a remuneration certificate rarely reduces the solicitor's costs by more than half, so normally a client will in the end pay at least half of the costs.

2.5.12 Article 12: miscellaneous

This article sets out various provisions which are not easy to classify. Note in particular that:

- if the application for a certificate has been made the client can pay the bill without invalidating the application;
- if the solicitor and client agree in writing, the client will *not* lose his or her right to a remuneration certificate by paying the bill or by asking 'out of time' for the solicitor to obtain a remuneration certificate;
- the solicitor has the right to take security for the payment of costs (this provision mirrors article 6 of the old Order).

2.5.13 Article 13: refunds of money due to an entitled person, and interest on refund moneys

This article is new; it specifies the implied duty to refund any overpayment arising from a remuneration certificate being issued for a smaller sum than that shown on the certificate, where costs have already been paid in full. The solicitor must make the refund immediately unless he or she 'appeals' the certificate by applying for taxation of the bill within one month of receiving the certificate.

The article also flags up the possibility that the refund may carry interest under the Solicitors' Accounts Rules or under trust law, since the money to be refunded will have been held by the solicitor for a period 'on behalf of' the client or the estate.

2.5.14 Article 14: interest payable on unpaid costs

The provisions of this article mirror article 5 of the old Order, with additions. Since in estate cases money will have been taken by deduction these provisions only apply in respect of clients who have not paid the whole of the bill. As with the old Order a solicitor who has given a client the information required before suing on the bill may charge interest at the judgment debt rate on the unpaid amount from one month after delivery of the bill. Note in particular:

- the solicitor and client may agree that interest will run from before or after the date of delivery of the bill, or that interest will be charged at a higher or lower rate than the judgment debt rate (interest runs from one month after the date of delivery of the bill unless the solicitor and client agree otherwise);

- if the solicitor delays in applying for a remuneration certificate interest may not be charged for the period between one month after the client's request and the date on which the solicitor makes the application to the Law Society;
- interest is chargeable on the amount certified unless either the application is withdrawn or there is a taxation of the bill; in which case it is chargeable on the full amount in the bill or the taxed amount respectively.

2.5.15   Article 15: applications

This article requires the solicitor to supply the file and any other information or documentation required for the purpose of providing a remuneration certificate.

2.6   SPECIMEN 'NOTICE OF RIGHTS'

This specimen information for entitled persons is not part of the Order and you may use any form of words which complies with the requirements of the Order.

Remuneration certificates

(1)   If you are not satisfied with the amount of our fee you have the right to ask us to obtain a remuneration certificate from the Law Society.

(2)   The certificate will either say that our fee is fair and reasonable, or it will substitute a lower fee.

(3)   If you wish us to obtain a certificate you must ask us to do so *within a month* of receiving this notice.

(4)   We may charge interest on unpaid bills and we will do so at [the rate payable on judgment debts, from one month after delivery of our bill].

(5)   (a)   If you ask us to obtain a remuneration certificate, then, unless we already hold the money to cover these, you must first pay:

- half our fee shown in the bill;
- all the VAT shown on the bill;
- all the expenses we have incurred shown in the bill – sometimes called 'paid disbursements'.

> (b) However, you may ask the Law Society [see Appendix 6 for contact details] to waive this requirement so that you do not have to pay anything for the time being. You would have to show that exceptional circumstances apply in your case.
>
> (6) Your rights are set out more fully in the Solicitors' (Non-Contentious Business) Remuneration Order 1994.
>
> **Assessment of costs**
>
> You may be entitled to have our charges reviewed by the court. (This is called 'assessment of costs'.) The procedure is different from the remuneration certificate procedure and it is set out in Solicitors Act 1974, ss. 70, 71 and 72. Where appropriate it refers to the new Practice Rule 15.

2.7 RELEVANT FACTORS WHEN GIVING COST INFORMATION FOR NON-CONTENTIOUS WORK

2.7.1 Introduction

The rest of this chapter draws together and updates the existing guidance available to the profession about giving costs information to clients, particularly with regard to estimates, quotations, or other costs indications.

2.7.2 Solicitors' Costs Information and Client Care Code 1999

The Solicitors' Costs Information and Client Care Code is designed to ensure that clients know the name and status of the person(s) responsible for both the day-to-day conduct and overall supervision of their matters which is an ongoing requirement that lasts throughout the retainer. It also requires that clients are at all relevant times given appropriate information as to the issues raised and progress of those matters.

Firms are required to maintain their own procedures for dealing with complaints about the service received and in practical terms, such complaints usually manifest themselves at the time of billing. The new Code requires that in addition to the requirement to inform the client of the name of the person handling the case and to operate a complaints handling procedure, solicitors will also be required to give 'appropriate' information as to the costs of any matter (both professional fees and disbursements). The full text of the new Code is set out in Chapter 3.

What is 'appropriate' is explained in the Code.

2.7.3 Lexcel

The Practice Management Standards under Lexcel were last revised in July 2000. The standards encourage compliance with the Code and can be viewed at **www.lexcel.lawsociety.org.uk**.

2.7.4 Client care letter

The best way of ensuring compliance with Rule 15 and the Code is to send the client, as soon as possible after instructions are taken, a comprehensive client care or terms of business letter

The Law Society has designed a series of sample letters to assist with compliance with the new Code. There is no reason why practitioners should not devise their own letter to suit the particular needs or circumstances of the client. From the Committee's standpoint, the existence of such a letter is *prima facie* evidence of compliance with the Code.

2.7.5 Agreements under Solicitors Act 1974, s.57 (as amended)

Solicitors who enter into a written agreement signed by the client concerning their costs or remuneration (including hourly rates) will find that these can only be challenged through the courts as they are outside the scope of the remuneration certifying procedure. However, to qualify as such an agreement, the terms must be precise and unambiguous (*Chamberlain* v. *Boodle & King* [1982] 3 All ER 188).

Depending on the wording used, solicitors may find that if the client signs and returns a client care or terms of business letter of the type referred to above, then a s.57 agreement may have been entered into.

If a solicitor is involved in a costs dispute, care should be taken by the solicitor to make sure there is no s.57 agreement in existence. If there is, then the solicitor may be inviting further difficulties with the client by telling them about remedies which are not, in fact, available.

2.7.6 Other Law Society advice

In November 1999 the Law Society published the booklet *Non-Contentious Costs*, available from the Practice Advice Service (see Appendix 6) or the website. This states that when charging for non-contentious work solicitors must consider the Solicitors' (Non-Contentious Business) Remuneration Order 1994, art. 3. It suggests the following guidelines for charging in Probate and Estate Administration. They are only guidelines and the overall consideration is still that the charges are fair and reasonable.

1. *Hourly rate.* This should be an inclusive figure incorporating the fee earner's expense rate and any care and conduct uplift.

2. *Value element.* Account may be taken of the value of the assets in the estate. The guidelines are as follows:

Consider the value, nature and number of assets

The deceased's home

The value of the deceased's home, or as much of it as he or she owned, if it was shared with another person. Where the property is jointly owned, the value is reduced by half.

Apply the following percentages

- *Solicitor not acting as executor*

Value of gross estate less residence	1.0%
Value of residence	0.5%

- *Solicitor acting as sole executor or joint executor with another person*

Value of gross estate less residence	1.5%
Value of residence	0.5%

- *Solicitor not acting as executor but acting for corporate executor*

	General conduct of matter	Probate application only
Value of gross estate less residence	0.5%	[one-sixth of a per cent]
Value of residence	0.25%	[one-twelfth of a per cent]

- *Solicitor acting as joint executor with a corporate executor*

Value of gross estate less residence	[three-quarters of a per cent]
Value of residence	[three-eighths of a per cent]

When dealing with high value estates solicitors should consider reducing the value element percentage charged to ensure that the overall level of charge is fair and reasonable. For general guidance on this point see *Maltby* v. *D. J. Freeman* [1978] 2 All ER 913.

The guidance concludes by referring readers to an earlier Law Society publication, *An Approach to Non-Contentious Costs* (now out of print), on charging in respect of jointly owned property passing by survivorship and guidance on costs where PRs are separately represented.

The decision in *Jemma Trust Company* v. *Kippax Beaumont Lewis and Others* (2 September 2002) will be of great concern to probate practitioners. In a judgment on the costs charged in a high value administration Master Rodgers reviewed *Maltby* v. *D. J. Freeman* and came to the conclusion 'now that hourly rates are calculated, invariably, on the basis of sophisticated time recording material, that it is anachronistic and wrong to include an additional element in respect of value'. It is understood that the firm involved will appeal. In a recent survey carried out by the Probate Section, 73 per cent of those who responded said that they charged both an hourly rate and a value element. The result of the appeal will obviously be of great importance to probate practitioners.

2.7.7 Estimates, quotations or other indications of cost

The word 'indication' is used where appropriate to include quotations and estimates. It is advisable that indications are given by an authorised responsible member of a firm and that a standard procedure for giving indications is adopted within the firm. All such indications should be readily visible on the file.

All indications should be confirmed in writing to the client. The final amount payable should not vary substantially from the relevant indication unless the client has been informed in writing at the time that there was a change of circumstances.

If a solicitor wishes to give a qualified indication, e.g. by stating that it may be reviewed if the matter develops in an unforeseen manner or turns out to be more complex or difficult than originally envisaged, then such an indication will still be binding on the solicitor unless he informs the client immediately and in writing of the change in circumstances. The solicitor should point out that the original indication no longer stands and/or the client's instructions to proceed should be sought.

In cases where the solicitor's fee is to be paid by a third party, it may be that the indication has only been given to the third party and not to the solicitor's client. In such cases (depending on the overall circumstances) the same principles as set out above in relation to solicitor and own client indications will generally apply.

2.7.8 Consumer Protection Act 1987, Part III

Practitioners are reminded that indications could fall within the Consumer Protection Act 1987, s.20. Section 20 sets out the circumstances in which a misleading indication could give rise to a criminal offence.

2.7.9 Solicitors' (Non-Contentious Business) Remuneration Order 1994

Article 3 states that a solicitor's remuneration in non-contentious business 'shall be such sum as may be fair and reasonable having regard to all the circumstances of the case'.

The normal practice of the Appeals and Adjudication Committee would be to regard any indication of the likely cost of the matter as a material consideration to be taken into account in the giving of a certificate if it appears that the indication was given as an incentive to the client to give instructions to that solicitor, or that the client relied on the indication.

The Committee will therefore normally hold an indication (whether oral or written) to be binding upon the solicitor giving it. Similarly, it is the policy of the Committee to view a material breach of Rule 15 and the Solicitors' Costs Information and Client Care Code 1999 as a circumstance to be taken into account in assessing a fair and reasonable fee under the above Order.

Where there is a dispute as to whether an oral indication has been given, the Committee will try to ascertain from the available documentation and circumstances whether the claim that an oral indication was given can be justified.

2.7.10   Office for the Supervision of Solicitors (OSS)

A material breach of Rule 15 and the Code could lead to a finding (by the Committee) that the solicitor has provided inadequate professional services (IPS) or, in a serious or persistent case, a finding (after reference to the Solicitors' Disciplinary Tribunal) of professional misconduct. Similarly, the exceeding of costs without appropriate notice or warning could, depending on the particular circumstances of the case, result in the fee being reduced to the indication figure if the matter is subject to an IPS investigation.

It therefore follows that the principles applied to remuneration certificates apply equally to IPS investigations in the context of costs indications.

2.7.11   Change of circumstance

A solicitor is required to notify the client immediately, and in writing, if a change of circumstances has occurred so that the original qualified indication no longer applies. It is appreciated that some special circumstance, e.g. a contract race, may make it impractical for the solicitor to revise the indication in the way contemplated by the statement.

Solicitors should take extra care in these circumstances to ensure that the client does not rely on the indication if it has become misleading.

2.7.12   Split transactions

Where a transaction has a number of parts (e.g. the purchase of a property, the creation or discharge of a mortgage or the registration of title) the indication, unless it states otherwise, will be deemed to include all of these matters. The view that an indication only covers the basic transaction and that a charge can be raised in addition for ancillary matters such as registration of title is not acceptable and this may well be (depending on the circumstances) a misleading indication.

2.7.13   Petty disbursements

The practice of adding petty disbursements such as postage, telephone calls
and faxes to the final bill is generally unacceptable. Petty disbursements are
considered to be part of the overheads of the firm. They are expenses of the
firm and should be included in the calculation of the fee even if there is an
indication that petty disbursements will not normally be allowed, unless there
is a specific agreement to the contrary.

Where a transaction is likely to involve substantial telephone work, faxing
or photocopying, it should be made clear to the client if such items are to be
charged in addition to any indication of costs.

2.7.14   Abortive matters

In general, where an indication has been given for a completed transaction
and it does not proceed to completion, the charge for the abortive work
should be made on a *pro rata* basis. In the context of conveyancing, an indication given for a sale will normally be held to include all abortive sales unless
the solicitor has revised his indication at the appropriate time.

In a purchase transaction, it is in both the solicitor's and the client's interests that the extent of the indication is revised in writing as soon as abortive
matters make it clear that the original indication is no longer appropriate.

In all abortive matter cases, the Appeals and Adjudication Committee will
look closely at the available evidence and decide the scope of the indication

[See at 15.7 below in connection with estates which turn out to be
insolvent.]

2.7.15   Approximations

Where an indication is expressed in forms such as 'about £500', or 'approximately £500', it would normally be expected that the final fee charged would
be within 10 per cent of the indicated figure. Any fee outside that tolerance
may (depending on the circumstances) be viewed as a substantial variation
resulting in the original approximation restricting the solicitor's fee.

2.7.16   Time limits

When confirming an indication, it is advisable to make clear the time period
within which the indication will remain valid. Failure to do so may well
(depending on the circumstances of the case) result in the solicitor being held
to what he considers to be an out-of-date figure, particularly where it is clear
that the client still viewed the indication as an incentive to instruct the
solicitor and relied upon it.

CHAPTER 3

Client care

Peter Johnson

Publications on client care are included in Appendix 5. *Keeping Clients* and a booklet entitled *Handling Complaints Effectively* can be found on the Law Society's website at **www.clientcare. lawsociety.org.uk** (see also Appendix 6 for Practice Standards Unit contact details).

3.1 PRACTICE RULE 15 AND SOURCES OF INFORMATION

The Solicitors' Practice (Costs Information and Client Care) Amendment Rule 1999 came into force on 3 September 1999. The amended rule provides for a replacement Rule 15 as follows:

Rule 15 (Costs information and client care)

Solicitors shall:

(a) give information about costs and other matters; and
(b) operate a complaints handling procedure

in accordance with a Solicitors' Costs Information and Client Care Code made from time to time by the Council of the Law Society with the concurrence of the Master of the Rolls, but subject to the notes.

Notes

(i)   A serious breach of the code, or persistent breaches of a material nature, will be a breach of the rule, and may also be evidence of inadequate professional services under section 37A of the Solicitors Act 1974.

(ii) Material breaches of the code which are not serious or persistent will not be a breach of the rule, but may be evidence of inadequate professional services under section 37A.

(iii) The powers of the Office for the Supervision of Solicitors on a finding of inadequate professional services include:

(a) disallowing all or part of the solicitor's costs; and

(b) directing the solicitor to pay compensation to the client up to a limit of £1,000. [Law Society note: This limit has now been raised to £5,000.]

(iv) *Non-material breaches of the code will not be a breach of the rule, and will not be evidence of inadequate professional services under section 37A.*

(v) *Registered foreign lawyers practising in partnership with solicitors of the Supreme Court or registered European lawyers, or as members of recognised bodies which are limited liability partnerships, or as directors of recognised bodies which are companies, although subject to Rule 15 as a matter of professional conduct, are not subject to section 37A. However, such solicitors, registered European lawyers and recognised bodies are subject to section 37A for professional services provided by the firm.*

The amended rule also provides for a Code that gives detail to the replaced Rule 15 as follows (including consolidated amendments to April 2001):

SOLICITORS' COSTS INFORMATION AND CLIENT CARE CODE 1999

Code dated 3 September 1999 made by the Council of the Law Society with the concurrence of the Master of the Rolls under Rule 15 of the Solicitors' Practice Rules 1990, regulating the English and Welsh practices of solicitors, registered European lawyers, registered foreign lawyers and recognised bodies in giving information to clients and operating complaints procedures.

1. Introduction

(a) This code replaces the written professional standards on costs information for clients (see paragraphs 3–6) and the detail previously contained in Practice Rule 15 (client care) (see paragraph 7).

(b) The main object of the code is to make sure that clients are given the information they need to understand what is happening generally and in particular on:

(i) the cost of legal services both at the outset and as a matter progresses; and

(ii) responsibility for clients' matters.

(c) The code also requires firms to operate a complaints handling procedure.

(d) It is good practice to record in writing:

(i) all information required to be given by the code including all decisions relating to costs and the arrangements for updating costs information; and

(ii) the reasons why the information required by the code has not been given in a particular case.

(e) References to costs, where appropriate, include fees, VAT and disbursements.

2. Application

(a) The code is of general application, and it applies to registered foreign lawyers as well as to solicitors of the Supreme Court and registered European lawyers (subject to note (v) to Practice Rule 15). However, as set out in paragraph 2(b), parts of the code may not be appropriate in every case, and solicitors should consider the interests of each client in deciding which parts not to apply in the particular circumstances.

(b)   The full information required by the code may be inappropriate, for example:

     (i)   in every case, for a regular client for whom repetitive work is done, where the client has already been provided with the relevant information, although such a client should be informed of changes; and

    (ii) if compliance with the code may at the time be insensitive or impractical. In such a case relevant information should be given as soon as reasonably practicable.

(c)   Employed solicitors should have regard to paragraphs 3–6 of the code where appropriate, e.g. when acting for clients other than their employer. Paragraph 7 does not apply to employed solicitors.

(d)   Solicitors should comply with paragraphs 3–6 of the code even where a client is legally aided if the client may have a financial interest in the costs because contributions are payable or the statutory charge may apply or they may become liable for the costs of another party.

(e)   The code also applies to contingency fee and conditional fee arrangements and to arrangements with a client for the solicitor to retain commissions received from third parties.

3. Informing the client about costs

(a)   Costs information must not be inaccurate or misleading.

(b)   Any costs information required to be given by the code must be given clearly, in a way and at a level which is appropriate to the particular client. Any terms with which the client may be unfamiliar, for example 'disbursement', should be explained.

(c)   The information required by paragraphs 4 and 5 of the code should be given to a client at the outset of, and at appropriate stages throughout, the matter. All information given orally should be confirmed in writing to the client as soon as possible.

4. Advance costs information – general

The overall costs

(a)   The solicitor should give the client the best information possible about the likely overall costs, including a breakdown between fees, VAT and disbursements.

(b)   The solicitor should explain clearly to the client the time likely to be spent in dealing with a matter, if time spent is a factor in the calculation of the fees.

(c)   Giving 'the best information possible' includes:

     (i)   agreeing a fixed fee; or

    (ii) giving a realistic estimate; or

   (iii) giving a forecast within a possible range of costs; or

   (iv) explaining to the client the reasons why it is not possible to fix, or give a realistic estimate or forecast of, the overall costs, and giving instead the best information possible about the cost of the next stage of the matter.

(d)   The solicitor should, in an appropriate case, explain to a privately paying client that the client may set an upper limit on the firm's costs for which the client may be liable without further authority. Solicitors should not exceed an agreed limit without first obtaining the client's consent.

(e)   The solicitor should make it clear at the outset if an estimate, quotation or other indication of cost is not intended to be fixed.

Basis of firm's charges

(f) The solicitor should also explain to the client how the firm's fees are calculated except where the overall costs are fixed or clear. If the basis of charging is an hourly charging rate, that must be made clear.

(g) The client should be told if charging rates may be increased.

Further information

(h) The solicitor should explain what reasonably foreseeable payments a client may have to make either to the solicitor or to a third party and when those payments are likely to be needed.

(i) The solicitor should explain to the client the arrangements for updating the costs information as set out in paragraph 6.

Client's ability to pay

(j) The solicitor should discuss with the client *how and when* any costs are to be met, and consider:

    (i) whether the client may be eligible and should apply for legal aid (including advice and assistance);

    (ii) whether the client's liability for their own costs may be covered by insurance;

    (iii) whether the client's liability for another party's costs may be covered by pre-purchased insurance and, if not, whether it would be advisable for the client's liability for another party's costs to be covered by after-the-event insurance (including in every case where a conditional fee or contingency fee arrangement is proposed); and

    (iv) whether the client's liability for costs (including the costs of another party) may be covered by another person, e.g. an employer or trade union.

Cost-benefit and risk

(k) The solicitor should discuss with the client whether the likely outcome in a matter will justify the expense or risk involved including, if relevant, the risk of having to bear an opponent's costs.

5. Additional information for particular clients

Legally aided clients

(a) The solicitor should explain to a legally aided client the client's potential liability for the client's own costs and those of any other party, including:

    (i) the effect of the statutory charge and its likely amount;

    (ii) the client's obligation to pay any contribution assessed and the consequences of failing to do so;

    (iii) the fact that the client may still be ordered by the court to contribute to the opponent's costs if the case is lost even though the client's own costs are covered by legal aid; and

    (iv) the fact that even if the client wins, the opponent may not be ordered to pay or be capable of paying the full amount of the client's costs.

Privately paying clients in contentious matters (and potentially contentious matters)

(b)   The solicitor should explain to the client the client's potential liability for the client's own costs and for those of any other party, including:

    (i)   the fact that the client will be responsible for paying the firm's bill in full regardless of any order for costs made against an opponent;

    (ii)   the probability that the client will have to pay the opponent's costs as well as the client's own costs if the case is lost;

    (iii)   the fact that even if the client wins, the opponent may not be ordered to pay or be capable of paying the full amount of the client's costs; and

    (iv)   the fact that if the opponent is legally aided the client may not recover costs, even if successful.

Liability for third party costs in non-contentious matters

(c)   The solicitor should explain to the client any liability the client may have for the payment of the costs of a third party. When appropriate, solicitors are advised to obtain a firm figure for or agree a cap to a third party's costs.

6. Updating costs information

The solicitor should keep the client properly informed about costs as a matter progresses. In particular, the solicitor should:

(a)   tell the client, unless otherwise agreed, how much the costs are at regular intervals (at least every six months) and in appropriate cases deliver interim bills at agreed intervals;

(b)   explain to the client (and confirm in writing) any changed circumstances which will, or which are likely to affect the amount of costs, the degree of risk involved, or the cost-benefit to the client of continuing with the matter;

(c)   inform the client in writing as soon as it appears that a costs estimate or agreed upper limit may or will be exceeded; and

(d)   consider the client's eligibility for legal aid if a material change in the client's means comes to the solicitor's attention.

7. Client care and complaints handling

Information for clients

(a)   Every solicitor in private practice must ensure that the client:

    (i)   is given a clear explanation of the issues raised in a matter and is kept properly informed about its progress (including the likely timescale);

    (ii)   is given the name and status of the person dealing with the matter and the name of the principal, or director (in the case of a recognised body which is a company), or member (in the case of a recognised body which is a limited liability partnership) responsible for its overall supervision;

    (iii)   is told whom to contact about any problem with the service provided; and

    (iv)   is given details of any changes in the information required to be given by this paragraph.

Complaints handling

(b) Every principal in private practice (or, in the case of a recognised body, the body itself) must:

    (i) ensure the client is told the name of the person in the firm to contact about any problem with the service provided;

    (ii) have a written complaints procedure and ensure that complaints are handled in accordance with it; and

    (iii) ensure that the client is given a copy of the complaints procedure on request.

3.2 MORE THAN A COMPLAINTS PROCEDURE

Although the Rule refers to a complaints handling procedure being in place client care is more than setting up a means for dissatisfied clients to resolve their problems, important though that is. Client care means focusing your own and your firm's attention on clients' needs. This may be through simple steps which you can adopt immediately (like meeting clients in reception, rather than having them 'sent up' – recent research shows that this seemingly minor factor is the single thing clients appreciate most). It may be through something which involves a major review of your work and how you do it, intended to improve the quality of service offered (and save you time and effort), such as practice-wide standardisation of procedures or computerisation.

References to client care crop up throughout this Handbook, explicitly and otherwise. One of the aims of the Handbook is to help reduce the time you spend on routine and repeated tasks, to free you for more satisfying and productive ones, including giving the best possible service to your clients. Examples of standard letters, leaflets and checklists for wills and probate clients have been included or are recommended. (Solicitors in private practice may adapt or adopt those included for the purpose set out on page iv but not for any other purpose.) More generally, help with assessing how you do what you do is also included (for example, the checklists on client care in this chapter). Some of the dozens of inexpensive books on business management (and managing your personal workload) available in general bookshops are listed in Appendix 5. See also Chapter 19.

When introducing changes, it is important to recognise that any change, even for the better, is stressful; and that results are more likely to be lasting if you have a clear idea of your goal but set about reaching it in stages: consolidate progress before moving ahead.

Many practices and individual solicitors have faced enormous pressures in the last few years, particularly from changes forced on them by the last recession and clients' altered expectations. Workloads may have increased or decreased sharply. Client care need not be just another worry; it can help you stand back from what you do and where you are and offers the opportunity to make some changes you have chosen.

3.3   WHAT DOES PRACTICE RULE 15 MEAN FOR YOUR FIRM?

Practice Rule 15 obliges firms to tell clients:

- who is responsible for their matter and, in particular, what their status is;
- the name of the supervising principal;
- the person to approach in the event of any problems with the service provided.

In addition, every principal in private practice must operate a complaints handling procedure. The Office for the Supervision of Solicitors (OSS) expects that procedure to be employed effectively and in a manner that provides the best possible opportunity for the complaint to be resolved by the firm if it is not to be asked to justify how it complied with Rule 15. Additionally firms now need to have a suitable complaints procedure that can be given to the client (see Code para. 7(b)(iii)). This also means that firms may also wish to provide guidance for all members of staff on how to handle a complaint (see specimen guidance in [2001] *Gazette*, 3 May, 49 and the booklet *Handling Complaints Effectively*, available at **www.clientcare.lawsociety. org.uk**.

If a client raises a problem with it, the OSS will establish whether there are grounds for complaint, tell the client what the OSS can and cannot do, and ask if the complaint has been put to the firm involved. The OSS generally expects clients to do this first. The OSS will encourage the client to raise their complaint with the firm if the client has not done so.

If the client remains unhappy, the OSS assesses the response from the firm and tells the client if this is satisfactory. If not, it investigates.

If the OSS does investigate a complaint, it will try to resolve it by agreement. If this cannot be done, a more formal investigation will take place and it will discuss the firm's complaints handling procedures. If appropriate, improvements may be recommended but if there are serious shortcomings, it may seek a sanction for breach of Rule 15.

3.4   COMMUNICATIONS AND CLIENT CARE

The emphasis in much of the Law Society's work in recent years has been on client care, and helping firms to provide high quality services. The OSS has had a dedicated client care and compliance team for several years who have been at the forefront of many initiatives to help firms. This team has now been superseded by the Practice Standards Unit based at Redditch.

Communicating clearly with clients is a vital part of good client care. Using pre-prepared information such as leaflets, brochures, information sheets and standard letters saves time, helps ensure consistency throughout the practice and provides an ice-breaker for new clients.

The following checklist (originated by the OSS) includes reminders about what to do and when to do it.

3.5 CHECKLIST: BETTER CLIENT COMMUNICATION

1. At the first appointment

- Cover preliminary points:

  - Ensure that the client is clear about the fee earner's status.
  - Identify the supervising partner.
  - Agree the objective with your client and consider, if appropriate, whether the likely outcome justifies the expense or risk involved.
  - Identify any special client needs and discuss and manage client's expectations.
  - Explain the action you will be taking, especially the next step and any action the client must take.
  - Discuss the timescale involved, including when you are next likely to contact the client.
  - Give the client the best information possible about the likely cost.
  - Run through how costs will be met – legal aid/insurance, instalments, direct debit, etc.
  - Discuss and explain any payments on account (both initial and future).
  - Point out any other reasonably foreseeable payments the client may have to make, and when.

- Tell the client the likely cost and/or basis of charging, and what will happen if the matter doesn't proceed or proves abortive.
- Give the client your firm's standard costs information guide and standard information leaflet with relevant information about the firm's services.
- Point out who should be contacted about any problem with the service.
- Record the instructions.
- Note any agreed fee (+/− VAT/disbursements), and what it covers.
- Confirm oral estimates in writing.
- Mark the file if a limit on costs has been agreed.
- After the first interview confirm the client's instructions in a client care letter, incorporating the Rule 15 essentials; who is acting/supervising, costs information and contacts for service problems.

2. During the case

- Keep the client regularly informed of progress (and promptly return phone calls).
- If there is delay or there is likely to be delay, tell the client why.
- Explain important and relevant documents.
- Tell the client if a change of staff will affect his matter.
- Explain if a costs forecast needs revising and the revised forecast. (This must be done in writing.)
- Review with the client whether the likely outcome will justify the continuing expense or risk.
- In continuing matters, report the costs incurred at least every six months or even monthly if the client would prefer a personal budgeted approach.
- Review whether any agreed costs limit has been reached.

3. At the end of the matter

- Write confirming the matter has been completed.
- Explain any continuing consequences.
- Render your bill as promptly as possible. See Principle 14.07 in the *Guide to the Professional Conduct of Solicitors 1999*.
- Account promptly for all client funds held by you (together with interest as appropriate).
- Hand over all papers and property to which the client is entitled (subject to any lien if a bill has not been paid).
- Take speedy action on any post-completion matters.
- Consider asking the client whether the matter was complete to their satisfaction.

3.6 STANDARD INFORMATION

Three examples of standard information for clients, which set out basic details about what to expect, in different styles, are included here. At 3.7 below is an example of a client information leaflet, prepared by the OSS and slightly edited. At 3.8 below are the parts relevant to probate of the specimen leaflet in the OSS's guide, *Keeping Clients*. Finally, at 3.9 below is a specimen letter for estate administration clients. (Solicitors in private practice may adapt or adopt these for the purpose set out on page iv but not for any other purpose.)

In addition to general information about your firm, you might want to provide specific information about wills and probate. Law Society Publishing produces a booklet available in packs of 25, *Making a Will Won't Kill You*, and other organisations such as Age Concern have useful information for consumers on their website (see Appendices 5 and 6 respectively).

In addition to providing the standard information to clients the OSS recommends issuing a copy of the client care letter to residuary beneficiaries. This is especially relevant where solicitors are themselves acting as personal representatives. The beneficiaries will then be aware of how matters are being handled and this may avoid problems.

Bear in mind that residuary beneficiaries have a right to complain about your services and if found wanting the OSS has power to award a financial penalty against you by reducing your bill. Residuary beneficiaries are also entitled to require you to obtain a remuneration certificate so questions as to costs should always be discussed and beneficiaries kept informed.

3.7   SPECIMEN CLIENT INFORMATION LEAFLET

A guide for our clients

We want the best relationship between us as we help you with your matter and this leaflet explains:

- the name of the person looking after your matter and/or the supervising partner;
- when our office is open;
- where people can be reached in an emergency outside office hours;
- our costs and the service we promise you;
- how you can help us; and
- what to do if you are unhappy about the way your matter is being dealt with.

Your instructions to us are being looked after by Mr/s _____ who is a partner/consultant/assistant solicitor/trainee solicitor/legal executive. If he or she is unavailable Mr/s _____ will be pleased to take a message for you.

The supervising partner is Mr/s _____.

Our office is open from _____ to _____ each weekday and from _____ to _____ on Saturdays.

If an emergency arises when the office is closed please ring Mr/s _____.

Our promise to you

We aim to reply to correspondence within two working days.

At the outset we will confirm in writing to you:

- your instructions to us;

- any advice we have given;
- the approximate time the matter will take to finalise;
- what action we will be taking;
- when you are next likely to hear from us;
- any action we need you to take;
- the best information we can give as to the likely cost and how it will be met; and
- any further information we need from you.

During the conduct of your matter we will:

- keep you informed of progress;
- advise you of any delays or anticipated delays and explain the reasons;
- explain the effect of any important documents;
- inform you if a costs forecast needs revising;
- explain any changes of staff affecting your matter; and
- if you so wish, send you copies of important letters (but it will cost more if you ask for copies of all letters).

At the end of your matter we will:

- write confirming its conclusion;
- explain any continuing consequences;
- render our bill as promptly as possible;
- account to you for all money due to you; and
- you can ask for any papers and property to which you are entitled, subject to our right to retain them in certain unusual circumstances, for example if our bill has not been paid.

How you can help us

- Give us clear instructions.
- Tell us if you have any important time limits.
- Make sure we have understood each other correctly. Ask us if you are not sure about anything.
- Deal promptly with any important questions which may arise.
- Keep in regular touch. Do not feel afraid to ask for a progress report if you are worried about anything or do not hear from us when you expect to do so.
- Help us plan our working day. For example unless it is urgent, write to us rather than telephone, and make an appointment if you want to see someone. Remember, avoiding unnecessary calls and appointments helps us keep costs down for you.

We will be pleased to give you costs information at any time. When we write confirming your instructions we will give you the best information we can about the likely cost, including our terms for payment of bills and right to charge interest on an unpaid bill. Ask us about anything you would like amplified or explained.

Standard costs information

Our charges

When taking your instructions we will:

- discuss how your legal charges are to be met and whether you are eligible for legal aid – we can make the application for you;
- give you the best information we can about the likely overall costs including a breakdown between fees, VAT and disbursements, either by:
  - agreeing a fee with you;
  - providing you with an estimate of costs; or
  - explaining how our costs will be worked out.

Value Added Tax (VAT) and all the payments out which we make on your behalf (called 'disbursements') will be added to our final account.

We will confirm these arrangements in writing, explain what work they cover, tell you about other foreseeable payments which are likely to be necessary, and set out our terms of payment for bills and our right to charge interest on an unpaid bill. You can:

- set a limit on the costs to be incurred without further agreement with you (this is not the same as an 'agreed fee'); and
- ask us for details of what costs have been run up at any stage.

We will tell you what costs have been incurred at least every six months where a matter takes some time or at any other interval agreed with you and at your request.

Unless you are on legal aid we may ask you for a payment on account of our costs for disbursements, especially for court or tribunal work. We may need to ask you for further payments as the matter progresses.

What to do if you are dissatisfied

Tell us if you feel you are not receiving the service you hoped for. We want to know if you are dissatisfied. We can try to put it right, and will look into it promptly and thoroughly.

Mention it first to the person looking after your matter.

If you are still unhappy after that you can complain to Mr/s _____ who will investigate it and contact you to talk about the problem. It will help if you put your complaint in writing (keeping a copy for yourself) explaining what action you want us to take. If you would prefer to discuss your concerns over the telephone or in a face to face meeting please say so and we will try to accommodate your wishes. Afterwards he/she will write confirming your complaint, the discussion, and what we will be doing about it. This will be at no extra cost to you.

Note: Only if a client complains should solicitors disclose details of their firm's complaints handling procedure and only if they fail to resolve the complaint after taking every step to do so should they inform the client of how to seek assistance from the OSS (see Appendix 6 for the OSS Helpline for clients).

3.8   SPECIMEN CLIENT INFORMATION: ESTATE ADMINISTRATION

These are the paragraphs relating to probate, slightly edited, from the specimen information leaflet for clients in the OSS's guide *Keeping Clients*.

(a)   Charges

Our charges will be calculated according to:

- the time spent by solicitors and legal staff in dealing with the estate, and
- a 'value element'. This is a percentage of the gross value of the estate, as the monetary value involved is one measure of the extent of responsibility falling on the firm.

We review our charging rates [every six months/every year]. It is our practice to write to you about changes in these rates and tell you the dates after which the changes will apply.

We give below an explanation of the 'time' and 'value' factors.

Time

- For meetings, discussions and other work progressing the administration of the estate, the hourly charging rates (excluding VAT) of our solicitors and legal staff are:

	£
partners	_____
other solicitors	_____
trainee solicitors	_____
legal executives	_____

VAT will be added at the current rate.

If less than one hour is involved, we calculate the time spent in units of six minutes. (One six-minute unit equals 10 per cent of the hourly rate.)

- Telephone calls and letters are treated as follows:
  - telephone calls (made and received by us) are recorded in units each of six minutes;
  - short and routine letters (written and received) are counted as six minutes each.

Value

The 'value element' is calculated as follows:

- ___ per cent on the gross value of the estate (excluding the value of the deceased's home if this was owned); and
- ___ per cent on the value of the deceased's home.

Additional expense

Other expenditure will be necessary in dealing with the estate. This will include:

- Probate Registry fee (for issuing the grant)   £_____ (no VAT)
- Commissioner's fee (the charge for swearing the personal representatives' oath)   £_____ (no VAT)
- Valuers' fees (if necessary)   £_____ (plus VAT)
- Additional court copies of the grant document   £_____ (no VAT)

(b) Amount of work

It is difficult at the beginning of the administration of most estates to say how much work will be involved, but we estimate at present that about ____ hours' work, spread over several months, will be needed. We will be able to give you a more accurate estimate after we have prepared the application for the grant of representation in about ___ days' time. We will write to you immediately if it becomes clear that substantially more time will be needed than we expect.

(c) Bills

We usually submit bills at intervals during the administration of estates. This will keep you informed about charges. If you approve them, both the interim and final bills can be paid from estate funds automatically and you do not need to make payment personally.

The first interim bill is normally submitted after the grant has been obtained. If it is likely to be some time before we can finalise the tax position and complete the administration, we normally submit a second interim bill during the course of the administration. Our final bill will be presented when the administration is completed.

(d) Staff

The partner with ultimate responsibility for this matter is _____. It will be handled on a day-to-day basis by _____, [a solicitor/a trainee solicitor/a legal executive]. We want to offer you and all our clients a friendly and efficient service, but if any difficulty should arise, please raise the matter first with [him] [her]. If you still have problems, please contact _____, the partner responsible.

Should you still be unhappy with the situation please refer the matter to_____, [address and telephone number], who will investigate and contact you to talk about the problem. [He][She] will then write to you about the matter and the action being taken.

(e) Handling the administration

Grants of representation

Unless the estate is very small and with no freehold or leasehold property (such as a house or flat) the personal representatives will have to obtain a grant of representation from the Probate Registry showing their entitlement to deal with the estate. We will probably be able to tell you straightaway if a grant is needed, and we shall handle all the necessary paperwork for you.

If the deceased left a will, the application is to the Probate Registry for a grant of probate; if the deceased did not make a will and therefore died 'intestate', the application is for a grant of letters of administration.

If a will was left, this should set out who is to inherit the estate. If there was no will, the law sets out who is entitled to inherit and we should be able to tell you at a very early stage which members of the family are entitled to the estate and in what proportions and shares.

First steps

The first stage of our work is to prepare the papers for the application for the grant. We try to complete this promptly. You should be hearing from us within the next seven to 14 days. We will also tell you then how quickly we expect to receive the documents from the Probate Registry.

We usually write as soon as possible to all the beneficiaries named in the will, or to those family members entitled on an intestacy, to tell them of their legacies and entitlements. When writing, we also try to indicate when we expect to be able to make payment.

We will arrange for payment of the funeral account and other bills in due course. *Would you please therefore send the funeral account and other unpaid bills and accounts to us as soon as possible?*

Inheritance tax

We do our best to tell you as quickly as possible whether or not there is likely to be any inheritance tax (IHT) to pay, and if so, advise on how the tax is to be paid. We shall deal with this when we write to you about obtaining the grant.

It may be helpful to have some very general guidance on IHT. None is payable if the value of the net estate is less than £223,000. Above this amount, IHT is payable at the rate of 40 per cent on the net value of the rest of the estate. There is no tax at all, whatever the value of the estate, on property going to a widow or widower, or to a registered charity. The value of this exempt property is deducted from the value of the whole estate before the tax calculation is done. So gifts to husbands and wives and charities can take an estate out of the tax bracket.

However, if there is likely to be a large amount of IHT to pay, either on the estate now or by the family in the future, we will discuss this with you and, if necessary, the others involved, before the grant is obtained, to consider whether or not action can be taken to reduce the amount payable either now or in the future.

If you have any questions or difficulties at any time, do not hesitate to get in touch with us. In the meantime, I await the bills and accounts and [list other documents] mentioned in para. e(ii) above.

Note: It is becoming increasingly common for probate practitioners along with those practising in other areas of law to agree a fixed fee for the work at the outset. This can still include a percentage of the estate's value but a fixed fee provides simplicity with certainty for all concerned and minimises the chances of a dispute over costs.

3.9 SPECIMEN INTRODUCTORY LETTER FOR PRs

This is a specimen standard letter for new PR clients.

Dear

THE ESTATE OF THE LATE Mr/s _____

Thank you for asking this firm to carry out the administration of Mr/s _____'s estate.

When we [met/spoke on the telephone] [yesterday,] we discussed a number of the steps which have to be taken and I enclose a leaflet which explains in more detail some of the duties you will be taking on in acting as Mr/s _____'s [executors/administrators]. Please let me know if I can add to this in any way.

(a) Questionnaire

I enclose a questionnaire listing information I shall need to start work. Simply let me have the information in the way that is easiest for you – this will probably be by making notes on the leaflet and sending it back to me with the papers it mentions. I can photocopy any papers that you send me, and your completed questionnaire, and return these to you, if you wish.

We may already have much of the information asked for on our files. If so, please indicate this on the form together with the name of the person here to whom I should speak.

Please let me know if you want any help in connection with the funeral or with making property safe.

(b) Mr/s _____'s will

If you do not have a copy of [Mr/s _____'s] will, I shall be sending one to you very shortly. If you think there may be a later will, or codicil, please let me know as soon as possible.

(c) Mr/s _____'s estate

We will have to establish the value of what Mr/s _____ owned when [he/she] died and the amount of money [he/she] owed in outstanding bills. The questionnaire includes suggestions about property Mr/s _____ may have owned and which may not otherwise immediately come to mind. A similar list of bills which may be due to be paid is also included. Please let me have any relevant documents and papers you trace.

(d) The administration of the estate

It may be helpful if I briefly outline what has to be done before work is completed and the estate can finally be wound up. As the [executors/administrators] you have the responsibility of administering the estate properly. This means establishing the extent of the estate, paying the debts and distributing the balance. The law requires that this be done with due diligence. It is my job to help you do this [with the assistance of colleagues within the firm]. We shall handle all the following steps on the basis of the information you provide:

- Estimating the value of the estate after all the bills are paid and identifying any problems there may be before the beneficiaries can be given their entitlements.
- Estimating the length of time it will take to deal with everything; we shall tell you how long we expect this to be and, as far as possible, what the cost will be.
- Dealing with any inheritance tax (IHT) due – this has to be paid before we can get the grant of representation from the Probate Registry.
- Sending copies of the grant to banks, building societies and others holding money and property. Some items may need to be sold and, of course, I will discuss this with you. (Larger and more valuable items may have to be professionally valued. Fees for this and other work for the estate will be paid from money in the estate.)
- Collecting and paying estate money into our client account (where it will be subject to the protection of the Law Society's rules regarding solicitors' firms' handling of clients' money). This also helps us to start to prepare the accounts, which will show the assets of the estate and the payments of bills and legacies. I should be able to let you know how matters stand at any particular time, should you wish it.
- Once the bills have been paid, it will be possible to start paying smaller legacies under the will. The final stages of my work involve obtaining confirmation from the Inland Revenue that no more tax is due, finalising the accounts, handing over the remaining entitlements to the beneficiaries and getting their receipts [and setting up the necessary trusts under the [will] [intestacy].

I hope this outline of what has to be done is helpful. Please contact me if I can be of assistance in any way at any stage. If I am not available, my secretary _____ or my colleague _____ would be happy to take a message. Finally, I look forward to receiving the following from you [list the items] mentioned in para(s) _____.

Yours sincerely

[*Note*: The *Questionnaire for Personal Representative Clients* is available from Law Society Publishing (see Appendix 5) and complements this letter.]

CHAPTER 4

Estate administration and the Financial Services and Markets Act 2000: a review

Peter Camp

This review is intended to give a brief outline of the relevance of the Financial Services and Markets Act 2000 to wills and probate work and to raise the issues that should be considered. First, terminology and sources are covered, then where to find more information; finally, some of the basic points are outlined.

4.1   TERMINOLOGY AND SOURCES

The Financial Services and Markets Act (FSMA) 2000 prohibits the undertaking of 'regulated activities' without authorisation. Since the Act came into force on 1 December 2001 the only regulating authority has been the Financial Services Authority (FSA). The Law Society is no longer able to regulate solicitors as a recognised professional body. However, exemptions and exclusions in the new legislation mean that few solicitors will need to be authorised by the FSA. It is, however, important for firms to identify the exact nature of the exemptions and exclusions. Undertaking regulated activities without authorisation and outside the statutory exemptions or exclusions is a criminal offence.

The main statutory exemption for professionals is contained in Part XX of FSMA 2000. Solicitors will be able to rely upon Part XX since the Law Society is a 'designated professional body' (DPB). However the Society has been required to issue rules regulating solicitors who use the Part XX exemption. The rules are the Solicitors' Financial Services (Scope) Rules 2001 ('the Scope Rules') and the Solicitors' Financial Services (Conduct of Business) Rules 2001 ('the COB Rules').

Solicitors conducting regulated activities (whether mainstream activities or exempt activities) must also comply with the Money Laundering Regulations 1993 now contained in *The Guide to the Professional Conduct of Solicitors 1999* ('the Guide') at Annex 3B. Guidance on money laundering may be obtained from Professional Ethics at the Law Society (see Appendix 6). See also Annex 16D of the Guide for the text of the Blue Warning Card on money laundering.

4.2 MORE INFORMATION

Probate work is, generally speaking, the area where most solicitors come into contact with regulated activities, FSMA 2000 and the Scope and COB Rules. It is, therefore, important that solicitors are aware of the compliance requirements and also the investment business opportunities involved.

If you wish to gain a wider knowledge of this area the following publications would be useful (see Appendix 5 and Appendix 6 for more information):

- P. Camp, *Solicitors and Financial Services: A Compliance Handbook* (Law Society, 3rd edn, 2002);
- *Financial Services and Solicitors*, an information pack available from the Law Society website or from Professional Ethics (August 2001);
- *Professional Firms: the Need for Authorisation under the Financial Services and Markets Act 2000*, FSA Guidance (August 2001).

The Professional Ethics Division offers confidential guidance on the Practice Rules and the Scope and COB Rules, including whether or not authorisation is required.

4.3 THE BASICS

What follows is, necessarily, a brief indication of the relevant aspects and the guidance and the Rules will give more detailed information.

4.3.1 Do you need to be authorised?

If you are carrying out probate and trust work, you are likely to be potentially undertaking regulated activities but the exclusions and exemptions contained in the legislation mean that most solicitors will not need to be authorised by the FSA.

4.3.2 What are 'investments' and what is a 'regulated activity'?

'Investments' are defined in the Financial Services and Markets Act 2000 (Regulated Activities) Order (RAO) 2001, SI 2001/544. Examples include stocks and shares, unit trusts and life policies. (National Savings products are outside the scope of FSMA 2000.) The activities constituting 'regulated activities' are also defined in RAO 2001: examples include dealing and arranging deals in investments, giving investment advice and the discretionary management of investments. The activities of 'sending dematerialised instructions' and 'custody of investments' are also potentially regulated activities. 'Custody of investments' involves safeguarding *and* administering investments and this is likely to be relevant to firms conducting probate/trust work. Further guidance is available from Professional Ethics.

4.3.3   What exclusions apply?

Under the terms of RAO 2001 there are exclusions for dealing and arranging deals where the activities are carried out using an authorised person providing an authorised person has advised on that activity. However, of greater relevance to trust and probate practitioners are the exclusions contained in RAO 2001, art. 66 which apply to arranging deals, discretionary management, investment advice, sending dematerialised instructions and custody of investments where the activity is being carried out by a trustee or personal representative. Note that these exclusions are not available where a firm is simply acting for outside trustees or personal representatives. However, where a member of the firm is a trustee or personal representative (whether alone, with another member of the firm or with an external trustee or personal representative) these exclusions are valuable. Practitioners must check carefully the conditions contained in art. 66. Where they apply the firm will not be carrying on regulated activities and will be subject to no compliance requirements other than those applicable to solicitors generally.

4.3.4   What exemptions apply?

Whilst RAO 2001, art. 66 is invaluable for those matters where a member of the firm is a trustee or personal representative, it will offer no assistance in those circumstances where the firm is simply acting for outside trustees or personal representatives. Here, an alternative solution must be found to avoid the need for authorisation. Under Part XX of FSMA 2000 certain professionals can undertake 'exempt regulated activities' without the need for authorisation. The exempt regime is available where the member of the profession is regulated by a DPB. The Law Society is such a body. Certain conditions must apply before regulated activities can be treated as exempt. These include the requirement that the activities must be incidental to the provision of other professional services, and that the activities are of a type not prohibited by the rules of the DPB. The Scope Rules of the Law Society contain a number of prohibitions. Most of these prohibitions will not be relevant to probate practitioners. However, where the Part XX regime is relied upon, care must be taken to ensure that the specific prohibitions relating to 'packaged products', 'securities' and other 'contractually based investments' are identified. In most cases these prohibitions apply to recommendations and arrangements to *buy* such investments. Investment activities undertaken by probate practitioners usually relate to the disposal of investments. However, trust practitioners may need to take care in relying upon the Part XX regime as a result of these Scope restrictions.

4.3.5   The 'incidental' nature of probate

If a solicitor is involved only in winding up estates on behalf of outside personal representatives, then the investment business work is likely to be 'incidental' to the main activity, which is the administration. The effect of this is that the work will be capable of falling within Part XX of FSMA 2000 and the requirements for compliance are very few: see below.

4.3.6   Compliance requirements

Where the statutory exclusions apply, as noted above, no special compliance requirements will apply. Where a solicitor relies upon the Part XX regime, the COB Rules will apply. These rules are designed to be simple and generally will not impose a major burden upon practitioners. However, it is necessary for probate practitioners who rely upon Part XX to familiarise themselves with the Rules. The Rules cover obligations relating to status disclosure, record-keeping, systems for safe custody and confirmation of execution only business.

4.3.7   Investment business opportunities

If a firm decides to offer investment services to its clients, either by seeking authorisation or by using an exclusion or exemption, then there are a number of investment business opportunities deriving from probate work. Examples include offering investment advice to beneficiaries and tax planning for beneficiaries.

4.3.8   Relevance of the Solicitors' Practice Rules

Solicitors who are involved in investment business activities (whether benefiting from a statutory exclusion or from the 'exempt' regime under Part XX of FSMA 2000) are bound by the Solicitors' Practice Rules. As with any aspect of a solicitor's practice, the Rules will apply, but of particular relevance to probate work and investment business services are Practice Rules 2, 3, 5, 10 and 12. (See the Guide, paras 27.19 onwards.)

4.3.9   Relevance of the Solicitors' Accounts Rules 1998

Solicitors are also subject to the Solicitors' Accounts Rules 1998. Brief guidance on these is included in Chapter 5.

Solicitors' Accounts Rules 1998

Professional Ethics, the Law Society

5.1 INTRODUCTION

The Solicitors' Accounts Rules 1998 ('1998 Rules') were made by the Council of the Law Society with the approval of the Master of the Rolls on 22 July 1998 and had to be implemented by 1 May 2000.

The 1998 Rules replaced the Solicitors' Accounts Rules 1991, the Solicitors' Accounts (Legal Aid Temporary Provision) Rule 1992 and the Accountant's Report Rules 1991. They include explanatory notes which form part of the Rules.

The 1998 Rules were rewritten for three main reasons:

- the old Rules had been subject to many piecemeal amendments over the years and as a result were becoming more and more difficult to interpret;
- the Professional Ethics division of the Law Society received more questions on the old Rules than on any single other subject;
- a number of gaps in the old Rules had been identified.

The 1998 Rules were published by the Law Society in the *Solicitors' Accounts Manual* (8th edn, 2001) and the latest version is available at **www.guide-on-line.lawsociety.org.uk**.

5.2 AN OUTLINE OF THE RULES

5.2.1 Who is governed by the Rules?

The Rules apply to solicitors, registered European lawyers, registered foreign lawyers and recognised bodies. They do not apply to solicitors who are employed by, for example, a local authority or to a solicitor when carrying out the function of a coroner or other judicial office or a sheriff or under-sheriff (Rules 4 and 5).

All of the partners in a practice are required to ensure compliance with the 1998 Rules by fellow partners and everyone else in the practice, and to remedy breaches (Rules 6 and 7). (This duty extends to directors of recognised bodies which are companies, and to members of recognised bodies which are limited liability partnerships.) The case of *Weston* v. *The Law Society, The Times*, 15 July 1998 is a reminder that solicitors are under a heavy obligation in securing compliance with the 1998 Rules. The Court of Appeal confirmed that it was appropriate to strike off a solicitor where no dishonesty was alleged but the partner in question was guilty of breaches through his partners' activities of which he was unaware. Lord Bingham referred to 'the duty of anyone holding anyone else's money to exercise a proper stewardship in relation to it'.

The Law Society's Guidelines – published as Appendix 3 to the 1998 Rules – state that compliance with the Rules is the equal responsibility of all partners. Responsibility for day-to-day supervision may be delegated to individual partner(s) but it is not acceptable to delegate total responsibility to a cashier or book-keeper.

Liquidators, trustees in bankruptcy, Court of Protection receivers and trustees of occupational pension schemes are subject to some of the record-keeping requirements of the 1998 Rules (Rule 9 and see at 5.4 below). The reason for this extension of the Rules is to protect the vulnerable against defalcations and to protect the profession from claims on the Compensation Fund.

Similarly solicitors who operate joint accounts with clients or operate the accounts of clients are subject to certain record-keeping requirements (Rules 10 and 11 and see at 5.3 below).

Reporting accountants are regulated by Part F of the 1998 Rules.

5.2.2 Classification of money (Rule 13)

All money held or received in the course of practice falls into one of the following categories.

Client money

Client money is money held or received for a client and all other money which is not controlled trust money or office money.

A 'client' is defined by Rule 2 as a person for whom the solicitor acts. However, client money includes money held for non-clients as a bailee, agent, or donee of a power of attorney. It also extends to money held as stakeholder, liquidator, trustee in bankruptcy or Court of Protection receiver.

Client money also includes money received:

- for unpaid professional disbursements;
- for other unpaid disbursements where the solicitor has not incurred a liability to pay them;
- on account of costs;

- as commission paid in respect of a client unless the solicitor is entitled to retain it.

Professional disbursements include the fees of counsel, other lawyers, and other professionals, agents or experts instructed by the solicitor – this will include interpreters, translators, process servers, surveyors and estate agents instructed by the solicitor. It does not include travel agents' charges.

Controlled trust money

Controlled trust money is money held or received for a 'controlled trust'. A controlled trust is one where the solicitor is the sole trustee or co-trustee only with one or more of his or her partners or employees. See Rule 2(2)(h) for controlled trusts and registered foreign lawyers, registered European lawyers and recognised bodies. Note that if the trust is not a controlled trust, for example because there is a lay co-trustee, the money is client money. There is no longer a category of 'trust' money as there used to be under the 1991 Rules.

Office money

Office money is money which belongs to the solicitor or practice. It includes:

- money held or received in connection with running the practice, for example PAYE or VAT on the firm's fees;
- interest on general client accounts;
- money received for profit costs where a bill or written notification of costs has been sent;
- money received to repay the solicitor for disbursements already paid;
- money received for disbursements which are unpaid but for which the solicitor has incurred a liability to pay (e.g. items settled by an account such as Land Registry search fees, taxi fares); however, unpaid professional disbursements are expressly excluded and money received for them is client money;
- money received for an agreed fee;
- money held in the client account but earmarked for costs and awaiting transfer.

5.3 USE OF CLIENT ACCOUNT

A solicitor who holds or receives client money and/or controlled trust money must keep one or more client accounts.

5.3.1 What is a client account? (Rule 14)

A client account is an account of the practice kept at a bank or building society in England and Wales. It must include the word 'client' in the title. There are two types of client account:

- a separate designated client account which is a deposit or share account for a single client, or a current, deposit or share account kept for a single controlled trust;
- a general client account which is any other client account.

As from 6 January 2000, a client account may comprise a building society share account as well as a deposit account (Rule 14(4)(b)).

5.3.2 What money goes into the client bank account? (Rule 15)

Rule 15(1) states that you must pay all client money and controlled trust money without delay into a client account.

There are some exceptions, for example when a client instructs you not to pay in money (Rule 16(1)) or where a controlled trustee operating in accordance with his/her powers pays money into a non-client account or retains it as cash (Rule 18(c)).

Rule 15(2) states that no other money may be paid into the client account. Again there are exceptions so, for example, you can use your own money to open or maintain the client account and can advance money to the client where you are holding too little money for a client or controlled trust to fund a payment.

5.3.3 When can money come out of the client account?

This is governed by Rule 22. The situations in which you can withdraw client money and controlled trust money include:

- making payments on behalf of the client or trust;
- paying disbursements on behalf of the client or trust;
- reimbursing yourself for money spent on behalf of the client or trust;
- transferring to another client account.

The money you take out of a general client account must not exceed the total you hold for that client or controlled trust in all the general client accounts.

There is one exception to this which is where you hold money in a separate designated client account for a client or trust. You can withdraw from a general client account in excess of the amount held there for the client or trust provided you make a transfer from the separate designated client account immediately.

Note: You can withdraw money from the client account to meet the cost of disbursements that you have already paid from the office bank account without sending a bill. You can only withdraw money for your professional charges once you have sent the bill or other written notification of costs or agreed a fee under Rule 19(5). Once you have sent your bill the money due for professional charges becomes office money and you must transfer it within 14 days. See at 5.3.6 below.

5.3.4 Mixed receipts (Rule 20)

Where you receive office money mixed with either client or controlled trust money, you either split the cheque or pay the whole amount into the client account.

If you pay it all into the client account you must transfer all office money out of the client account within 14 days. (But see also Rule 19 (at 5.3.5 below) in the case of costs payments.)

5.3.5 Special rules for dealing with money received for bills (Rule 19)

There are four possibilities:

- Identify the type of money received and deal with it appropriately:
    - if the money is all office money, put it all in the office account;
    - if the money is all client money, put it all in the client account;
    - if the money is a mixture, deal with it under Rule 20 – either splitting it or paying it all into the client account.

- Where the money is all office money and/or client money in the form of unpaid professional disbursements for which you have incurred a liability to pay, in this one circumstance you can pay client money into the office bank account for a limited period (Rule 19(1)(b)). To fall within Rule 19(1)(b) the receipt must consist only of office money and client money for unpaid professional disbursements (see Rule 2 for definition). You must have already incurred liability for the disbursement. If you do not pay the disbursement by the end of the second working day following receipt, you must transfer the client money to the client bank account. The advantage of this option is that it simplifies dealing with receipts of costs, allowing more to be paid straight into the office bank account and resulting in fewer transfers between client and office bank account.
- Irrespective of the type of money, pay it all into the client bank account and transfer out any office money within 14 days of receipt. This may be done where the person dealing with the money is uncertain as to its correct classification. This option allows the money to be banked

promptly pending a decision as to how it should be treated. It is also a useful option where a client wishes to make direct payments into your bank account. You can give the client the number of the client bank account and all payments can be made into that account.

- There are two special dispensations for money received from the Legal Services Commission (LSC):

  - provided the LSC gives instructions in writing, advance payments for work to be carried out may be paid into the office bank account;
  - a payment for costs may be paid into the office bank account even when mixed with client money for unpaid disbursements, provided the disbursements are paid or money representing them transferred to the client bank account within 14 days of receipt.

There is a special rule for payments from a third party. Where the LSC has already paid any costs to a solicitor (or has paid professional disbursements direct) and costs are subsequently settled by a third party, the entire third party payment must be paid into the client bank account.

Any balance belonging to the solicitor must be transferred to the office bank account within 14 days of the solicitor sending a report to the LSC containing details of the third party payment. The amount retained in the client bank account must be recorded as held for the LSC (either on the individual client's ledger account or on a separate ledger in the LSC's name).

It must be kept there until the LSC informs the solicitor that it has recouped an equivalent sum from subsequent legal aid payments due to the solicitor. The retained sum must be transferred to an office bank account within 14 days of notification.

Standard monthly payments have been introduced since the 1998 Rules were issued. They are not yet dealt with in the Rules. Interim guidance is available at **www.lawsociety.org.uk**. It gives solicitors the choice of holding standard monthly payments in either the office or client bank account, but suggests that consideration should be given as to how professional disbursements are to be settled.

5.3.6 Time limit on transfers (Rules 19–21)

The 1998 Rules impose a standard 14-day time limit on all transfers needing to be made from the client bank account (apart from the two-day period for unpaid professional disbursements under Rule 19(1)(b)). The reason for imposing the time limit on transfers is to prevent unclaimed costs concealing a shortfall on the client account.

5.3.7   Transfers between clients (Rule 30(2))

You are required to obtain the written authority of both clients in the case of private loans between clients. This does not apply to loans made by an institutional lender.

5.3.8   Authority for withdrawals from client account (Rule 23)

A withdrawal of funds from client account may be made without the bank which actually makes the transfer having to hold a written authority, for example, it can be done by telephone. However, before the transfer is made there must be in existence a specific authority in respect of the particular withdrawal, signed by one of the persons specified in Rule 23(1). It is also important that there are appropriate safeguards such as passwords. Note that in the case of a withdrawal by cheque, the signature on the cheque is usually the specific authority *but not if the cheque is blank*.

5.3.9   Who may authorise withdrawals from client account? (Rule 23)

Withdrawals from client account may be authorised by:

- a solicitor with a current practising certificate or a registered European lawyer;
- a three-year FILEX employed by a solicitor, registered European lawyer or recognised body;
- a licensed conveyancer employed by a solicitor, registered European lawyer or recognised body where the office deals solely with conveyancing;
- a registered foreign lawyer who is a partner in the practice, or director of the practice (if it is a company), or member of the practice (if it is a limited liability partnership).

5.4   RECORD-KEEPING REQUIREMENTS (RULE 32)

You must keep records to show all dealings with client money, controlled trust money and office money relating to any client or controlled trust matter. The dealings must be recorded on a cash account (or record of inter-client transfers) and on a client ledger account for each client or controlled trust. The current balance for each client must be shown or be readily ascertainable.

The records must show all dealings with client money and controlled trust money. It is, therefore, important to record any change in the person(s) for whom money is held.

For example, during or at the end of an administration beneficiaries will become entitled to funds. Normally there will be a cash payment to the beneficiaries which will be recorded as a cash payment from the client account on behalf of the personal representatives. However, the beneficiary may ask you to retain funds for them in the client account. In such a case you must record – on the client ledger accounts and also on the transfer record – that money is no longer held for the personal representatives but is now held for the beneficiary. Separate client ledger accounts are necessary.

5.4.1 Relaxation of requirements when acting for both institutional lender and borrower (Rule 32(6))

To regularise the practice of a solicitor opening one ledger account where he or she is acting for both lender and borrower in a conveyancing matter, Rule 32(6) permits the opening of only one ledger account, provided that the funds belonging to each client are clearly identifiable on the ledger. The permission does not extend to private loans.

Rule 32(6) is expressed to apply to mortgage *advances*. There is no mention of mortgage *redemptions*. If a solicitor holds money for a lender after completion of a sale, it will only be necessary to open a separate ledger account for the lender if you have been instructed by the lender to act in the redemption.

5.4.2 Record-keeping when acting for controlled trusts

You must keep full records of all dealings with controlled trust money unless you use an outside manager to run the trust on a day-to-day basis. In such a case the manager must keep and retain appropriate accounting records which must be available for inspection by the Law Society.

5.4.3 Record-keeping requirements for liquidators, etc. (Rule 9)

Provided liquidators, trustees in bankruptcy, Court of Protection receivers and trustees of occupational pension schemes comply with their own statutory rules and regulations, they will be deemed to have complied sufficiently with the Solicitors' Accounts Rules so long as they also comply with the limited record-keeping requirements of Rule 9. They must:

- keep a central record of bills;
- retain for at least six years any records kept under the statutory rules;
- keep or register such records centrally;
- make such records available for monitoring and inspection by the Law Society;
- produce such records to the reporting accountants to enable them to check compliance.

5.4.4 Record-keeping requirements for joint accounts (Rule 10)

The 1998 Rules in general do not apply to solicitors operating joint accounts but various record-keeping requirements do (to protect against fraud). Solicitors must:

- keep a central record of bills;
- retain statements and passbooks (or duplicates and copy entries) for at least six years;
- keep or register such statements and passbooks (or duplicates and copy entries) centrally;
- make such records available for monitoring and inspection by the Law Society;
- produce such records to the reporting accountants to enable them to check compliance.

5.4.5 Record-keeping requirements for client's own account (Rule 11)

The 1998 Rules in general do not apply to solicitors operating a client's own account (for example, under a power of attorney) but various record-keeping requirements do (to protect against fraud). Solicitors must:

- receive and keep statements and passbooks (or duplicates and copy entries) for at least six years;
- keep or register such statements and passbooks (or duplicates and copy entries) centrally;
- make such records available for monitoring and inspection by the Law Society;
- produce such records to the reporting accountants to enable them to check compliance.

5.4.6 Regular bank reconciliations (Rule 32(7))

You are required to prepare bank reconciliations for all general and designated accounts containing client and controlled trust money at least once every five weeks (in effect monthly).

However, where you keep controlled trust money in a passbook-operated separate designated client account, you need only prepare a reconciliation for that money every 14 weeks. There is no requirement to check that interest has been credited since the last statement or entry in the passbook.

5.4.7 Retention of paid cheques and bank statements etc. (Rule 32(9) and (10))

Paid cheques must be retained for two years. You need not arrange for your bank to return paid cheques, if you arrange in writing that the bank keep paid cheques for two years. Other authorities for withdrawals from the client account must also be kept for two years (Rule 32(10)).

Bank statements and all other records must be kept for six years (Rule 32(9)). These requirements extend not just to client accounts but to others such as non-client accounts where client or controlled trust money is held.

5.5 RULES ON INTEREST (RULES 24–27)

You must account to a client for all interest earned on separate designated client accounts. You are required by Rule 25(1) to aim for a reasonable rate of interest on such money.

Where money is not held in a separate designated client account the general rule is that you must account to the client for a sum in lieu of interest. However, there are the following exceptions where there is no need to account:

(a) if the amount calculated is £20 or less;
(b) (i) if the amount held does not exceed the amount and the time for which it is held does not exceed the period set out in the table:

Amount £	Time / (Weeks)
1,000	8
2,000	4
10,000	2
20,000	1

(ii) if the amount held exceeds £20,000 but is held for one week or less, unless it is fair and reasonable to account having regard to all the circumstances;

(c) on money held for the payment of counsel's fees, once counsel has requested a delay in settlement;
(d) on money held for the LSC;
(e) on money held in the client account as a result of an advance from the solicitor to the client to cover a payment for which the client had insufficient funds;
(f) if there is an agreement to contract out of the interest provisions of the 1998 Rules.

You are still allowed to retain any interest earned on client money held in a general client account over and above the amount you are required to pay out. It is expressly provided in Rule 13 that interest earned in this way is office money. However, there is a problem if the general client account includes controlled trust money (see Rule 15, note (vi)).

Trustees are subject to the legal duty not to profit from their trust and must obtain the best reasonably obtainable rate of interest. You have three options in respect of controlled trust money:

- you can place the money in a separate designated client account in which case all interest earned belongs to the trust;
- you can set up a general client account just for controlled trust money. The interest will be credited to the office bank account in the normal way but you must immediately allocate it to each controlled trust;
- you can continue to mix controlled trust money with client money in a general client account so long as you are able to comply with your legal duty and ensure that you do not profit from your trust.

A client may fail to present a cheque for payment promptly. Note (vii) to Rule 24 states that whether or not it is reasonable to recalculate the amount due will depend on all the circumstances of the case. You can make a reasonable charge for any extra work carried out but only if you are legally entitled to make a charge for such work.

When calculating the amount due to a client in lieu of interest, Rule 25(1) requires you to account for a 'fair' sum. It need not necessarily reflect the highest rate of interest available but it is not acceptable to look only at the lowest rate of interest available. Rule 25(2) provides that the sum must be calculated:

- on the balance(s) held over the whole period for which cleared funds are held;
- at a rate not less than whichever is the higher of:

  – the rate payable on a separate designated client account for the amount(s) held, or
  – the rate payable on the relevant amount(s) if placed on deposit on similar terms by a member of the business community
  – at the bank or building society where the money is held.

5.6 ACCOUNTANT'S REPORT RULES 1991

The Accountant's Report Rules 1991 are now incorporated in the 1998 Rules as Part F.

Changes made in December 1995 stemmed from the Law Society's attempts to reduce the costs of default. It became apparent from the reports of the then Monitoring Unit and from inspections carried out by the then Solicitors' Complaints Bureau's Investigation Accountants that some reporting accountants were not carrying out their duties effectively and that serious breaches of the Rules and in some cases fraud had not been identified.

Reporting accountants must have registered auditor status together with membership of one of the accountancy bodies currently listed in the 1998 Rules. To enable the Law Society to maintain accurate records you must inform the Society of any change in the reporting accountant.

You have to produce a letter of engagement for accountants incorporating the terms set out in Rule 38(1). The letter (and a copy) have to be signed by the solicitor (or a partner, director or member) and by the accountant. The letter has to be kept for three years and produced to the Law Society on request.

Accountants are also required to report on any substantial departure from the Guidelines for Procedures and Systems for Accounting for client money.

In addition to the requirements for testing already contained in the 1998 Rules, reporting accountants have to complete and sign a Law Society check-list which the solicitor must keep for three years and produce to the Law Society on request. The checklist is intended to be an assurance to the solicitor and to the Law Society that the work required to be done has indeed been done. It does not impose any additional obligations on accountants.

A solicitor who has operated a client's own account as signatory must deliver an accountant's report for the accounting period within six months of the end of the period (Rule 35). The reporting accountant will check compliance with Rule 11.

The reporting accountant will have to check that records, statements and passbooks are being kept as required by liquidators, Court of Protection receivers, etc. (Rule 9). The reporting accountant will also check the requirements for joint accounts (Rule 10). (There is a useful article on the new reporting Rules by Amanda Reade in [1997] *New Law Journal*, 15 August.)

From 1 September 2000, the reporting accountant must also look at the solicitor's certificate(s) of insurance and note on the report whether or not there appears to have been indemnity insurance for the period covered by the report.

5.7   HOW DO THE 1998 RULES AFFECT PROBATE WORK?

When you are doing trust and/or probate work you will handle client money and controlled trust money. You will have to pay money into the appropriate bank accounts and follow the rules as to withdrawals. In particular, you will have to classify money correctly as client, controlled trust or office. The rules relating to client money and controlled trust money are much more similar than they used to be but there are still some differences.

5.7.1 Client money or controlled trust money?

Remember that this is the only choice. There is no longer a category of 'trust' money. Controlled trusts are trusts where a solicitor is the sole trustee or is a trustee with a partner or employee. Rule 2(2)(h) also sets out the circumstances where a controlled trust may arise, where one or more of the trustees are registered European lawyers, registered foreign lawyers or recognised bodies. As the notes to the 1998 Rules point out, this definition, which is statutory, gives rise to some anomalies. For example, an assistant solicitor who is a sole trustee is a controlled trustee; two assistant solicitors who are the only co-trustees are not; an assistant and a partner are controlled trustees; a sole solicitor trustee who is a director of a recognised body which is a company is a controlled trustee; two or more directors of a recognised body which is a company are not. Where a trust is not a controlled trust any money received for the trust is client money.

5.7.2 Which bank account?

Client money can go into the general client account or a separate designated client account. It can also be retained in cash or paid into a non-client account if the client so instructs.

Controlled trust money can go into the general client account or a separate designated client account which can be a current, deposit or share account. It can also be paid into a non-client account if the trustees' powers permit it or be retained in cash in the performance of the trustees' duties.

5.7.3 Reconciliation

Where money is paid into a general client account it will be subject to the requirement for reconciliations at least once every five weeks.

This requirement will apply to controlled trust money in separate designated client accounts unless the account is passbook-operated in which case the requirement is at least once every 14 weeks. Such a reconciliation is necessary even where the controlled trust money is held in a non-client account under Rule 18.

5.7.4 Records

The record-keeping requirements for controlled trust money are the same as those for client money. However, where controlled trustees instruct an outside manager to run the business or property portfolio of an estate or trust, the manager must maintain, and then produce, appropriate records for inspection by the Law Society.

Remember that if you are acting as a Court of Protection receiver, operating a joint account or operating the client's own account, you will be required to keep records and have them checked by the reporting accountant.

5.7.5 Interest

Remember that if you pay controlled trust money into the general client account, you must be careful not to profit from your trust (as outlined at 5.3.3 above).

In addition there may be problems for solicitors in calculating how much interest is due to clients. You may have completed the administration and sent cheques to beneficiaries. If the beneficiaries fail to cash those cheques, you may be under an obligation to pay the client interest unless the amount falls into one of the exceptions set out in Rule 24(3). The notes to the Rule say that whether or not a solicitor has to recalculate interest will depend on the circumstances of the case.

PART II

Probate, Wills and the Law

This Part includes guidance on certain legal aspects of probate work, and ends with a brief outline of the basics of succession law. The Handbook is not intended to be a legal textbook, however, and Appendix 5 includes relevant works.

CHAPTER 6

Liability for a client's fraud

Steven Fennell

6.1 INTRODUCTION

You may, in good faith, assist a client in a financial transaction which you imagine at the time to be perfectly proper, but which turns out to involve a fraud on a third party. You will then want answers to two questions – can you:

- be held liable in any way to the injured third party? and
- disclose details of the client's transaction to the third party once you discover (or more likely suspect) the client's wrongdoing.

This chapter gives basic guidance on both of these issues. The first section deals with the extent of liability for a client's fraud in the light of the leading cases. The second section deals with the solicitor's duty of confidentiality. The third section suggests what action solicitors should take when they know or suspect that a client has involved them in a fraudulent transaction. The last section is a summary of the points made.

6.2 EXTENT OF LIABILITY FOR A CLIENT'S FRAUD

6.2.1 How liability can arise

A number of recent cases illustrate the way in which a solicitor (or other professional adviser) can become drawn into a client's improper scheme, and face a claim. In one case, for example, the defendant solicitor acted for several members of the same family in relation to a complex network of family trusts, which included his appointment as trustee. The assets had been acquired by the father of the principal beneficiaries, who was also a trustee and beneficiary under certain of the trusts. The solicitor was asked to exercise his powers as trustee to support the business run by the father, which involved a substantial risk to the assets of the trust. The solicitor was one of the defendants sued by the other members of the family after the business collapsed and the father was declared bankrupt (*Walker* v. *Stones* [2000] 4 All

ER 412). The court had to decide whether the solicitor was guilty of a breach of his own fiduciary duties, or guilty of assisting others to contravene their own obligations.

In another example, the client had two solicitors acting for him. Funds were transferred from the first solicitor to the second, in breach of an undertaking given by the first firm. The client then instructed the second solicitor to use them in a manner inconsistent with the first firm's undertaking. The court again had to decide whether this assisted in a breach of fiduciary duty in circumstances in which the second firm should be liable (*Twinsectra Ltd* v. *Yardley and others* [1999] Lloyd's Rep 438).

A final illustration involved a firm of accountants acting for an oil company, which was being defrauded by its in-house accountant. The dishonest accountant had been diverting payments due to the company to a series of shell companies, which the defendant accountants set up and eventually liquidated. They took instructions from a French lawyer, and did not discover the nature of the transactions in which they had assisted until the oil company sued them. They thought that they had been involved in a scheme to circumvent exchange controls. Again, the court had to decide whether they were liable for the losses suffered by the company (*Agip (Africa) Ltd* v. *Jackson* [1991] Ch 54).

In all three cases, the professional advisers were found to be liable for the losses suffered, although in none of the cases had they been personally enriched beyond the payment of fees. It is all too easy to imagine solicitors becoming involved in similar transactions.

6.2.2 Liability for receipt and liability for assistance

There are two main ways in which liability can arise:

- for receiving the proceeds of fraud through:

    - unjust enrichment and the common law of restitution;
    - the tort of conversion;
    - a proprietary constructive trust in equity;

- for assisting in the fraud through:

    - personal liability under a constructive trust imposed on the basis of:
    (a) knowing receipt and dealing;
    (b) dishonest assistance in a breach of trust;
    - breach of contract;
    - the tort of negligence.

Each of these will be examined in turn.

6.2.3   Liability for receiving the proceeds of fraud

Liability for unjust enrichment

In *Lipkin Gorman* v. *Karpnale Ltd* [1991] 2 AC 548 the House of Lords set out the conditions under which a claim for unjust enrichment can succeed:

- the defendant must be enriched;
- the enrichment must be at the claimant's expense;
- the enrichment must be unjust, which means that there must be a factor, such as mistake or duress, which renders the enrichment reversible, not simply that the enrichment is 'unfair'; and
- there must be no defence.

Liability does not depend on fault by the defendant: the fact of enrichment, combined with the lack of a defence (such as *bona fide* purchase or change of position), will justify the court giving judgment for the claimant.

The application of these tests means that, in practice, solicitors and other professional advisers are unlikely to incur liability to make restitution. There will normally be no enrichment beyond the receipt of fees: while substantial sums may pass through a client account, the professional is not enriched by this, and so no liability will arise.

Receipt of fees from the misdirected funds is clearly an enrichment, but *bona fide* purchase should provide a defence. Provided that the advisers have acted in good faith and without notice of the fraud, their services will amount to good consideration for the receipt of the fees, and they will not be liable to return them.

Change of position is also a defence, and so a firm which has relied upon the receipt of fees may be able to show that it is inequitable to be asked to return them. In practice, change of position is unlikely to add anything to the defence of *bona fide* purchase: if the firm cannot show that it acted in good faith and charged no more than a proper fee for the job, it is unlikely to succeed on a defence of change of position.

Liability for conversion

It is easier to incur liability as a result of handling chattels (including cheques and bankers' drafts) on behalf of a client. Liability can arise under the tort of conversion, which applies to any dealings with a chattel inconsistent with the rights of the person entitled to immediate possession. A person who deals with a stolen cheque or bankers' draft will be strictly liable for its face value if there is anyone entitled to immediate possession (*Morrison* v. *London County and Westminster Bank* [1914] 3 KB 356; *International Factors Ltd* v. *Rodriguez* [1979] QB 315; *Lipkin Gorman* v. *Karpnale Ltd* (above)). There is no defence of change of position, although the Bills of Exchange Act 1882 provides limited defences based on acting in good faith and for value.

The endorsement of negotiable instruments such as cheques and bankers' drafts is now far less common than it used to be, as a result of the Cheques Act 1992 and the use of 'account payee only' on negotiable instruments, and the increasing use of direct transfers. A detailed account of the law of conversion as applied to bills of exchange is therefore unnecessary, and it is enough to warn solicitors not to handle indorsed cheques or bankers' drafts from clients unless they are absolutely sure that the client has good title. The client should be asked to transfer the money in a more conventional way.

Liability under a proprietary constructive trust

A proprietary constructive trust is a trust attaching to property, or its proceeds, which can be traced from the claimant to the defendant under the equitable rules of tracing. Liability arises here because the defendant is in possession of property which belongs, in equity, to the claimant. The defendant will not be liable if he is a *bona fide* purchaser for value without notice, and neither will he be liable if he no longer has the property or its proceeds.

The greatest risk for a professional in relation to this form of liability is to be faced with competing claims on clients' monies, for example with a third party claiming that funds held in a client account are in fact the traceable proceeds of a fraud which the client has received. In such a situation, a professional faced with a claim which is not obviously hopeless should consider making an application to court for directions: paying the money to the client with notice of the claim attaching to it might lead to liability for knowing assistance in a breach of trust, as described below.

6.2.4 Personal liability as a constructive trustee

Personal and proprietary claims distinguished

The use of the term 'constructive trust' to describe two entirely different situations has caused confusion for a long time. In deciding a claim based on a proprietary constructive trust, the court has to ask whether a person takes property subject to or free from an equitable claim. The court looks at whether the defendant had *notice* of the equity, whether he gave value, and whether he still has the property or its traceable proceeds.

In deciding a claim based on a personal constructive trust, the court must ask whether the defendant is to have imposed upon him the personal burdens and obligations of a trustee. Liability will arise where the defendant has either received trust property or become involved in a breach of trust in circumstances in which it is equitable for him to be treated as a trustee. The court therefore looks at the defendant's *knowledge*, rather than the more technical rules of actual and constructive *notice*. Liability is not limited to the traceable assets still in the defendant's hands: the defendant will be liable for the total foreseeable loss suffered by the claimant as a result of the breach of trust in which the defendant assisted, or the total amount knowingly received by the defendant. This will be subject to an allowance for anything subsequently recovered by the claimant. The claimant will not be able to claim anything in respect of losses which were not caused by the breach of trust in which the defendant assisted, or as a result of which the defendant received funds (*Target Holdings Ltd* v. *Redferns* [1995] 3 All ER 735; *Heinl* v. *Jyske Bank (Gibraltar) Ltd* [1999] Lloyd's Rep 511).

Liability for knowing receipt and dealing

To be liable for knowing receipt and dealing, defendants must receive or apply the trust property for their own benefit. Consequently, a professional who simply receives trust property on behalf of a client, and passes it on, cannot be held liable under this head, because there is no beneficial receipt (*Agip (Africa) Ltd* v. *Jackson* (above)).

Again, the difficulty for professionals arises where their fees are paid out of the property claimed by the claimant. In the earliest case to address this issue, *Carl Zeiss Stiftung* v. *Herbert Smith and Co. (No. 2)* [1969] 2 Ch 176 the question was whether the solicitors involved could retain the fees which had been paid to them for defending a claim that their client held all of its assets on trust for the claimant. The court held that as the firm acted honestly and provided full consideration, it could not be liable for knowing receipt. The approach in *Carl Zeiss Stiftung* v. *Herbert Smith and Co.* was approved (obiter) by the House of Lords in *Royal Brunei Airlines* v. *Tan* [1995] 3 WLR 64, in which Lord Nicholls characterised the situation as one of genuine doubt, in which the firm had not acted dishonestly in accepting remuneration from one of two genuine claimants.

In *Twinsectra Ltd* v. *Yardley* (above) the court required the defendant solicitor to return fees which he had been paid in circumstances in which he knew involved a deliberate misapplication of trust property. The facts of the case are discussed in more detail below, but in relation to liability for receipt the case only shows that a dishonest recipient cannot retain professional fees paid from misapplied funds. It does not address the issue of whether liability can arise where the recipient has some degree of knowledge, but is not dishonest.

There has been considerable confusion as to whether dishonesty is the standard of liability for knowing receipt. The recent case of *BCCI* v. *Akindele* [2000] 4 All ER 221 made it clear that dishonesty is not an essential element of a claim for knowing receipt. It is enough that the defendant should receive property in circumstances in which his state of knowledge makes it unconscionable to retain it. Nourse LJ suggested that this will allow the courts to adopt a commonsense approach, although it could certainly be suggested that in the absence of reported decisions on the application of this test, it will be difficult to predict the nature and degree of knowledge which will give rise to liability in any given case. In particular, there is now a possibility that professionals may be required to repay fees which were received honestly, but in circumstances where they had sufficient notice of the claimant's interest to make the receipt 'unconscionable'. In cases of doubt, professionals are likely to be best advised to insist upon payment from another source, or where they already hold the funds when the claim is notified to them, it could well be appropriate to make an application to the court for directions (*Finers* v. *Miro* [1991] 1 All ER 182).

Liability for dishonest assistance

While dishonesty is not an essential element in a claim for receipt of trust property, it remains the most important element in liability for assistance (*Royal Brunei Airlines* v. *Tan* [1995] 3 WLR 64). A person who helps another to misapply trust property will be liable to the beneficiaries if he does so dishonestly; no liability arises if the assistance is provided honestly, even if the defendant acted negligently.

If the defendant acts dishonestly, he will be liable even if the breach of trust itself is not dishonest. Lord Nicholls in *Royal Brunei Airlines* v. *Tan* gives the example of trustees who innocently wish to deal with the trust funds in their care in such a way as to amount to a breach of trust, who instruct a solicitor to act for them. If the solicitor acts in the knowledge that a breach of trust is being committed, he or she will be liable to the beneficiaries.

The defendant must, of course, assist in the breach of trust. A person who is peripherally involved in a transaction and who does not further the breach of trust in any way will not incur liability, even if he or she is aware of the breach (*Brinks Ltd* v. *Abu Saleh and others (No. 3)*, *The Times*, 23 October 1995, where the wife of one of the individuals involved in laundering the proceeds of the Brinks Mat robbery was not liable for knowing assistance simply because she travelled abroad with her husband while he was disposing of the proceeds of the crime).

Three further points need to be clarified in relation to the notion of dishonesty.

THE MEANING OF 'DISHONESTY'

In *Royal Brunei Airlines* v. *Tan* (above) the Privy Council took the view that the technical definitions of dishonesty which apply in the criminal law should not be used for civil claims. Instead, 'dishonesty' is defined as simply 'not acting as an honest person would in the circumstances', or 'conscious impropriety'. Difficulties arise when the defendant has taken a risk, or acted where he or she knows that there is an element of doubt, but again, a commonsense approach should be taken: 'The honest person is expected to attain the standard which would be observed by an honest person placed in those circumstances. It is impossible to be more specific' ([1995] 3 WLR 64, 74, per Lord Nicholls). Honest people may, for example, take advice, or even advise of the risks but continue to act: it is all a question of fact.

Dishonesty is not simply a question of whether the defendant knew that what he was doing was wrong. In *Al Sabah* v. *Grupo Torras SA* (2 November 2000) the Court of Appeal explained that a person can also be dishonest if what he does is dishonest by objective standards, even if the defendant's own standards of honesty are lower than those of society in general so that the defendant genuinely believes that he has done nothing wrong. The defendant can further be guilty of 'blind eye' dishonesty by lending his assistance to a transaction after deliberately closing his eyes and not asking questions for fear of learning something he would rather not know.

A number of recent cases have demonstrated that the courts are willing to find solicitors to be objectively dishonest when their conduct falls far short of the standards which the profession sets for itself. For example, in *Walker* v. *Stones* (above) the defendant solicitor argued that even if he had committed a deliberate breach of trust by applying trust property for the benefit of a company controlled by the beneficiaries' family, rather than the beneficiaries themselves, he could not be dishonest if he had a genuine if misguided view that this was all for the benefit of the beneficiaries. The Court of Appeal rejected this view, holding that a solicitor trustee should be liable where his so-called 'honest belief', though actually held, is so unreasonable that, by any objective standard, no reasonable trustee could have thought that what he did or agreed to do was for the benefit of the beneficiaries.

Similarly, in *Twinsectra* v. *Yardley* (above) the defendant solicitor had received money from another firm retained by his client, knowing that the payment to him was a breach of the undertaking given by the other firm to the claimant. The High Court held that the defendant had been 'misguided', but had not been dishonest, by accepting the funds and then applying them in accordance with his client's instruction. This was rejected by the Court of Appeal, which held that no honest solicitor would knowingly encourage or assist another solicitor in a deliberate breach of an undertaking, and so by deliberately closing his eyes to the interests of the beneficiary of the undertaking, the defendant acted dishonestly.

KNOWLEDGE OF IMPROPRIETY

A defendant will normally be held to be dishonest provided that he knows that something illegal or improper is being planned: he does not need to know the precise details of the fraud itself. For example, in *Agip (Africa) Ltd* v. *Jackson* (above) the defendant accountants thought that they were assisting in a scheme to contravene Tunisian exchange controls, rather than a fraud on the claimant, but were nevertheless held to have acted dishonestly.

ASKING QUESTIONS WHEN SUSPICIONS ARE AROUSED

It will be rare for dishonest clients to inform their advisers of the nature of their plans. They are much more likely to make up a more or less plausible excuse for what they want to do. In such a case, it will be no defence for a solicitor who fails to question a dubious scheme to say that the client would have produced a convincing answer if asked. Liability depends on whether the defendant acted honestly, which includes consideration of the answers actually received when the scheme is questioned. It is not possible to refute a claim of 'blind eye' dishonesty by saying that the fraudster would have been sufficiently inventive to come up with a plausible explanation if asked for one.

VICARIOUS LIABILITY AND PARTNERSHIP LIABILITY

In *Dubai Aluminium Co. Ltd* v. *Salaam* [2000] 1 WLR 910, the court had to consider whether the partners of a solicitor liable for dishonest assistance in a breach of trust were vicariously liable for his acts. It was argued that the Partnership Act 1890, s.10, which imposes vicarious liability for 'any wrongful act or omission of any partner acting in the ordinary course of the business of the firm, or with the authority of his co-partners', only applies to torts, and not to liability as a constructive trustee. The Court of Appeal rejected this view, and held that the partners were vicariously liable, and that s.10 extended to liability for being an accessory to a breach of trust. However, s.10 only imposes liability for acts done in the course of business of the firm. The court held that deliberate involvement in a dishonest scheme is not within the ordinary course of a solicitors' practice, and so as the other partners had done nothing to suggest that the dishonest partner was acting with their authority, they were not liable for his actions. The situation would be different if the solicitor acted for trustees who, entirely innocently, wanted to do something which amounted to a breach of trust. In such a case the advice given would be within the scope of a firm's business, and so the partners would be vicariously liable.

This approach was followed by the Court of Appeal in *Walker* v. *Stones* (above) where it was held that the decision by the solicitor trustee to misapply trust property was not within the scope of the firm's practice, with the result that the claim against the other partners in the firm was struck out.

Leave to appeal to the House of Lords has been granted in the *Dubai Aluminium* case, and so the issue of vicarious liability is likely soon to be re-examined in detail.

Breach of contract and negligence

Solicitors engaged in financial transactions will clearly owe a contractual duty to safeguard the client's financial interests. Thus, if the client is a company, the solicitor will have a duty to make inquiries and take further action if there is a suspicion that it is being defrauded by its executives. This is not to say that the solicitor must regard everyone with suspicion: the relationship between a legal adviser and the individuals giving instructions must be one of trust. The solicitor must merely make inquiries if a reasonable person in his or her position would have doubts about the transaction.

The extent of the solicitors' duty of care in tort to third parties is less clear. The recent cases on solicitors' involvement with dishonest clients have indicated that the principal test for liability is dishonesty on the part of the solicitor, and the courts have taken care to emphasise that negligence is an inappropriate test for liability. Thus it is unlikely that the courts would find that a duty of care exists in favour of third parties, and liability will be confined to dishonest assistance rather than careless involvement, except possibly for cases involving closely related parties, such as groups of companies, where a solicitor retained by a subsidiary may owe a duty of care in tort to the parent company.

6.3 FRAUD, PRIVILEGE AND CONFIDENTIALITY

6.3.1 Nature of the problem

A solicitor who fears that he or she may inadvertently have become involved in a fraudulent transaction is placed in a difficult position with regard to client confidentiality. If the solicitor has acted properly, there should be no liability in relation to past actions. However, the solicitor may incur liability by continuing to act after his or her suspicions have been aroused, and assistance previously provided to the client may allow that client to continue to defraud innocent persons in the future.

6.3.2 Decision of the Court of Appeal in *Finers* v. *Miro*

The leading case on the options available to an inadvertent participant in a fraud is the decision of the Court of Appeal in *Finers* v. *Miro* [1991] 1 All ER 182. The solicitors in that case helped their client to set up a complex series of trusts which made his ownership of his assets difficult to detect, and did so in such a way that they found themselves holding the assets as bare trustee for the client. The solicitors honestly believed that the client's aims were simply to prevent foreign states from nationalising his property. They then discovered a report from a committee of the United States House of Representatives which accused the client of defrauding a now-insolvent American insurance company. The solicitors feared that the assets in the trusts were the proceeds of the fraud, and applied to the court for directions under RSC Ord. 85 (which has not yet been replaced by the Civil Procedure

Rules). In particular, they wanted the court to rule on whether the liquidator of the insurance company should be notified of the application. The Court of Appeal held that the liquidator should be notified.

The solicitors accepted that they did not have conclusive proof that the client was guilty of the fraud: their aim was to have the court determine what they should do as a result of their suspicions. The court held that the liquidator should be notified of the existence of the trusts, because, on the evidence available, there was proof on the balance of probabilities that the alleged fraud had been committed.

The court held that communications between a solicitor and client for the purpose of furthering a client's fraud are not confidential. Committing a fraud is not part of the solicitor-client relationship, and so professional duties do not arise. Professional obligations are regarded as never having arisen if solicitors discover in the course of acting that clients have been using them to commit a fraud, and so disclosure can be made without the client's consent.

Fraud for these purposes covers all forms of dishonesty, as long as the conduct in question amounts to real dishonesty and not merely disreputable conduct or a failure to maintain good ethical standards (*Gamlen Chemical Co Ltd* v. *Rochem* (CA, 1977) per Goff LJ, followed in *Finers* v. *Miro* (above)).

A solicitor can disclose information if he is consulted by a client who wants help to plan, execute or conceal a fraud. If the fraud is already complete, and the client is seeking advice which would not further it or conceal it, the solicitor cannot disclose the fraud to the injured party. The solicitor would be in breach of both the legal duty of confidentiality and the rules of professional conduct if any disclosure were to be made without a court order.

6.3.3 Privilege and confidentiality

The position of solicitors is complicated by the fact that information may be privileged as well as confidential. The two concepts are distinct: privilege is much narrower than confidentiality, as it relates only to the inadmissibility of solicitor–client correspondence in litigation. *O'Rourke* v. *Darbyshire* [1920] AC 581 is authority that as fraud is outside the solicitor–client relationship, information relating to the solicitor's furtherance of a fraud is not privileged.

6.4 ACTION BY SOLICITORS INVOLVED IN DISHONEST TRANSACTIONS

Having outlined the basic legal position in relation to fraud and confidentiality, the next issue is the appropriate course of action for any solicitor who fears that a client has been using his or her services to defraud an innocent third party.

6.4.1 Professional rules

The Guide to the Professional Conduct of Solicitors 1999 provides the following guidance in the first paragraph of the commentary to Rule 16.02 ('The duty to keep a client's confidences can be overridden in certain circumstances'):

> The duty of confidentiality does not apply to information acquired by a solicitor where he or she is being used by the client to facilitate the commission of a crime or fraud, because that is not within the scope of a professional retainer. If the solicitor becomes suspicious about a client's activities the solicitor should normally assess the situation in the light of the client's explanations and the solicitor's professional judgment.

This summarises the general law, and emphasises the need to seek the client's explanation before taking any further action. A telephone call to Professional Ethics at the Law Society, or the policy adviser in the Representation and Law Reform directorate (see Appendix 6 for details) is likely to be the next step. Any such communication would be treated in confidence.

6.4.2 Legal problems

The recommended approach to the legal problems of inadvertent involvement in fraud is as follows. If the solicitor has been honest throughout the transaction, he or she will have incurred no liability for assisting the client, and the worst that could happen would be that the solicitor might be ordered to return any fees received. If suspicions arise, the solicitor can avoid liability for dishonesty simply by refusing to act further.

If a solicitor has strong *prima facie* evidence of fraud, disclosure may be justifiable. In difficult cases, the Law Society or the Solicitors Indemnity Fund may be approached for guidance, but neither can give legal advice, which must be sought from specialist solicitors and/or counsel. The Court of Appeal in *Finers* v. *Miro* has suggested that disclosure may be justified where on the balance of probabilities it appears that the solicitor's services have been used improperly, but it is hard to see how disclosure could be justified without first giving the client the opportunity to explain the situation. In practice, the issues involved in disclosing a transaction against the client's wishes are likely to be so difficult to resolve that an application to the court for directions may provide the only solution.

The greatest problem arises when a firm cannot simply refuse to act because it is still holding some of the proceeds of the suspected fraud. The solution, again, when the client has failed to satisfy the solicitor of the honesty of the transaction, is to apply to the court for directions on how to apply the funds held on trust. This happened in *Finers* v. *Miro*, where the court held that it had jurisdiction to give directions for the administration of a bare trust, even where the apparent beneficiary opposes the application and asks for the funds to be paid direct to him or her. An application to the court is therefore necessary if the client tells the solicitor to pass the money on to someone else.

6.5 SUMMARY

As this area of law is difficult and complicated, a brief summary of the general principles may be useful.

- The starting point is that a solicitor who receives any money (including fees) for his or her own benefit will be liable to return that money if he or she has acted dishonestly, or if he or she had sufficient knowledge of the rightful owner's interest to make it inequitable to retain that money.
- A solicitor should therefore consider requiring payment from a third party if there is doubt as to the beneficial ownership of the funds claimed by the client.
- A solicitor is unlikely to owe a duty of care in tort to a person defrauded by his client. Duties of care are likely to arise only where there is an extremely close relationship between the client and the third party, such as a parent and subsidiary company.
- If a solicitor dishonestly assists in a fraudulent transaction, he or she is likely to be liable for the full extent of the injured party's losses in all cases.
- A dishonest solicitor's partners or employer will be vicariously liable for his or her actions.
- Solicitors who have doubts as to the honesty of a client's transactions should always ask the client for an explanation. If the explanation is satisfactory, the solicitor can continue to act: the law does not expect solicitors to distrust their clients and look for evidence of dishonest conduct; neither does it require a solicitor to be given every last detail of a transaction as long as the transaction is *prima facie* lawful.
- Solicitors who have *prima facie* proof on the balance of probabilities that they have been inadvertently involved in the commission of a fraud can disclose this information to the injured party, but it would be wise to consult the Law Society or take independent advice from specialist counsel before doing this, and to consider an application to the court for directions.
- Fraud covers all forms of dishonesty, but not simply disreputable conduct.
- If the solicitor only has suspicions which do not amount to *prima facie* evidence, it would be wrong to make any disclosure. As a matter of pro-

fessional conduct and self-interest, the solicitor should consider refusing to act any further.

- Significant risks are involved in handling indorsed cheques and bankers' drafts, and the situations in which these are properly used are increasingly rare. Solicitors should consider asking the client to provide funds in a more conventional manner.
- Finally, it must be emphasised that the law in this area is subject to rapid change. This chapter sets out the general principles as they were understood in February 2002. Solicitors should ensure that their knowledge is kept up to date.

CHAPTER 7

Appointing guardians of children

Gillian E. Cockburn and David Hodson

This is a revised version of an article which first appeared in the *Gazette*. We are most grateful to the authors for updating it.

7.1 INTRODUCTION

A guardian of a child is someone who is appointed to take over responsibility for a child in the event of the death of the child's parent or other carer. The appointment is not only necessary if a child has property or money but also to provide day-to-day care for the child, as the guardian will have the right to decide on the child's upbringing, health care, religion and education. It is very important to ensure that the right person or persons are appointed as guardians in accordance with the law.

The law on the appointment of guardians changed radically as a result of the Children Act 1989 ('the 1989 Act') which came into effect from 14 October 1991. It is essential for the will drafter and probate practitioner to understand the main elements of the 1989 Act and in particular the concepts of parental responsibility and residence orders. In some cases it may also be important to liaise with a family law practitioner to find out what court orders have been made concerning a child which may in turn affect the appointment of guardians under the will.

7.2 WHO MAY APPOINT A GUARDIAN?

This is governed by s.5 of the 1989 Act, which provides that guardians may be appointed by:

(a) a parent with parental responsibility for the child (s.5(3)); or
(b) an existing guardian of the child (s.5(4)); or
(c) a court in family proceedings (s.5(1) and (2)).

Except as set out below, the appointment in (a) and (b) becomes effective when the person who makes the appointment dies. At that time the guardian will acquire parental responsibility for the child.

7.2.1 Parental responsibility

The 1989 Act defines parental responsibility for a child as all the rights, duties, powers, responsibilities and authority which by law a parent of a child has in relation to that child and his or her property (s.3(1)).

7.2.2 Who has parental responsibility?

If the child is legitimate (or has been legitimated, or is adopted), the parents (or adopting parents) will each have parental responsibility (s.2(1) and (3)) and both may appoint guardians for the child in the event of their respective deaths (s.5(3)).

If:

- the parents of a child were not married to each other at the time of the birth; and
- the child has not been legitimated by the parents' later marriage or adopted,

the mother alone has parental responsibility for that child (s.2(2) and (3)). The father does not have automatic parental responsibility and so will not be able to appoint a guardian of the child on his death. However, the father may *acquire* parental responsibility (and therefore be able to appoint a guardian) in the following ways:

- through a court order granting him parental responsibility (s.4(1)(a)); or
- by entering into a parental responsibility agreement with the child's mother (s.4(1)(b)); or
- by being appointed, either by the mother or by the court, to assume parental responsibility after the mother's death.

The agreement must be in accordance with the Parental Responsibility Agreement Regulations 1991, SI 1991/1478, reg. 2 as amended by the Parental Responsibility Agreement (Amendment) Regulations 1994, SI 1994/3157. The agreement must contain the names of the child's parents and of the child to whom the agreement is to relate, and must contain the signature of both parents and be witnessed. Both parents must have their signature witnessed at court by a JP or court official and provide evidence of their identity (including a photograph and signature). The mother must also provide the child's full birth certificate. The agreement will only take effect once it has been filed at the Principal Registry of the Family Division in London. The agreement may be brought to an end only by a court order (s.4(3)). It should be noted that a parental responsibility agreement can only be made with an unmarried father and not with any other family member.

By the Adoption and Children Bill 2002, it is intended to provide that parental responsibility shall also be acquired by an unmarried father if he is registered as the father on the child's birth certificate. The birth certificate will therefore also need to be checked. Step-parents can also acquire parental responsibility by agreement or court order.

The Bill also introduces a concept of 'special guardians'. They are appointed by the court, can only apply from a limited category of persons connected with the child, and have to give three months' prior notice of the application to the relevant local authority which then prepares a report. It is akin in some ways to adoption. A special guardian has parental responsibility and is entitled to exercise parental responsibility to the exclusion of any other person with parental responsibility apart from other special guardians. It is likely therefore, but not yet certain, that their testamentary appointments will take priority over those of others with parental responsibility. A special guardian may appoint another individual to be the child's guardian in the event of his or her death. Until the Bill is passed, the complete position will not be known but this aspect must be carefully considered when looking at testamentary provisions.

7.2.3 Who can be a guardian?

Subject to 7.2.4 below, a parent with parental responsibility for a child, or a properly appointed guardian, may appoint another individual to act as guardian for the child on his or her death (s.5(3) and (4)). Although the 1989 Act refers to an individual in the singular, more than one individual may be appointed in accordance with the Interpretation Act 1978, s.6(c). In addition, the 1989 Act also contemplates the subsequent appointment of further guardians (s.6(1)). However, the term 'individual' would not include a trust corporation, local authority or other non-individual.

7.2.4 Residence orders

A residence order is a court order settling the arrangements to be made about the person with whom a child is to live (s.8(1)). It also affects the testamentary appointment of guardians and so needs to be considered by the will drafter.

A residence order can be made jointly in favour of both parents, or a parent and another carer of the child (s.11(4)). It may be made in the context of divorce, judicial separation, or nullity proceedings. It can be made in free-standing applications under the 1989 Act, for example to unmarried parents, grandparents or others who are given leave of the court to apply (s.10). It is not an automatic replacement of the care and control orders made under the pre-Children Act law; in many respects it is wider and more flexible. Also, unlike parental responsibility which is bestowed by law on all parents except as set out in 7.2.2 above, residence orders can only be granted by a court.

However, residence orders are not automatically granted post-divorce to, say, the parent who has the child primarily living with him or her. By s.1(5), the court shall not make any order in respect of the arrangements for a child unless it considers that doing so would be better for the child than making no order at all. In practice, many family law courts are not making residence orders and other child orders on divorce if the arrangements between the parents for the child are working well. Will drafters should therefore enquire of clients whether there is an existing residence order and not presume that there is one simply because a child is living with a particular parent following a divorce or other family law proceedings.

7.3 APPOINTMENT OF A GUARDIAN

If, on the death of the appointor (even if the parents are separated or divorced):

- there is a surviving parent with parental responsibility; and
- the deceased did not have a residence order in his or her favour,

the appointment of the guardian *does not take effect until the death of the surviving parent* (s.5(8)). Then effective appointments by both parents will take effect simultaneously: this can lead to conflicts between the two separately appointed guardians which the court may have to resolve.

This also represents a change from the previous law under which the parent of a child could appoint a guardian to act jointly with the surviving parent. Now such an arrangement would only take place if the deceased parent with parental responsibility had a residence order in his or her favour and in force at the date of his or her death (s.5(7)) or (if the Adoption and Children Bill is passed as anticipated) he or she was the child's only (or last surviving) special guardian.

If:

- on the death of the appointer the child has no surviving parent with parental responsibility; or
- immediately before the death of the appointor, a court residence order was in existence in the appointor's favour regarding the child; or
- (if the Adoption and Children Bill is passed as anticipated) he or she was the child's only (or last surviving) special guardian

then the appointment of the guardian takes immediate effect on the death of the appointor (s.5(7)).

A properly appointed guardian of a child may also appoint another individual to take his or her place as the child's guardian on his or her death (s.5(4)). However, if there is a surviving parent with parental responsibility and the guardian does not have a residence order in his or her favour (or was not the last surviving special guardian) then the appointment by the guardian will only take effect on the death of the surviving parent (s.5(8)).

7.3.1 How is a guardian appointed?

Under the 1989 Act, the appointment by a parent or guardian will not be effective unless it is made in a written document and dated. It must also be signed by the person appointing the guardian, except in the case of a document signed at the appointor's direction, in which case it must be signed in the presence of two witnesses who each then attest to the execution of the document (s.5(5)). An appointment made by will (or other testamentary document) signed at the appointor's direction must be properly witnessed as required under the provisions of the Wills Act 1837, s.9.

The court can also appoint a guardian (on specific application or in general family proceedings) if either:

- a child has no parent with parental responsibility; or
- a residence order has been made in favour of a parent or guardian who has died whilst the order was still in force (s.5(1)).

The former applies to orphans, or to children of unmarried fathers without parental responsibility. The latter applies even though the child may have a surviving parent, albeit without a residence order. In practice, the court is only likely to appoint a non-parent as sole guardian when the deceased, having a residence order in his or her favour, did not make a lifetime appointment and a third party is likely to be better able to care for the child than the surviving parent. (The full circumstances in which courts appoint guardians is beyond the scope of this Handbook.)

7.3.2 Can the appointment be revoked or refused?

During the lifetime of the person who has made the appointment, he or she may revoke the appointment in the following ways:

- by a further appointment of a guardian which is clearly inconsistent with the continuation of the first appointment (s.6(1));
- by specifically revoking the appointment in writing, subject to the same conditions for the appointment of guardians as set out in 7.3.1 above (s.6(2));
- if the appointment is made other than in a will or codicil, by destroying the original written document which provided for the appointment

of the guardian, with the intention of revoking the appointment (s.6(3)); or

- by revoking the will or codicil which contains the appointment (s.6(4)).

The court has power to revoke the appointment at any time under s.6(7). In addition, the person who is appointed guardian may refuse the appointment by any document in writing signed by him or her made within a reasonable time of his or her first knowledge that the appointment has taken effect (s.6(5)).

It should be noted that the Law Reform (Succession) Act 1995, which came into effect from 1 January 1996, contains provisions amending Children Act 1989, s.6 to revoke, on divorce, any appointment of a former spouse as guardian in a will. If such a parent has parental responsibility, his or her right over any children would be unaffected. However, any appointment by will of a step-parent (without parental responsibility) as guardian is affected by any later divorce. The result is that, unless there is anything in the will to the contrary, the appointment of a step-parent as guardian in such circumstances would be revoked. This would not apply if the step-parent had parental responsibility.

7.3.3 Pre-Children Act 1989 orders

As noted at 7.2 above, s.5(3) of the 1989 Act provides that a parent with parental responsibility may appoint a guardian. What is the position then, in respect of orders made under previous enactments?

Transitional provisions contained in Sched. 14, para. 4 to the 1989 Act specify that, in the case of an order in force made under Family Law Reform Act 1987, s.4 giving the father parental rights and duties in relation to a child, that order is deemed to be an order under Children Act 1989, s.4 giving the father parental responsibility for the child.

In addition, Sched. 14, para. 6 provides that where an order is in force, made under specified enactments (Domestic Proceedings and Magistrates' Courts Act 1978; Children Act 1975; Matrimonial Causes Act 1973; Guardianship of Minors Acts 1971 and 1973; Matrimonial Causes Act 1965; Matrimonial Proceedings (Magistrates' Courts) Act 1960) which determines custody and/or care and control of and/or access to a child or any matter regarding a child's education *and* the child's father and mother were married at the time of the child's birth, each parent is deemed to have parental responsibility in accordance with Children Act 1989, s.2. Where such an order is in force and the child is not legitimate, s.2 applies with the following modification: where the existing order gives the father custody or care and control of the child, the court is deemed to have made an order under s.4(1) giving him parental responsibility for the child.

The transitional provisions also cover the question of residence orders, specifying that, for any reference in s.5 of the 1989 Act to a residence order in favour of a parent or guardian, there is to be substituted a reference to any existing order by virtue of which the parent or guardian has care and control of the child.

In practice, the Children Act 1989 has now been in force for 11 years and there will be fewer and fewer children with pre-Children Act orders.

7.3.4   Effect of the 1989 Act on appointment of guardians by will or codicil

An appointment of a guardian may still be made in a will or codicil as these documents are written instruments under s.5(5). Although an appointment may be made in any written document, there is an advantage in appointing in a testamentary document as such documents are likely, by their nature, to be preserved, easily identifiable and be considered by those dealing with the estate of the appointor on death. However, as substitute or additional guardians may also be appointed in other written documents, the probate practitioner cannot assume that the guardians appointed in the will are the only guardians and enquiries should be made as to any other appointments which might take effect either instead of, or in addition to, the appointment in the testamentary document.

Even if a guardian is appointed in the will or codicil, the appointment may be revoked in any written document in accordance with ss.5 and 6 of the 1989 Act. Thus a will may be valid, apart from the appointment of guardians, which may have been revoked in a later non-testamentary document. The converse situation could never arise, i.e., a revoked will but a valid appointment of guardians due to the provisions of s.6(4), so that if a will or codicil is revoked, the appointment of a guardian contained in the testamentary document will also be revoked.

It is advisable, when dealing with an estate involving minors, to check whether there are any other written documents which may have revoked an appointment of guardians in a will or codicil.

However, it is possible to have an invalid will (e.g. if the formalities for signing and witnessing the will have not been complied with) containing a valid appointment of guardians. The appointment will be valid provided that the invalid will qualifies as a document in writing, is signed by the appointor, and is dated.

It has been common in the past for both parents to appoint a guardian or guardians to take effect on the death of the second parent. In general, it is no longer necessary that such a specific condition should be included within a will because under the terms of the 1989 Act, where both parents have parental responsibility (and there is no residence order in force), the appointment will not take effect until the second death.

At any one time more than one person may have the right to appoint a guardian for a child but the appointment of guardians on death will not, in general, take effect until the child's last surviving guardian or parent with parental responsibility dies. The situation may then arise of two or more separately appointed guardians acting. This should be taken into account by the probate practitioner.

As will be noted from 7.3 above, the position will be further complicated if there are any residence orders in force with respect to the child. Will drafters and probate practitioners should also take this into account. If clients are at all unclear as to the existence of residence orders, the prudent will drafter should make enquiries of the court or of a family law practitioner to ascertain the correct position.

If the will drafter is acting for the mother of a non-marital minor child, enquiries should be made as to the existence of any parental responsibility agreement, as the father of the child may then be able to appoint testamentary guardians. As the significance of parental responsibility is of such importance for the appointment of guardians, and the requirements for parental responsibility agreements are strict, it may be prudent for the will drafter or probate practitioner, in appropriate cases, to check the existence of a valid agreement at the Principal Registry. Enquiries should be directed to the Children Section (see Appendix 6). A fee of £20 is payable for every 10 years searched. Cheques should be made payable to HM Paymaster General. In addition, assuming the provisions of the Adoption and Children Bill 2002 are enacted unchanged, the child's birth certificate should be checked to see if the unmarried father has acquired parental responsibility by being registered on the child's birth certificate.

There is no provision in the 1989 Act for successive appointments by the original appointor (i.e., 'I appoint Jane Smith as guardian of my minor children and when she dies then I appoint her husband William Smith as guardian'). However, there seems to be no prohibition on substitutional appointments taking effect if the first choice as guardian does not survive the appointor (i.e. 'I appoint Jane Smith as guardian of my minor children but if she has pre-deceased me then I appoint her husband William Smith as guardian').

There are often a number of clauses included in wills giving executors, trustees and appointed guardians certain rights and powers in relation to financial provision for minor beneficiaries under the will. If the will refers to provision for the child being made to the child's guardian, care should be taken by executors and trustees as well as those administering estates to ensure that the named guardian is properly and effectively appointed.

CHAPTER 8

Time for probate

Gillian E. Cockburn

This is a revised version of an article which first appeared in the *Gazette*. We are most grateful to Gillian Cockburn of Cockburns, Guildford for revising and updating it.

Time limits are of crucial importance in probate and estate planning. This chapter considers, in brief, some of the more important time limits that practitioners should bear in mind during the administration of an estate.

8.1 OBTAINING THE GRANT

In general, a grant of probate will not issue from the probate registry within seven days of the date of death and a grant of letters of administration will not issue within 14 days of the date of death. In exceptional cases, a district judge or probate registrar may give leave for the grant to issue earlier but the applicant will first have to explain the need for expedition by way of a letter accompanying the application (Non-Contentious Probate Rules (NCPR) 1987, SI 1987/2024, Rule 6(2)).

8.1.1 Caveats

If a caveat is entered to prevent a grant of representation being issued in an estate it should be remembered that the caveat will only remain in force for a period of six months from the date of entry (NCPR 1987, Rule 44(3)(a)–(c)). It may be extended for further periods of six months but each application for extension must be made in the last month prior to the expiry of the caveat.

8.2 RECTIFICATION OF THE WILL

It is possible to correct errors in wills of testators dying on or after 1 January 1983 provided the court is satisfied that the will fails to express the testator's intentions as a result of either a clerical error or a failure by the drafter to understand the testator's intentions (Administration of Justice Act (AJA) 1982, s.20). An application for rectification of a will must be made within six months of the date that representation to the estate is first taken out. The court does have power to consider applications outside the six-month period but the applicant has to show that there was a very good reason why the application was not made within the time limit. If there is a possibility of rectification the personal representatives should not distribute the estate within the six-month period referred to above. (See AJA 1982 regarding distributions once the six-month period has expired.)

8.3   FAMILY PROVISION CLAIMS

(See also Chapter 10.) Certain individuals have the right to apply for financial provision from the estate of a person who dies domiciled in England and Wales (Inheritance (Provision for Family and Dependants) Act (IPFDA) 1975, s.1). A claim must be made within six months of the date that representation to the estate is first taken out (IPFDA 1975, s.4). If there is a possibility of a claim the personal representatives should not distribute the estate within this period. (See IPFDA 1975, s.20 for more on distributions.) The court does have power to allow a claim to be made outside the six-month period but this power is rarely exercised.

8.4   INTEREST AND LEGACIES

(See also Chapter 16.) Personal representatives must administer the estate properly and should not unduly delay the payment of legacies. Personal representatives who delay payment without good reason may find themselves personally liable to pay interest to aggrieved beneficiaries. In certain cases, legatees have the right to interest at 6 per cent per annum (RSC Ord. 44, Rule 10) on their legacies, if they are paid late as follows:

- General pecuniary legacies should be paid within one year ('the executors' year') from the date of death. Where they are paid outside that period they must carry interest calculated from the first anniversary of the death (when the right to receive the legacy arose). Any interest paid will come from the residue of the estate (from monies which might otherwise have passed to the residuary beneficiaries).
- Specific legacies do not carry the right to interest but they do carry any income arising from the gift, subject to the wording of the will.
- Immediate legacies will carry interest from the date of death if it is clear from the will that the testator or testatrix intended that the payment should be made immediately on death. Legacies (whether immediate or

contingent) provided for the maintenance of the testator's or the testatrix's children will also carry interest from the date of death.

- Future or contingent legacies will in general carry interest from the date the future event or contingency occurs.
- Residuary gifts do not carry interest in accordance with these provisions. However, residuary beneficiaries are entitled to a share in any income the estate generates after payment of estate liabilities and legacies.

8.5 ADVERTISING FOR CREDITORS

Personal representatives should consider advertising for creditors and potential beneficiaries before starting to distribute the estate (Trustee Act 1925, s.27). The point during the administration at which the advertisement is inserted will depend on a number of factors, varying with each estate. The advertisement gives notice of the personal representatives' intention to distribute to those who may have claims against the estate. A suitably worded advertisement should be inserted in the *London Gazette* and in a newspaper circulating in any area where the deceased owned land. In addition, the personal representatives should also consider advertising elsewhere if there are any special factors affecting the estate. The advertisements must give claimants at least two months to notify the personal representatives of their claim. After the advertisements have been inserted, and assuming that no claimants have come forward in the two-month period the personal representatives may distribute the estate with reference only to claims known to them at the time of distribution.

8.6 INTESTACY

Under the intestacy laws, the surviving spouse has the following rights, both of which should be exercised within 12 months of the date that representation to the estate is first taken out:

- to redeem the life interest and instead receive a capital sum (Administration of Estates Act 1925, s.47A as amended by Administration of Justice Act 1977); and/or
- to have the deceased's interest in the matrimonial home appropriated as part of the surviving spouse's interest in the estate (Intestates' Estates Act 1952, Sched. 2).

8.7 INHERITANCE TAX

8.7.1 Payment of tax

The due date for payment of inheritance tax (IHT) on death is six months after the end of the month in which the death occurs (Inheritance Tax Act (IHTA) 1984, s.226). Late payment will result in interest charges under ss.233 and 234. However, when the application for the grant of representation is made, any IHT payable on the non-instalment option assets (e.g. money, chattels, quoted shares, etc.), must be paid at that time even if prior to the due date.

IHT on instalment option assets (as set out in IHTA 1984, s.227) may be paid by 10 equal yearly instalments if the personal representatives so elect. If this election is made, the first instalment is due six months after the end of the month in which the death took place and the remaining nine instalments on successive anniversaries of that six-month date. The election is usually made within the Inland Revenue account but it may also be made separately at a later date. In practice there does not appear to be any specific time limit within which this election should be made.

8.7.2 Delivery of accounts

An account must be delivered to the Inland Revenue within 12 months of the end of the month in which the death occurs or, if later, three months from the date the personal representatives first act (IHTA 1984, s.216). Regulations may be made under s.256 dispensing with this requirement in certain cases (e.g. excepted estates). Failure to deliver an account within the time limit may render the personal representatives liable to penalties (IHTA 1984, ss.245 and 245A, as amended by Finance Act 1999, s.108).

8.7.3 Reliefs and exemptions

If an estate includes a holding of qualifying investments (usually quoted shares) which are sold within 12 months of the date of death for less than the probate value, the personal representatives, or other person liable for the tax, may apply to have the lower sale price substituted for the probate value (IHTA 1984, ss.178 and 179). In addition if land or an interest in land is sold within four years of the date of death for less than the probate value, the personal representatives, or other person liable for the tax, may be able to substitute the lower sale price for the probate value (IHTA 1984, ss.190 and 191). In the case of deaths on or before 15 March 1990 the sales must be made within three years following the death.

91

8.7.4 Variations and disclaimers

It is possible to vary the terms of a will or the provisions applicable to an estate under the intestacy laws so that the varied provisions take effect (for IHT and/or capital gains tax (CGT) purposes) as if those provisions had been included in the deceased's last will (IHTA 1984, s.142 and Taxation of Chargeable Gains Act (TCGA) 1992, s.62(6) and (7), as amended by Finance Act 2002). A variation must be made in writing by the people who would otherwise benefit from the varied assets within a period of two years from the date of the death. For instruments made on or after 1 August 2002, formal elections to the Board of the Inland Revenue are no longer necessary. Instead of elections, a statement must be contained within the instrument made by all the relevant parties that they intend IHTA 1984, s.142(1), and TCGA 1992, s.62(6) to apply to the variation. If more tax is payable as a result of the variation then a copy of the deed must be delivered to the Board of the Inland Revenue within six months of the date of the deed informing them of the additional payment tax to be paid.

A disclaimer of an interest under a will or under the intestacy laws must also be made in writing and within two years of the date of death. No elections are necessary for the disclaimer to be treated as though made by the deceased for IHT or CGT purposes.

8.7.5 Property settled by will

Capital distributions or appointments from a discretionary will trust within two years of the date of death (or any shorter period stated in the will) will be treated as having been made under the deceased's will and taking place at the date of death (IHTA 1984, s.144). This provision only applies if the capital distribution or appointment is an event which would otherwise have been chargeable to IHT. Thus a capital distribution or appointment from the property within the first three months after death would not qualify (IHTA 1984, s.65(4)).

8.7.6 Quick succession relief

If the deceased's estate was increased by a chargeable transfer within five years of the date of death then quick succession relief will be available to reduce the IHT payable on the death (IHTA 1984, s.141). The reduction is a percentage of part of the IHT paid on the earlier transfer. The percentage applicable will depend upon the period between the transfer and the date of death.

8.7.7 Overpayments of tax

Claims for repayment of overpaid IHT (including interest) must be made within six years of the payment of the tax (IHTA 1984, s.241). However, if too much tax was paid as a result of a mistake of the Inland Revenue then a repayment can be claimed within 20 years.

8.7.8 Underpaid tax

The Revenue will not bring any proceedings for underpaid tax once a period of six years has expired from the later of:

- the date when the payment of tax or the last instalment was made and accepted; and
- the due date for payment of the tax or last instalment (IHTA 1984, s.240).

This restriction on the Revenue will not apply if there is any fraud, wilful default or neglect on the part of the person liable for the tax.

8.7.9 Events prior to death

There are a number of important time limits for probate practitioners in relation to pre-death events. For instance, chargeable transfers and potentially exempt transfers made within a period of up to seven years before death must be taken into account by the personal representatives in the calculation of the IHT due on the transferor's estate at death (IHTA 1984, s.7 and s.3A).

Gifts with reservation may also have to be taken into account when calculating the IHT due on death if the gifts are either still subject to the reserved interest at the date of death or alternatively the reservation was released within seven years before the date of death (Finance Act 1986, s.102 and Sched. 20).

There may also be a liability to IHT payable by the transferees of these different types of lifetime transfers following the death of the transferor within the seven-year period. Any additional IHT payable by a transferee as a result of the death will be due for payment six months from the end of the month in which the death occurs, but payment by instalments may be available in certain cases (IHTA 1984, s.226).

However, if the transferee does not pay within 12 months of the end of the month in which the death occurs the Revenue may look to the personal representatives for payment of the tax (IHTA 1984, ss.200, 204: see also Chapter 15 on personal representatives and IHT). It is important, therefore, for the personal representatives to make full enquiries to discover any lifetime transfers. If any are discovered, the estate should not be fully distributed until the tax due on these transfers has been settled and an appropriate certificate of clearance issued by the Capital Taxes Office.

8.8 CAPITAL GAINS TAX

Personal representatives are entitled to the individual's annual CGT exemption for the tax year of death and the following two tax years (TCGA 1992, s.3(7)). After that time an annual CGT allowance will not be available unless the personal representatives qualify in another capacity, e.g. as trustees. It should be noted that under the self-assessment regime (i.e. for 1996/97 onwards) the due date for payment of CGT is now 31 January following the end of the tax year in which the gain was made.

8.9 INCOME TAX

8.9.1 Appeals

An appeal against an income tax (or CGT) assessment or an appeal against an amendment to a self-assessment must be made in writing and lodged within 30 days of the issue of the assessment or notice of amendment (Taxes Management Act (TMA) 1970, s.31). *Inland Revenue* v. *Wilkinson* [1992] STC 454 demonstrates the importance of making a formal appeal against tax assessments. An application for postponement of payment of some or all of the tax assessed may be made at that time. The Revenue may allow appeals to be made outside the 30-day period but they are under no obligation to do so.

8.9.2 Returns

During the course of the administration it may be necessary to submit income tax returns. In order to avoid the possibility of automatic penalties and surcharges (see at 8.9.3 below) always make enquiries of the Inland Revenue about the deceased's income tax affairs and do so as soon after the death as possible. To avoid interest and penalties under the self-assessment regime completed returns must be submitted to the Inland Revenue by 30 September following the end of the tax year (if the taxpayer wishes the Inland Revenue to calculate the tax due). If the taxpayer calculates the tax himself then the return should be submitted to the Inland Revenue by 31 January following the end of the tax year (or if the return is issued after the end of October, then within three months of the date of service of the return). Taxpayers who do not submit self-assessment returns by the due date will be subject to an automatic penalty of £100 (TMA 1970, s.93). A further penalty of £100 will be charged if the return is still outstanding after a further six months. In cases of more serious delay other penalties will be charged. It should be noted that, in general, a self-assessment return is not considered to have been submitted unless it is complete. Thus 'to be advised' figures are not acceptable (although best estimates may be).

8.9.3 Payment of tax

Under the self-assessment regime, tax must be paid in full by 31 January following the end of the tax year. In addition, payments on account in two equal instalments for the current tax year may be required to be paid by 31 January in the tax year and the following 31 July. A balancing payment may then be required on the following 31 January. Interest will be charged on overdue tax plus a 5 per cent surcharge if the balancing payment is outstanding more than 28 days after the due date (TMA 1970, s.59C). A further 5 per cent surcharge may be payable if the tax is still unpaid more than six months after the due date.

8.10 PREVENTING PROBLEMS

Missing just one time limit could prove to be an expensive error involving an application for extension of the normal time limit, interest charges, and even a claim for damages. It may also spoil a good solicitor–client relationship.

How can a practice guard against missing an important time limit? It is clear that there are too many time limits to rely on memory alone. The use of a central diary (whether handwritten or on computer) operated by a responsible member of the practice may be of considerable benefit. Fee-earners could provide the diary-keeper with a list of their important dates, perhaps by completing a pro forma list. The diary-keeper would then be responsible for reminding each fee-earner of the date well in advance of the time limit concerned. If a fee-earner was unexpectedly absent, his or her important dates would not be missed as the diary-keeper would be able to bring the date to the attention of another member of the practice. Used in this (or a similar) way, a central diary system could prove to be invaluable in the running of an efficient and trouble-free probate practice.

CHAPTER 9

Probate and benefits

Meg Andrews

9.1 INTRODUCTION

Some clients may not be concerned about potential inheritance tax liability
or how best to invest their legacy, but more practically how they are going to
cope financially without the deceased.

9.2 FUNERAL COSTS

The first problem is often: how is the funeral to be paid for? One does come
across the enterprising client who has withdrawn the money for the funeral
refreshments and flowers using the deceased's cashpoint card, or paid for the
funeral using an enduring power of attorney before the bank is aware of the
death, but clearly this should not be encouraged.

For a family used to paying cash on the nail, the prospect of a bill of over
£1,000 hanging over them can be distressing. The suggestion that they take
the funeral account to the deceased's bank or building society as soon as they
receive it, may be all that is required. Where someone has a collection of
small accounts, closing them all by cheques payable to the funeral director
can be cheaper than a collection of statutory declarations in lieu of a grant.

Unfortunately, some financial organisations make a habit of referring the
bereaved customer to a solicitor as soon as they find out a will is involved,
when the bank's own small estates procedure would be perfectly appropriate.
The fairest thing to do in those circumstances (unless there is a pending flota-
tion, when other considerations may apply) is to refer the client back to the
institution involved, perhaps having telephoned the branch manager first. On
the other hand, where a bank has actual knowledge of the state of the personal representative's own finances, they may insist on a grant for a very
modest estate, in order to protect their position and that of the beneficiaries.

If the deceased was a member of a trade union or hospital fund, it is worth
contacting the organisation before the funeral arrangements are made. Some
will only pay funeral benefits if the claim is made before the funeral, while
others, especially if a funeral bond is involved, may wish to specify a

particular funeral director. Many make their cheque payable to the funeral director, rather than the family, which can present problems if the family have already clubbed together to pay the bill.

The Social Fund will pay the costs of a basic funeral, if the person responsible for paying for it is on income support, in receipt of income based jobseeker's allowance, council tax benefit, housing benefit, disabled person's tax credit or working families tax credit. The funeral payment will cover the costs of a burial plot and interment or cremation costs, including the doctors' certificates, the cost of a hearse and up to £600 for any other funeral expenses. The claimant's capital may preclude a claim if it exceeds the prescribed amount (normally £500 or £1,000 if the claimant is over 60).

The application can be made immediately or up to three months after the funeral. The application form asks for some detailed information about the relationships between the claimant and the deceased and the deceased and other members of his or her family, to confirm that the applicant is the appropriate person to have responsibility for paying for the funeral. The Social Fund will be able to recover its costs from the estate, if it turns out that there are liquid assets after all. The application form can be obtained from the local social security office or downloaded from the Internet at **www.dwp.gov.uk**.

9.3 BEREAVEMENT

9.3.1 Bereavement payment

Although moves are afoot to improve the situation of cohabitants, both single sex and so called 'common law' marriages, in death married couples are treated more favourably than they are in life. Since April 2001, a surviving spouse of either sex has been able to claim a tax-free lump sum bereavement payment of £2,000. This is not means-tested, but is conditional on the deceased spouse having paid appropriate national insurance contributions and either not being entitled to state retirement pension when he or she died or the surviving spouse being under retirement age at the date of death.

9.3.2 Bereavement allowance

If the surviving spouse is over 45-years-old at the time of death, he or she may be entitled to bereavement allowance, a taxable weekly benefit, for 52 weeks from the date of death. Again, this can be conditional on the deceased having paid appropriate national insurance contributions, but will also be paid if death was caused by their employment. The amount payable (rates correct at October 2002) depends on the age of the surviving spouse, with those aged over 55 getting the full rate of £75.50 per week and those aged between 45 and 54 getting only part of this (£22.65 per week if the surviving spouse was 45 at the time of bereavement). Unfortunately the rate is fixed and does not go up if the bereaved spouse crosses an age threshold during the year in question. Current rates and claim forms can be found at **www.dwp.gov.uk**.

9.4 ORPHANS

If the surviving spouse has children entitling them to child benefit, or was expecting the deceased's child, then widowed parent's allowance will be paid instead of bereavement allowance. Unlike bereavement allowance, this includes state earnings related pension, if the claimant qualifies, and an allowance for each dependent child, as well as a basic allowance for the claimant at the (October 2002) rate of £75.50 per week. The widowed parent's allowance continues for as long as the claimant meets the conditions, generally until the youngest child leaves school.

A lone parent who was not married to the deceased may, like a widow or widower, be entitled to income support, help with rent in the form of housing benefit or council tax benefit. Those receiving income support are also eligible for budgeting loans to buy things for the home or Social Fund crisis loans if immediate help is needed in an emergency. If the child is under five, income support also entitles the claimant to cold weather payments. Other triggers for this last benefit are the claimant being disabled or over 60.

Child benefit is not means-tested and is payable to any bringing up children, while the child is under 16, or under 19 and studying full-time either A level, NVQ level 3 or an equivalent qualification, or under 18 and actively looking for work or a training place while registered for work or training with the Careers Service or Connexion Service. It is paid in respect of each child, at the rate of £15.75 a week for the first child and £10.55 a week for others.

If the carer is not the child's parent, he or she may also be entitled to guardian's allowance, if both parents are dead, or one has died and the other is in prison or cannot be found or the parents were divorced. Guardian's allowance redresses the balance slightly between the eldest and subsequent children, the rate being £9.65 for the eldest and £11.35 per week each for the others.

9.5 INCAPACITATED DEPENDANTS

Sadly it is often the ostensibly fitter half of a couple who dies first and it is only then apparent how much care the surviving partner has been receiving. If he or she is under pension age, then there may be an entitlement to incapacity benefit, if the right to statutory sick pay has expired. This benefit is dependent on National Insurance contributions, unless the claimant became unable to work between 16 and 20 years of age, or under 25 if the claimant was in education or training when under 20. Rates (at October 2002) vary between £53.50 and £85.85 per week, depending on the age of the claimant, the length of time he or she has been incapacitated and the level of incapacity.

Attendance allowance is available to those over 65 who have needed help looking after themselves for at least six months or who have received a terminal diagnosis. The need may be for daytime care, help at night, or both, with the rate payable depending on the need (£56.25 per week for day and night attendance or if there is a terminal diagnosis, or £37.65 per week if day or night care is required). Attendance allowance is not means-tested or taxed and does not count as income for income support assessment purposes.

The claim forms can be completed on behalf of the claimant, so that the fact of a terminal diagnosis need not be disclosed to them.

9.6 OTHER SOURCES OF HELP

Apart from state help, it is worth looking at what pension rights the deceased had or what pensions the deceased was receiving. Most pension schemes make provision for widows or widowers and dependent children of any age and more will now pay pensions to cohabitants. The old-fashioned schemes where a widower was only entitled to a pension from his late wife's pension if he was disabled are no longer found. If the deceased had not reached retirement age, an employer's pension scheme will generally provided that a lump sum or pension is payable at the discretion of trustees, who will be guided by any letter of wishes signed by the deceased. In the absence of any such expression, trustees generally follow the intestacy rules, but you may be able to persuade them to pay money into a purpose-built discretionary trust, if this would avoid the beneficiary losing means-tested benefits.

It is always worth checking the death certificate to see what the deceased died of, or what illnesses he suffered from at the time of his death. The number of industrial diseases for which compensation can be claimed is growing all the time. If the deceased was a miner's widow, it is wise to ask if her late husband suffered from emphysema, as his claim for compensation did not necessarily die with him and may not have been recognised at the time of his death.

Many types of employment have their own charities attached, from the Royal Agricultural Benevolent Association to the Solicitors Benevolent Association. The Civil Service has its own charity, which offers emotional as well as financial support, as do each of the services. Counsel and Care is a charity which specialises in pointing people, including legal advisers, in the direction of appropriate charities who may be able to assist elderly people in financial need or requiring help or advice (see Appendix 6).

Benefit advice can be given under the Legal Help Scheme or, of course, *pro bono*.

CHAPTER 10

Inheritance (Provision for Family and Dependants) Act 1975 Claims

Dawn Goodman and Sue Medder

This chapter was written by Dawn Goodman, who heads Withers' specialist contentious trust and probate team and Sue Medder, a solicitor on the team. We are most grateful to them for doing so.

10.1 IPFDA 1975 AND WILLS

You cannot guarantee to exclude the possibility of a claim under the Inheritance (Provision for Family and Dependants) Act (IPFDA) 1975 but there are some simple steps you can take when drafting the will which may reduce the likelihood of a claim or, if one is made, reduce its chances of success.

10.1.1 Check background facts

Establish the extent of all your client's family and dependants. There is no point in skating round the issue of a client's secret relationships and non-marital children, only to find that claims are made against the estate after he or she is dead.

10.1.2 Ask questions

Your client may have dependants who are not immediately obvious to him or her as such. Examples are gratuitous payments to a niece or nephew, or accommodation provided for a mother-in-law, companion, or even an elderly nanny or other former member of staff.

10.1.3 Options

If your client has been providing for people who could claim against the estate as dependants, but who do not fall within any of the other categories of claimant under the IPFDA 1975 – spouse, former spouse who has not remarried, cohabitant, children (including adopted and non-marital children and those treated as children of the family) – the client should be advised that the chance of a claim could be reduced by:

- making provision by will or otherwise for them; or
- ceasing to maintain them.

If the second option is taken, you should also advise your client to make it clear to any dependants that he or she no longer assumes responsibility for their maintenance. A memorandum can be left with the client's will explaining that maintenance has ceased but it is preferable for the client to send a letter (keeping a copy) to each dependant explaining that maintenance (or the assumption of responsibility) is ceasing.

Some clients will say they are making no or little provision for their wife or husband because she or he has adequate personal assets. This may reflect a misunderstanding on the client's part about what would be regarded for these purposes as adequate assets, so make further enquiries and ensure that your client understands the position. It may be prudent to remind your client that one of the criteria the court will use for assessing what is reasonable provision is what the wife or husband would have received if the marriage had been terminated by divorce rather than death. Recent ancillary relief decisions have seen an increase in the level of financial awards and undoubtedly this will have some impact on the level of provision the court views as appropriate in IPFDA 1975 claims brought by spouses. See the favourable decisions for spouses in *Re Adams* [2001] WTLR and *Stephanides* v. *Cohen and Stephanides* LTL 22/5/2002.

10.1.4 Ex-spouses

A former spouse may make a claim if he/she is receiving maintenance at the time of the ex-spouse's death. It is best to try to forestall the claim by making some provision. It is sensible to check whether your client is bound by the terms of any ancillary relief orders for transfer of matrimonial assets, ongoing maintenance payments, or obligations to provide by will or life assurance: if the latter you should check whether the policy is still valid.

10.1.5 Leaving a memorandum

If your client fears a claim under the IPFDA 1975 but does not wish to make provision for the potential claimant, he or she should be encouraged to leave a memorandum with the will explaining why no provision was made, unless your client's reasons for making no provision are unreasonable, in which case the memorandum could do more harm than good.

There appears to be a trend in IPFDA 1975 actions towards the introduction of parallel claims – proprietary estoppel, declarations as to beneficial interests, mutual will obligations, claims based on a contractual relationship with the deceased – to bolster inheritance claims. Such claims are based on a combination of the deceased's intentions and of fact. The claim will only be made after the deceased's death. Often there are no independent witnesses so the surviving claimant is free to give their version of the deceased's intentions, unchallenged.

With this in mind, it may well be appropriate for a detailed attendance note of the initial instructions to be copied to the client with the draft will. The client should be asked to confirm the attendance note details are correct when confirming instructions to engross the will. The attendance note should be kept, as with any memorandum, with the will. At least then there is an accurate record of the testator's intention.

10.1.6 People with special needs

If your client has dependants with mental or physical disabilities, and is assuming that the state will support them, warn your client that the local social services department can make an application on behalf of the dependants for provision from the estate. You may wish to consider with your client the advantage of making provision for such a dependant in the form of a discretionary trust.

10.1.7 Cohabitees

If your client is living with someone as a cohabitee, your client should be advised that a will may be necessary to provide for his or her partner. Cohabitees cannot claim under the intestacy rules and will not be able to make a claim under the IPFDA 1975, if:

- they were not living together for two years prior to the death;
- they were not dependent;
- they were a same sex couple.

They can be severely disadvantaged. This includes gay and lesbian couples and any others where marriage is never an option.

Law Reform (Succession) Act 1995, s.3, includes new guidelines which the court should consider when applications are made by cohabitees. They are:

- the age of the applicant and the length of the period during which the applicant lived as the husband or wife of the deceased and in the same household as the deceased; and
- the contribution made by the applicant to the welfare of the family of the deceased including any contribution made by looking after the home or caring for the family.

10.1.8 Caveats

Sometimes a claimant lodges a caveat against the issue of the grant – this is wrong use of a caveat and you should be able to have it warned off.

10.2 WHAT SHOULD BE DONE IN THE EVENT OF A CLAIM

If a claim has been issued, personal representatives (PRs) should be cautious about how they administer the estate. Broadly speaking, PRs faced with a claim should pay debts and funeral expenses and collect in the assets of the estate; but they should not distribute until the claim has been disposed of.

10.2.1 Small legacies or cases of hardship

If there are small legacies which are unlikely to be affected by the claim, or beneficiaries are experiencing hardship, PRs can seek agreement of the parties affected, including the claimant, to payment of legacies or a distribution to relieve hardship (*Re Ralphs, Ralphs* v. *District Bank* [1986] 1 WLR 1522). If consent is not forthcoming, an application can be made to the court for directions (CPR Sched. 1 and RSC Ord. 85, Rule 2), preferably with the claimant making an application for an interim payment in the contest of a potential IPFDA 1975 claim.

If the converse applies and it is the claimant who is suffering hardship, and the beneficiaries will not agree to a distribution, the claimant can apply under IPFDA 1975, s.5 for an interim payment.

10.2.2 Time limit

Claimants have six months from the issue of the grant to put in a claim, so PRs will not be liable if they distribute the estate more than six months after obtaining the grant if no IPFDA 1975 application has been issued. However, claimants can apply for leave to apply out of time. *McNulty* v. *McNulty* [2002] WTLR 737 is a recent example of a successful application.

A Trustee Act 1925, s.27 advertisement does not protect PRs who distribute after two months has expired from the date of advertisement but within six months from the grant of probate.

10.2.3 PRs as claimants

Obviously, as a solicitor for the PRs, you cannot act both for potential claimant and potential defendant(s) in the IPFDA 1975 claim. If a PR or proposed PR is, say, a widow who does not think that her late husband's will or the application of the intestacy rules provides for her adequately, then she must be independently advised by another firm on whether or not to claim.

In this situation your firm can continue to act in the administration with the agreement of all PRs. The PR who is claiming as a claimant and the PRs who are defending the claim as beneficiaries should instruct two firms other than yours, i.e. there will be three firms involved. Any PRs who are not claimants or beneficiaries can be represented by you in the litigation. The PRs as a body should adopt a neutral role and not attempt to defeat the claim. Without this approach being seen to be followed, the administration of the estate is likely to grind to a halt while the claim is pending.

A claimant who is one of the proposed PRs can have power reserved. It is not necessary to renounce if he or she is going to make a claim. A PR who has taken out a grant and proposes to claim need not be removed from office.

10.2.4 Sole PRs

If the intending claimant is the sole PR, he or she might prefer not to take out the grant (although power might be reserved). In such a case, the grant may have to be taken out by the person next entitled, or by a nominee of the intending claimant pursuant to Supreme Court Act 1981, s.116.

10.2.5 PRs as beneficiaries

The PRs are also often beneficiaries who are resisting a claim. Although PRs should adopt a neutral stance, leaving it to the claimant and the beneficiaries to fight the matter out, beneficiary PRs are not obliged to be neutral *in their capacity as beneficiaries*. They must not pay the costs of defending the claim out of the estate: such costs are their personal liability.

Difficulties arise where one or more PRs are professionals and another is a beneficiary who wishes to contest the claim. If all PRs are content to accept your advice, or counsel's, on how to handle the claim, and are not causing costs to be incurred unnecessarily (for example, by refusing to settle a meritorious claim), you should not have a conflict of interest in acting for all the PRs.

Nevertheless, it is much better to ensure that the PR with the beneficial interest is separately represented in his or her capacity as beneficiary.

(There is a useful article by John Ross Martyn in [2002] *Solicitors Journal*, 15 March, dealing with the need for neutrality on the part of PRs and the question of costs.)

10.3 HOW TO HANDLE A CLAIM

If you learn about a claim which appears meritorious before proceedings are issued (and the would-be claimant is either in time or is likely to get an extension) consider asking the beneficiaries (if *sui juris*) if they are willing to enter into a deed of variation. You must advise them to obtain independent advice.

Once the claim is issued, the PRs should promptly provide the information required by CPR, Sched. 1 and RSC Ord. 99 unless all parties agree to freeze the obligation to respond by witness statement in order to save costs.

PRs must comply with their obligations to bring to court matters within their knowledge which may be relevant to the court's exercise of its discretion. Equally, they should maintain a neutral position with regard to the merits of any claim and not usurp the function of the beneficiary defendants.

Although PRs have extensive common law and statutory powers (see Trustee Act 1925, s.15) to compromise claims against the estate, provided that they act in good faith, these powers do not extend to compromising an IPFDA 1975 claim because the claim, instead of being against the estate, is to become a beneficiary in the estate. The PRs ought to leave the claimant and the beneficiaries to negotiate a settlement but should indicate:

- their readiness to assist by providing up-to-date information on the composition and administration of the estate;
- their desire to be involved at the final stage of negotiations to ensure that the agreement reached between the parties is workable from the administrative point of view and that the PRs' own position on costs is protected.

Solicitor PRs should be concerned to ensure the part they play is as limited as possible. The estate should not be put to unnecessary additional expense.

It may be appropriate for PRs to seek directions from the court that the beneficiaries' advocate represent them during proceedings.

10.3.1 Charitable beneficiaries and IPFDA 1975

(For more on charitable beneficiaries see Chapter 16.) A charity can agree to a compromise of proceedings through its duly authorised officer. The charity may need separate advice on whether to agree a compromise and if in doubt can seek an order from the Charity Commissioners or a letter of opinion or advice under Charities Act 1993, ss.26 and 29, but this is not normally necessary.

In some cases, charities may feel a moral obligation to renounce part of their entitlement and under Charities Act 1993, s.27 the Charity Commissioners have powers to authorise charity trustees to give effect to a perceived moral obligation. Charities cannot give effect to a moral obligation without such authority. The Charity Commission has produced a very useful leaflet CC7, *Ex Gratia Payments by Charities* (available from their website – see Appendix 6).

10.3.2 Costs

Unless the PRs have acted unreasonably (such as by adopting too proactive a stance) or for their own benefit rather than that of the estate, they should receive their costs out of the estate, on the indemnity basis (CPR, Rule 48.4). PRs and trustees should be aware of the new provisions in CPR Part 48 Practice Direction, paras. 50A.1 to 50A.3, which list the criteria that the court will use in assessing whether the costs were properly incurred. However it is not generally necessary for a PR to obtain the court's consent to adopt a neutral stance when defending an IPFDA 1975 claim.

The PRs will also be expected to act in accordance with the overriding objective of CPR, Rule 1.1(2) in dealing with the claim and will be expected to do so in a way which is proportionate to the amount of money involved, the importance of the case, the financial position of each party, and the complexity of the issues. In making costs orders the court will give consideration to whether the parties have complied with the overriding objective. The draft Pre-Action Protocol for the Resolution of Probate and Trust Disputes (a copy of which can be obtained at **www.actaps.com**) sets out guidelines for the conduct of parties to contentious probate and trust actions.

A successful claimant's costs are usually paid from the estate, commonly on the standard basis; conversely, an unsuccessful claimant's costs are not always borne by him or her. Frequently, an unsuccessful claimant is not ordered to pay the costs of the PRs or other defendants. PRs should be aware of the effect on the estate of costs orders in favour of a number of parties and it may be appropriate to bring this to the attention of the claimant and beneficiaries.

10.3.3 Wasted costs

Solicitors for the PRs should be aware that, if they have acted improperly and unreasonably or have been negligent, and in consequence any party to the proceedings has incurred additional costs, they can be disallowed their costs or asked to meet all or any wasted costs of another party (Supreme Court Act 1981, s.51(6) as amended; CPR, Sched. 1, RSC Ord. 44, Rule 14(1)). An example of causing wasted costs would be the negligent provision of incorrect information about the size and nature of the estate when preparing the PR's witness statement under CPR, Sched. 1, RSC Ord. 99, Rule 5.

The case of *Ridehalgh* v. *Horsefield and another (No. 2)* [1994] 3 WLR 462 considered the question of when a wasted costs order might be sought against the opposing solicitor or barrister. In *Wall* v. *Lefever, The Times*, 1 August, 1997 the Court of Appeal said that the wasted costs jurisdiction would only be used where the conduct of the professional advisers was clearly improper, unreasonable or negligent.

CHAPTER 11

Contentious probate

Henry Frydenson

11.1 INTRODUCTION

The proportion of contentious work in private client departments is growing rapidly. The growth is partly the result of an increasingly litigious society and partly the result of the fact that there is more wealth around for people to argue over.

Practitioners who find that more work of this type is coming their way may be interested in joining the Association of Contentious Trusts and Probate Specialists. The purposes of the Association include raising the standard of contentious work and developing a common approach. Members agree to endeavour to act in accordance with a voluntary Code of Conduct. Under this Code members agree where appropriate to try to use the full range of solutions, in particular alternative dispute resolution, and where possible to encourage the use of the same legal team where parties have common interests.

Application forms are available from Robert Hunter of Allen and Overy on 020 7330 3000.

11.2 IDENTIFICATION OF ISSUES

When advising a client it is important to identify the points which are likely to be in issue.

If there is a will there will be two possible questions relating to the will:

- Is the will valid? This may require considering any of the following questions: Have the formal requirements for making a will been complied with? (See Wills Act 1837, s.9.) Did the testator have the capacity to make a will? Do claims of undue influence or lack of knowledge and approval arise?
- How is a particular provision in a will to be construed?

11.3   METHODS OF ATTACK

Where a person is unhappy with the terms of a deceased's will or the provisions which would arise on intestacy there are various grounds of possible attack. Before considering these grounds in detail you should always give thought to what the outcome of a successful attack will be. For example, the overthrow of a will may result in intestacy or in the provisions of an earlier will remaining in effect. There is absolutely no point in overthrowing the later will if your client will have no rights on intestacy or under the earlier will.

Consideration must also be given to the all-important question of costs (see at 11.6.5 below).

11.3.1   Lack of due execution of the will

The burden of proving that the will was executed in accordance with Wills Act 1837, s.9 (as substituted by the Administration of Justice Act 1982, s.17) is on the party seeking to establish the validity of the will.

It may be possible to challenge the will on the following grounds:

- the signature was not made by the testator in the presence of two witnesses present at the same time, but see *Couser* v. *Couser* [1996] 1 WLR 1301;
- the two witnesses did not subscribe or acknowledge their signatures to the will in the presence of the testator;
- the signature of the testator was not intended to give effect to the will;
- the signature which appears on the will was not in fact made by the testator himself or for him, or in his presence, or by his direction.

11.3.2   Lack of testamentary capacity

The test of testamentary capacity is still that established in 1870 in *Banks* v. *Goodfellow* (1870) LR5QB 549. A person may suffer from a mental disorder and yet still be able to fulfil that test.

Mental states are presumed to continue, so if a person is normally mentally capable it will be presumed, provided the will appears rational, that he had capacity when he made the will. However, this presumption is rebuttable by evidence. Where a person lacks general mental capacity, the person putting forward the will has to prove testamentary capacity.

The difficulty in bringing a case where lack of capacity is alleged is to gather together sufficiently convincing evidence. It is very important to try to get together the evidence before advising the client on the likelihood of success.

11.3.3　Lack of knowledge and approval

The burden of proving that a testator knew and approved the contents of his will, rests with the person seeking to prove that will. However, where a testator reads through a will (or has had the contents read to him) there is normally a presumption that he knew and approved the contents of the will.

There is no presumption if the testator was deaf and dumb or blind or if there were suspicious circumstances (such as where a major beneficiary prepares the will or is active in arranging its execution). See *Richards* v. *Allan* [2001] WTLR 1031. The burden of proof is then upon the person attempting to set up the will to remove any such suspicions and to prove positively that the testator knew and approved of the contents of the will.

It is usually preferable to plead lack of knowledge and approval rather than to allege undue influence. Once you can show suspicious circumstances the burden of proving knowledge and approval falls on the person putting forward the will. In a case of undue influence the person alleging it must prove it. There can be adverse costs consequences where an allegation of undue influence fails.

11.3.4　Undue influence

Undue influence is one of the most difficult allegations to sustain, since the primary witness – the deceased – is by definition unavailable to give evidence and not able to assist the court.

Where you allege fraud or undue influence and lose, you will be particularly at risk of a costs order being made against your client.

It should be clearly understood that there is nothing inherently wrong with influence by itself; people who make wills are influenced by various factors when deciding on what they will include in their will. What the law will not allow is *undue* influence.

As mentioned above, proving undue influence in relation to a will is extremely difficult whereas sustaining an allegation of lack of knowledge and approval is somewhat easier. However, you are not allowed to disguise what is in reality a plea of fraud or undue influence as a lesser plea of lack of knowledge (*Re Stott* [1980] 1 WLR 246).

11.3.5　Beneficial interest under resulting or constructive trust

It may be possible to claim a beneficial interest under a resulting or constructive trust.

11.3.6 Claim under Inheritance (Provision for Family and Dependants) Act (IPFDA) 1975

If your client falls within one of the categories set out in IPFDA 1975, s.1 it may be possible to make a claim under the Act.

11.4 PRACTITIONER'S TOOLS

11.4.1 Law Society Ruling of September 1959

There is often a need for information about the circumstances in which a will was made. Solicitors are under an obligation to provide information about wills which they have prepared.

In accordance with the Law Society Professional Purposes Committee Ruling of September 1959 there is an obligation on a solicitor who prepares testamentary instruments to state the circumstances relating to the preparation of these instruments. The Law Society's recommendation was considered in *Larke* v. *Nugus* [2000] WTLR 1033 by the Court of Appeal in an appeal from the decision of Browne Wilkinson J.

11.4.2 Caveats

(See Non-Contentious Probate Rules (NCPR) 1987, Rule 44.) A caveat is a notice issued out of the Principal Probate Registry or a district registry or sub-registry preventing a grant from being issued. If a person does not wish to prevent the issue of a grant but wishes to be notified when a grant is made, a standing search is appropriate.

11.4.3 Citations

(See NCPR 1987, Rules 46 and 47.) Where a probate dispute can be seen on the horizon, those named as executors may well have a natural reticence to do anything. In addition, very often if the validity of a last will is called into question, the executors may be unhappy to release earlier wills.

In all these cases it is necessary to seek the assistance of the Principal Probate Registry by way of a citation. A citation is a document issued out of the Principal Probate Registry or a district registry and can be issued for any one of the following reasons:

Citation to accept or refuse a grant

Where there is a delay in obtaining the grant and the person entitled does not renounce his entitlement to do so, a citation may be issued.

111

Citation to take probate

Where the executor has intermeddled in the estate and thereby accepted office but has not applied for a grant within six months of death, the citation is to take the grant. The citor may be any person with an interest in the estate. NCPR 1987, Rule 47 allows a grant to the citor as an alternative to an order directing the executor to take a grant within a specific time.

Citation to propound a will

Where the validity of a will is doubted, a person entitled on intestacy or under an earlier testamentary document may cite the executors and persons interested under the alleged will to propound it. It should be noted that a citation is not appropriate for executors appointed by a will doubting the validity of a codicil.

The procedure with a citation is to lodge it in draft form with the district judge/district probate registrar so that he can settle it.

There are alternatives to the citation procedure which may be more effective. Citations are often used to try to force someone who is being dilatory to do something. However, even if the citation is successful in the short term, future progress may still be slow.

11.4.4   Subpoena procedure

(See NCPR 1987, Rule 50.) If the original will/codicil is in the possession of a person who will not release it and is thus preventing an application for a grant by the person entitled, an application may be made under Supreme Court Act 1981, s.123 for the issue of a subpoena by the district judge/registrar. The application must be supported by an appropriate affidavit. The effect of the subpoena is to require the person in possession of the will to file it in the registry. The subpoena must be served personally and endorsed with the penal notice. Committal is not normally the result of disobedience. More usually the person is ordered to attend for examination as to possession of the testamentary document.

If a person is not in possession of the will but has knowledge of it, s.122 allows the court to require the attendance of such a person for examination. It is a contempt of court not to comply. This could apply to the witnesses to a will who have declined to swear an affidavit of due execution.

11.4.5   Supreme Court Act 1981, s.116

Where there are appropriate circumstances the court can pass over the persons entitled to a grant and appoint such person or persons as the court feels expedient. This form of application is particularly useful where those entitled to a grant cannot be traced or where it is desired to appoint some person who is not interested in the estate as beneficiary or creditor.

The application is made *ex parte* under NCPR 1987, Rule 52 to a district judge or probate registrar, supported by an affidavit. It is possible to pay a fee of £5 to have the affidavit approved by the registrar.

11.5   TYPES OF PROBATE ACTION

11.5.1   Probate action re validity of a testamentary document

The action is commenced by the executor or someone else with an interest under the document or someone opposing a grant. Persons entitled on intestacy may put an executor to proof of the will. The attesting witnesses may be called for examination or to swear an affidavit of due execution.

11.5.2   Action regarding interests

An interest action is one in which a person's interest in opposing a will or claiming the right to letters of administration is disputed. Such an action may involve proof of a person's entitlement, for example by production of a birth certificate. Such actions are often about validity of a marriage or legitimacy. The applicant in an interest action will ask the court for a declaration against the person who is claiming entitlement to a grant and instead to make an order in his favour. If the court can be persuaded to make an order, the person who was not entitled to the grant will have their right 'cleared off' and the grant will issue to the person who is properly entitled to administer the estate.

11.5.3   Action regarding revocation of a grant

Such an action would be appropriate where a grant has been improperly obtained by a person not entitled or where the will is invalid. On an intestacy the action may force a person who has obtained letters of administration to prove his entitlement. If a will is subsequently found the action will be to revoke the earlier grant and pronounce the will's validity. The court will be asked to pronounce against any earlier will and in favour of the later document which will in turn enable a correct application for a grant to then be made.

Where a grant has been obtained by mistake, e.g. a filing department has produced the wrong will which has then been proved, an application should be made by the person who obtained the grant with an affidavit specifying the error. The district judge/registrar will then make an order revoking the grant and a further correct application may then be made (see NCPR 1987, Rule 41).

In a revocation action the original grant should be filed within seven days of the claim form or within 14 days of service on the defendant of the original grant.

11.5.4   Action for the removal of personal representative

This form of action was introduced by Administration of Justice Act 1985, s.50. If the application by summons does not request the appointment of a substituted personal representative, the court will not allow the estate to be unrepresented. The applicant will swear an affidavit giving reasons for the removal and as to the suitability of the replacement personal representative who must consent to act. An example of this would be where a partner in a firm is an executor and then leaves the firm. It would be appropriate for him to be removed and replaced with another partner. The Civil Procedure Rules 1998 (CPR), Part 57 require every personal representative to be joined as a party and for the grant to be lodged in court.

Under Supreme Court Act 1981, s.116 as stated above the court has discretion to appoint as administrator any person it considers expedient even if the person entitled, for example on intestacy, would thereby be passed over.

A district registrar or district judge may be willing to contemplate revoking a grant where a personal representative refuses or neglects to participate properly in the administration of an estate. (See Chapter 15.)

11.5.5   Appointment of a judicial trustee

Applications are governed by the Judicial Trustees Act 1896 and the Judicial Trustees Rules 1983, SI 1983/370.

This can be a more expensive exercise than the appointment of a new personal representative under Administration of Justice Act 1985, s.50 but may be the more practical solution where, for example, the sole personal representative has a beneficial interest in the estate and there has been a substantial breakdown in confidence and/or communications between him and the other beneficiaries.

Where an application is made in relation to an estate, the Judicial Trustees Act 1896, s.2(7) provides that the court may, if it sees fit, proceed as if the application were made under Administration of Justice Act 1985, s.50.

The judicial trustee has all the powers and discretions of a properly appointed personal representative but the court has wide powers to give directions as to the custody of the funds in the estate. Following the appointment of the judicial trustee the trustee or any beneficiary interested can apply to the court for further directions by letter.

11.5.6   Breach of trust or breach of fiduciary duty

Executors who, through negligence and default, have caused loss to an estate will clearly be open to an action by a beneficiary of the estate. Such neglect or default might consist of failures to carry out the provisions of the will; making distributions to persons not named in the will; a failure to maintain neutrality between the beneficiaries on the one hand and the claimants on the other; executors who derive a personal benefit from the estate; or failure to obtain sufficient information regarding the estate.

11.5.7   Claims relating to the administration of Estates and Trusts

It is possible to apply to court under CPR Part 64 for:

- the court to determine any question arising in the administration of an estate or in the execution of a trust;
- an order for the administration of an estate or the execution of an estate to be carried out under the direction of the court (an 'administration order').

It is unusual for the court to take over the administration of an estate or trust. It will only do so if it considers that the issues between the parties cannot properly be resolved in any other way. It is more likely to give directions on specific points.

The Practice Direction which accompanies Part 64 gives the following examples of the types of claims which may be made for specific directions under Part 64:

- the determination of any question as to who is included in any class of persons having:

  - a claim against an estate;
  - a beneficial interest in an estate;
  - a beneficial interest in any property subject to a trust;

- the determination of the rights or interests of any person claiming:

  - to be a creditor of an estate;
  - to be entitled under a will or intestacy;
  - to be beneficially entitled under a trust;

- a claim for an order requiring a trustee to:

  - provide and, if necessary, verify accounts;
  - to pay into court money which he holds in that capacity;
  - to do or not to do any particular act;

- a claim for an order approving any sale, purchase, compromise or other transaction by a trustee;
- a claim for an order directing any act to be done which the court could order to be done if the estate or trust in question were being administered under the administration of the court.

Claims under Part 64 can be made by beneficiaries, trustees, personal representatives or other interested parties. They must use a Part 8 claim form.

11.5.8   Summons to deliver an inventory and account

This is an extremely useful procedure. It is available in the probate registry and is therefore relatively cheap. Every deponent to an oath leading to a grant of administration swears 'to exhibit on oath . . . a full inventory of the estate and when so required render an account of the administration'. (See Administration of Estates Act 1925, s.25(6).)

This means that anyone with a beneficial interest in the estate can apply by summons at any time for an inventory and account. The summons issues out of the registry from which the grant issued and should be supported by affidavit.

When you ask for an inventory it is a good idea to ask for an order for your costs. If you attend the summons with an idea of the costs incurred the registrar can assess costs there and then which avoids the 7.5 per cent taxing fee which would otherwise be payable.

The probate registry's jurisdiction is limited to ordering an inventory and account. If you want an administration order you will have to go to the Chancery Division under CPR Part 64.

11.5.9   *Beddoes* summons

A problem often faced by personal representatives is whether in the administration of an estate they should defend a claim brought against them, initiate an action on behalf of the estate or compromise a claim on behalf of the estate. A personal representative who brings or defends a claim without obtaining leave of the court may find himself exposed to the costs that arise. A personal representative can obtain protection by applying to the court for directions. This is often referred to as a *Beddoes* order from the case of *Re Beddoes* v. *Cottam* [1893] 1 Ch 547. The decision as to the granting of a *Beddoes* order is a matter which the court will decide in its absolute discretion in each case. A *Beddoes* order is not given as of right by the court.

The case of *Singh* v. *Bhasin and another* [2000] WTLR 275 is a salutory illustration of the risks of not seeking an order.

In some cases it will also be prudent for executors to seek directions from the court under CPR Part 64.

11.5.10   Rectification under Administration of Justice Act 1982, s.20

Under Administration of Justice Act 1982, s.20, the court may order that a will be rectified so as to give effect to the testator's intention. There are two grounds for such rectification:

116

- in consequence of a clerical error; or
- in consequence of a failure to understand the testator's instructions.

It is important to appreciate that s.20(1)(b) applies where the testator's instructions are not understood which is not the same as a failure to carry out those instructions. Thus, rectification will not be available where the testator or his solicitor does not understand the meaning and effect of words used, unless it is unclear what the testator's instructions were or he had failed to inform his solicitor.

If the person seeking rectification has obtained the grant and has the will in his possession, he must lodge them with the court when the claim form is issued. If a defendant has the probate or letters of administration in his possession or under his control, he must, lodge it in the relevant office within 14 days after the service of the claim form on him.

11.5.11 Claims against solicitors

If rectification is not available due to an error by the solicitor who prepared the will, the disappointed beneficiary may have a claim against the solicitor.

11.6 CPR PART 57

With effect from 15 October 2001 there is a new CPR Part 57 and Practice Direction dealing with probate claims, claims for the rectification of wills and claims to replace or remove a personal representative. For this purpose a 'probate claim' is:

- a claim for the grant of probate or letters of administration;
- a claim for the revocation of such grant, or
- a claim for a decree pronouncing for or against the validity of an alleged will not being a claim which is non-contentious (or common form) probate business (such matters being dealt with by Supreme Court Act 1981, s.128).

Non-contentious probate business remains outside the scope of the CPR and is still governed by the RSC.

[*Note*: Transitional Provisions
Contentious probate proceedings for the rectification of wills started before 15 October 2001 continue to be dealt with by the Practice Direction which supplements CPR Part 49. Applications for the removal or substitution of personal representatives made before that date continue to be dealt with under CPR, Sched. 1, Ord. 93, Rule 2.]

11.6.1 Commencing a probate claim under CPR Part 57

Probate claims issue from:

- Chancery Chambers at the Royal Courts of Justice; or
- a Chancery District Registry; or
- a county court which has a Chancery District Registry (at present this means Birmingham, Bristol, Cardiff, Leeds, Liverpool, Manchester, Newcastle-upon-Tyne or Preston) if:

  - an application for grant has been made in the Principal Registry of a district probate registry, and
  - the value of the net estate after payment of expenses and debts does not exceed the county court limit (currently £30,000).

You must use the CPR Part 57 procedure for probate claims. CPR Part 57 Practice Direction, para. 2.1 sets out the requirements for the probate claim form (Form N2). It is a standard claim form save that it is headed 'In the estate of X deceased (Probate)'. The notes for the claimant (Form N2A) are helpful and set out most of the special requirements.

11.6.2 Response to probate claim

The defendant must file an acknowledgment of service on the new Form N3. Moreover, if the particulars of claim are served with the claim form, the defendant must file the acknowledgment of service form within 28 days of service of the claim form.

11.6.3 Lodging testamentary documents and filing of evidence of them

Any testamentary documents (previously known as testamentary scripts) in the possession or control of any party must be lodged with the court. Unless the court directs otherwise, these documents must be lodged by the claimant when the claim form is issued and by a defendant when he files his acknowledgment of service.

In addition, the claimant and every defendant who acknowledges service must in written evidence describe any testamentary document of which he has knowledge or if he does not know of any such document, state that fact. Also, if the claimant/defendant has knowledge of any testamentary document which is not in his possession or control, the claimant/defendant must give the name and address of the person in whose possession or under whose control it is. If he does not know the name and address of such persons, he must state that fact. There is a prescribed form for written evidence set out in the CPR Part 57 Practice Direction.

In cases of urgent need, the court may permit the claimant to issue the claim form against an undertaking to the court to lodge the documents and file the evidence within such time as the court may specify.

11.6.4 Contents of claim form

The claim form must contain a statement of the nature of the interest of the claimant and each defendant in the estate.

A plea of want of knowledge and approval must be particularised as must a claim that a will was not duly executed, that the testator was not of sound mind, memory and understanding or that the execution of the will was obtained by undue influence or fraud.

CPR Part 57 also deals with revocation actions, judgments in default, summary judgment, discontinuance and settlement, rectification of wills, substitution and removal of personal representatives.

It is important to appreciate that CPR Part 57 and its Practice Direction are not a comprehensive reformulation of procedure and accordingly practitioners must bear in mind the other relevant provisions of the CPR.

11.6.5 Costs

Supreme Court Act 1981, s.51 provides that in contentious probate actions all parties' costs are at the discretion of the court.

It is, however, true to say that a 'wind of change' has been blowing for some time in relation to the old 'rule of thumb' that, if the proceedings were reasonable, costs would usually come out of the estate. The issue of costs is now looked at very carefully, and the party who loses can often find himself saddled with *inter partes* standard costs (and on occasion with indemnity costs) particularly if it is found that he has instituted untenable or unreasonable proceedings. A prudent practitioner will therefore always keep the question of costs under review and where appropriate make without prejudice offers in accordance with the Calderbank principle.

CHAPTER 12

Wills and best practice

Lesley King with Helen Clarke

12.1 DRAFTING POINTS

12.1.1 Appointment of solicitors-executors

Probate registries report frequent problems with the wording of clauses appointing solicitor-executors. An appointment of 'one of' or 'two of' the partners in a firm is void for uncertainty. The appointment should be of 'the partners' in the firm at the date of the deceased's death and express the wish that only two should prove.

The clause included in *Williams on Wills*, 8th edn (Sweet & Maxwell, 2002) (as B3.8 Alternative Form), has the approval of the Principal Registry of the Family Division. The commentary usefully outlines the issues.

It is important to use Form B3.10 where a firm is contemplating incorporation. The clause provides for the appointment of partners or 'in the event of such firm being incorporated' at the date of death it appoints 'the directors, members and beneficial owners of any share of the incorporated practice' at the date of death.

In the absence of such a provision Williams says that 'there would be a question whether the appointment would still be effective'. To protect themselves firms would, therefore, have to ask testators to execute codicils appointing members of the incorporated practice as executors in place of partners.

12.1.2 Sole practitioners

Sole practitioners should include in their own wills an appointment of a special executor to deal with the affairs of the practice. Suitable clauses were published in the *Probate Section Journal* (November 2001). They are also available from the Sole Practitioners' Group (see Appendix 6).

12.1.3 STEP: standard conditions for wills

On behalf of the Society of Trust and Estate Practitioners (STEP, address in Appendix 6) barrister James Kessler has prepared a set of standard administrative clauses for wills and settlements (see Appendix 5). STEP's aim in publishing the standard provisions was to enable wills and settlements to be shortened, and to provide 'the necessary standard powers . . . in language which is lucid, contemporary and easily understood' by non-lawyers.

A Practice Direction from the Principal Registry of the Probate Division dated 10 April 1995 allows wills incorporating the STEP provisions by reference to be proved in the normal way without providing the text of the provisions themselves.

If incorporating the STEP provisions it is helpful to place a copy of the provisions with the will. The testator may not die for many years by which time the provisions may have been amended several times. Life will be much simpler for the person dealing with the administration if the relevant provisons are to hand.

12.1.4 Clauses excluding liability for negligence in respect of professional executors/trustees

Many people feel that it is inappropriate to include in wills and settlements clauses which seek to limit a solicitor's or other professional trustee's liability, when acting as an executor or trustee, to loss or damage through fraud or dishonesty and to exclude liability for negligence. Solicitors should in any event be fully insured against their own negligence.

However, in *Armitage* v. *Nurse* [1997] 3 WLR 1046, CA and *Bogg* v. *Raper*, *The Times*, 22 April 1998, CA, the Court of Appeal stated that such clauses were not contrary to public policy nor to the nature of a trust. Millett LJ stated that although many people felt such clauses had gone too far, it would require legislation to change their validity.

Bogg v. *Raper* confirmed that a solicitor who prepares a will or settlement which appoints him or her or a partner as an executor or trustee and which then restricts or excludes liability for negligence, does not receive a benefit. The clause merely limits liability.

Whatever you may think about the correctness of such clauses in general, there are clearly special cases where it would be reasonable for the trust document to exclude or restrict liability for negligence (for example assets held overseas in countries with unreliable legal systems, long-running and serious family or other disputes, continuing litigation).

12.1.5 Mutual wills

For wills to be mutual wills there must be evidence of an agreement between two people that

- they will each leave their property in a particular way (not necessarily to each other, *Re Dale* [1994] Ch 31), and
- *neither party will revoke unilaterally.*

121

The mere fact that the wills are 'mirror-images' does not make them mutual.

In fact the agreement is impossible because wills *cannot* be made irrevocable. Each party is always free to revoke. Revocation may be out of the hands of the survivor as where a later marriage revokes an earlier will.

However, revocation will not assist the survivor as equity will intervene.

If the first party to die has carried out his/her part of the agreement, the law imposes an obligation on the survivor to give effect to the agreement. In effect assets of the survivor are held under a trust.

Apparently the trust is a floating one during the lifetime of the survivor and crystallises on the survivor's death (*Re Goodchild* [1996] 1 WLR 694 confirmed by the Court of Appeal [1997] 1 WLR 1216). There is some uncertainty as to how the trust works. What if the survivor spends or gives away everything? Mutual wills may provide little protection for the agreed beneficiary as there may be few assets left by the time the surviving testator dies.

Birch v. Curtiss [2002] WTLR 965 confirms the need for evidence of an agreement that the wills were to be irrevocable. Rimer J accepted that there may well have been an agreement between the husband and wife as to how the husband was to leave his property after the wife's death. However, there was no evidence of an agreement not to revoke. Therefore, the wills were not mutual and the husband was free to leave his property as he wished.

Always include an express statement if there is such an agreement.

Even more importantly, however, consider including a statement that there is no such agreement in other wills. This makes the true position clear to the clients. It will also help deter disgruntled family members from incurring the expense and ill feeling of challenging the will of the survivor.

12.1.6 Wills and public funding

The making of wills and matters of trusts law generally are amongst the services that cannot normally be publicly funded as part of the Community Legal Services scheme. However, the Lord Chancellor issued a direction under the Access to Justice Act 1999, s.6(8) authorising the Legal Services Commission (LSC) to fund certain services which would normally be excluded.

In relation to wills the Lord Chancellor has authorised the LSC to fund legal help where the client is:

(a) aged 70 or over; or

(b) a disabled person within the meaning of the Disability Discrimination Act 1995; or

(c) the parent of a disabled person (as defined in (b) above) who wishes to provide for that person in a will; or

(d) the parent of a minor who is living with the client but not with the other parent, and where the client wishes to appoint a guardian for the minor in a will.

Applications for funding under this direction must still satisfy all r
criteria in the Funding Code and regulations.

12.2 CAPACITY

12.2.1 The 'golden rule'

Questions of capacity frequently arise in connection with the validity of a
will. In cases where there is room for doubt the solicitor drafting a will should
have considered the question of capacity at the time. If capacity is in question the solicitor should consult the client's medical practitioner as to the
client's capacity in general and should try to have the doctor present at the time
the will is signed so as to be able to give an opinion on the client's capacity at
that point. In *Buckenham* v. *Dickinson* [1997] CLY 661 the court pronounced
against a will where the solicitors had not followed the 'golden rule' applied
in *Kenward* v. *Adams* [1975] CLY 3591 and followed in *Re Simpson* (1977) 121
SJ 224, that a medical practitioner should be present where there are doubts
as to a testator's capacity. Templeman J (as he then was) said in *Kenward* v.
Adams:

> In the case of an aged testator or a testator who has suffered a serious illness, there
> is one golden rule which should always be observed, however straightforward
> matters may appear, and however difficult or tactless it may be to suggest that pre-
> cautions be taken: the making of a will by such a testator ought to be witnessed or
> approved by a medical practitioner who satisfies himself of the capacity and under-
> standing of the testator, and records and preserves his examination and findings.
>
> There are other precautions which should be taken.
>
> If the testator has made an earlier will this should be considered by the legal and
> medical advisers of the testator and, if appropriate, discussed with the testator.
>
> The instructions of the testator should be taken in the absence of anyone who
> may stand to benefit, or who may have influence over the testator.
>
> These are not counsels of perfection. If proper precautions are not taken
> injustice may result or be imagined, and great expense and misery may be
> unnecessarily caused.

It is important to take these precautions. Where a will is successfully challenged for lack of capacity, a solicitor who failed to take appropriate steps to
check capacity may be made liable for the costs suffered by the estate. See the
comments made in *Worby* v. *Rosser* [1999] Lloyd's Rep PN 814 and *Corbett*
v. *Bond Pearce* [2001] EWCA Civ 559.

12.2.2 ACTAPS checklist

The Association of Contentious Trusts and Probate Practitioners has published a checklist on capacity. We have reproduced it below with their kind
permission.

RISK ASSESSMENT

Factors to be taken into account in the assessment of mental capacity/undue influence

By Christopher Allen, consultant with Lawrence Graham and Member of the Association of Contentious Trust and Probate Specialists Committee

A 'Golden Rule' was reemphasised by Mr Justice Templeman (as he then was) in *Re Simpson deceased* (*Solicitors Journal*, 1 April 1977). Templeman J there said that the events of this case, which involved the disputed will of an old and infirm testator 'constrained him to repeat the warning he had given in *Kenward* v. *Adams, The Times*, 29 November 1975, that the making of a will by such a testator ought to be witnessed and approved by a medical practitioner who satisfies himself as to the capacity and understanding of the testator and makes a record of his examination and findings'.

The points in issue were recently reinforced by *Re Morris, Trustees of Great Ormond Street* v. *Rushin and others* (Lawtel, 15 May 2000). In referring to the rule, Rimer J stated that the rule must always be observed 'however straightforward matters appear and however difficult or tactless it may be to suggest that precautions be taken'. The desirability of review and discussion of earlier wills with testators and for instructions to be taken in the absence of a potentially influential beneficiary were also emphasised.

In the light of these cases and *Killick* v. *Pountney, The Times*, 30 April 1999, ACTAPS with assistance from Susan Midha of the Probate Section has drawn up a suggested checklist which has now been adopted by the Probate Section.

Possibly there has been diffidence about producing a 'Code of Conduct' lest the already heavy duties placed on practitioners be further increased. It seems to me to make little difference what one calls the following; we have Lord Templeman's 'Golden Rule' and individually we have to decide how to apply it in the many and various situations with which we are faced.

Preliminary notes

1. The test of testamentary capacity remains that established in *Banks* v. *Goodfellow* (1870) LR5QB 549, namely:

    (a) the testator must not be affected by any disorder of mind or insane delusion. A disorder which operates only in respect of a particular individual may amount to lack of capacity although it must be sufficient to affect the testator's judgment – mere eccentricity or irrationality does not in itself invalidate the will;

    (b) he should appreciate the nature and consequences of making a will, e.g. understanding that the will operates only on death, that it can be changed or revoked and beneficiaries might die before him. He should generally be aware of the purposes of appointing executors;

    (c) he must understand the extent of his property (in general terms). He ought also to realise that his estate may reduce (or increase) over time and know if any assets are jointly owned;

    (d) the testator should consider the moral claims of those persons for whom he ought to make provision.

2. Lack of capacity and vulnerability to undue influence may go hand in hand but equally one may exist without the other. It is felt helpful to separate them

because the precautionary measures to be taken by the practitioner (e.g the attendance of a doctor) are not necessarily the same in each case.

3. The following constitute important areas for practitioners to raise with their clients. It should, however, be noted that the list is not exhaustive, nor are all items compulsory (e.g in the case of an elderly and very alert client whom the practitioner has known for many years) but there may well be additional points to be raised in particular cases.

Capacity

Client's name and date of birth	
Have you any reason to doubt your client's testamentary capacity?	
Are you aware of any medical problems of your client? What are they?	
Is your client taking any medication and if so what?	

If in the light of the above, you feel that your client's capacity may be questioned:

Have you advised the client of the importance of having either a medical report or medical witness or both if he/she has any medical or other condition which could invalidate the will?	
Have you kept contemporaneous file notes?	

Undue influence

Do you consider there are any issues of vulnerability or suggestibility in the client or do you feel that the client might be subject to undue influence as defined by case law?	
Who contacted you to see the client or to draft the will?	
Who else was present when the instructions were given?	
Has your client made an earlier will or wills?	
What changes is your client making?	

Was the client able/prepared to tell you why the changes were being made?	
Attach a brief family tree.	
What relationship do the main beneficiaries have with your client?	
Has your firm acted for the client (or his or her family) before?	

If there seems to be a problem:

Did you discuss the existence of lifetime gifts with the client? If so, were they made to someone with whom your client had a 'special relationship' as defined in case law? Has that person subsequently benefited under the will?	
Who was present, apart from the witnesses, when the will was executed?	

12.2.3   Instructing medical practitioners

Denzil Lush in an article in [1996] *Gazette*, 24 January, points out that capacity is not an absolute concept. It is relative to the particular transaction. Thus, the lawyer has a duty to explain to any doctor involved the test relevant to the particular activity. We have set out below a form of letter which may be adapted and used when writing to a client's general medical practitioner for a report as to mental capacity. The letter was originally prepared for the Law Society's *Elderly Client Handbook* by Gordon R. Ashton (see Appendix 5) and we are most grateful to Gordon Ashton for allowing us to reproduce it. The letter assumes that the solicitor has already attended the client and received preliminary instructions but that there is a doubt as to mental capacity which may need to be resolved.

Dear Dr_____ Our client and your patient: Mrs _____ of _____ We act for your patient and are presently advising her in regard to the preparation of a new will. [We have previously made several wills for her the last one being some ___ years ago.] She has [only a small estate] [a fairly substantial estate] – [*amplify if there are any complications*].

We seek from you a report as to the mental capacity of your patient t this will. The legal test of capacity in these circumstances is wheth understands first, that she is giving her property to persons of her choice on her death, second, the extent of that property and third, the nature and extent of her obligations to relatives and others. Your report should relate specifically to these questions and you may if you wish qualify the report by stating that you do not express any further opinion with regard to the mental capacity of your patient. Legal tests of capacity vary according to the nature of the transaction, and there is no universal test of capacity. However, you may form your view on the balance of probabilities and do not need to be satisfied beyond reasonable doubt.

If the capacity of this patient tends to fluctuate please mention this in your report and we may then need to ask you to be one of the witnesses so as to confirm your view of capacity at the time of signature. You will no doubt need to attend on her before preparing your report and we confirm that we shall be pleased to pay your reasonable fee for such attendance and the preparation of the report. She is presently at [her home] and expecting you to contact her there.

Yours sincerely

The Law Society and the British Medical Association joined together in 1995 to publish *Assessment of Mental Capacity: Guidance for Doctors and Lawyers* (see Appendix 5) which is extremely useful reading and provides answers to many awkward questions. It sets out the specific legal tests of capacity to make particular decisions or carry out legal transactions, and explains how these relate to the medical practicalities of assessing capacity.

Mind has issued two booklets on wills and trusts to help people with mental health problems gain greater financial control of their lives. *Find Peace of Mind* is a step-by-step guide to wills. *Making Provision* is aimed at parents and carers of people with mental health problems and explains how the carers can make financial provision for such people. Both can be obtained from the Legacy Officer at Mind (see Appendix 6).

12.3   NEGLIGENCE AND WILLS

As we all know clients are much swifter to allege negligence than used to be the case. There are a number of problem areas in connection with taking instructions for a will.

12.3.1 Preparing a will for someone who lacks capacity without making adequate checks

As we saw at 12.2.1 above a solicitor who does not take appropriate steps to satisfy himself that a client has appropriate capacity may be liable to the estate for the costs of a successful challenge to the validity of the will. See *Worby* v. *Rosser* [1999] Lloyds Rep PN 814.

12.3.2 Failing to take steps necessary to make the will effective

A solicitor may be held liable to a disappointed beneficiary who cannot benefit under a will because the solicitor has not taken steps necessary to ensure that an asset is part of the estate (for example, failing to sever a beneficial joint tenancy). In *Carr-Glynn* v. *Frearsons* [1998] 4 All ER 225 the Court of Appeal held that the solicitor was negligent because she had allowed the testatrix to execute a will at a time when neither she nor the testatrix knew whether the testatrix was able to leave her interest in her house to the desired beneficiary. The solicitor should have advised the client that it was possible to serve a notice of severance as a precaution irrespective of whether the property was actually owned as beneficial joint tenants or tenants in common.

12.3.3 Failing to clarify the property owned

Clients do not always remember how they own property. In *Re the Estate of Ronald Ernest Chittock (Deceased)* [2002] EWCA Civ 915, the matrimonial home was believed to be in joint names but eight months after the death of the husband (partially intestate) it was discovered that it had been in his sole name.

Property in joint names may be held on a resulting trust for the original purchaser. In *Carlton* v. *Goodman* [2002] 2 FLR the Court of Appeal found that although a property had been conveyed into joint names, it was in fact in the sole beneficial ownership of the deceased.

Proprietary estoppel may mean that someone else can claim an interest in property 'owned' by the client. See *Gillett* v. *Holt* [1998] 3 All ER 917, *Campbell* v. *Griffin and West Sussex County Council* [2001] WTLR 981, *Jennings* v. *Rice* [2002] WTLR 367.

Does the client have a power of appointment over trust property? If it is a general power of appointment, an ordinary residuary gift will be sufficient to exercise it without any express reference to the power. The client may not realise this and may believe that, because the power has not been expressly exercised, the trust property will pass to the person entitled in default. In *Gibbons* v. *Nelsons* [2000] PNLR 734, the court found that a solicitor was in breach of duty in not clarifying the client's wishes in such circumstances.

Try to resolve any ambiguities or uncertainties when taking instructions. Where there is any doubt, you should record that the will has been prepared on the basis of the information provided by the client.

Be aware that serving a notice of severance is not the only way of severing a joint tenancy. Law of Property Act 1925, s.36(2) expressly preserved the pre-1925 methods of severance. *Williams* v. *Hensman* (1861) 1 John & H 558 lists three methods:

(a) an act of any one of the persons interested operating upon his own share may create a severance as to that share;
(b) mutual agreement;
(c) any course of dealing sufficient to intimate that the interests of all were mutually treated as constituting a tenancy in common.

You may be taking instructions from a client who appears to be the sole beneficial owner of property as a result of survivorship. However, there may have been an earlier severance by conduct. See *Re Woolnough, Perkins* v. *Borden* [2002] WTLR 595.

As in *Re Woolnough* you may be consulted by two clients who are beneficial joint tenants but who indicate by the instructions they give for their wills that they are treating the joint tenancy as at an end. Make sure that there is clarity as to when the severance takes place. Is it when the instructions are given or when the wills are signed? Consider preparing a signed statement or notice of severance on the spot.

12.3.4   Failing to prepare a will sufficiently quickly

The speed required depends on circumstances. In *X* v. *Woollcombe-Yonge* [2001] WTLR 308 a solicitor was alleged to have been negligent where a testatrix, known to be suffering from terminal cancer, died before he had prepared a will. He had intended to have the will ready for signature one week after taking instructions. Neuberger J held that on these facts the amount of time taken was not unreasonable. It was significant that although the testatrix was terminally ill, she was not expected to die in the near future. Neuberger J went on to say that:

> Where there is a plain and substantial risk of the client's imminent death, anything other than a handwritten rough codicil prepared on the spot for signature may be negligent. It is a question of the solicitor's judgement based on his assessment of the client's age and health.

12.3.5 Failing to keep an appointment

A solicitor who cancelled an appointment to visit a client in hospital for execution of the client's will was held to be negligent in *Hooper* v. *Fynemores (a firm)* [2001] WTLR 1019:

> there is a positive duty on the solicitor to satisfy himself that the additional delay caused by his (not the client's) request is not to the client's detriment.

12.3.6 Allowing a testator to execute a will conditionally

In *Corbett* v. *Newey* [1996] 3 WLR 279 solicitors allowed a testatrix to sign a will but not to date it. Her intention was that the will was not to come into effect until she had completed certain lifetime gifts. The will was held to be conditional and the solicitors therefore compensated the disappointed beneficiaries.

12.3.7 Failing to offer the testator an opportunity to execute the will under supervision

In *Esterhuizen* v. *Allied Dunbar* [1998] 2 FLR 668 Longmore J said:

> It is in my judgement not enough just to leave written instructions with the testator. In ordinary circumstances just to leave written instructions and to do no more will not only be contrary to good practice but also in my view negligent.

To protect themselves solicitors should have in writing an offer in the following terms:

- the client can visit the solicitor's office for execution;
- if the client prefers, the solicitor will visit the client's house with a member of staff;
- if the client prefers, the client can make his/her own arrangements.

Although the safest course is clearly to follow *Esterhuizen*, it is worth noting that in the earlier case of *Gray and others* v. *Richards Butler (a firm)* [2000] WTLR 625 Lloyd J found that a solicitor who had not offered to oversee execution had not been negligent in the circumstances of the case. He referred to the 'very clear terms of the attestation provision of the will' and went on to say that:

> What steps are appropriate in discharge of these various duties in any given situation may depend on who the client is and the view that the solicitor has formed, or ought to have formed if acting with reasonable competence, as to the ability of the client to understand and follow advice as to the relevant procedures.

12.3.8 Failing to inspect a will returned after execution

In *Ross* v. *Caunters* [1979] 3 All ER 580 Megarry V-C accepted that the solicitors had breached their duty by *inter alia*:

- not checking the will after execution;
- not noticing that one of the witnesses was a spouse of a beneficiary;
- not bringing that fact to the attention of the testator.

In *Gray* the court accepted that there was nothing about the particular will under consideration which should have aroused suspicion. However, the case proceeds on the basis that solicitors have a duty to inspect a will that has been returned.

12.3.9 Failing to offer a client advice required for the transaction being carried out

In *Hurlingham Estates* v. *Wilde & Partners* [1997] STC 627, Lightman J had to consider whether or not a property lawyer had entered into an effective agreement with his client to exclude any obligation to advise on the tax aspects of a property transaction. He concluded that there was insufficient evidence of such an agreement. It ought to have been recorded in a letter to the client so that the client could have considered the implications and discussed them with others but it had not been. He also held that to be effective such a limitation on liability would require fully informed consent on the part of the clients.

He went on to consider whether, in the absence of an effective retainer limiting liability, a solicitor carrying out a commercial conveyancing transaction for a client has an obligation to advise on tax implications. Obviously this is an issue for probate practitioners too.

Lightman J said that the test was whether, having regard to all the circumstances, the solicitor should reasonably have appreciated that the client 'needed his advice and guidance in respect of the tax liabilities to which entry into the transaction would expose it'.

A solicitor cannot gain protection from liability by claiming to rely on counsel's opinion. In *Estill* v. *Cowling, Swift & Kitchin* [2001] Lloyd's Rep PN 378 an estate suffered unnecessary inheritance tax because a discretionary trust was established in inappropriate circumstances.

Arden J said that he endorsed the approach taken in *Locke* v. *Camberwell Health Authority* [1991] 2 Med LR 249 that a solicitor does not abdicate his professional responsibility when he seeks the advice of counsel.

The principles to be derived from the relevant authorities were, he said, as follows:

1. In general, a solicitor is entitled to rely upon the advice of counsel properly instructed.

2. For a solicitor without specialist experience in a particular field to rely on counsel's advice is to make normal and proper use of the Bar.

3. However, he must not do so blindly but must exercise his own independent judgment. 'If he reasonably thinks counsel's advice is obviously or glaringly wrong, it is his duty to reject it . . .' (per Taylor LJ, (at page 254, with whom Sir George Waller and Parker W agreed).

Arden J went on to consider what in his view a reasonably competent solicitor would do to give himself sufficient general knowledge of the subject. He said:

as respects the tax considerations, he would have read some general outline of the tax implications of setting up a trust, and (having discovered IHT applied to all transfers of value subject to exemption) looked to see what exemptions were available. The point was not some obscure point of tax law. It was a basic principle of IHT which had been discussed in the professional press at the time, particularly when the law was changed to make transfers to IIP trusts PETs. As it was, Mr Anderson did no research of his own . . . His conclusion that a transfer of value to the settlement was a PET was negligent.

12.4 WILLS PROCEDURE CHECKLIST

Some practitioners like to use a checklist with their clients. Others prefer to have one available for their own use as an *aide-mémoire*. The following checklist was compiled after discussions with the various probate registries around the country. It draws attention to common mistakes which can lead to delay in obtaining the grant and other points, certain of which are mentioned in this Handbook, which can easily be overlooked. Probate registries report difficulties in relation to the drafting of clauses appointing solicitor-executors (see at 12.1.1 above).

The Law Society used to publish a comprehensive Will Preparation Checklist, to be used while taking instructions, as an *aide-mémoire* of the topics to cover and record of those instructions. This checklist is no longer available separately but is reproduced below.

1. Did you obtain full, clear instructions from the client?
2. Was there any reason to suspect a later challenge to the client's testamentary capacity?   If so, did you ask questions to satisfy yourself?   And record them in a full written attendance note?
3. Did you check the client's eligibility for public funding: age; capacity; intention?
4. Did you check that any charity mentioned is really charitable? And the correct charity name, number and address? And that the estate is likely to be solvent and all the legacies can be paid?

5. Have you explained to the client (in no particular order):

- the pros and cons of appointing members of the family/solicitors/ others as executors?
- the implications of the clauses extending or varying the executors' general law powers and duties?
- the impact of the general law on the will (e.g. effect of marriage)?
- the implications of any charging clause?
- the need for parents to appoint guardians of minor children?
- the position of single parents under the Children Act 1989?
- the law relating to specific, general or demonstrative legacies, where appropriate, e.g. the need to review specific legacies if the property the subject of the gift alters or is sold or destroyed?
- the terms and effect of any residuary gifts made?
- whether there will be any secret or half-secret trusts?
- whether the will is to be mutual, i.e. not to be revoked unilaterally?
- the effect of mutual wills? (are they appropriate for the client?)
- whether the will incorporates any document – was that intended?
- the general law concerning the payment of tax, testamentary expenses or other liabilities (especially those items which will not be paid out of residue)?
- the tax planning considerations which affect the terms of the will, e.g. lifetime gifts within seven years of death?
- the likelihood of a claim under the Inheritance (Provision for Family and Dependants) Act 1975 and, if any, what should be done?
- about the position of a cohabitee (with and without an interest in the home)?
- the consequences for the beneficiaries if the residue is much larger (say because of an unexpected windfall) or smaller (say because a property has had to be sold to pay for care) than anticipated?
- the advisability of making an enduring power of attorney and discussed with the client a procedure for making the will available to the attorney (to avoid problems such as accidental ademption)?
- the need to sever a joint tenancy if the client wants to make a gift of property held as beneficial joint tenant.

6. Have you agreed the arrangements for valid execution of the will, and advised the client accordingly? Have you offered to inspect the will after execution?

7. What is to happen to any previous wills or codicils? It is advisable to destroy them so as to avoid any possible confusion.

8. Have you asked the client if there are any other practical or legal steps they want to consider in relation to their financial and other arrangements – writing a life insurance policy in trust, drawing up an enduring power of attorney making an advance directive or living will?

9. Was the will executed within a reasonable time? If not, have you:

- explained to the client the implications of not executing the will, i.e. intestacy or non-revocation of existing will?
- sought instructions about new provisions, if the client is unhappy about the terms or effect of the draft will?
- ensured that existing provisions have not been overtaken by events in the intervening period?

10. After the will has been executed, have you:

- checked it was executed and witnessed properly by people who are neither beneficiaries nor married to beneficiaries?
- kept a copy for your files?
- if you are holding the original, have you given a copy to the client?
- advised on the importance of placing the will where it will be found, and telling executors and family where it is?
- advised on the desirability of the client placing a Personal Assets Log (available from the Law Society – see Appendix 5) with their papers?
- explained to the client that it is necessary to review a will every two to five years and sooner if there is a major change of financial or personal circumstances?
- agreed the extent of your retainer? Is the client aware that you will/will not be reminding them of the need to review their will in five years' time or in any other situation, and will/will not be notifying them about tax changes affecting provisions made?
- if partners of the firm have been appointed as executors have you a separate record of this so that the client can be approached if a partner leaves, retires or dies?

12.5 SOLICITOR'S DUTY AFTER WILL EXECUTED

This guidance was approved by the Law Society's Standards and Guidance Committee and Property and Commercial Services Committee in 1991.

1. It is for clients to ensure that their wills are kept up to date and solicitors may help clients to do this by retaining in a manual or computer database (note the requirements of the Data Protection Act 1984 and European legislation in relation to manual records and databases) the names of clients for whom they have drawn up wills in the past. Solicitors may write to these clients from time to time reminding them of the need to review a will regularly and of their firms' services.

2. The preparation of a will for a client is in the ordinary case an entire contract so that when the work is completed and the final bill is submitted, the relationship of solicitor and client may be assumed to have ended as far as will preparation is concerned. Of course, the relationship of solicitor and

client may continue with that client on other matters. Where solicitors have a continuing relationship with clients, they may wish to consider agreeing with those clients whether or not the client wishes the firm to maintain a watching brief on legal changes or tax changes which might affect their will; the Society considers that it would be appropriate for a charge to be made for such a service in addition to charges for preparation of a will.

3. Without specific instructions from the client, a retainer for will preparation would not entail the solicitor in maintaining any such 'watching brief', but it is possible for a solicitor by his or her conduct to change a retainer so that a client comes to have a reasonable expectation that such a watching brief will be maintained. Solicitors would be well advised to ensure that these matters are clear between themselves and their clients.

4. Many firms store clients' wills as a free service and a courtesy to their clients. The storage of a will does not of itself create a retainer. Solicitor and client may agree otherwise.

5. In relation to wills stored by firms, should a solicitor or clerk named as executor or executrix in such a will retire, move to another practice, or die, or otherwise become unable or unwilling to act, the firm should consider writing to the testator or testatrix at the client's last known address detailing the changed circumstances. Informing clients of such internal changes to a firm is not considered to be any indication that a watching brief on matters of law has been agreed upon, but is, rather, part of the necessary changes which follow retirement or resignation, etc., of a solicitor from a firm, such as changes to the notepaper.

6. Some firms may retain large numbers of wills for clients from whom they have not heard for many years. Solicitors wishing to clarify the position in relation to these wills may wish to consider writing to a testator or testatrix at the last known address. However, even if no reply is received, such wills should never be destroyed as they remain the clients' property or the property of the clients' PRs.

There was an interesting article by James Sunnucks in [1995] *New Law Journal*, Probate Supplement, 29 September, where he pointed to an Australian case (*Hawkins* v. *Clayton* [1988] CLR 539) which holds that a solicitor retaining a will has a duty to take reasonable steps to find the executor.

12.6 RETAINERS GENERALLY

Also note the cases of *Cancer Research Campaign* v. *Ernest Brown & Co.* [1997] STC 1425, *Gibbons* v. *Nelsons* [2000] PNLR 734 and *Gray* v. *Buss Murton* [1999] PNLR 882, all of which emphasise the importance of clarity in the terms of a solicitor's retainer. In *Gibbons* v. *Nelsons* Blackburne J stressed that a solicitor has a general duty to the client when preparing a will and the burden is on the solicitor to demonstate any limitation on that retainer:

Although the burden of proof rests with the claimant to establish what the scope was of the solicitor's retainer, once the claimant establishes that the solicitor was retained to prepare a will, the burden must, I think, shift to the solicitor to show, if he can, that his responsibility for the preparation of the will did not extend to advising the client on some aspect of the will relevant to the claim.

In *Gray* v. *Buss Murton*, Rougier J said that any ambiguity in the retainer would be determined in favour of the client. It is the solicitor's duty to clarify precisely the terms of any retainer.

Lightman J in *Hurlingham Estates Ltd* v. *Wilde & Partners* [1997] STC 627 emphasised the need for a client to give informed consent to any limitation in the retainer and to the importance of a clear written record of any agreement to limit the retainer.

12.7   INTERNET WILLS

12.7.1   Using the Internet

An increasing number of solicitors' firms now have their own website and are offering a variety of legal services including will drafting via the Internet. Important issues which are now beginning to be raised in respect of the use of this modern technology when taking instructions and preparing wills include the solicitor's duty of care in relation to e-commerce.

Some solicitors are keen to use the Internet to its full potential and have readily embraced the e-commerce age, whilst others are more cautious and some are openly hostile to the idea of preparing wills via the Internet. As the legal and technical difficulties surrounding electronic signatures are resolved it will become possible for wills and other documents to be completed and executed online. The possibility of wills executed electronically has serious implications, so it is perhaps worth reviewing the advantages and disadvantages of using the Internet for the preparation of wills.

The type of legal services offered by legal firms via the Internet varies. At present most firms use their websites to promote their services to existing and new clients and to provide legal knowledge. Some firms offer a more interactive site which enables the client to download forms and to complete and return questionnaires and information to the firm. Relatively few firms at present return the will electronically for the client to sign.

12.7.2   Advantages of using the Internet for wills

The Internet provides easy access for computer literate clients possibly on a 24-hour basis and is heavily used by the younger generation who consider it an essential part of their life. Giving instructions via an interactive site is likely to appeal to the under 35s who overall tend to resist making wills. Some firms may regard a sophisticated IT set-up as a marketing tool promoting a modern image of solicitors and may specifically target a younger generation and encourage them to make wills.

It *may* be possible to offer a less expensive service as overheads and reduction in staffing could cut costs in the long term. It should, however, be noted that the start-up costs of setting up a truly interactive site would not be insignificant and can require a considerable amount of time and effort to develop an accurate and responsive system.

The Internet knows no boundaries, therefore the actual drafting of wills can be carried out at a different location where the overheads are cheaper. This may result in more flexible working practices for staff as if the instructions are received via the Internet there is no need for the staff to be located in a central office. Accessibility problems may be overcome for disabled clients or staff if they choose to use the Internet instead of attending at the solicitor's office. A considerable amount of information can be presented to the client via the website which they can access in the privacy of their home and at their own speed.

However, appropriate face-to-face access should continue to be made available as a significant proportion of clients for the foreseeable future are likely to choose to have a meeting in person at the solicitor's office when discussing complex issues.

12.7.3 Disadvantages of using the Internet

A will is not a commercial contract; it is a unilateral document which may not become operative for many years. To create a valid will the statutory requirements of the Wills Act 1837, s.9 and an adequate level of testamentary capacity must be satisfied. What sets a will apart from other forms of commercial transactions is the fact that by the time the will is challenged the testator (and possibly the witnesses) will be dead and unable to verify the will.

Without a personal interview with the client it would be difficult to spot underlying problems or the 'hidden agenda'. There is a potential risk of fraud or coercion of clients, particularly if they are vulnerable or elderly.

It can be very time-consuming for the client to access the appropriate information on the taxation system, information concerning claims under the Inheritance (Provision for Family and Dependants) Act 1975 or complexities which can occur where second marriages are involved. There is a real risk that the clients may lack the ability to either use properly or understand key explanations and definitions in the computer software, i.e. 'children' include illegitimate and adopted children but not step-children.

It is essential that any website is regularly maintained and upgraded. Regrettably some existing sites run by solicitors include out-of-date tax information (including references to capital transfer tax!) and misleading and sometimes incorrect advice.

Issues of mental capacity cannot be easily resolved. If you have not had a meeting with your client when taking the instructions and discussing the same, how would you be able to confirm to any court in the event of a dispute that the client did actually have the necessary mental capacity to make a will?

If the final will is downloaded by the client it will be impossible for the solicitor to ensure that the pages have in fact been printed correctly on suitable quality paper.

Some databases recorded in old computer formats are already obsolete and it is now impossible to retrieve the data. There is also evidence that floppy disks and CDs degrade after a relatively short period. An electronic will should be capable of being stored for at least 75–80 years and easily retrievable. At present there is no technical standard or guarantee that data can be stored for any long-term period, i.e. 50 years or more.

12.7.4 Confidentiality

The client understandably will expect confidentiality but *this cannot and should not be guaranteed.* Many large global organisations have set up complex security systems, which have then been compromised by computer hackers. Nevertheless solicitors will be keen to try and emphasise that they can make the website as secure as possible. Possible means of doing this will be by using a guaranteed encrypted system, or software, which includes other security devices to protect the information from being intercepted.

Protecting personal information and privacy are likely to be key issues for most clients. Fear of their credit card being misused and invasion of their privacy are likely to be factors, which will cause clients to resist purchasing products online. Therefore any solicitors firm wishing to encourage clients will need to consider confidentiality and security very seriously. Some firms have had their information systems independently audited and arranged for an attempted penetration to check the levels of security. An American security company challenged hackers to break into its security system which it described as the 'Fort Knox' of computer security. It took the hackers one day to access the main server and claim their prize of £35,000.

Verifying the authenticity of the message and the sender/recipient is important. Videocameras linked into the computer are likely to become increasingly important in the future alongside electronic keys and electronic signatures as a means of confirming the identity of the client. Such systems have cost implications for solicitors and their clients, but as the market for these goods increases so some of the costs are likely to fall.

12.8 E-COMMERCE STATUTORY FRAMEWORK

12.8.1 Introduction

The UK government, as a member of the European Union, is required to implement the Electronic Commerce Directive 2001/31/EC, which requires all Member States to ensure that their legal systems permit contracts to be executed by electronic means. The Directive was adopted by the EU on 8 June 2000 but has not yet been fully implemented by the United Kingdom.

The Electronic Communication Act (ECA) 2000, which partly came into force on 25 May 2000, seeks to create public confidence in e-commerce by:

- confirming the legal status of electronic signatures;
- creating a statutory framework for the approval of cryptography providers;
- providing a system to facilitate the removal of any legal barriers against the use of electronic communications.

12.8.2 What is an electronic or digital signature?

ECA 2000, s.7(2) defines an 'electronic signature' as something which incorporates or is linked to electronic data or an electronic communication with the purpose of establishing the authenticity or the integrity of the communication or data.

ECA 2000 did not attempt to define the basis on which an electronic signature would be treated as valid. ECA 2000, s.7(1) states that electronic signature and the certification by any person of the signature are deemed to be admissible in any legal proceedings, but it is left to the courts to decide what evidential weight to give to an electronic signature.

A paper signature can be treated as a record of the intention of the signatory to be committed to a course of action. An electronic 'signature' can be used to verify the identity of the person and to bind them in the same manner as a manual signature. An electronic signature is not a scanned image of the individual's normal signature.

Electronic Signature Regulations 2002, SI 2002/318 came into effect on 8 March 2002 with the purpose of implementing the provisions of the Electronic Signatures Directive 1999/93/EC. The regulations include a definition of an 'advanced electronic signature' by reference to certain specific requirements and is intended to encourage their legal recognition throughout the EU. The electronic signature is treated as an 'advanced electronic signature' if the signature:

(a) is uniquely linked to the signatory;
(b) is capable of identifying the signatory;

(c)   is created using means that the signatory can maintain under his sole control; and

(d)   is linked to the data to which it relates in such a manner that any subsequent change of the data is detectable.

The term digital signature is somewhat misleading as the 'signature' consists of complex information which is encrypted. The system relies on the signature having been approved by way of a digital certificate issued by a certification authority. The system relies on 'keys' which are in fact complex mathematical algorithms; the complexity of the algorithms means that only the specific individual should be able to sign the email or other electronic document. There are public and private keys, which when matched together enable encrypted information to be decrypted and read. So the keys enable information to be encrypted with a public key which can then be simply sent via the Internet and only be decrypted with a private key.

The government, financial institutions and commerce are all trying to create secure systems which will enable fully integrated electronic business to be conducted via the Internet. The whole area of digital and electronic signatures is likely to continue to change dramatically in the next few years. At the moment there is no specific legislation which prohibits the use of an electronic signature to effect the creation of a will, although it still has to satisfy the requirements of the Wills Act 1837, as amended.

12.8.3   Privacy and Data Protection Act 1998

Solicitors when they collect and store personal information are required to comply with the obligations set out in the Data Protection Act 1998. These include:

- an individual must be informed that personal data is being collected and held by the solicitors' firm;
- the individual must be informed that use may be made of that personal data;
- the solicitor must take appropriate measures to ensure secure access (storage and transmission of the data);
- the information collected must be processed and stored in a fair and accurate manner.

The Seventh Principle contained in Data Protection Act 1998, Sched.1, Pt II requires appropriate technical and organisational measures to be taken against unauthorised or unlawful processing of personal data and against accidental loss or destruction of or damage to the personal data. This means that if you are in receipt of personal information about a person you will have an obligation to ensure the reliability of all the employees that have access to that personal data to ensure that it is not misused. Non-compliance is an offence and directors/officers of the company can be held personally liable.

If a firm fails to comply with the provisions of the Act it may be liable to claims for compensation from the party providing the data as well as to criminal proceedings (Data Protection Act 1998, s.13).

12.8.4 Consumer Protection (Distance Selling) Regulations 2000

Firms intending to develop a website which is more than an information portal will need to comply with the Consumer Protection (Distance Selling) Regulations 2000, SI 2000/2334 which became operative from 31 October 2000. These regulations were primarily aimed at mail order catalogues, telephone sales and other types of 'distance selling' but the regulations also affect faxes, newspaper advertisements, the Internet and contracts that are not made face to face. The regulations only apply to transactions involving consumers; they do not apply where the services are being offered to a business.

The regulations set out the minimum requirements concerning the information which must be supplied to the client/customer by the supplier. A solicitor or legal firm which is offering to sell legal service or legal knowledge to a consumer or lay client over the Internet is deemed to be a supplier of legal services.

The regulations include an automatic seven-day cooling-off period and unless time is specifically extended, all contracts must be completed within 30 days.

The right to return 'goods' to the supplier after they have been received by the consumer does not apply if the goods that are supplied are customised for that particular client (reg. 13(1)(c)). Most wills should be capable of being treated as specific to the client and therefore should not be caught by the right of return.

A cooling-off period should, however, be incorporated into the firm's terms and conditions of business regardless of whether the transaction is over the Internet or in written form.

12.8.5 Contractual implications of wills via the Internet

The Internet may not recognise geographical boundaries but anyone providing services via the Internet needs to define in which country or legal jurisdiction they wish any contractual disputes to be decided. It is also necessary to define the place of performance of the contract or the provision of services. Failure to define the terms clearly could result in the case being heard in another country and the legislation of that country being applied. Although this problem is less likely to apply to wills than the purchase of other goods, such as books or videos, it is obviously preferable to avoid uncertainty wherever possible. An EU Council Regulation 44/2001 on jurisdiction and the recognition and enforcement of judgements in civil and commercial matters imposes additional restrictions if there is a consumer contract.

12.8.6 Duty of care limiting liability

Using email, a website or other Internet facilities to provide legal services does not negate the basic duty of care which a solicitor owes to a client. E-commerce is simply a different modern method of delivering solicitor's services.

Email and the Internet may increase the pressure for you to respond to the client immediately but it does not reduce the professional standard of care that a solicitor is expected to adhere to.

Different levels of information may be agreed or may be appropriate for different clients. Ideally the client should normally be told in appropriate language at the *outset of a matter or as soon as possible thereafter* the issues in the case and how they will be dealt with. In particular the immediate steps to be taken in a transaction must be clearly explained.

It may be helpful to provide linked specialist text for the client to access explaining particularly complex issues, i.e. parental responsibility if the parents are unmarried or when and why you recommend including a life interest trust.

Drafting questionnaires

The emphasis therefore is on *informing* the client. So if you require the client to complete an online questionnaire they need to understand the legal language used.

> This questionnaire is only appropriate if your assets and possessions do not exceed the inheritance tax threshold – £250,000 for tax year 2002/2003.

This statement assumes that the client understands what is meant by the term *assets*. Many clients and members of the public might query what from a legal perspective appears to be a straightforward question. The client might want to ask the following questions:

- Does that include my half share in the house I own jointly with my wife – I thought that was tax-free and did not count?
- What about my life policies – I think they go to my children if I die – are they included?
- I also have a timeshare in Grand Canaria – I wonder if that is included?

The example given above demonstrates that even a simple statement concerning the assets requires a considerable amount of knowledge and information in order for the client to make a reasoned judgement. If you choose to gather such information electronically, detailed additional information and checks need to be included and this can make the process time-consuming and off-putting to the client.

Very few wills are straightforward, in fact more and more wills are becoming complex. Second or third marriages, children from different partners and a variety of pension schemes and investments mean taking a detailed profile in order to prepare the will.

It is unlikely that the Internet is going to be the appropriate method for preparing complex wills which involve tax planning.

12.8.7 Can you limit your liability?

Some solicitors who are already using the Internet to provide will services have tried to limit their liability to the information provided in the will questionnaire;

> We will prepare your will strictly on the basis of the information provided in the will questionnaire and cannot be held responsible for an incorrectly drafted will based on inaccurate information provided.

It is understandable that a solicitor does not want to be held liable if the client has provided inaccurate or inadequate information which the solicitor has then relied upon to draft the will. However, if the solicitor has failed to provide an adequate level of information to assist the client in completing the questionnaire, the clauses attempting to limit liability are unlikely to be given effect by the courts.

In the tax case of *Hurlingham* v. *Wilde & Partners* referred to above at 12.3.9 there appeared to be a widening of the obligations of the solicitor to a client.

The *Hurlingham* case cannot be viewed as an isolated case as it has now been followed in the case of *Gladis Muriel Estill and others* v. *Cowling Swift & Kitchin and others* referred to above at 12.3.9. It should be noted that both the cases of *Hurlingham* and *Estill* refer to express agreements. This would seem to indicate that simply sending your terms of engagement or a retainer letter whether through the post or via email may not always be enough.

There are also certain implied duties, which a solicitor cannot exclude. The problem for the draftsperson is ascertaining which tasks should be included or excluded.

Some IT experts argue that if a basic 'no frills' service is offered it is unreasonable for the client to expect a high level of information or service. However, by holding themselves out as a solicitor, a standard of care of that of a competent solicitor will be expected irrespective of the standards offered by other Internet sites which may be offering a will-making service. An interesting question will be whether the courts when dealing with other Internet sites offering will-drafting services will be willing to follow the principles for-mulated in the case of *Allied Dunbar* v. *Esterhuizen* [1998] 2 FLR 668, where the court stated that a commercial company, Allied Dunbar, had to apply the same standards of care as a solicitor when carrying out a will-making service.

Where a retainer has been agreed, the status of the parties may be signifi-cant. An elderly client who does not have detailed knowledge of tax or trust law is unlikely to be expected to understand the significance of clauses which seek to limit the solicitor's areas of responsibility under a retainer unless it can clearly be shown that the client understood the consequences of the clauses. It is arguable that in these circumstances the duty towards the client will widen and a solicitor should take additional time and effort if necessary to explain the terms of the retainer to their client. If you communicate only by email how can you assess the situation?

12.9   INTERNET SERVICES OFFERED BY FIRMS

12.9.1   Larger firms

In recent years private client work has been eschewed by some of the large commercial firms in the city of London and elsewhere, individual private client work not being regarded as cost effective. However, some larger firms are now returning to private client work, and some commercial firms are also developing highly sophisticated IT systems capable of carrying out a high volume of legal work via the Internet.

It is anticipated that some large legal firms will develop will-drafting pack-ages for their institutional clients, which the clients can then market through their individual high street shop or premises. Instructions will be taken in the commercial premises of the company or institution from the individual and then emailed back to the legal firm to implement. The legal firm does not actually deal with the individual client directly. The legal firms acting on behalf of the institutions are hopefully aware of the potential risks in draft-ing wills via the Internet but they are likely to make a commercial judgement based on risk assessment. If the volume of business generated is sufficiently large they will be prepared to take the commercial risk of having to deal with some potential problems/claims.

Certainly the level of financial investment enables sophisticated security systems and rigorous quality checks to be undertaken which may not be realistically cost effective for smaller firms to undertake.

12.9.2   Small firms' potential use of the Internet

Some small firms have viewed the Internet as a possible way of widening their client base without the need to purchase costly additional premises. An increasing number of smaller firms have readily seized on the opportunity to set up a low cost website and offer wills on the Internet.

Potential problems that may occur will be the failure to maintain and to upgrade the website at regular intervals. The ability to set up a website and claim an expertise in will drafting is very easy to do; the question is whether or not some of the solicitors' firms have the necessary levels of competence actually to draft the documentation.

There is an expectation by courts when considering negligence claims against solicitors and by clients themselves (perhaps even more so because they are using the Internet) that the work will be completed quickly and this may place considerable pressure on a small firm with limited resources.

12.9.3   Areas to define and limit when using the Internet

Foreign assets

Foreign assets such as a holiday home in France or Spain require careful thought and specialist advice. In most circumstances, therefore, the retainer should explain that such specialist advice is not provided as part of the will-making service offered through this particular Internet service. The Internet has no geographical boundaries and the issues concerning domicile and residence may be relevant. A client's email address will not necessarily give any indication of where they are resident although this could affect the legal advice you should offer.

The solicitor may if appropriate suggest that the client have a meeting in person to discuss the matter further, but they should make it clear that an additional charge will be made.

Inheritance tax advice

In most circumstances a solicitor will be expected to ascertain the extent and the nature of the testator's estate. If the estate is well below the nil-rate band for tax purposes is it reasonable to try and exclude tax advice?

Some solicitors' firms who are already offering legal services over the Internet have sought to restrict their liability to give tax advice by excluding such advice in the terms of their retainer. If the *Hurlingham* and *Estill* decisions are followed such a clause may not be enough as you need to establish that the client had informed consent. So if a solicitor is seeking to try to limit liability for tax advice the solicitor should still provide at least a résumé of tax principles and this information must be up-to-date.

It may be prudent to include a clause within the terms of the agreed retainer with the client defining clearly that the advice given and the prepared will are based on the law at a definite moment in time and that the firm does not accept responsibility to notify the client of any future changes in the law or any legal decisions which might affect the terms of the will.

Due execution of the will

Clients using the Internet for will drafting are perhaps less likely to be willing to attend in person at the solicitor's office to execute the will. Provided the client is willing and able to understand instructions on how to execute the will and the solicitor has provided a clear set of written instructions, the solicitor in normal circumstances should have discharged his duty of care. The danger lies in the fact that having taken instructions via the Internet you may not have identified possible complications and if there are unusual circumstances any exclusion in the retainer is unlikely to be effective.

As problems concerning the correct execution of the will have been a fertile area of litigation in recent years with cases such as *Esterhuizen*, the risk of failing to provide adequate instructions should not be underestimated.

Printed documentation

Where the will-drafting service is via the Internet an additional issue may arise concerning the printing of the will as well as the execution of the will.

In these circumstances any retainer should very clearly state the potential risks and seek to define whether or not the solicitor is responsible for checking the will if it is returned. However, there is still the risk that the courts would not accept the retainer as being reasonable in all circumstances.

12.9.4 Is it worth the risk?

Many solicitors are already carrying out an increasing amount of their legal work via the Internet and this is likely to increase further. However, wills by their nature are very specialist documents, which require specific procedures, i.e. careful drafting and correct execution in order to be valid. There is real danger that firms that do not have specialist knowledge will simply set up websites offering services without considering the dangers and risks and this in turn will lead to negligence claims at a later date.

Even for the experienced practitioner the time required to provide the detailed information for the client which is essential should not be underestimated. Furthermore such information will still not negate the obligation to explain, if necessary in person, complex issues to clients who are vulnerable or have special needs.

It is inevitable that the Internet increasingly will be used to deliver a wide range of legal information, knowledge and services to the public. Although cost is undoubtedly a factor for some individuals, superstition and a reluctance to make decisions are also key inhibitors which cause people to delay making a will and these are likely to remain the same whether the will is created via the Internet or made in person.

At the moment there is definite lag between the development of increasingly sophisticated forms of software and the ability to translate that technical knowledge into a product which clients feel confident to trust and use. Electronic signatures may be appropriate for contracting to purchase the weekly shopping online, but the creation of a will is quite different. What IT does offer is the ability to store and then easily retrieve specific information about the client which enables the firm to provide a more client-focused service, i.e. the client database can be programmed automatically to generate a reminder letter to the client of the need to review the will/enduring power of attorney after a given period of time. Such a system can, however, be counter-productive if there is insufficient staff available to respond to the work generated.

The use of the Internet to prepare and send draft wills is likely to increase over the next five years. The creation and recognition of totally electronic wills using electronic signatures is a more complex matter and is unlikely to be widely implemented in the near future.

12.9.5   Further advice and information

- The Wills and Equity Committee published guidance in connection with the preparation of wills on the Internet, which was published by the Law Society in May 2000 and appeared in (2000) 14 *Probate Section Newsletter* (June).
- The Law Society has also prepared guidelines for best practice in respect of electronic mail and these were published in [2000] *Gazette*, 8 June.
- The Department of Trade and Industry website at **www.dti.gov.uk** contains useful information concerning electronic signatures and other e-commerce issues.
- *E-commerce – A Practical Guide to the Law* (Gower, 2001) by Susan Singleton, a solicitor specialising in e-commerce, is a useful reference.

Points and actions to consider regarding wills via the Internet include the following:

- You could choose to ignore the Internet and continue with traditional service.
- Consider your market carefully – do you do a lot of simple wills or are they complex?
- Litigation involving wills has increased dramatically in recent years – do you have the necessary expertise and the IT knowledge to provide the service?
- You could create a website of services offered by the firm, plus information for clients and a checklist that the client can download to use to

collate information before a face-to-face meeting (this could be an effective marketing tool).

- You could create an interactive website enabling clients to complete a questionnaire to send to the firm but then still post the will to the client.
- You could set up a totally electronic system, with payment by credit card and the will dispatched electronically.
- Any information on the website must be accurate and regularly updated.
- Insurance-loading may become an issue in the future.
- Be careful about relying on retainers and make sure you have written agreement from the client and that they understand the terms of the agreement.

12.10   ADVANCE DIRECTIVES AND 'LIVING WILLS'

12.10.1   Introduction

'Advance directives or statements' and 'living wills' are different terms for the same thing. They are documents intended to allow individuals to specify the extent and nature of the medical treatment they would or would not find acceptable should they lose capacity in the future. The term 'living will' can be confusing since such documents have no connection with ordinary wills but this term is probably too well established to change.

Gordon Ashton, in *Elderly Client Handbook* (published by the Law Society – see Appendix 5) considers these documents in detail.

Competent patients can authorise or refuse consent to treatments, both contemporaneously and in advance, but cannot make legally enforceable demands about specific treatments they wish to receive.

The recent case of *Re B* [2002] 2 All ER 449 reviewed the authorities and states very clearly that a mentally competent patient has an absolute right to refuse consent to medical treatment for any reason, rational or irrational, or for no reason at all.

The difficulty with advance directives is that they are normally in issue in cases where the patient is unable to speak to make his/her wishes known.

The following cases support advance directives: *Re T (Adult: Refusal of Treatment)* [1992] 3 WLR 782, *Airedale NHS Trust* v. *Bland* [1993] 2 WLR 316, HL and *Re C* [1994] 1 All ER 819. In *Re T* the Court of Appeal said that an anticipatory choice will bind a medical practitioner if it is:

- clearly established, and
- applicable in the circumstances.

The British Medical Association (BMA) published a statement in 1992 on advance directives. It stated that the BMA 'strongly supports the principle of an advance directive' and points out that 'patients have a legal right to decline specific treatment, including life prolonging treatment'. It stresses 'the significant ethical and legal difference between the concept of an advance statement and the issue of euthanasia . . . [which] is illegal' and emphasises that its conclusion on advance directives should not be seen as supporting euthanasia.

This distinction was supported by the House of Lords Select Committee on Medical Ethics, HL Paper 21–I, HMSO (1994), which commended the development of advance directives, but recommended no change in the law to permit euthanasia. Its recommendations led to a Code of Practice from the professions entitled 'Advance Statements about Medical Treatment', BMA (1995). The Code restates the law with explanatory notes and gives health professionals the protection of guidance and an accepted body of professional opinion.

The Law Commission published a report *Mental Incapacity*, Law Com. No. 231 (1995), which also supported the use of advance directives, and called for legislation in order to clarify the current common law position that an advance refusal of treatment made with capacity survives any supervening incapacity. No such legislation has been forthcoming.

In its report *Withholding and Withdrawing Life-prolonging Medical Treatment* (BMA, 2nd edn published 2001) the BMA claimed that:

> A valid advance refusal of treatment has the same legal authority as a contemporaneous refusal and legal action could be taken against a doctor who provides treatment in the face of a valid refusal.

Living will documents are not like normal testamentary documents. Their validity is determined by the patient's capacity, not the document. There are obviously strong reasons for using a written document but an oral living will could be just as binding.

Information on the assessment of capacity to consent to or refuse medical treatment is contained in the book published by the Law Society/BMA, *Assessment of Mental Capacity* (1995). There is an interesting article on this subject by Anne Wilkinson of the University of Bristol in [1997] *New Law Journal*, 12 December.

One of the difficulties with advance directives is the requirement that they be 'applicable to the circumstances'. In *Re B*, Ms B had executed a living will in 1999 after she had first become ill. It said that if she was unable to give instructions, she wished treatment to be withdrawn if she was suffering from 'a life-threatening condition, permanent mental impairment or permanent unconsciousness'. When she became paralysed from the neck down and needed ventilation, the doctors concluded that the terms of the directive were not specific enough to authorise withdrawal of ventilation. Although she was able to make her wishes known, the doctors argued that she had lost her mental capacity to make decisions as to her treatment. The Court of Appeal did not agree and Ms B was allowed to reject ventilation.

An alternative to consider is a health care proxy document. In this a competent patient appoints an agent to make health care decisions for him or her, should the patient become incompetent. There is a common misconception that the next of kin are normally responsible for making treatment decisions. This is not so. In *Re T*, Lord Donaldson pointed out that the responsibility lies with the doctor:

> There seems to be a view in the medical profession that in emergency circumstances the next of kin should be asked to consent on behalf of the patient and that, if possible, treatment should be postponed until that consent has been obtained. This is a misconception because the next of kin has no legal right either to consent or to refuse consent. This is not to say that it is an undesirable practice if the interests of the patient will not be adversely affected by any consequential delay. I say this . . . because contact with a next of kin may reveal that the patient has made an anticipatory choice which, if clearly established and applicable to the circumstances . . . would bind the practitioner.

12.10.2 Specimen living will

There are numerous precedents for living wills and advance directives in existence. The *Elderly Client Handbook* by Gordon R. Ashton contains one example, drafted by Denzil Lush; [1999] *Trusts and Estates Law Journal* (September) has another in an article by Chris Docker of the Voluntary Euthanasia Society of Scotland and others are obtainable from the Voluntary Euthanasia Society and the Terence Higgins Trust.

We have reproduced the precedent from the *Elderly Client Handbook* below and are most grateful to Gordon Ashton and Denzil Lush for allowing us to do so.

THIS LIVING WILL

is made on   _____

by me   _____

of   _____

born on   _____

I WISH these instructions to be acted upon if two registered medical practitioners are of the opinion that I am no longer capable of making and communicating a treatment decision, AND that I am:

- unconscious, and it is unlikely that I shall ever regain consciousness; or
- suffering from an incurable or irreversible condition that will result in my death within a relatively short time; or
- so severely disabled, physically or mentally, that I shall be totally dependent on others for the rest of my life.

I REFUSE any medical or surgical treatment if:

- its burdens and risks outweigh its potential benefits; or
- it involves any research or experimentation which is likely to be of little or no therapeutic value to me; or
- it will prolong my life or postpone the actual moment of my death with no further benefit to me.

I CONSENT to being fed orally, and to any treatment that may:

- safeguard my dignity; or
- make me more comfortable; or
- relieve pain and suffering,

even though such treatment might unintentionally precipitate my death.

If I change the terms of this document I will notify the undermentioned person(s) so every effort should be made to contact (one of) them before relying on it.

[name(s), address(es), telephone number(s) and e-mail address(es)]

SIGNED by me	_____
in the presence of:	_____
Name;	_____
Address:	_____
Occupation:	_____

In the article in *Trusts and Estates Law Journal* referred to above Chris Docker discusses three options which exist when preparing a living will. We are very grateful to the *Trusts and Estates Law Journal* and to Chris Docker for permission to reproduce this section of the article.

Some options include:

- drawing up a living will from scratch;
- using a simple standard text;
- using a more sophisticated document.

The first option is desirable in some ways, but the practical pitfalls mean that it is inadvisable without very extensive research. One of the most common errors is to draw up a complicated document with extensive checklists. These might look very impressive to the lay person, but the medical pitfalls mean that they are unconvincing in practice – the exact details of medical exigencies can rarely be predicted in such accurate detail.

The second option could mean simply photocopying the form apppearing with this article, or using the text from it as a basis for a document on the firm's notepaper. The form includes all the minimum requirements recommended by the BMA. Usually, when people first think of making a living will, they want to make a very simple statement.

Later on, clients may wish to put effort into completing a more sophisticated document (the third option) which enables them to state their wishes more precisely, and probably gives them greater protection. These documents can be obtained at relatively low cost from The Scottish Voluntary Euthanasia Society [see Appendix 6] or the Terence Higgins Trust [Appendix 6]. Both of these sources provide well-researched documents which apply anywhere in the UK. The one from VESS comes as part of a pack with medical stickers, a carrying wallet, an emergency medical card and an advice booklet.

If solicitors draw up their own version of a living will, then, like all legally binding forms for use by lay people, it should be well designed, clear and straightforward. Lord Donaldson in *Re T* commented on the desirability of using different sizes of typeface, underlining, and colour print.

The BMA says that the minimum information to be included is as follows:

- the person's full name;
- their address;
- the name and address of their GP;
- whether advice was sought from health professionals;
- their signature;
- the date the will was drafted and reviewed;
- the signature of a witness;
- a clear statement of wishes, either general or specific;
- the name, address and telephone number of the person's nominated contact, if they have one.

Within the Law Society these matters are the responsibility of the Mental Health and Disability Committee, in the Policy Directorate.

EAGLE (Exchange on Ageing, Law and Ethics) has published further articles on the topic. There is also a useful section by Chris Docker in Tolley's looseleaf title *Finance and Law for the Older Client*. The website **www.euthanasia.org** is also useful.

CHAPTER 13

The law – on probate and succession: a review

Lesley King

There are many excellent works covering the law relating to probate and succession already available (see Appendix 5). This Handbook is not intended to be a legal textbook but a summary of the principal legal issues may be helpful generally, and also as a pointer to some of the grounds on which you may find the validity of a will, or parts of it, being challenged.

13.1 IS THE WILL VALID?

Check the following matters.

13.1.1 Age

Was the testator or testatrix over 18 (or on active service)?

13.1.2 Mental capacity

Requirements

Did the testator or testatrix understand:

- the nature of his or her act and its effects;
- the extent of his or her property; and
- the moral claims which ought to be considered?

For the classic statement of the test of testamentary capacity, see *Banks* v. *Goodfellow* (1870) LR5QB 549.

Proof of capacity

Capacity is presumed unless the contrary is shown. There is a presumption in favour of a duly executed will if it is rational on the face of it, i.e. those opposing it must produce evidence to suggest lack of capacity. It will then be for those putting forward the will to establish capacity. A will fails if the person putting it forward cannot discharge the burden of proof (see *Vaughan* v. *Vaughan* [2002] EWHC 699)..

If the testator or testatrix generally lacked mental capacity (e.g. he or she was mentally ill), lack of capacity is presumed; this can be rebutted.

The time for testing capacity is normally when the will is executed. However, if the testator or testatrix was competent when giving instructions, but not at actual execution, the will is nonetheless valid if he or she recalls giving the instructions and believes the will to accord with them: *Parker* v. *Felgate* (1883) 8 PD 171.

13.1.3 Intention

Requirements

The testator or testatrix must intend:

* to make a will; and
* to make the particular will executed. He or she must, therefore, know and approve its contents: *Guardhouse* v. *Blackburn* (1886) LR1P&D 109.

Attestation clause

Whilst an attestation clause is not required by Wills Act 1837, s.9, if such a clause is included and recites that the formalities of s.9 were observed, it will raise the presumption of due execution. Further, the inclusion of such a clause will normally avoid the necessity of providing the registrar with an affidavit of due execution.

Proof of intention

Knowledge and approval of the particular will are presumed from the fact that the testator or testatrix had capacity and executed the will, unless:

* he or she was blind or illiterate or the will has been signed by someone else on his or her behalf (e.g. in the case of someone totally paralysed). Here the registrar must be satisfied that the testator or testatrix had knowledge of the will's contents and execution;
* suspicious circumstances are present (e.g. the will substantially benefits the person who prepared it). Here, the greater the degree of suspicion, the stronger must be the affirmative proof to remove it: *Fulton* v. *Andrew* (1875) LR7HL 448, *Wintle* v. *Nye* [1959] 1 WLR 284. If there is a question of suspicious circumstances, is there a careful and full record of events? In some cases the burden of proof may be so heavy as to be impossible to discharge, as in *Wintle* v. *Nye* itself.

The two recent cases of *Fuller* v. *Strum* [2002] 1 WLR 1097 and *Hart* v. *Dabbs* [2001] 1 WLR 527 suggest that where a will is simple and straightforward and the testator had an opportunity to read it, the court may well accept that he knew and approved the contents even where a beneficiary was concerned in the preparation of the will.

Rebutting the presumption of knowledge and approval

If knowledge and approval are presumed, those opposing the will must prove that such knowledge and approval were absent by establishing that:

- the testator or testatrix was induced to make the will by force, fear or fraud; or
- he or she was subjected to undue influence and so did not make the will voluntarily. In the case of a will, undue influence must be tantamount to coercion, i.e. the testator or testatrix being driven to make the will against his or her wishes, e.g. by physical threats or actual violence; or incessant nagging may suffice: *Wingrove* v. *Wingrove* (1885) 11 PD 81. However, persuasion (appeals to sentiment, ties of kindred, etc.) is permissible.

Motives are irrelevant.

13.1.4   Mistake

Mistake will invalidate a will, or that part of it included by mistake, but only if the relevant words are present without the testator's or testatrix's knowledge: it will not save a disposition where the testator or testatrix was mistaken as to the effect or meaning of the words used. Thus, he or she is deemed to know and approve the technical language used by the person drafting the will: even though that person was mistaken as to its legal effects, such language must be admitted to probate, *Re Horrocks* [1939] P 168.

Conversely, a mere clerical slip or error (such as a typing mistake) will generally be omitted from probate unless it has been brought to the testator's or testatrix's notice: *Re Morris* [1971] P 62.

13.1.5   Formalities

Wills Act 1837, s.9 states:

No will shall be valid unless:

(a) it is in writing and signed by the testator, or by some other person in his presence and by his direction; and

(b) it appears that the testator intended by his signature to give effect to the will; and

(c)   the signature is made or acknowledged by the testator in the presence of two or more witnesses present at the same time; and

(d)   each witness either:

(i)   attests and signs the will; or

(ii)   acknowledges his signature, in the presence of the testator (but not necessarily in the presence of any other witness).

Whereas previously the signature had to be at the foot or end of the will, the rule now is that in (b) above. The emphasis is on giving effect to the will as far as possible whilst not opening the door to fraud.

Signature is given a wide meaning: a mark, an initial, and even a thumb print have all been held to suffice but not a seal. Even an incomplete signature will do: *Re Chalcraft* [1948] P 222, *Re Cook* [1960] 1 All ER 689. See also *Weatherhill* v. *Pearce* [1995] 1 WLR 592. Presence is also given a wide meaning: see *Couser* v. *Couser* [1996] 1 WLR 1301.

13.2   HAS A DOCUMENT BEEN INCORPORATED?

To be incorporated as part of a will an unexecuted document must be:

- in existence at the date of execution of the will;
- referred to in the will as already existing; and
- clearly identified in or identifiable from the will.

Care should be taken to avoid reference in a will to an existing document if incorporation is not intended. The registrar may require production of any such document, with evidence of possible incorporation.

The consequence of incorporation is that the document incorporated will be open to public scrutiny, as it will be admitted to probate with the will.

13.3   ARE TWO WILLS MUTUAL?

See paragraph 12.15 for a for a discussion of the requirements for mutual wills.

Be aware that once one testator dies with a will in the agreed terms, the property of the survivor becomes subject to a trust. The property will pass to the agreed beneficiary even if the surviving testator makes a new will purporting to leave the property elsewhere.

Re Hobley Deceased, The Times, 16 July 1997 shows that there can be difficulties in deciding whether or not the first testator has died with a will in the agreed terms where there has been any kind of alteration to the agreed will.

There is a useful article on cases on mutual wills in [1997] *Trusts & Estates*, November, 83.

13.4 TYPES OF LEGACY

Legacies may be categorised as follows.

13.4.1 Specific

This is a gift of property forming part of the testator's or testatrix's estate at death and distinguished in the will from other property of the same kind, e.g. 'my race horse Red Rum', 'my dwelling-house Blackacre, or such other dwelling-house in which I shall reside at the date of my death'.

Even a gift of money may be a specific legacy (*Re Wedmore* [1907] 2 Ch 277) although this is relatively rare.

13.4.2 General

This is a gift of property not distinguished in the will from other property of the same kind, e.g. 'to X the sum of £5,000; to Y £5,000 shares in ICI'. Whilst most general legacies are of money, it is not essential that they be so – although clearly an attempt to give a general legacy of some types of property would create problems and might well be void for uncertainty (e.g. 'to X a horse'. How does one define a horse, what value, etc?).

13.4.3 Demonstrative

This is a general legacy payable out of a specific designated fund, e.g. '£1,000 payable out of my paid-up share account with X Building Society'. Here, in so far as the fund is still in existence at the testator's or testatrix's death, it will be treated as a specific legacy. In so far as it is not, it will be treated as a general legacy and abate accordingly should there be insufficient in the estate to discharge debts without recourse to the other general legacies.

The distinction between specific, demonstrative and general legacies is particularly important because:

- a specific legacy is subject to ademption; a general one is not, e.g. if Red Rum (see above) has been sold, given away, or has died during the testator's or testatrix's lifetime, the legatee will get nothing unless there is a substitutional provision (as in the case of the gift of Blackacre (again, see above));
- a general legacy must be applied for payment of debts before a specific one;
- a demonstrative legacy is only treated as a specific legacy in so far as the designated fund remains at the testator's or testatrix's death.

157

13.4.4 Pecuniary

This is a gift of money which may be specific, general or demonstrative. Administration of Estates Act 1925, s.55(i)(ix) defines a pecuniary legacy as including:

> an annuity, a general legacy, a demonstrative legacy, so far as . . . not discharged out of the designated property, and any other general direction by a testator for the payment of money, including all death duties free from which any devise, bequest or payment is made to take effect.

Thus a legacy specified to be free of tax or free of expenses will be treated as a legacy conferring an extra benefit, the amount of which would be equivalent to the tax or expenses being paid out of the estate.

13.4.5 Residuary

This is what is left after all debts, liabilities, legacies and other expenses have been paid.

Where residue is left to be divided between an exempt and a non-exempt beneficiary (e.g. a charity and a member of the deceased's family) problems arise as to how the burden of tax should fall. See the discussion of *Re Benham* in paras. 16.31–40.

With regard to legacies to institutions (including charities) you need to know whether or not the institution is charitable, as the cy-près doctrine only applies to charities, and charities are not bound by the rule against perpetuities. This means that a charity can generally take an interest under a will no matter how distantly in the future it vests.

The Charity Commission (see Appendix 6) may be able to advise if problems arise. More information on charitable beneficiaries is included at para. 16.28 onwards.

13.5 IS INTEREST PAYABLE?

Legacies should be paid with due diligence and usually within the executors' year. Even where the will directs earlier payment, this cannot be compelled.

Interest (payable from residue) normally runs from the time when payment is due (or otherwise if so provided by the will, e.g. 'and I direct that the said legacy shall carry the interim income'). It appears that the rate of interest is 6 per cent per annum as this is the rate which would apply if there were a judgment in the matter (see *Williams on Wills*, 8th edn (Sweet & Maxwell, 2002) (Appendix 5)).

Exceptionally, interest runs from death where the legacy is:

- charged on realty;
- in satisfaction of a debt charged on unconverted realty;
- to the testator's or testatrix's minor child(ren); and
- to any other minor if the will shows an intention that the income is to be used for maintenance or education.

13.6 PROVISION ON INTESTACY

(*Note:* The statutory legacies quoted are applicable for deaths on and after 1 December 1993.)

13.6.1 Deceased was married at death

The Family Law (Succession) Act 1995 introduced a survivorship period for spouses of 14 days in respect of deaths occurring on or after 1 January 1996:

(a) If the intestate leaves issue (e.g. children and/or grandchildren) the spouse takes:

   (i) personal chattels absolutely (as defined by Administration of Estates Act 1925, s.55(1)(x)); and
   (ii) £125,000 plus interest at the rate of 6 per cent from death until payment (free of tax, with costs and interest coming from the residue); and
   (iii) a life interest in half the residue, the remainder and the other half going to the children on the statutory trusts.

(b) If the intestate leaves no issue, but does leave a parent or brother or sister of the whole blood or their issue, the spouse takes:

   (i) the personal chattels absolutely; and
   (ii) £200,000 plus interest as above; and
   (iii) half the residue absolutely.

(c) If the intestate leaves no issue, no parents, no brothers or sisters of the whole blood or their issue, the spouse takes the whole estate absolutely.

13.6.2 Deceased was unmarried (or divorced or widowed)

The estate goes to the intestate's:

(a) issue on the statutory trusts; if none,

(b) parents; if none,

(c) brothers and sisters of the whole blood on the statutory trusts, failing whom to remoter relations and, if none, to the Crown or the Duchy of Cornwall. The Treasury Solicitor will deal with the estate in these cases (see at 15.3 below). The Treasury Solicitor has a discretion to make payments from the estate to anyone unrelated but close to the deceased during his or her lifetime.

'Personal chattels' excludes any which are used for business purposes. It also excludes money or securities for money, but has been held to include, for example, valuable collections.

Under the statutory trusts (Administration of Estates Act 1925, s.47), a child of the intestate has a contingent interest in the estate. This is satisfied if the child reaches 18 or marries before that. A child dying under 18, unmarried, is treated as never having existed.

If a child of the intestate does not survive him or her, but leaves a child or children, then that child or those children will take his, her or their deceased parent's share (in equal shares if more than one), again contingently on attaining 18 or marrying before that.

13.6.3 Spouses: special rights

The surviving spouse may elect (generally within 12 months of the grant) to:

- redeem any life interest in the estate in return for a lump sum (Administration of Estates Act 1925, s.47). If the spouse so elects for inheritance tax purposes, this does not count as a transfer of value by the spouse. He or she is treated as if, instead of being entitled to the life interest, he or she had been entitled to the lump sum from the outset;
- take the matrimonial home, or the deceased's share in it, in or towards satisfaction of any absolute or capitalised interest in the estate (Intestates' Estates Act 1952, Sched. 2). The value of the house is taken at the date of appropriation, not of death: *Re Collins* [1925] 1 WLR 309. To qualify, the surviving spouse must be living in the house concerned at the intestate's death.

Exceptions to the surviving spouse's right to take the matrimonial home include cases where the intestate's interest in the property was a tenancy expirable (by notice or otherwise) within two years of death and where the house forms part of a commercial unit, such as a farmhouse on a working farm or a flat in a family hotel.

If the value of the matrimonial home is more than the spouse's statutory legacy, the spouse may make up the shortfall.

The surviving spouse may *require* personal representatives to make this appropriation, in direct contrast to the position under Administration of Estates Act 1925, s.41, under which PRs may (whether the deceased died testate or intestate) appropriate his or her property in (or towards) satisfaction of interests in the estate, subject to the consent of the other beneficiaries, if the need for this has not been dispensed with in the will.

13.6.4 Hotchpot

The Law Reform (Succession) Act 1995 abolished the rules as to hotchpot in their entirety for deaths occurring on or after 1 January 1996.

13.7 JOINT PROPERTY

Joint property can cause a number of problems for solicitors.

In *Carr-Glynn* v. *Frearson* [1998] 4 All ER 225, the testatrix wished to leave her interest in a house to her niece. She was uncertain whether her interest was held as joint tenant or as tenant in common with her nephew. The solicitor explained to her that the will would be ineffective if the house was held as joint tenants and that it would be necessary to sever the joint tenancy. The solicitor offered to obtain the title deeds to check. The client said that she would do it herself but did not do so. When she died, it was discovered that the house had been held as joint tenants so the will was ineffective.

The Court of Appeal found the solicitor negligent: the service of a notice of severance was part of the will-making process. The niece was as much an intended beneficiary of the severance as she was of the new will. The solicitor should have explained that it was possible to serve the notice of severance as a precaution without any need to check the title deeds:

> She did not tell the testatrix that the doubt, identified in her letter of 6 February 1989, could and should be laid to rest by the service of a notice of severance before or at the same time as the will was executed; that there was no need to obtain the deeds before serving the notice; and that there was nothing to be gained, and potentially much to be lost, by delay.

It is important to check the basis of ownership and, if there is any doubt, advise service of a notice of severance.

Re Woolnough, Perkins v. *Borden* [2002] WTLR 595 confirms that it is possible to sever a joint tenancy in any of the ways possible before the Law of Property Act 1925 (see para. 12.3.3).

In *Re Woolnough* a brother and sister had made wills leaving their interest in a house owned as joint tenants to the other for life with a gift over to a third party. After the sister's death the brother left the house to charity. If the joint tenancy had already been severed, only half of the value of the house was in his estate. If it had not, the whole value of the house was his.

The fact that the two had made wills giving each other a mere life interest in the property was sufficient to amount to an agreement to sever:

> It is not a case of one of them acting behind the back of the other. The reference in the Will to a half share makes it clear that they were treating their share as disposed of by their Wills.

It would not, of course, have amounted to severance had one joint tenant alone made a will dealing with the half share.

When administering an estate there may be cases where it is necessary to investigate whether or not there was an earlier severance by consent. Although an estate may appear to have acquired the entire interest in a property by survivorship, there may have been severance by consent at an earlier stage.

13.8   RELEVANT STATUTES

13.8.1   Law of Property (Miscellaneous Provisions) Act 1994

The Law of Property (Miscellaneous Provisions) Act 1994 came into effect on 1 July 1995. Helpful articles on this, by Philip Rossdale and Robin Towns, appeared in [1995] *Solicitors' Journal*, 28 July and [1995] *New Law Journal*, Probate Supplement, 29 September. The 1994 Act affects sales of land by personal representatives (PRs) and also vests intestates' property pre-grant in the Public Trustee (instead of the President of the Family Division).

13.8.2   Trusts of Land and Appointment of Trustees Act (TLATA) 1996

TLATA 1996 came into force on 1 January 1997. It prevented the creation of new trusts for sale and strict settlements in respect of land and introduced the 'trust of land'. Trustees of land have all the powers of an absolute beneficial owner including the power of sale. Property of an intestate is no longer held on a trust for sale.

Where a will creates a continuing trust, s.11 imposes an obligation on trustees of land to consult beneficiaries of full age with an interest in possession when exercising any function in respect of land.

Section 12 gives a beneficiary with an interest in possession a right to occupy land in certain circumstances.

Section 13 allows trustees to regulate the respective rights of beneficiaries where more than one has an interest in possession.

All of these provisions can be varied by the will.

Helpful articles appear in [1996] *Solicitors' Journal*, 1154 on the will drafting implications of TLATA 1996, in [1996] *Family Law*, December, 736 on the provisions of the Act relating to joint ownership, expansion of trustees' powers and beneficiaries' right of occupation and in [1997] *Conveyancing*, July/August, 263 on drafting to restrict trustees' powers.

13.8.3   Trustee Delegation Act 1999

The Trustee Delegation Act 1999 came into force on 1 March 2000. It prescribed a new short form of power of attorney, amended Powers of Attorney Act 1971, s.25 and repealed Enduring Powers of Attorney Act 1985, s.3(3).

In *Inland Revenue Commissioners* v. *Eversden and another (Executors of Greenstock, deceased)* [2002] EWHC 1360 (Ch), [2002] STC 1109 Lightman J suggested that TLATA 1996, s.12 and s.13 had affected the legal position of co-owners. However at the time of writing the case is listed for appeal.

Trustee Act 1925, s.25 as amended by Powers of Attorney Act, s.9, allows trustees to delegate all powers and discretions but subject to various restrictions. The appointment cannot be an enduring power; cannot exceed 12 months (although the appointment can be renewed); cannot be to a sole trustee; the donor remains liable for the acts of the attorney; notice of the delegation must be given to all co-trustees.

Enduring Powers of Attorney Act 1985, s.3(3) allowed trustees to delegate all trustee functions and contained none of the Trustee Act 1925, s.25 safeguards. In particular it allowed a sole co-trustee to be appointed as attorney despite the rule that two trustees are required to give a good receipt for capital money. There was a feeling that s.3(3) had gone too far in removing the safeguards of the Trustee Act 1925, s.25, hence the changes introduced by the 1999 Act.

The main effects of the Trustee Delegation Act 1999 are as follows:

- Section 7 confirms and strengthens the rules that capital money must be paid to, and a valid receipt for capital money must be given by, at least two trustees, and that a conveyance or deed must be made by at least two trustees to overreach any interests affecting a legal interest. In effect two individuals must always act. So, for this purpose a trustee acting on his own behalf and as attorney for all the other trustees only counts as one person. The provisions relating to delegation must be read subject to this.
- Prior to the 1999 Act co-owners could not delegate by using a general power of attorney. They had to use a Trustee Act 1925, s.25 trustee power of appointment or an enduring power. Section 1 of the 1999 Act allows trustees with a beneficial interest in the trust property (for example, co-owners) after 1 January 2000 to use a general power of attorney to delegate their trustee functions in relation to land, the proceeds of sale of land and income arising from it. The effect is that they are freed from the restrictions of s.25 so there is no limit on the length of time the delegation can last, it can be to a sole co-trustee and notice need not be given to co-trustees. In a typical husband and wife co-ownership, one could delegate to the other. However, under s.7 of the 2000 Act there will still need to be two individuals to give a good receipt for capital money. If the attorney wanted to sell, there would have to be another trustee appointed.

- Section 8 gives an attorney who cannot sell because there is no other trustee, power under an amended Trustee Act 1925, s.36 to appoint a further trustee. However, s.8 is a complicated section and only applies where there is a registered enduring power under which the attorney is authorised to exercise the donor's trustee functions.
- Enduring Powers of Attorney Act, s.3(3) is repealed so that from 1 March 2000 onwards trustees who do not have a beneficial interest in the trust property can now only delegate their powers and discretions by complying with the requirements of Trustee Act 1925, s.25. The delegation can be by an ordinary s.25 trustee power or it can be by enduring power. However, whichever route is used s.25 limits the delegation to 12 months. The only advantage to using an enduring power is that the incapacity of the trustee will not revoke it. The attorney will also be able to appoint an additional trustee under s.8 of the 1999 Act.

Helpful summaries of the Trustee Delegation Act 2000 appear in [2000] *Solicitors' Journal*, 3 March, (2000) 64 *Conveyancer* and [1999] *Gazette*, 20 July. (2002) 33 *Trusts and Estates Law Journal*, 13 contains an interesting letter suggesting including in wills and trusts a wider power for specified persons to remove trustees who are becoming mentally incapable and, in appropriate cases, to appoint a replacement.

13.8.4 Trustee Act 2000

The Trustee Act 2000 came into force on 1 February 2001. It implies a set of default powers into trusts unless the trust document specifies differently by exclusion, modification or widening and irrespective of whether the trust was created before or after 1 February 2001. The powers implied are a general investment power, power to use agents, nominees and custodians and a general power to insure. These are dealt with at 13.10 below.

The Trustee Act 2000 makes various changes to the law on charging clauses. Under s.28:

- a trustee of a non-charitable trust who acts in a professional capacity (defined as one providing services in connection with the management and administration of trusts) can charge for work that a lay person could do without express authorisation in the charging clause;
- a charging clause is no longer treated as a legacy so:
  - a partner in a firm with the benefit of a charging clause can witness the will without losing the benefit of the clause;
  - the charges will not abate with other pecuniary legacies where there are insufficient funds (so it is no longer necessary to provide for this expressly in the clause).

Under s.29 a trustee of a non-charitable trust who is acting in a professional capacity can charge reasonable remuneration for his services without a charging clause provided a majority of co-trustees authorises it. This does not apply to a sole trustee (other than trust corporations).

The Act also imposes a general duty of care. Whenever the duty applies, the trustee must exercise such care and skill as is reasonable in the circumstances, having regard in particular:

- to any special knowledge or experience that he has or holds himself out as having, and
- in the case of a professional trustee, to any special knowledge or experience it is reasonable to expect him/her to have.

13.9 APPOINTMENT AND REMOVAL OF TRUSTEES AND PERSONAL REPRESENTATIVES

13.9.1 Retirement

There is no power for a personal representative (PR) who has taken a grant simply to retire from the office of executor in favour of another person. However, where a will appoints a person to act as executor *and* trustee, it will be possible for that person to retire from the office of trustee.

When does a PR become a trustee?

This can be a difficult question. Once the PR has ascertained the amount of residue available to the residuary beneficiary and, if appropriate, obtained approval of the estate accounts it is likely that the PR then holds the remaining assets as trustee. If, however, other assets or liabilities were discovered, the PR would have to deal with these assets or liabilities as PR since that office is never lost.

In what circumstances can a trustee retire and/or appoint new trustees?

The circumstances may be covered by the will. If not, the provisions of Trustee Act 1925, ss.36 and 39 will apply. These sections allow a trustee to retire provided this does not result in there being a sole remaining trustee and provided the continuing trustees consent. Continuing trustees can appoint replacement or additional trustees. The PRs of a sole trustee who has died can appoint replacements.

13.9.2   Removal of PRs by the court

Under Administration of Justice Act 1985, s.50 the court has a discretion to appoint a new PR or PRs in the place of existing PRs or any of them, or to terminate the appointment of one but not all of the PRs (unless appointing at least one substituted PR).

The court's jurisdiction under s.50 is not limited to cases of conflict between PRs. It can be used where a PR wishes to retire.

Where the court has ordered the administration of the estate under its supervision (a comparatively rare event) it has power to appoint PR(s).

The court has power to remove PRs and appoint new ones under Trustee Act 1925, s.41 where without an order it is 'inexpedient, difficult or impracticable' to appoint a new trustee or new trustees (including PRs). Such appointees may be 'in substitution for or in addition to any existing trustee or trustees'. The wording of s.41 is sufficiently wide to enable the court to remove PRs and trustees from office for other than the common causes – residing permanently abroad, becoming mentally disordered, becoming bankrupt or being convicted of serious crime. In *Probate Disputes and Remedies* (Sweet & Maxwell, 1997) Dawn Goodman and Brendan Hall state that:

> The court will not exercise this jurisdiction lightly and will generally do so only:
>
> (a)   when there has been a breach of duty and the court thinks that the estate will not be safe, or will not be administered in accordance with the will or the intestacy rules;
>
> (b)   where it is in the interests of the beneficiaries that the personal representatives be removed; or
>
> (c)   where there is considerable friction between the personal representatives.

In *Letterstedt v. Broers* (1884) 9 App. Cas. 371 the court was at pains to point out that there are no hard and fast rules and that the main guide in these cases must be the welfare of the beneficiaries. In the majority of cases an application is made under the AJA 1985, s.50 rather than under the Trustee Act 1925, s.41.

There is power under Judicial Trustees Act 1896, s.1 for the court to appoint a judicial trustee but this is rarely used.

The Law Society has power under the Solicitors Act 1974 to apply to court for the appointment of a new trustee in substitution for a solicitor who is a controlled trustee. This would be a step of last resort.

13.9.3   Trusts of Land and Appointment of Trustees Act (TLATA) 1996, s.19

It is worth noting that under TLATA 1996, s.19, beneficiaries who are of full age and capacity and between them entitled to the whole beneficial interest can compel the retirement of the existing trustees and the appointment of trustees of their choice.

In the past, beneficiaries who were at odds with their trustees could not simply change the trustees (*Re Brockbank* [1948] Ch 206). In such circumstances they had to bring the trust to an end and then resettle the property with trustees of their choice, but this would frequently have had adverse capital gains tax (CGT) consequences. The new provision is subject to contrary intention in the will or trust instrument. However, for most people the CGT advantage will outweigh the concern over arbitrary replacement of trustees so only rarely will it be appropriate to exclude the s.19 power.

It is important to note that because of the requirement for full age and capacity and absolute entitlement to the whole beneficial interest there will be comparatively few occasions where s.19 will be relevant.

13.10 POWERS AND DUTIES OF EXECUTORS AND TRUSTEES: A SUMMARY

13.10.1 Powers

Unless the powers of executors and trustees are extended or varied by the will, they are limited to the powers given to them by statute. The main statutory powers are set out below.

Trustee Act 2000, s.3 gives a general power to invest in anything other than land as if the trustees were absolute owners. The power is in addition to any express power but subject to any restrictions contained in the trust instrument. However, nothing in a trust instrument made before 3 August 1961 will be treated as restricting or excluding the general power of investment. While this power will make little difference to modern, professionally drafted trusts, it will make an enormous difference to trusts arising on intestacy and to older or home-made trusts.

The Act does have important implications for all trustees even those acting under express investment clauses as it imposes additional duties.

Section 4(1) provides that when exercising *any* power of investment trustees must take into account the statutory investment criteria which are:

- the suitability to the trust of investments of the type proposed and of that particular investment as an investment of that type, and
- the need for diversification of investments of the trust, in so far as is appropriate to the circumstances of the trust.

Section 4(2) provides that trustees must review investments from time to time and consider whether they should change investments.

Unless the trustees reasonably conclude that it is unnecessary or inappropriate in all the circumstances to do so, they must obtain and consider proper advice before investing and when reviewing (s.5).

Trustee Act 2000, s.8 gives power to acquire freehold or leasehold land in the United Kingdom. This can be for investment or residence by a beneficiary. It does not provide power to buy land abroad or an interest in land.

Trustee Act 2000, ss.11–27 authorise the appointment of agents, nominees and custodians subject to certain safeguards. Trustees will not be liable for the acts of their appointees unless they fail to exercise reasonable care and skill in the appointment or in keeping the arrangements for employment under review.

Section 14 provides that where trustees wish to delegate their asset management function, they must do so in writing and must prepare a policy statement giving guidance as to how the agent is to carry out its functions. The statement should deal with such matters as:

- attitude to risk;
- the balance to be maintained between income and capital;
- level of liquidity;
- attitude to capital gains (undesirable if the life tenant is very elderly and there is a possiblity of tax free uplift on death in the relatively near future);
- willingness to be exposed to foreign currency.

There is a helpful article on the relationship between trustees and investment managers by Robert Smeath in *Private Client Business* [2001] Nov/Dec, 371 and one by Toby Harris outlining the main provisions in the *New Law Journal, Wills and Probate Supplement* [2002] 21 June, 945.

Administration of Estates Act 1925, s.19 as substituted by Trustee Act 2000, s.30, gives trustees a general power to insure any trust property against all risks and to pay the premiums out of income or capital.

Administration of Estates Act 1925, s.39 gives PRs all the powers of trustees of land (generally the powers of an absolute owner).

Administration of Estates Act 1925, s.41 gives power to appropriate assets.

Administration of Estates Act 1925, s.42 enables payment of a minor's gift to be made to a trust corporation or at least two trustees, if the minor is absolutely entitled. The section is less important since the Children Act 1989. This provides that all parents with parental responsiblity have the same rights, powers and duties as guardians appointed under the Children Act. These rights are set out in s.3 and include the right to receive property in their own name for the *benefit of the child*.

Trustee Act 1925, s.31 gives power of maintenance in relation to income.

Trustee Act 1925, s.32 gives power of advancement in relation to capital.

13.10.2   Exercise of powers

These powers are fiduciary. A sole, or sole surviving, executor or executrix may act alone in all cases. Where there is more than one executor or executrix, authority is joint for land (i.e. all must execute any deed) and joint and several for some personalty (i.e. just one may deliver an asset (e.g. jewellery) to a beneficiary and get a good receipt and discharge).

The Law of Property (Miscellaneous Provisions) Act 1994 covers aspects of sales of land by PRs, including the contract for sale: see at 13.6.5 above

13.10.3   Duties

The executors must safeguard the estate and with due diligence:

* collect and realise the assets;
* pay the debts and legacies;
* distribute the residue of the estate among the beneficiaries.

13.11   FOREIGN ASSETS AND DOMICILES

13.11.1   Foreign assets

Some of your clients may own property abroad because of a family connection; others because they have bought second homes or businesses. Potentially disastrous consequences can ensue if those clients are not fully advised about local laws regulating the inheritance of land and other property. In certain civil law jurisdictions, for example, children are automatically entitled to a fixed share of the estate regardless of any will to the contrary.

You need to be aware of the possibility both when preparing wills and when dealing with estates. You may need to instruct a solicitor in the United Kingdom with the necessary knowledge and experience or a local lawyer in the jurisdiction. The Law Society can help with the names of appropriately qualified lawyers (contact the International division, see Appendix 6).

13.11.2   Wills for clients with foreign assets

Sometimes an English will dealing with foreign property can put the testator or testatrix's wishes into effect, but it is often helpful for the client to make a will in accordance with the requirements of the other jurisdiction to deal specifically with those assets. Once a client has a foreign will you need to take care that any new English will does not start with a standard revocation clause revoking *all* other wills.

13.11.3 Dealing with the estates of clients with foreign assets

If the deceased died domiciled in England and Wales, but with assets in another country, a foreign will may have been made. A lawyer of that country may have to be instructed. Usually it is necessary to extract the grant in England and Wales first and then send it accompanied by a sealed and certified copy of the will to a local practitioner. This does not apply in a country where the Colonial Probates Act 1892 applies, or in Scotland or Northern Ireland.

The publications listed below may also be of interest – those dealing with conveyancing often contain a section on wills and probate.

Property in France

Make Yourself at Home in France (French Chamber of Commerce, 2000), which can be ordered through their website at **www.ccfgb.co.uk**, or telephone 020 7304 4040.

Property in Portugal

Buying a Home in Portugal, David Hampshire (Survival Books Ltd, 2002).

Property in Spain

The Complete Guide to Buying Property in Spain, Tony Foster (Property Search Spain, 2002); *Living and Working in Spain*, David Hampshire (Survival Books Ltd, 2000).

13.11.4 Foreign domiciles

If the deceased died domiciled outside England and Wales, but left assets in England and Wales (unless the Colonial Probates Act 1892 applies, or the deceased was domiciled in Scotland or Northern Ireland) it will be necessary to obtain a grant in England and Wales: see Non-Contentious Probate Rules 1987, Rule 30.

PART III

Practical Probate

This Part deals with some of the practical aspects of probate work which have caused difficulty in the past. It starts by covering inheritance tax, then deals with problem-solving, preparation of the accounts and some of the issues arising from distribution, and it ends with a series of checklists which take you from the beginning of the administration right through to the closing of the file.

CHAPTER 14

Inheritance tax

Lesley King with David Wright

14.1 CONTACTING INLAND REVENUE CAPITAL TAXES

For details on contacting Inland Revenue Capital Taxes, see Useful Addresses in Appendix 6.

14.2 INHERITANCE TAX RATES 1997–2002

(For transfers to non-exempt beneficiaries.)

14.2.1 Transfers on deaths occurring on or after 6 April 1997 and lifetime transfers taking place within three years of death

The table gives the IHT threshold limits, beyond which the 40 percent rate applies.

For deaths after 5 April	*IHT Threshold £*
1997	215,000
1998	223,000
1999	231,000
2000	234,000
2001	242,000
2002	250,000

14.2.2 Lifetime transfers taking place between three and seven years of death

There is a tapering relief available on such gifts but it takes the form of a reduction in the tax which would otherwise be payable. Thus, it only becomes effective if the total of the lifetime transfers made between three and seven years of death exceeds the limit of the nil rate band.

Years before death in which transfer made	*Percentage of death rate tax payable*
3–4	80%
4–5	60%
5–6	40%
6–7	20%

Note: Gifts made between seven and 14 years before the death, although themselves not liable to tax, may affect the rate of IHT applicable to gifts within the seven-year period.

14.2.3   Annual exemption

£3,000 (plus £3,000 for the previous tax year if unused).

14.2.4   Reliefs

Business property relief/agricultural property relief

Each at 100 per cent or 50 per cent of the value of the property transferred, depending on the nature of the assets and subject to minimum ownership requirements.

Woodlands relief

The value of trees or underwood growing in non-agricultural woodlands can be left out of account by election and the tax deferred until disposal of the timber.

National Heritage property

Exempt from inheritance tax if so designated by the Revenue and undertakings regarding the property are given and complied with. The notes to IHT 200 explain in detail how to deal with Heritage property. If you need more information, write to the Heritage section at the Nottingham office or telephone the Heritage section Helpline (see Appendix 6 'Useful addresses').

Quick succession relief

Available on a sliding scale when a transfer on death takes place within five years of an earlier transfer on which tax was paid, the point on the scale depending on date of the second death.

14.3   THE INLAND REVENUE ACCOUNT

14.3.1   Is one necessary? Excepted estates

The following edited extracts are taken from the Revenue's leaflet IHT 12 and are reproduced with their permission. The leaflet is extremely helpful and you should make sure you have a copy of it. Note that we have not reproduced the whole of the leaflet.

WHEN IS AN EXCEPTED ESTATE GRANT APPROPRIATE?

Introduction

Section 256 of the Inheritance Tax Act 1984 permits the Revenue to make regulations dispensing with the requirements to deliver an account for inheritance tax. We have made regulations under this section. If an estate meets the conditions in the regulations, it is an 'excepted estate'. If an estate is 'excepted', you do not have to deliver an account of the estate to obtain a grant of representation. The regulations are amended from time to time to update the qualifying conditions and the financial limits. Most recently they have been amended in 1998, 2000 and 2002.

Which estates are excepted?

For deaths after 5 April 2002, there are two options depending on the domicile of the deceased at death. Where the deceased was **domiciled in the UK** at death (the Channel Islands and Isle of Man are **not** in the UK), the estate is an excepted estate where

- the gross value of the estate, including the deceased's share of any jointly owned assets (whether passing by survivorship or under the will) and any 'specified transfers' does not exceed £220,000, **and**
- if the estate includes assets held in trust, their gross value does not exceed [£75,000], **and**
- if the estate includes foreign assets, their gross value does not exceed £100,000, and
- if there are any 'specified transfers', their chargeable value does not exceed £100,000, **and**
- the deceased had not made a gift with reservation of benefit.

Where the deceased was domiciled outside the UK at death [and after April 5 2002], the estate is an excepted estate where

- the deceased's UK estate consists **only** of cash or quoted shares or securities passing under a Will or intestacy or by survivorship in a beneficial joint tenancy and the gross value does not exceed £100,000, **and**
- the deceased's domicile of origin was outside the UK, **and**
- the deceased was neither resident nor domiciled in the UK for income tax purposes at any time during the period of 20 years ending with the year of assessment in which the death occurred. [. . .]

'Specified transfers' are chargeable transfers of cash, quoted shares or securities. For deaths [occurring] after 5 April 2002, this term also includes transfers of land from one individual to another, but only where the transferor did not retain any interest or benefit in the assets transferred. Land includes the fixtures, fittings and any household goods that are transferred with the property at the same time to the same donee.

The cash limit for 'specified transfers' is

Date of death
After 5 April 1996 and before 6 April 1998   £50,000
After 5 April 1998 and before 6 April 2002   £75,000
After 5 April 2002   £100,000

In working out the value of any 'specified transfers', you should deduct any exemptions that are available. [. . .]

When can the Revenue insist on delivery of an account?

If you have taken out an excepted estate grant, we can still insist on delivery of an Inland Revenue account. We will do so in a sample of estates. If we require delivery of an account, we will give notice in writing within 35 days of the issue of the grant of representation. The regulations require that we give this notice to the [legal personal representatives] rather than any solicitor acting for them.

What if I find out after taking out the grant that the estate is not excepted?

If you have taken out an excepted estate grant and then find out that the estate did not meet the conditions, you must tell us. If this happens we may insist on delivery of an account even though the 35-day period has [elapsed]. [. . .]

If you need a grant for a death before 18 March 1986 or if you need details of the excepted estate regulations for deaths before 1 April 1991, you should contact our Helpline on 0115 974 2650.

See also Appendix 6 for address.

14.4   WHERE AN ESTATE IS NOT EXCEPTED

Practitioners must complete IHT 200 together with the relevant supplementary pages, the probate summary (D18) and worksheet. The Inland Revenue publishes a helpful *Practitioners' Guide* (IHT 215) which can be found on the website at **www.inlandrevenue.gov.uk**.

14.5   REVENUE LEAFLETS

The Inland Revenue has produced a series of leaflets about inheritance tax:

IHT 2   Inheritance tax on lifetime gifts
IHT 3   An introduction
IHT 8   Alterations to an inheritance following a death
IHT 11   Payment of inheritance tax from National Savings or from British Government stock on the Bank of England Register
IHT 13   Inheritance tax and penalties

14.6 ADDITIONAL REMINDERS

14.6.1 Calculation of the tax and interest

Practitioners should note the following:

- Personal representatives have a duty to complete their Inland Revenue account form properly. They have a legal responsibility to pay the full amount of tax for which they are liable, before they send the account to the probate registry with their application for a grant of representation. Practitioners acting as, or on behalf of, personal representatives are expected themselves to calculate the correct amount of tax due.
- Interest on unpaid inheritance tax as from 6 November 2001 is 3 per cent.
- There may be circumstances where it is necessary to apply for a grant quickly and there is not time to obtain final valuations. You should phone the Capital Taxes Helpline and explain your problem. In *IRC* v. *Robertson* [2002] STC 182I a solicitor who submitted an account containing estimated values was held by the Special Commissioner to have acted properly because he paid the extra tax required within six months from the end of the month of death. However, it is preferable to avoid the possibility of any argument by making arrangements in advance.
- Practitioners should supply Capital Taxes with as much information as possible with the account to enable more focused enquiries to be raised after the grant has been issued. Both Capital Taxes and practitioners want to provide a good speedy service to their respective customers. It will save time if the IRA contains a statement of the basis of an ownership claim rather than waiting for Capital Taxes to raise enquiries.

14.7 DEATH OF A LIFE TENANT: CT APPROVED STANDARD LETTER

Capital Taxes approves the letter below to notify them of a life tenant's death. They add that applications for clearance on IHT 30 should not be made until these can be issued. There is no point in submitting the IHT 30 with, for example, the IHT 100.

As a result of the changes to the excepted estates rules, some estates that include assets held in trust may still qualify as excepted estates (see **14.3**). Inland Revenue Capital Taxes will return any Accounts IHT 100 in connection with trust assets the gross value of which does not exceed £100,000, if it is not clear whether the estate as a whole may qualify as an excepted estate.

The Director
Inland Revenue Capital Taxes
DX 701201 Nottingham 4

[Date]

Dear Sir

The Trust of Mr Fred Bloggs (Settlement 1953/Will dated 10/4/55)
Date of Death: 1/5/58
Your Reference: F/123456/53
Life Tenant: Mrs Freda Payne
Date of Death: 25/10/02

The Life Tenant of this Trust has died. We enclose a copy of the Trust Instrument.

We also enclose a completed form IHT 100 with supporting schedules. Please acknowledge receipt.

The Life Tenant's Estate will be dealt with by:
    Morse & Co, Solicitors, Lewis House, 22 Burt St, Oxford OX1 20X

*[We have not yet been able to ascertain the value of the Life Tenant's free estate.]
OR
*[We understand that the value of the deceased's free estate is about £200,000.]

We look forward to receiving an assessment or, in due course, confirmation that we may lodge form IHT 30.

Yours faithfully

(Jaguar & Co)

---

* Include as necessary: this will help Capital Taxes decide whether to issue a provisional assessment immediately. They can only do this if they know the value of the free estate.

14.8   PRODUCING YOUR OWN INLAND REVENUE FORMS

Capital Taxes has provided information for firms wanting to generate IHT account forms using their own computers (see Inland Revenue booklet 10/02 *Guidelines for Producing Substitute Inheritance Tax Forms*). The following extracts may be of interest.

Legislation

Section 257(1) of the Inheritance Tax Act 1984 explains the legal provisions for submitting accounts ... Basically, you must complete the correct form as prescribed by the Board of the Inland Revenue.

Inland Revenue (Capital Taxes) acts on behalf of the Board. We will accept an accurate facsimile of the prescribed form in order to satisfy this section of the Act. In the rest of this leaflet, we will use the word 'original' to indicate the 'prescribed form'.

What must the substitute form show?

To satisfy the Act, the substitute form must show all the text that appears on the original. You should not reproduce the Inland Revenue logo.

What about layout and style?

You must reproduce the same layout and style as on the original.

How will our staff know that the form is acceptable?

You will need to obtain official approval for each different type of inheritance tax form you intend to use.

We will give an approval reference. You should make sure that this appears on the bottom right hand corner of the first page of each form you complete. This is an example of the format: 'CT approval ref. A1/01'.

Is there anything else that must appear on the form?

You must show the correct identifier on the bottom left hand corner of the first page. A version of IHT 200 could show 'IHT 200 (substitute)(S&J)'. *The 'S&J' represents an abbreviation of a firm's name (e.g. Smith and Jones).*

Design notes

1.   Colour

Your substitute should not be colour-printed. Also, you do not need to print it onto coloured paper.

Where the original form has different tints of colour, you should use differing degrees of monochrome shading.

2. Logo

You **must not** reproduce the Inland Revenue logo on any substitute that you produce. You should, however, include the text part of the header (i.e. the 'Inland Revenue Capital Taxes' part).

3. Paper

You should use the same size paper as the original (A4).

You should print on paper of a reasonable standard as the forms will need to survive for many years. You may print either single or double-sided.

4. Text

You **must** reproduce **all** of the text that appears on the original. Your text must also follow the same patterns of bold and italic as on the original.

Our standard font for forms is Stone Sans. You should use a similar sans-serif alternative, such as Helvetica or Arial.

You should use all the same font sizes as the original and any other special styles (e.g. IHT 200 uses some white text on a dark background in its headings).

5. Page content

Each page on your substitute must contain the same information in the same order as the original. You should show page numbers clearly in the same place the originals show them.

6. Lines and boxes

You should try to achieve the same size and positioning of boxes as on the original.

It is important that your version keeps to the same proportional layout as those on the original. You should try to make sure that any boxes and lines are the same length and thickness.

7. I am happy with my form, what happens next?

You should print out two blank copies of your form and send them to us at the address shown [below].

The Forms Adviser will tell you about changes you must make. When you reach the required standard, the Forms Adviser will give you a unique reference. You must show the reference on each form that you send to us. [. . .]

Copyright

Her Majesty's Stationery Office (HMSO) have changed their Copyright practices as part of a drive to make it easier for people to access and re-use government information. The Inland Revenue are no longer required to issue Copyright Licences to people who wish to market our forms commercially and we will therefore no longer be sending these to producers of substitute forms.

Copyright permission to reproduce substitute forms appearing on the Inland Revenue website is given on our Copyright webpage www.inlandrevenue.gov.uk/copyright/index.htm.

Forms not appearing on our website are normally covered by the new 'Click-use' Copyright Licence, which you can obtain from HMSO's website www.hmso.gov.uk.

These changes do not affect the Inland Revenue approval process. We still need to see drafts of your proposed substitute Inheritance tax forms for approval before these are brought into use. We will notify design approval by letter in the normal way.

Crown Copyright applies to Inland Revenue Inheritance Tax forms. HMSO do not intend to seek payment from producers of substitute versions, but the Crown copyright should be acknowledged when these are released to the end-users.

What forms are appropriate for substitutes?

Accounts and inventories	Other forms
IHT 200	C4
IHT 100	IHT 30
IHT 101	IHT 35
C1	IHT 38
C2	Mis 1G

I want to use computerised forms but do not want to do all the work myself

Ask our Forms Adviser to send you a list of the software firms who operate under licence. You can contact them yourself and choose the package that suits your needs.

See Appendix 6 ('Useful contacts') for contact details of Forms Adviser.

14.9 PAYING PRE-GRANT IHT

It is always worth asking whether the deceased's bank will pay pre-grant inheritance tax directly to the Inland Revenue. Many banks will do this.

14.9.1 Interest on loans

The interest payable on qualifying loans taken out by the PRs to pay IHT pre-grant is deductible for income tax purposes from income in the PRs' hands in respect of a period of one year from the making of the loan.

14.9.2 Sources of funding

It is common to look to the deceased's bank for a loan to finance the payment of IHT, but other alternatives – such as encashing National Savings certificates (no grant being needed for this), or investments in nominee names, approaching the deceased's building society or asking family members – may be worth considering. However, the process is not quick and can slow down the obtaining of a grant quite substantially. The Revenue's booklet IHT 11 gives guidance on paying IHT from National Savings.

Below are two specimen letters which solicitors in private practice may adapt or adopt for the purpose set out on p.iv, but not for any other purpose. The first letter is to a bank seeking a global loan facility; the second letter is to a building society seeking the early release of funds.

14.9.3 'Global' loans facility – letter to bank

This is an edited version of a letter used by one practice to obtain special favourable facilities. If such an arrangement is established, consider in each case whether there are any issues which would make it advisable to suggest that clients seek separate independent advice on the arrangements for the loan on to them: for example, is this the cheapest arrangement currently available? Also, explain the details the bank will want and obtain the client's consent to passing on the information shown in item 6 of the specimen letter.

The Manager   Your Ref [   ]
[   ] Bank [etc.]   Our Ref [   ]
                                                 Date   [   ]

Dear

GLOBAL PROBATE LOANS FACILITY
I should like to discuss a new facility to enable us to arrange short-term bridging loans for clients to meet inheritance tax and probate registry fees.

As you will be aware, personal representatives have to pay inheritance tax and probate registry fees when they apply for a grant of representation (whether of probate or letters of administration) to a deceased's estate. In a typical situation, no funds will be available from the estate until the grant has been issued, which means a loan has to be arranged, usually from the deceased's bank.

The personal representatives may well not be familiar with the deceased's bank, and may therefore instruct us to make the necessary arrangements. In such cases, it would save my firm time and paperwork if we were able to arrange the necessary loan through your bank on an agreed basis.

I would estimate that, on average, the loans would be repaid after approximately six to eight weeks, or nine to 11 weeks if quoted securities have to be sold, allowing for the settlement period and registration with the company registrars.

May I suggest that the basis on which your bank may agree the provision of this facility might be along the following lines:

1. **'In principle' agreement**. I accept that the bank will need to treat the provision of this facility as being an 'in principle' agreement because each loan, for reasons including taxation, branch monitoring and the liabilities of the borrowers, will be set up separately but taken within the 'umbrella' limit. I would hope that the advantage of having this agreement in place would be that the setting up of such accounts could be negotiated with you

---

locally on an immediate basis, rather than suffering delays while nego-
tiating and setting up relevant arrangements with the deceased's bank in
each instance.

2. **Global limit**. Having regard to the normal volume of estate administration
    conducted by this firm, I would suggest that this should be £[100,000].

3. **Availability**. I anticipate that the bank would wish the facility to be
    expressed to be available for 12 months and that it will be described by
    you as being technically 'repayable on demand'. If this be the case, I
    should appreciate your confirmation that the only likely circumstances
    under which such a demand might be made would be if for some reason
    the lending had become 'unsatisfactory'.

4. **To whom available**. The facility would be available to the personal repre-
    sentatives of deceased persons where this firm is acting for them.

5. **Purpose**. To enable the personal representatives to deal with the estate's
    liability to inheritance tax and probate registry fees.

6. **Account arrangements**. I anticipate that you will wish the firm to complete
    the bank's form of application to open an account on each occasion and
    it would be helpful if we could be supplied with a stock of these. If you
    wish, having obtained the agreement of the personal representatives, the
    firm can provide the bank with the application form, the appropriate
    Inland Revenue forms (IHT 200, IHT 201, IHT 202) confirming the
    amount due by way of inheritance tax and the details of the estate assets.

7. **Drawdown**. Each facility will be drawn as a separate loan, although partial
    drawings against that loan would need to be permitted.

8. **Interest**. I suggest that the rate of interest payable on the amount of each
    facility outstanding from time to time might be [2 per cent] per annum
    above the bank's base rate from time to time in force. Presumably inter-
    est will be calculated on a daily basis and charged at quarterly intervals
    to each separate loan facility.

    Please confirm that it will be possible, on request, for the bank to
    apportion the interest between the amount of loan drawn for payment of
    inheritance tax (on which tax relief can be claimed) and any part of the
    loan taken up for other outgoings such as the Probate Registry fees –
    which do not attract income tax relief.

9. **Arrangement fee**. I would hope that in view of this firm's connection with
    your bank no arrangement fee will be charged in respect either of the
    setting up of this facility or the taking up of each individual loan within it.

10. **Repayment and security**. Repayment would normally be made either from
    liquid assets, e.g. cash accounts, building society accounts, stocks and
    shares, etc., or from the sale proceeds of assets of the estate. As regards
    security, if each account is opened in the name of the firm and designated
    with the name of the estate, the firm will be responsible to the bank for the
    payment of each loan facility. We will, of course, secure our own position
    with the personal representatives in the context of this liability.

11. **Discretionary arrangements**. There will be occasions when the size of the estate is such that the amount required by way of loan would be too large to take under the global 'umbrella' facility. In such circumstances I would expect that we would approach you on behalf of the personal representatives to negotiate terms for a similar facility for the estate and which might involve a discounted rate of interest. I appreciate that you would not necessarily be able to provide as quick a response in this case.

If this facility is provided, my firm will be able to offer an improved service to its clients and the bank will derive benefit as well. I hope that I have covered everything which is relevant in this letter but please let me know if there is any further information you require.

Yours sincerely [etc.]

14.9.4 Release of funds – specimen letter to building society

The Manager   Your Ref [   ]
[   ] Building Society [etc.]   Our Ref [   ]
                                                 Date   [   ]

Dear

THE LATE MRS VICTORIA JONES
Mrs Jones' personal representatives would like to arrange for a withdrawal from her account[s] no[s] _____ [to pay] [the funeral expenses] [the inheritance tax] [Probate Court fees] [so the grant of representation can be obtained].

The payments needed are:

[Funeral expenses: £____, payable to _____]
[Inheritance tax: £ ____, payable to Inland Revenue.]
[Probate Court fee: £____, payable to HM Paymaster-General.]

We hope that you will be able to agree the personal representatives' requests. If so please send the forms they must sign.

We will register the grant with you when we have it.

Yours faithfully [etc.]

14.10 INLAND REVENUE NEWSLETTER

Inland Revenue Capital Taxes produces a quarterly newsletter for its customers. If you want to receive this, write to David Wright, Customer Services Manager, at the address given in Appendix 6.

CHAPTER 15

Probate problems

Lesley King

15.1 MISSING BENEFICIARIES

If you cannot trace beneficiaries, try the following:

- Instruct genealogists to trace the beneficiaries. Firms divide into those that charge on a time costing basis and those that charge the beneficiary a share of their inheritance. It is normally cheaper to use a firm that charges on a time costing basis and, therefore, preferable for the benefici-aries and the estate. The Law Society's Wills and Equity Committee reviewed the use of genealogists some years ago and said that it was per-missible to use firms which charge a fee to beneficiaries if traced, *provided* it was appropriate in the context of the size and overall circumstances of the estate. However, improvements in research technologies and tech-niques make establishing the existence of entitled kin much more straight-forward now than it was even a few years ago so it should not normally be necessary to use a firm that charges the beneficiary. In the case of a gift to a wide class of relatives, for example 'my nieces and nephews', personal representatives should be very cautious about accepting an assurance from one part of a family that 'X died without any children'. It is neces-sary to check or risk distributing assets wrongly.
- If you hold a date of birth, it may be possible for the Office for National Statistics on payment of a fee to forward a letter to the beneficiary at the last address they hold. Address it to him or her, care of Traceline in Southport (see Appendix 6).
- Trustee Act 1925, s.27 advertisements and searches should be made as early as possible in case they reveal helpful information.

If you have no success, there are the following options:

- You can take personal indemnities from the other beneficiaries (but from a risk management point of view, these are of doubtful value).
- You can apply to court for a *Benjamin* order which will allow the estate to be distributed on the basis of certain assumptions, usually that a particular person died without issue.

- You can apply to court for permission to make payment without reservation to meet costs.
- You can take out missing beneficiary insurance but as the case of *Evans* v. *Westcombe* [1999] 2 All ER 767 shows, you must insure for an amount large enough to cover the payment of interest should the missing beneficiary appear. Only a limited number of firms now offer this insurance and, before providing it, they will normally require that genealogists attempt to trace the beneficiaries.
- The entitlements may be paid into court under Trustee Act 1925, s.63 if appropriate: see *Underhill and Hayton: Law Relating to Trustees* (Butterworths, 2002) (see Appendix 5).

You may be consulted by a beneficiary who has been approached by an heir locator who is offering to inform them of an entitlement in return for a substantial part of the inheritance. It may be worth looking at the list of recent *bona vacantia* estates published by the Treasury Solicitor to see if the client can recognise a name.

The courts are not well disposed towards heir locators who charge extravagant amounts and there are cases where such agreements have been set aside.

In *Rees* v. *De Bernardy* [1986] 2 Ch 437 Romer J set aside such an agreement on the basis that it was champertous and an improvident bargain on the part of the beneficiaries obtained as a result of the defendant taking an unfair advantage of the beneficiaries. There are two Irish cases: *McElroy* v. *Flynn* [1991] ILRM 294 and *Fraser* v. *Buckle* [1996] 2 ILRM 34 in which arrangements were set aside. See, however, an interesting article by David Capper in [1997] *Modern Law Review* 286 in which he regrets the failure of the Irish Supreme Court to examine whether public policy requires heir locator agreements to be void for public policy in the present day and considers the arguments for and against.

15.2   UNCLAIMED CLIENT ACCOUNT MONEY

If money has been unclaimed for a long time, the Professional Ethics Division (see Appendix 6) can advise.

15.3   DECEASED WITH NO RELATIVES

Is there a will appointing you executor? If so, you can take the steps set out at 15.1 above to trace claimants. Where the deceased is intestate, you should consider whether it is appropriate for you to take any steps other than to refer the matter to the Treasury Solicitor's Bona Vacantia Division (see Appendix 6) (or in the Duchies of Cornwall and Lancaster to the corresponding Crown

Agent, Farrer & Co). There may be reasons which justify your involvement. If so, there are two main possibilities.

If there is any danger to the assets of the estate, you can apply to the court for a limited grant *ad colligenda bona*. This is a limited grant issued where there is a pressing need for a grant and it is not possible to wait for the issue of a full grant. It can issue to anyone irrespective of whether or not that person has any right to take out a general grant to the estate. It is not necessary to say whether there is a will or an intestacy nor to do any of the usual clearing off. A caveat does not prevent the issue of an *ad colligenda* grant. However, it is normally limited to 'collecting and getting in and receiving the estate and doing such acts as may be necessary for the preservation of the estate' and ends when a full grant issues.

If you apply for an *ad colligenda* grant, you will need to set out the grounds justifying the application (for example, land which needs to be made secure against vandals or squatters, debts which need to be paid to avoid interest or penalties, volatile assets such as shares which need to be dealt with).

There may be no immediate danger to the estate and yet you may want to take out a grant; perhaps because you had a professional relationship with the deceased going back many years or perhaps because you are concerned that a creditor, who is proposing to take out a grant, is an unsuitable person. You can apply to the court under Supreme Court Act 1981, s.116 for a grant in your favour under the court's discretionary power. The registrar will require evidence showing that it is appropriate in the circumstances to make such a grant.

In circumstances where you cannot justify applying for a grant, you take two risks if you incur costs trying to trace relatives:

1. **You may be unsuccessful.** If no relatives are found, you will have to refer the matter to the Treasury Solicitor who may not be able to reimburse solicitors who have incurred expenditure without instructions. However, Nicholas Beetham of Title Research says this:

   > Of all the apparently bona vacantia estates we see each year, very few will prove to be genuinely so. Even disregarding that families through the first half of the twentieth century were typically larger than they are today, for a person to die without leaving any such kin is most unusual. In addition, the resources now available to probate practitioners make establishing the existence of entitled kin a more straightforward exercise than it was just a few years ago.

2. **You may be successful.** You may successfully trace the kin but they will have no obligation to reimburse you for the expense you have incurred.

If the Treasury Solicitor traces kin, they may be unwilling to reimburse costs in respect of extensive work done before they were found. Therefore, if it appears that no relations survive, make contact with the Treasury Solicitor for advice as soon as you can.

It is possible to apply for 'ex gratia' payments in exercise of the Royal Bounty to redress hardship or for some other good cause. The Treasury Solicitor will consider claims against an estate by persons who are not kin on grounds such as:

- services rendered;
- a testamentary document invalid as a will;
- an unmarried partner;
- a factual relationship such as a step-child brought up by the deceased.

If the Treasury Solicitor succeeds in identifying a member of the deceased's family, the estate is no longer *bona vacantia*. The Treasury Solicitor will not adjudicate between claims nor become involved in subsequent disputes between kin.

15.4   CLIENTS AND BENEFICIARIES LACKING MENTAL CAPACITY

The Guide to the Professional Conduct of Solicitors 1999 ('The Guide'), Principle 24.04 and Commentary 1–3 cover the position if a client lacks capacity. Your retainer is terminated when a client loses capacity. See also *Assessment of Mental Capacity* (Law Society/BMA, 1995).

If a beneficiary is mentally incapacitated (and cannot therefore give a good receipt) it may be appropriate to consider the appointment of a receiver through the Court of Protection, or payment into court under Trustee Act 1925, s.63.

On very difficult points, guidance may be obtained from the Practice Advice Service and the Professional Ethics Division (see Appendix 6). The *Elderly Client Handbook* by Gordon Ashton (published by the Law Society) may also assist (see Appendix 5).

15.5   DISABILITY

One of the most difficult disabilities for wills and probate solicitors to deal with is visual impairment. The RNIB offers a visual awareness course which gives guidance on best practice for helping clients with impaired vision. A benefit of attending the course is that the RNIB's Wills and Legacies Advisory Service is then able to recommend the firm to the visually impaired.

As a result of the Disability Discrimination Act 1995, solicitors must ensure that they do not discriminate against disabled people by, for example, refusing to provide a service or providing one at a lower standard. All service providers, including solicitors, must ensure that their services are provided in a way that makes them accessible to disabled people.

15.6 PERSONAL REPRESENTATIVES AND PERSONAL LIABILITY

15.6.1 PRs' liability for unpaid IHT on PETs

The primary liability for inheritance tax (IHT) on lifetime gifts is on the transferee. However, personal representatives have a secondary liability where tax on lifetime transfers is unpaid 12 months after the month of death. To clarify the position, the following edited note was published in [1989] *Gazette,* 22 November:

> Personal representatives are liable for:
>
> - the inheritance tax payable on potentially exempt transfers (PETs) where the transferor dies within seven years of the transfer, if the tax has remained unpaid by the transferee for 12 months after the end of the month in which the death of the transferor occurs (Inheritance Tax Act 1984, s.199(2)); and
> - any additional tax on inter vivos chargeable transfers payable as a result of the death.
>
> A similar problem for personal representatives exists where property is treated as part of the death estate by virtue of the reservation of benefit rules. Such property will be treated as part of the donor's estate on death (Finance Act 1986, s.102(3)).
>   The Solicitors Indemnity Fund Ltd (SIF) confirmed that where a solicitor incurred a civil liability in the course of his or her private practice then, subject to the provisions of the indemnity rules currently in force, that liability would be indemnified by the Indemnity Fund but only to the extent that otherwise funds are unavailable.
>   Further enquiries should be referred to your insurers.

Subsequently, following representations from the Law Society, the Inland Revenue confirmed in a letter of 11 February 1991 that, without prejudice to the application in an appropriate case of Inheritance Tax Act 1984, s.199(2):

> The Capital Taxes Office will not usually pursue for inheritance tax personal representatives who:
>
> - after making the fullest inquiries that are reasonably practicable in the circumstances to discover lifetime transfers; and so
> - having done all in their power to make full disclosure of them to the Board of Inland Revenue,
>
> have obtained a certificate of discharge and distributed the estate before a chargeable lifetime transfer comes to light.

The problem for personal representatives is determining what the Revenue will regard as 'the fullest inquiries that are reasonably practicable in the circumstances'.

15.6.2 PRs' liability for unpaid tax on the death estate

PRs are liable for IHT on the deceased's death estate (excluding settled property). Liability is limited to the extent of assets which the PRs have received or should have received.

Note that PRs remain liable to the extent of assets which they received and handed on to the beneficiaries. The case of *Howarth's Executors* v. *CIR* [1997] STI 640 (and discussed in [1997] *Trusts and Estates,* June, 71) illustrates the danger to PRs. An employee of a firm of solicitors acted as co-executor in an estate. One of the assets of the estate was land on which the instalment option was exercised. The land was transferred to one of the beneficiaries on the undertaking that he would be responsible for the payment of the instalments. Before the end of the 10-year period, the beneficiary became bankrupt, leaving tax unpaid. The land was sold and, as the Inland Revenue had not registered the charge over the land, the purchaser took free of the charge. The solicitors' employee was held personally liable.

The moral is clear: be very careful about distributing assets where there is an outstanding tax liability. Indemnities from beneficiaries will be worthless where a beneficiary has no assets. PRs may wish to consider charging assets before transferring them to beneficiaries, for inheitance tax.

15.6.3 PRs' liability to creditors

PRs are always in danger of a claim from unsatisfied creditors arising after assets have been distributed to beneficiaries. They can protect themselves from unknown claims by advertising for claimants under Trustee Act 1925, s.27. However, sometimes they may know that a possible liability exists but be uncertain as to the amount. Section 27 is then of no help since it protects PRs only against unknown claims.

Unquantifiable liabilities may arise perhaps under leases where the deceased was a tenant or as a result of the deceased being a member of Lloyd's. Limited protection is available in respect of leases under Trustee Act 1925, s.26. For a discussion of possible liability for trustees arising from the ownership of leasehold property see [1997] *Trusts and Estates*, 94.

In many cases the only solution may be to apply to the courts for guidance. This is obviously an expensive option and PRs may wonder if the cost can be justified. In the case of *Re Yorke deceased, Stone* v. *Chatway* [1997] 4 All ER 907, Lindsay J gave guidance on this subject in the context of possible liability in the estates of deceased Lloyd's Names. He stated that as only a court order can give complete protection, it cannot be wrong for executors of Lloyd's Names to insist upon the protection of a court order. For a fuller discussion see [1997] *Trusts and Estates*, 92 and 94.

15.7 BANKRUPTCY

More and more firms are handling insolvent estates, which were once a rarity. An estate is only insolvent if the debts and liabilities cannot be paid, and is not insolvent if these can be settled, even if none of the legacies can be paid.

15.7.1 Sources of information

The legislation governing the administration of an estate which is insolvent is the Administration of Insolvent Estates of Deceased Persons Order (AIEDPO) 1986, SI 1986/1999. Berry, Bailey and Schaw-Miller, *Personal Insolvency – Law and Practice* (Butterworths, 2001) deals with this issue. A useful outline of the law can be found in Williams, Mortimer and Sunnucks on *Executors, Administrators and Probate* (Sweet & Maxwell, 2000). Briefer outlines of practice can be found in Philip Rossdale, *Probate and the Administration of Estates* (Sweet & Maxwell, 1996) and Tolley's looseleaf title *Administration of Estates* (see Appendix 5). There is also a useful article by Mathew Pintus in [2000] *Trusts and Estates*, March.

15.7.2 A brief outline of procedure

When conducting the administration of an insolvent estate, there are three possibilities:

(a) administration by the personal representatives under the directions of the court pursuant to an administration order (CPR Part 64). This means that the administration is dealt with by the PRs under the direction of the court. The courts are not anxious to undertake such a role and professional advisers rarely consider this route;

(b) administration in bankruptcy following an insolvency administration order made by the bankruptcy court. Creditors or PRs can petition. In either case the order vests the estate in the Official Receiver. Subsequently a trustee in bankruptcy will be appointed. The trustee does not have to be a qualified insolvency practitioner (Insolvency Act 1986, s.292(2));

(c) administration by the personal representatives out of court. This is the most common method of administration. It is generally the most economic and straightforward method. Remember that creditors are entitled to take a grant. PRs do not need to be qualified insolvency practitioners (AIEDPO 1986, art. 4(3)).

There is little practical difference whether the estate is administered by a trustee in bankruptcy or by the PRs out of court. AIEDPO 1986 provides that, whichever method is used, the same rules apply to the respective rights of creditors, to provable debts, to the valuation of future and contingent liabilities and to the priority of debts.

However, a trustee in bankruptcy does have certain additional powers. A trustee can:

- challenge transactions made at an undervalue and transactions made to prefer some creditors at the expense of others;
- disclaim onerous property;
- apply for an order for sale of an asset in which third parties have an interest (typically the matrimonial home). Where the application is first made by the trustee in bankruptcy more than 12 months after the deceased's property vested in him, the court will assume, unless there are exceptional circumstances, that the interests of the creditors outweigh all other considerations (Insolvency Act 1986, s.335A(3)). PRs can also apply for such an order but there is no such assumption so they may have more difficulty.

It is possible for PRs to apply for the appointment of a trustee in bankruptcy if it becomes apparent that there are reasons justifying it at any stage of the administration.

PRs must be careful to pay debts in the order of priority set out in the Insolvency Act 1986. This is:

- bankruptcy expenses followed by funeral, testamentary and administration expenses;
- preferential debts (e.g. VAT arrears in the six months before death);
- ordinary debts;
- interest;
- deferred debts (e.g. a loan from a person who is the deceased's spouse at the date of death).

PRs will be personally liable if they pay an inferior debt before a superior one and there are insufficient funds for the superior one. They also incur personal liability if they pay one creditor in full when there are insufficient assets to pay all creditors in that class. However, in this case there is a defence if payment was made in good faith at a time when they had no reason to believe that the estate was insolvent.

15.7.3   Will you be paid?

The rules on solicitor/executors charging for administering estates have changed as a result of the Trustee Act 2000. Solicitors charges are no longer regarded as a legacy but instead s.35(3)(b) provides that charges are to be regarded as 'administration expenses'. As such they have priority over the preferential debts listed in the Insolvency Act 1986.

A trustee in bankruptcy can charge for his or her services and again the charges will be administration expenses and have priority over preferential debts. A trustee of an insolvent estate does not need to be an insolvency practitioner so any practitioner experienced in administering estates could consider being appointed.

Bear in mind that, although administration expenses have priority, the estate may be too small to cover them. Therefore, if there is a chance that an estate will be insolvent, try to assess the risk before committing a substantial amount of time to the estate. It may help if potential PRs complete a client questionnaire detailing assets and liabilities early in the administration process. The *Questionnaire for Personal Representative Clients* (available in packs of 25) is published by the Law Society (see Appendix 6). Solicitor-executors and, indeed, other executors, may want to renounce. It is important not to intermeddle in an estate which may be insolvent.

Terms of business letters (see Chapter 3 on client care) may incorporate a clause governing the position in relation to costs incurred if the estate turns out to be insolvent, say Professional Ethics at the Law Society. Even though they are entitled to an indemnity from the estate, PRs are personally liable for the solicitor's costs. (*Cordery on Solicitors* (9th edn) has a useful discussion on the position.)

15.7.4 Joint property

A Court of Appeal decision (*Re Palmer deceased (a debtor)* [1994] 3 WLR 420, CA) held that jointly held property passed to the co-owner on death as usual and was not available to the administrator of the estate.

The effect of this decision has been reversed by a new s.412A inserted into the Insolvency Act 1986 by the Insolvency Act 2000, s.12. The trustee of a deceased insolvent can now apply to the court to recover the value of the deceased's former interest in joint property from the survivor for the benefit of the estate. The trustee can only make the application where the petition for the insolvency order is presented after 2 April 2001 and within five years from the date of death. When deciding whether or not to make the order the court must have regard to all the circumstances of the case including the interests of the creditors and the surviving joint tenant but, unless the circumstances are exceptional, the court must assume that the interests of the creditors outweigh all other considerations.

15.7.5 Deceased Lloyd's Names

The well publicised problems at Lloyd's meant that many Names were faced with unquantifiable losses. To solve the problems Equitas was created. Names waived their claims against Lloyd's and in return received debt and litigation credits and reinsurance of outstanding open years into Equitas. All business for 1992 and prior years of account was reinsured to close with Equitas upon payment of the appropriate premium.

There is a possibility of claims being made against the Names (or their estates) if the resources of Equitas prove inadequate and it fails. This presents a problem for PRs who face the possibility of personal liability if they distribute the estate without providing for this contingent liability. The Society of Trust and Estate Practitioners (STEP) brought the test case (*Re Yorke deceased, Stone* v. *Chataway* [1997] 4 All ER 907) referred to at 15.6.3 above hoping that the judgment would remove the need for individual applications to be made for all estates in a similar position. The judgment did not achieve this. It approved the use of Equitas but said that PRs would face different levels of risk depending on the circumstances of the case and that they could only obtain full indemnity by applying to court for directions. He accepted that in appropriate cases, judged to be low risk, PRs could take indemnities or rely on insurance.

There is a streamlined form of application available which will be heard by a Master rather than a judge. This is dealt with in *Practice Statement: Chancery Division: Estates of Deceased Lloyd's Names* [2001] 3 All ER 765 which replaced the previous *Practice Direction: Distribution of Estates of Lloyd's Names*, 21 November 1997.

The procedure applies to cases where the only, or only substantial, reason for delaying distribution of the estate is the possibility of personal liability to Lloyd's creditors and:

- all liabilities of the estate in respect of syndicates of which the Name was a member for the years of account 1992 and earlier have been reinsured into the Equitas Group; and
- all liabilities of the estate in respect of syndicates of which the Name was a member for the years of account 1993 and later:
  - are in respect of syndicates which have closed by reinsurance in the usual way;
  - are protected by an Estate Protection Plan issued by Centrewrite Ltd; or
  - are protected by EXEAT insurance cover provided by Centrewrite Ltd.

The Practice Direction contains a specimen witness statement to support the claim form and a specimen draft order, although both are likely to need adapting to suit the circumstances of the case.

15.7.6 Bankrupt beneficiaries

There is a risk of personal liability for a PR who pays a legacy direct to a bankrupt beneficiary rather than to the trustee in bankruptcy. An article in [1993] *Gazette*, 24 February deals with this.

It is not usually necessary to enquire about financial status, but it is a different matter if PRs have notice that there may be a query about a particular beneficiary. A bankruptcy-only search under the Land Charges Act 1925 could be made (against any name a beneficiary might use) or the PRs could contact the Insolvency Service (see Appendix 6).

Bankrupts must tell their trustees in bankruptcy about acquisition of property. It seems, therefore, that PRs could safely hand over money to a bankrupt beneficiary on proof that the bankrupt has complied with his or her duties under the Insolvency Act 1986, in particular ss.307 and 312, to inform the trustee in bankruptcy of everything affecting the bankrupt's property.

Be alert to potential problems if a bankrupt beneficiary suggests that the money should be paid over in a way which is at all unusual. If concerned, consider seeking the assistance of the court under RSC Ord. 85 (or, as a last resort, paying money into court under Trustee Act 1925, s.63).

Makers of wills are reminded in the above article that they can revoke legacies to actually or potentially bankrupt beneficiaries, substituting discretionary trusts.

Rooney v. *Cardoona* [1999] 1 WLR 1388 was an interesting case on bankruptcy and life policies under Married Women's Property Act 1882, s.11. A life insurance company paid the proceeds of a joint life insurance policy to a bankrupt husband on the death of his wife. The husband was one of the two executors of the estate and the question was whether he had given a good receipt to the life insurance company. If he had not, the company would have to pay again to the trustee in bankruptcy. (The husband had effectively dissipated the money by the time the trustee heard of it.) The Court of Appeal held that the company had to pay again. The policy was accepted to be a Married Women's Property Act policy. Such a policy is not an asset of the estate. It is held by the executors as trustees for the beneficiaries. The signatures of *all* trustees are required to provide a valid discharge. These had not been obtained.

15.8 PRs SEPARATELY REPRESENTED

The following opinion was originally published in [1986] *Gazette*, 3 September, 2561–2 and may be of assistance if one PR wishes to seek separate advice from the other(s). (Text in italic has been superseded by the Solicitors' (Non-Contentious Business) Remuneration Order 1994, see Chapter 2.)

Costs: Personal representatives separately represented

The following notes are issued by the Law Society's Non-Contentious Business Committee. Since the Joint Agreed Case was reported in [1985] *Gazette*, 24 October, 2987, the number of enquiries which the Society has received from practitioners indicates a need to publish more detailed guidelines. The following guidelines have been settled by counsel but practitioners should note that the Society has no power to determine matters of law, and that matters of dispute may ultimately fall to be determined by the court.

1. The basic principle is that a personal representative is entitled to an indemnity from the estate in respect of costs and expenses properly incurred in the course of his office. Trustee Act 1925, s.23 expressly empowers personal representatives to employ and pay a solicitor to transact any business or to do any act required to be transacted or done in the administration of the estate.

2. The indemnity will not, however, be available (where there is more than one personal representative) to each personal representative who chooses to instruct his own separate solicitor, as the right to instruct a solicitor is limited by the overriding principle that personal representatives must act properly in exercising their rights and powers. In particular they must not make, or cause there to be made, any wasteful or unnecessary payments out of the estate.

3. Thus it is considered that in a normal case it is incumbent upon personal representatives to agree upon the joint instructions of solicitors.

4. In certain cases it may be proper for more than one firm to be instructed, where, for example, in the case of a large landed estate, different skills are required; in such a case it is unlikely that more costs would be incurred than if one firm dealt with all the work.

5. It is, of course, always open to a personal representative to seek independent legal advice separately from the advice given by the firm instructed on behalf of all the personal representatives, but in such circumstances he will normally not be entitled to an indemnity from the estate for the cost of doing so, and will have to pay such costs personally.

6. Mere personal animosity between personal representatives does not justify the appointment of a separate firm so as to increase the costs payable by the estate.

7. Exceptional circumstances justifying the instruction of a separate solicitor at the expense of the estate might include a case where a personal representative became aware of a devastavit or breach of trust by his fellow personal representative and required independent legal advice as to his position; or when the instructed solicitor refused or failed properly to carry out his instructions, thus necessitating the instruction of another firm (although here, strictly, no additional costs should be incurred, as the defaulting solicitor would not be entitled to recover his costs).

8. It is also open to personal representatives to agree that they should be separately represented provided that the estate does not thereby bear any additional costs. As the instruction of two firms in respect of the same work will inevitably involve extra work, it will avoid subsequent dispute if the personal representatives also agree in advance to bear personally the extra costs involved (and agree the proportions in which they will do so).

9. Any personal liability incurred by personal representatives may, of course, be charged to the estate with the concurrence of all the beneficiaries, provided that they are all *sui juris* and are properly advised.

10. Where a personal representative instructs a practitioner in circumstances where he knows that another firm is already acting for the estate he should be made aware of the likelihood that he will be personally responsible for his costs.

11. A distinction may need to be made between the fees charged to the personal representatives by the appointed firm of solicitors on the one hand and fees charged by a solicitor-executor on the other hand. Provided that the 'professional charging clause' expressly so provided a professional executor may properly charge for his time and trouble in acting as an executor, as distinct from his firm's charges for legal work transacted. More than one professional person may be appointed executor and may be entitled so to charge,

but such charges will in both cases be of a different nature from the fees of the firm jointly instructed by the personal representatives to do legal work.

12. Beneficiaries who take legal advice in connection with the administration of an estate will rarely be entitled to recover from the estate their costs so incurred, but they may be entitled to recover such costs from a defaulting personal representative who will not in such circumstances be entitled to recover them from the estate.

13. The Society is also asked from time to time to advise as to how the legal fees should be calculated in cases where more than one firm is involved in the administration of an estate. Opinions published in the Society's Digest in the past indicated a split of two-thirds/one-third; these were however published at a time when solicitors' fees were charged on a straight percentage of the value of the estate. *Since the Solicitors' Remuneration Order 1972 this element is only one of the factors to be taken into account in assessing what is fair and reasonable in each case; the two-thirds/one-third split is therefore no longer appropriate. The value element does still have to be taken into account, and will be recognised in the fair and reasonable charges of the respective firms, bearing in mind the amount of work carried out by each firm, the degree of responsibility involved and other factors set out in Article 2 of the Solicitors' Remuneration Order 1972.* This is subject to the overriding principle expressed in para. 8 above that the estate itself should not normally bear the additional expense occasioned by the employment of more than one firm.

15.9 UNSUITABLE PRS

PRs may be passed over under Supreme Court Act 1981, s.116: an application to the High Court may be made if it appears that the person apparently entitled to take the grant is unsuitable. The person next entitled to the grant will not necessarily be appointed.

An application for the removal of a PR may be made under Administration of Justice Act 1985, s.50. This section also gives the High Court power to appoint someone else to act. (See also at 13.9.1 above.)

The Family Division has power to revoke grants under R41. Normally the consent of the grantee is required before revocation can take place. However, 'in exceptional circumstances' a district judge or registrar can revoke a grant without the grantee's consent. Where an executor or administrator refuses or neglects to participate properly in the administration of the estate, it may be possible to get the grant revoked. It is worth contacting the registry to see whether or not the circumstances of the case would justify such an application. Where they do, it represents a simpler and cheaper solution than a s.50 application.

See also para. 13.9.

15.10   PROBLEMS FROM CLIENTS

15.10.1   Distressed clients

Clients coming for help and advice on probate may be suffering from grief
and distress. Bereavement can generate many and conflicting emotions, which
are not always expressed as one might expect. Sometimes clients' feelings spill
over, so that the conduct of the administration is affected, for example by a
family quarrel.

Helping bereaved clients, and coping with clients' feelings and emotions,
can be difficult for practitioners. This is an added (and often unrecognised)
source of stress for many practitioners, who may feel ambivalent about how
to respond to the client and how to deal with their feelings.

Christopher Clulow, Director of the Tavistock Institute for Marital
Studies in London, considered some of these issues in a number of short
articles in the series 'Only Connect' in the journal *Family Law* during
1992 and 1993. Although directed mainly to solicitors working with divorce,
the articles would be of great value and interest to all private client
practitioners.

It may be worthwhile ensuring that your office holds an up-to-date list of
local voluntary and other sources of help and support for distressed and
bereaved clients.

You may be approached by a client involved in a major tragedy. The Law
Society's Multi-Party Action Co-ordination Service exists to link the solici-
tors' firms instructed by those involved and their families and friends. The
Multi-Party Actions Information Service has two related objectives:

- to provide the public and their solicitors with basic information about
  current or recent actions, giving key dates and the names of either local or
  all participating firms as provided by those participating firms. The public
  should telephone the Law Society's public enquiry line and solicitors who
  want to refer clients should telephone Practice Advice (see Appendix 6);
- to maintain contact with participating firms in order to market them
  to potential clients and their solicitors and to communicate relevant
  information.

Firms already participating in or contemplating participating in an action
should telephone Practice Advice at the Law Society.

15.10.2   Dealing with sudden deaths abroad

Richard Bark-Jones, Partner at Morecroft Urquart, Liverpool and former
chairman of the Law Society's Wills and Equity Committee wrote the following guidance on dealing with sudden deaths abroad for the *Probate Section
Journal* shortly after the tragic events in New York of 11 September 2001:

The recent appalling events in the United States may mean that some of you have to help clients deal with the sudden death of a relative abroad. Here are some general pointers to help you handle the situation.

If the body is found

Follow the usual procedure ie arrange the issuing of the death certificate in the country of death. The British Embassy/Consulate is invariably helpful and can give some advice on local procedures.

The application for the grant will follow normal procedures.

If the body is not found, but its whereabouts are known

The first port of call will be the deceased's employers (if not self-employed or on holiday) who should be able to provide evidence as to the whereabouts of the deceased.

The second port of call will be the British Embassy/Consulate, which with the benefit of the information supplied by the deceased's employers, will advise on local procedures.

Assuming a death certificate is issued, the application for the grant should be straightforward as there is no difficulty in asserting death.

If no body is found and the whereabouts are not known

Steps 1 and 2 as above.

If no death certificate can be obtained in order to obtain the grant, the applicant can apply for leave to swear to the death on an ex parte application supported by a sworn Statement of Facts. This should set out all the known circumstances relevant to the disappearance and should list the deceased's assets and particularly any life policies (for obvious reasons).

On obtaining leave to swear to death, the application for a grant should be straightforward although the wording of the oath will be different.

15.10.3   Arranging funerals

Solicitors may be asked a variety of questions about funerals. Whose responsibility is it to arrange and pay for the funeral? Do PRs have to carry out the deceased's wishes? What if there is a dispute between surviving relatives? There are useful articles in [1999] *Solicitors' Journal*, 30 April by Philip Rossdale and in [1999] *Trusts and Estates Law Journal*, November by David Hershman and [2000] October by Mathew Knight. The following may be helpful.

Who is responsible for arranging the funeral?

Nobody owns a dead body (*R* v. *Sharpe*, 1875). This is presumably on the grounds of public health and public policy. However, there is a common law duty on an executor to arrange for the proper disposal of the deceased's remains.

As an executor's authority derives from the will and not from the grant, they are entitled to obtain possession of the body for the purposes of burial prior to the grant (by injunction under Supreme Court Act 1981, s.37 if necessary). Philip Rossdale said in his article above:

> In a case coming to my notice the threat of an application for an ex parte injunction resulted in the prompt release of the body to the executor. It is true that there is no property in a dead body to support a claim for damages . . . but that is no obstacle to an injunction for the delivery of the body: injunctions are awarded on different principles from damages.

An administrator also has a common law duty to dispose of the body but, as their authority derives from the grant, they may not be able to obtain an injunction for delivery of the body until they have obtained the grant.

A householder has a common law duty to dispose of a body. When the deceased lived alone the duty passes to the local authority (Public Health (Control of Diseases) Act 1984, s.46(1)). Local authorities will not pay if there are assets and may instruct solicitors (through their bereavement services department) to trace relatives to authorise the cost of the funeral. If the deceased died in hospital, the duty of disposal falls on the hospital authorities.

Are the deceased's wishes binding?

No. It was held in *Williams* v. *Williams* (1882) 20 Ch D 659 that a person has no property in their body after their death. Thus, a testator cannot dispose of his body by will and any wishes expressed in the will are not binding on the executors. Directions for a lavish funeral can thus be ignored with impunity. This is an issue which should be taken seriously when appointing executors. Many religious groups have strong views about burial or cremation (Judaism and Islam requires burial whereas Hinduism requires cremation) while some environmentalists regard cremation as an improper use of fuel. It is, therefore, important to appoint executors who will respect the deceased's wishes.

When are organs available?

A person can give written consent at any time or oral consent during his or her last illness to the use of organs for therapeutic purposes or for the purposes of medical education or research. The persons lawfully in possession of the body can then authorise the use of organs so long as they have no reason to believe the request was withdrawn.

If a solicitor is taking instructions for a will and the client expresses a wish to leave organs for donation, it is important for the solicitor to check whether the client only wants organs to be used for therapeutic purposes or whether the client is happy for organs to be taken for research or education purposes.

The clause in the will should be worded appropriately. Speed is of the essence in such cases so encourage the client to carry an organ donor card and to tell close relatives of his/her wishes.

If there is no evidence of the deceased's wishes, the person who has lawful possession of the body can authorise its use for organ donation or for research or education. However, they have to show that they made reasonable enquiries, have no reason to believe the deceased had expressed any objection and have no reason to believe that any surviving spouse or surviving relative will object.

Carrying a donor card is obviously helpful and many people are aware of this. Fewer people know about the possibility of registration with the United Kingdom Transplant Support Service Authority (UKTSSA 0117 975 7575). There is a helpful article by Jonathan Smith, a family law solicitor and mediator based in Litchfield in *Solicitors' Journal* [2002] 4 September, 781. UKTSSA will send solicitors registration forms which clients can complete and return.

Inquests and post-mortems

Fairly obviously, if there is reason to believe that there will be an inquest, no one can authorise the use of organs without the consent of a coroner. The same applies if a post-mortem is likely.

Alternative burials

Many people now consider burials in woods, fields or gardens. They can do this but will have to obtain the consent of the relevant local authority. This is because a body is treated as clinical waste and can, therefore, only be disposed of by a licensed operator in accordance with the Control of Pollution Act 1974 and the Environmental Protection Act 1990. If relatives want to bury the body in the garden, they will have to take advice from the Environment Agency which has a list of minimum distances from the site of a grave to water, cabling and wells or boreholes. The Department of the Environment, Transport and the Regions has said that it is not necessary to apply for planning permission to bury up to two people in a back garden. Permission would be required to bury any more. It is possible to apply for a certificate of lawfulness as regards planning law. The result of the application is recorded on a public register. If the application is refused, there is a right of free appeal.

Turning to the even more esoteric it is also possible to have a burial at sea. Readers wishing to know the details are referred to the Mathew Knight article above.

Cremation of body parts after post-mortem

Under the Cremation Regulations 1930, SR&O 1930/1016, there was a problem where body parts had been removed during post-mortem and not returned at the time of burial. When the body parts were returned, relatives were not allowed to cremate them if the body had been buried. The parts had to be buried with the body. Separate cremation of body parts was only permitted when the body itself had been cremated. Under the Cremation (Amendment) Regulations 2000, SI 2000/58 it is now irrelevant whether the body was buried or cremated. However, the new regulations do not *require* cremation. It will still be possible to bury the parts with the body or to have them disposed of as clinical waste.

Disputes between parents over child's funeral arrangements

In *Fessi* v. *Whitmore* [1999] 1 FLR 767, divorced parents were unable to agree on the funeral arrangements for their 12-year-old son. The boy lived with his mother in the Midlands but had contact with his father who lived in Wales. The boy was killed in an accident while visiting his father in Wales. The father had the boy cremated and wanted to scatter his ashes in the sea off the Welsh coast. The mother wanted to have the ashes interred in the Midlands with a service arranged in conjunction with the boy's school. The parties were unable to agree and an application was made to court. The court concluded that parents with parental responsibility both have an equal right and duty to arrange the child's funeral. Judge Boggis QC said that he was considering an issue where the parties had equal entitlement but conflicting proposals. This was akin to a dispute between trustees and he was, therefore, entitled to consider the issue and come to a conclusion 'which does justice and fairness to both sides'. He ordered that the remains should be disposed of in accordance with the proposals of the mother, in the Midlands. This was because there was a connection there with both sides of the family and this would provide a focus for all the family. For a fuller discussion of the case see the article by David Hershman in [1999] *Trusts and Estates Law Journal*, November.

15.10.4 Difficult clients

Sometimes clients are hard to please. It may just have to be accepted, but in a proportion of cases there may be some misunderstanding which could be discussed and perhaps removed. Asking such a client what the problem is, if appropriate, may be worthwhile, or a colleague may be able to assist. Prompt action may help to avert a complaint.

15.10.5 Are you being misled?

Not all clients are honest. If you suspect a client is misleading you or others involved, you need to discuss those concerns with the client, no matter how difficult this seems. There may be a completely reasonable explanation. The risks of involvement in another's dishonesty are analysed in Chapter 6. The Professional Ethics division may be able to help (see Appendix 6). See also the Green Card warning on property fraud and the Blue Card warning on money laundering (see Appendix I and *The Guide to the Professional Conduct of Solicitors 1999*, Annex 25G and 16D).

15.11 REQUESTS FROM CLIENTS

15.11.1 Request that you renounce

Following a death, if a solicitor has been appointed executor or executrix, the family may request that he or she renounce probate. This tends to happen especially when the family live in a different part of the country from the solicitor, or they consider the estate to be small and uncomplicated. The advice given by the Office for the Supervision of Solicitors (OSS) in these circumstances is that solicitors are not under any duty to renounce and may indeed be in possession of information imparted to them by the testator or testatrix which makes renunciation inappropriate; but that solicitors are free to agree to such a request and to renounce – the basic principle is the client's best interests.

15.11.2 Request for another firm to handle the work involved

This request is a variation on the request to renounce. If you have refused to renounce, there may be a request that the beneficiaries' chosen firm undertake the actual work instead of yours. This may be on a variety of grounds, but cost (the other firm is cheaper), convenience (the other firm is nearer) or familiarity (the other firm is the residuary beneficiary's own solicitors) are the most common.

The OSS suggests that the presumption would be that you, having been appointed executor or executrix by the deceased, would undertake the winding up of the estate. You are free to agree differently. If you do so, you will need to consider what, if anything, the charging clause in the will allows you. If you wish to insist on handling the administration, bear in mind you may be storing up a great deal of difficulty and ill-will for the future.

15.12   CHARGING CLAUSES

15.12.1   No charging clause

If a will does not contain a charging clause, Trustee Act 2000, s.29 allows a trustee who acts in a professional capacity in relation to the management or administration of the estate to charge reasonable remuneration provided that the co-trustees consent in writing. The provision is of no assistance to sole executors or administrators who will have to arrange the appointment of co-trustees.

Professional executors can charge for their time if the beneficiaries are all adult and *sui juris* and give their approval. According to Barlow, King and King, *Wills Administration and Taxation, A Practical Guide* (see Appendix 5), it is possible for a solicitor appointed executor or executrix to employ and pay individual partners in the firm, provided there is an express agreement that the solicitor-PR shall not participate in the profits nor derive any benefit from the charges: *Re Gates* [1933] Ch 913. However, it is better practice in such a situation to inform clients that this problem has arisen and seek their consent to a charge being made. If legal advice is to be taken by lay PRs, they will incur costs in any event.

15.12.2   Inappropriate charging clause

It is important to look carefully at a charging clause to check exactly who is entitled to charge and for what. Lay executors can charge if there is an appropriate charging clause but not otherwise. Charities complain that there is an increasing tendency for lay executors to seek to charge in circumstances where they are not able to do so.

A common form of clause is 'Any trustee engaged in a profession or business may charge'. This will allow any professional or business person to charge for any work done. The following clause is more limited: 'Any trustee who acts in a professional capacity may charge'. This will only allow a trustee to charge for professional services rendered. Thus, an accountant could charge for accountancy services rendered and an estate agent could charge for valuations provided.

15.13   SOLICITOR-EXECUTOR WITNESSES THE WILL

Trustee Act 2000, s.28 provides that a charging clause is no longer regarded as a gift for the purposes of Wills Act, s.15. Solicitors who witness a will which allows them to charge for their services will no longer forfeit the benefit of the charging clause.

15.14   CHARGING CLAUSE IN INVALID WILL

If a will proves to be invalid (for example, as a result of faulty execution) all legacies fail and naturally a solicitors' charging clause (being analogous to a legacy) also fails.

In *Gray* v. *Richards Butler* [1996] *Gazette*, 2 August, 29; [2000] WTLR 625, solicitors who had paid themselves under a charging clause contained in a will which proved to be invalid for want of due execution had to repay the residuary beneficiary of an earlier will. The court did exercise its inherent jurisdiction to order reasonable remuneration for work done by the firm which could have been undertaken for the earlier valid will.

15.15   TWO-YEAR DISCRETIONARY TRUSTS AND THE THREE-MONTH TRAP

Most practitioners are aware of the dangers of making appointments within three months of the testator's death. This was highlighted in the case of *Frankland* v. *IRC* [1996] STC 735 and discussed in articles in [1996] *Solicitors' Journal*, 4 October by Julie Evans and 25 October by Catherine Sanders.

15.16   DEALING WITH MISTAKES

See *The Guide to the Professional Conduct of Solicitors 1999* ('the Guide'), ch. 29. How one handles mistakes depends on the nature and significance of the error, and the applicability of the relevant principles in the Guide, but the following comments may also be of interest.

According to the Office for the Supervision of Solicitors (OSS), relatively minor errors are usually best dealt with promptly by being frank with the client. Most clients will appreciate openness at an early stage and an explanation. It seems that clients find a lack of frankness (or an impression of it, from an absence of explanation, or failure to answer questions or reply to letters, etc.) more irritating, and more likely to found a complaint, than a prompt apology and explanation of the problem.

More serious mistakes create different issues. First these should be discussed with your insurers. Second, clients may have to be advised to obtain independent advice (see Principle 29.09 and commentaries).

In either case, Professional Ethics and the Practice Advice Service (see Appendix 6) may be able to assist.

If solicitors acting for the other side have made an error which they refuse to deal with, or they do not reply to correspondence, it is open to you and/or your client to use the Rule 15 complaints procedure. If this does not resolve the matter, either you or your client may consider making a complaint to the OSS. Only the client, however, can ask for the complaint to be conciliated.

Conciliation can be an effective means of resolving less serious disputes – more information from the OSS (see Appendix 6).

A booklet entitled *Handling Complaints Effectively* can be obtained on the website at **www.clientcare.lawsociety.co.uk** or by telephoning the Practice Standards Unit on 01527 883264. Solicitors who require guidance on their firm's complaints procedures should contact Mike Frith at the Lawyer Line Service, tel. 0870 606 2588.

15.17 SOURCES OF HELP

15.17.1 The court

The court can assist in a number of ways: an application under CPR Part 64 may be made for help on a particular point, or for the court's assistance in the administration generally; a PR may be removed by the court under Administration of Justice Act 1985, s.50; and Trustee Act 1925, s.63 provides for payment into court, in appropriate circumstances, if trustees are unable otherwise to obtain good discharge. The court can also assist if it is impossible to trace missing beneficiaries (see at 15.1 above) and Administration of Justice Act 1985, s.49 allows the court to pronounce on the validity of wills if the consent of the beneficiaries has been obtained. Clearly, the cost of such an application means that approaching the court is not one's first recourse, but there may be in the end no other alternative. PRs' costs would usually be met from the estate (but see at 15.8 above for counsel's opinion on the costs of PRs separately represented). An excellent series of articles by Dawn Goodman of Withers appeared in [1994] *Solicitors' Journal*, August and September, on how to avoid problems and how the court can help. See also *Alsop Wilkinson (a Firm)* v. *Neary* [1996] 1 WLR 1220 on trustees and litigation.

In *Mark Niebuhr Tod* v. *Judith Cobb Lady Barton, William Godfrey Lukes Barton, Royal Society of Chemistry sub nom in the matter of Professor Sir Derek Harold Richard Barton, deceased* (unreported, 20 March 2002) an executor failed to recover his cost incurred in challenging a deed made between the residuary beneficiary and an annuitant commuting the annuity to a lump sum. The Society had made it clear before the commencement of proceedings that it and the annuitant accepted the validity of the deed and that there was, therefore, no need to refer the matter to court. The case is an illustration of how careful executors and trustees should be to avoid unnecessary cost. The courts are not prepared to order costs from the estate where the application was misconceived.

15.17.2 Treasury Solicitor

If it appears that the deceased left no family, the Treasury Solicitor is responsible for kin searches and dealing with the administration of the estate if none is found. (See at 15.3 above and Appendix 6 for the address, and an article in [1992] *Gazette,* 11 November, 32).

15.17.3 Official Solicitor

The Official Solicitor (see Appendix 6) deals with personal injury work for children and adults without mental capacity, and also acts for children in other cases, as next friend or guardian ad litem where appropriate. The Official Solicitor also acts as trustee, obtains grants of representation for the use and benefit of those without mental capacity, and is asked to administer estates of certain intestates to allow Inheritance (Provision for Family and Dependants) Act 1975 claims to be made. A most helpful article on the work of the Official Solicitor can be found in [1990] *Family Law* 53.

15.17.4 Court of Protection

The financial affairs of people lacking mental capacity to handle these personally are the responsibility of the Court of Protection. The Court publishes useful booklets for receivers and enduring attorneys (see address in Appendix 6).

15.17.5 Probate registries

The Principal Registry is encouraging registrars to make contact with practices in their catchment areas, for example by meeting local law societies, which were asked to appoint a liaison officer to further this link.

The Probate Registry offers a very reasonably priced oath-settling service in cases of difficulty. Kevin Donnelly, Probate Department Manager at the Principal Probate Registry wrote in [2002] *Probate Section Journal*, February:

> We are becoming equipped with the basis of a communication system which will in a relatively short time encompass all Probate Registries. I hope it should not be too long before you can contact Registries electronically, receive an electronic reply and (who knows) even have your documents settled that way. This will enhance the service to a considerable extent and perhaps even provide the basis for a different way of delivering the goods altogether.
>
> I talk of the future but I can offer these facilities in London now. I confess we have not settled a document electronically but it should be possible although I would ask that as the email facility is a little limited at present, this be used for urgent or complex cases.
>
> You will say you do not know the number: perhaps this is just as well as you might then try to get in touch. But if you really want to know, try **kevin.donnelly@ courtservice.gsi.gov.uk**. You never know, I might even be able to help.

15.17.6   Lawyer Line

The following article about the work of Lawyer Line appeared in [2001] *Probate Section Journal*, July. We have updated it and are grateful for permission to reproduce it:

> About five years ago the Office for the Supervision of Solicitors decided to offer a service to the profession whereby solicitors could obtain good advice over the telephone about how to deal with complaints they might receive about the standards of service afforded their clients. Since then the service has been operated with great success and appreciation by those who have made use of the facility.
>
> The service is presently operated, as it has been for the last three years by Michael Frith, who had 28 years experience in private practice before joining the SCB (as it then was) in July 1993, where he spent the next five years dealing with service complaints made against solicitors. Mike also goes around the country lecturing extensively on Complaints Avoidance and Complaints Handling.
>
> As far as service complaints in probate matters are concerned, Mike would tell you that these are mainly of three types. The first, and by far the most common, are concerned with delay – and what seems to be the main cause of the problem is simply failing to do the estate accounts and get the estate administered. It is as if, having done all the donkey work, the file is often put to one side, presumably on the basis that it is just a matter of routine to draw the estate accounts, and it is just forgotten about – or perhaps the solicitor just does not realise how time is passing! The same phenomenon manifests itself in conveyancing matters when solicitors fail to submit applications for registration at the Land Registry.
>
> The second source of complaints is estate accounts that are drawn incorrectly, not infrequently because of simple arithmetical error. In these cases it frequently transpires that had the Client Account been checked before the final accounts were drawn and the distribution made, the error would have been avoided altogether. The moral is obvious.
>
> The third cause of complaints is the overlooking of liabilities that need to be cleared or specific legacies, payment of which is overlooked. Either way, the result is that residuary beneficiaries are overpaid and the solicitor then has the embarrassing task of writing to them asking for monies to be repaid.
>
> A problem that, from the evidence of the numbers of calls on the subject made to Lawyer Line, is a constant worry to solicitors, is whether and when they need to deal with complaints from residuary beneficiaries. There is no room here to deal with that matter, but readers can refer to the article written by Mike on the subject in the February 2000 edition of the Gazette [see Chapter 20].
>
> Mike has also written a book dealing with the whole subject of Complaints Avoidance and Complaints Handling, which was published in September 2001 by EMIS Professional Publishing, which also deals in much greater detail with the advice referred to above.
>
> The Lawyer Line service is available by ringing 0870 606 2588.

15.17.7   The Law Society

(For addresses see Appendix 6.) The *Probate Section* caters for solicitors who have an interest in wills and trusts, tax planning, investment advice as part of financial planning, Court of Protection, care planning for elderly clients and estate administration. For more information see Appendix 4.

The *Practice Advice Service* answers solicitors' questions on legal practice problems in all areas of law. You can write or phone, asking for the Practice Advice Service.

The *Professional Ethics* department offers confidential advice on the application and interpretation of the rules and principles of professional conduct. This advice encompasses such issues as how the rules affect your plans to develop your practice, or your relationship with clients, the court and others with whom you have dealings. You can write or phone during office hours.

The *Solicitors' Assistance Scheme* helps solicitors who find themselves in difficulties or potential difficulties and for one reason or another prefer not to consult the Law Society. It is administered by the Professional Ethics Division and is therefore separate from the Office for Supervision of Solicitors. Members are volunteers, some on recommendation from local law societies, and they form a nationwide network of solicitors available for consultation by fellow solicitors in need of guidance and advice.

Many solicitors find that being able to talk about their problems to an understanding and objective listener, rather than seeking specific advice, can often help them reach decisions more easily. Consultation can vary from a telephone call to a series of interviews. Often solicitors in trouble prefer to contact a scheme member outside their own area of practice.

When appointing scheme members, local law societies are asked to consider those who are not officers of the local society. If scheme members take office after being nominated, they are asked to resign from the scheme until the end of their term of office.

The scheme is operated on a completely confidential solicitor–client basis. No charge is normally made for an initial interview, but thereafter it is open to the individual scheme member (or his or her firm) to make a formal arrangement with the solicitor concerned. The Law Society does not give any guidance as to charges, or at what stage these should be made, but prefers to leave the matter to the discretion of scheme members themselves, according to circumstances.

15.17.8 Insurers

Problems which may involve a claim against you need to be referred to your insurers. Your policy is likely to provide that you have a discretion whether to inform them of circumstances which you believe may result in a claim, and a duty to notify them of claims which have been made against you or which you learn will be made.

15.17.9   Specialist solicitors and counsel

Counsel's opinion may be necessary on a variety of matters. If the question is one of construction, Administration of Justice Act 1985, s.48 allows a barrister of 10 years' standing to give an opinion to the PRs on which the court may, without hearing argument, allow them to act.

Rather than approaching counsel, some practitioners may like to consider consulting another firm of solicitors. This is a practice which is becoming established in certain specialist fields such as pensions and contentious probate.

It may be particularly useful to approach a professional colleague if a difficulty also raises conduct or practice issues, since another solicitor will be more aware than counsel of the impact of the Practice Rules and issues relating to practice as a solicitor.

15.17.10   Within the office

We all, from time to time, have files we get bogged down with or which are a constant headache. Try making a deal with a colleague to exchange headache files once a month. You may be able to skip through something which has stalled a colleague for days – and vice versa.

15.17.11   Personal

Stress is a major cause of illness. Many solicitors face huge pressures and a heavy burden of others' expectations and responsibility at work. There are now numerous books on stress in paperback in general bookshops, which help to identify symptoms and suggest solutions.

15.18   PARTING COMPANY

Sometimes, solicitors and clients have to part company. Clients may terminate retainers on any grounds they wish. Solicitors may terminate retainers in more limited circumstances. These are set out in Principle 12.10 and commentaries of the Guide. They include a client's supervening incapacity and the breakdown of trust and confidence.

Lay and professional executors, or two or more lay executors, may disagree about a number of issues. Where executors cannot agree, one may seek independent advice. An opinion given by counsel in 1986 on costs issues arising out of such a step is included at 15.8 above. It is clear from this opinion that a PR seeking independent advice may not in every case find that his or her costs would be paid from the estate.

Other problems arise where it is clear, or feared, that a client intends to act dishonestly, for example, by saying outstanding tax is to remain unpaid. In certain cases, solicitors may decline to act. It is rare, but does sometimes arise, that a third party should be informed. Principle 16.07 of the Guide refers to such problems and in difficult cases the assistance of Professional Ethics (address in Appendix 6) is always available. Some of the issues are considered in Chapter 6. You should also be aware of the warnings given by the Law Society in relation to mortgage fraud and money laundering.

15.19 COPY DEATH CERTIFICATES UNACCEPTABLE

Probate paractitioners were concerned when HMSO issued Guidance Notes (No. 7, dated 27 October 1999, revised 4 January 2001) stating that because of the potential for photocopy documents to assist in the perpetration of fraud, their use was no longer acceptable. This obviously meant an increase in the cost of administering estates.

However, the Law Society has agreed a protocol with the British Bankers Association, the Building Societies Association and the Association of British Insurers. The agreement means that, instead of having to send original certificates to asset holders, solicitors can send a death certificate verification form giving a guarantee that they have in their possession and inspected an original. The protocol letter and form are set out below. Solicitors can reproduce the letter and form electronically. The form must remain unaltered although the letter can be modified.

At the time of writing it appears that Barclays Trust Company will not accept the protocol letters.

For use by Solicitors

DEATH CERTIFICATE VERIFICATION FORM[1]

Registration District	. . . .
Place of death	. . . .
Parish (if specified) & County	. . . .
Entry number	. . . .
Date of death	. . . .
Cause of death[2]	. . . .
Name of doctor[3] certifying death	. . . .
Name of informant[4]	. . . .

Name of registrar[5] . . . .

Date of birth[6] . . . .

Sex[7] . . . .

Maiden name[8] . . . .
(if applicable)

Previous married name . . . .
(if applicable/known)

Occupation . . . .

I/We certify that I/we have examined the death certificate of

(client's name) . . . .

(client's address) . . . .

. . . . and that the said certificate contains the information as recorded above. **A copy is kept on the client file for my/our information to which you may request access.**

Signed: (Partner) . . . . Date: . . . .

Full name . . . .

Firm Name . . . .

Firm Law Society number . . . .

[Firm's stamp]

Guidance notes

1 Only information contained in the certificate may be recorded on this form. Where information for a particular field is not recorded in the certificate, or not known, please state 'not recorded on certificate' or 'not known'. This form is not appropriate for use in lieu of an interim death certificate.

2 This information is important in the event of an early claim on an under-written policy. Each and every cause of death must be recorded as they appear in the certificate.

3 On occasion, usually in connection with an attempted fraud, the name of the doctor certifying the death may be important.

4 This information may be important in the context of an attempted fraud and in helping to identify if there is a spouse which may be relevant in the case of protected rights or guaranteed minimum pensions under pension plans where the provider has discretion over the beneficiary.

5 In some cases the signature may be illegible (and the name is not printed). If this is the case, please state 'signature illegible'. This does, at least, confirm that the Registrar has signed the certificate.

6 Identifies any possible mis-statements of age.

7 Allows comparisons with information provided at date of inception (gender is not always obvious from the forenames).

8 Confirms identity of a woman who has married since policy inception but omitted to provide this information.

Dear

Re: xxxxx deceased
Ref: xxxxx **[account/policy/pension number]**

We regret to inform you that xxxxx **[full name]** died on xxxxx at xxxxx. We act for xxxxx, who are personal representatives of xxxxx.

We are in possession of a certified copy of the entry of the death, the full details of which can be found in the attached schedule.* We confirm that we will forward the copy of the death certificate if the xxxxx **[bank/insurer/pension provider]** requires it.

We would be grateful if you would please note the fact of this death and take such action as is required.

We would be grateful if you could also provide precise details of all xxxxx **[accounts/insurance policy/assets]** held by you and their value as at xxxxx **[date of death]** for the purpose of administering the estate.

Yours faithfully

---

*Insurers/Pension providers will also require birth and marriage forms to be completed for certain purposes.

15.20 EXTRACTING A GRANT FOR NON-SOLICITOR PRACTITIONERS

You may be asked to make an application for a grant on behalf of a bank or will and administration company. Be cautious about accepting unsubstantiated figures. A company called Legacies (Will and Probate Services) Ltd was wound up in 2002 after an investigation by the DTI into its financial affairs. The company had instructed solicitors to obtain grants on its behalf on the basis that the estates involved were excepted (they were frequently not excepted). The company had then siphoned off £4.8 million due to beneficiaries of the estates to cover its own losses.

Solicitors who prepare an oath swearing that an estate does not exceed a stated figure when they have not made sufficient enquiries may find that they have themselves committed an offence and/or that they are implicated in the offences committed by others.

CHAPTER 16

Accounting and distributing

Lesley King

16.1 INTRODUCTION

Paragraphs 16.2–16.4, the specimen accounts for Victoria Thomas (at 16.3.1 below) and the explanatory notes which follow (at 16.3.2 below) are based on materials prepared by the College of Law for trainee solicitors. We are most grateful to the College for their help in allowing us to reproduce these edited sections.

An increasing number of firms are turning to computerised packages to produce their accounts (see Chapter 18). Even so, we have set out the essential elements of the accounts in this chapter.

16.2 ESTATE ACCOUNTS

16.2.1 The duty to account

Personal representatives (PRs) are reminded of their obligation to keep accounts by the wording of all the oaths leading to grants of representation (giving effect to Administration of Estates Act (AEA) 1925, s.25).

The accounts should give a clear and accurate statement of the estate property and income, and contain full details of all receipts and payments (for which the appropriate corresponding documentation should be available). Solicitor PRs are subject to the Accounts Rules (see Chapter 5) as well as the general law.

16.2.2 Form of accounts

The form of estate accounts varies. Some firms use the traditional 'side-by-side' format showing income and outgoings. Others, as here, a 'vertical' layout. The aim is always to give the PRs and residuary beneficiaries an explanation of the administration of the estate in an easily understandable form.

There is no prescribed layout or form for estate accounts, so you can use whatever format best suits the estate in hand, but the simpler and easier accounts are the better. They must, of course, give enough detail to allow a proper appreciation of all the transactions which have taken place.

The following elements are standard.

- *Introduction*: this is a narrative setting out:

  - the date of death, the date and place of issue of the grant of representation, and the PRs' names;
  - if there was a will, a summary of the gifts made; otherwise, an outline of the effect in the estate of the intestacy rules;
  - the value of the gross and net estates and the amount of any inheritance tax (IHT) paid;
  - details of any joint property passing by survivorship, variations made, elections under Inheritance Tax Act (IHTA) 1984, s.142, funds held back in respect of future tax liability and other relevant information.

- *Balance sheet*: you can group connected items under headings (such as 'legacies') for simplicity.

- *Estate capital account*: this shows the value of the estate at death, the transactions effected during the administration period and the balance remaining.

  - If the estate is complicated, this account can be drawn up in two parts: (1) the estate at death (based on the IHT account and any corrective account) and (2) the transactions taking place during the administration. The first part would show the gross and net estates at death, as agreed for probate and IHT purposes. The second part would record transactions which took place during the administration affecting the assets in Part 1.
  - The probate valuation figures are used in accounts for ease of comparison and because they give an acquisition cost (for CGT purposes) for the beneficiaries' future disposals of the assets.
  - Sometimes there will be differences between the IHT account(s) and the estate capital account, arising from the different tax treatment and legal nature of certain kinds of property (for example, reversionary interests, being 'excluded property', are left out of IHT accounts but appear, as assets, in the estate accounts; conversely, the deceased's share of jointly owned property passing by survivorship will be included in the IHT account but, as far as the estate accounts are concerned, will only be mentioned for information in the introductory narrative).

- *Estate income account*: this shows all the income received during the administration period. When tax is deducted at source (for example, company dividends) only the net amounts of income received need to be shown; otherwise put in gross receipts, with an entry showing the basic rate tax which the PRs have paid:

  - If equitable apportionments have been made, or if any income is apportioned to capital under the Apportionment Act 1870, show the full amount of the income the PRs receive, with the amount apportioned to capital being shown as an appropriation of part of the total.
  - This account should also show individually any interim payments of income to beneficiaries so that they can check these against the annual certificates of deduction of income tax you have given them (form R185E).
  - Show any interest paid on general legacies, and any income produced by property which was given specifically in the will, as deductions from the total income received. You can deal similarly with expenses attributable to income.
  - This account can be made up to each 5 April.

- *Beneficiaries' or distribution accounts*: these are usually only made available to residuary beneficiaries, and show how each one's share is derived.

- *Schedules or annexes*: more detailed information can conveniently be put here, to keep the main accounts uncluttered. Schedules may cover:

  - debts at death;
  - dividends received during the administration;
  - investments owned at death – this will usually be in two parts: (1) showing investments retained and appropriated to, or divided between, the beneficiaries, and (2) showing the investments which were sold, along with gains and losses.

- *Notes*: these may be helpful to draw attention to any aspects of the accounts which might otherwise be overlooked or unclear.

16.2.3 Planning for the end of the administration period

You should consider early on in the administration the discharge the PRs will eventually seek from the beneficiaries and whether any special arrangements need to be made, e.g. if any beneficiary lacks capacity. A discharge from residuary beneficiaries will only be valid if there has been full disclosure of the estate assets, the dealings with them and of the balances available for distribution. You should also anticipate the end of the administration period by, for example, settling all tax liabilities and arranging to withdraw funds from banks and building societies in good time.

PRs will want approval of the accounts from the residuary beneficiaries and may consider withholding some of the assets until this is forthcoming. Receipts for cheques or assets should be obtained and filed with the estate papers. (See at 16.7 below for guidance on obtaining receipts.)

16.3 SPECIMEN ACCOUNTS

The following specimen accounts for Victoria Thomas deceased illustrate the points made above, and are followed by notes, beginning at 16.3.2 below, explaining how these accounts were made up.

16.3.1 Victoria Thomas deceased

Miss Thomas died on 3 May 200–. Lowe Snow & Co. of Hixley held her will which was dated 15 August 1990 and (in summary) provided:

- revocation clause;
- executors: (1) Miss Emily Thomas and (2) Miss Amy Thomas both of 'Hillview', Hixley, Cheshire;
- charitable legacies (all registered charities):

  (1)   £1,000 to Cheshire Home of Rest for Horses,
  (2)   £250 to Hixley Dogs Home,
  (3)   £250 to Cheshire Donkey Sanctuary;

- receipts clause;
- residue, after debts, legacies, testamentary expenses – 'to such of them my said sisters Emily Thomas and Amy Thomas as shall survive me and if both equally between them'. (Gift over to RSPCA in event of both sisters pre-deceasing: both survived);
- clause dispensing with consents to appropriation.

It was duly executed and attested.

Victoria Thomas: estate for probate and IHT purposes		
	£	£
Spring Cottage	300,000.00	
Investments	39,412.00	
Halifax Building Society	4,100.00	
Cash in house	21.00	
National Westminster Bank	5,828.00	
Arrears of retirement pension	42.00	
Contents:		
sold gross	500.00	
other: estimated value 2,000	2,500.00	
GROSS ESTATE		352,403.00
Less		
Electricity	31.00	
Gas	52.00	
Income tax	295.00	
Funeral	525.00	903.00
NET ESTATE FOR PROBATE		351,500.00
Less		
Charitable legacies (exempt)	1,500.00	
ESTATE FOR IHT PURPOSES		350,000.00
IHT PAYABLE		
on first 250,000	NIL	
on £100,000 at 40 per cent		40,000.00
on delivery of account, on £50,000	5,714.29	
on Spring Cottage, on £300,000	34,285.71	

The solicitors sent a covering letter with the accounts to the two PRs:

Dear Miss Thomas,

YOUR LATE SISTER'S ESTATE

I enclose the estate accounts which include an outline of your sister's will, and the amount of the estate and of tax and other payments paid and so on.

We have not deducted income tax from the £150 this firm has allowed you as interest. You should, therefore, include it in your tax return for the tax year 200–/–.

Yours sincerely [etc.]

These are the accounts which were sent.

Accounts: Estate of Miss Victoria Thomas deceased

Included in these accounts are the following:

1. Introduction
2. Capital account
3. Estate income account
4. Beneficiary's account – Miss Emily Thomas
5. Beneficiary's account – Miss Amy Thomas
6. Schedule of investments showing probate values

Introduction

Miss Victoria Thomas, late of Spring Cottage, Tottenhall Road, Hixley, Cheshire died on 3 May 200–, aged 82. Probate of her will dated 15 August 1990 was granted on _____ to Miss Emily Thomas and Miss Amy Thomas, the executors named in the will.

In her will Miss Thomas left these charitable legacies:

(1)   £1,000 to the Cheshire Home of Rest for Horses,
(2)   £250 to the Hixley Dogs Home,
(3)   £250 to the Cheshire Donkey Sanctuary.

The estate remaining after payment of these legacies, and after payment of Miss Thomas's debts and funeral and testamentary expenses, was given to Miss Emily Thomas and Miss Amy Thomas equally.

The net estate for probate purposes amounted to £351,500.00. For inheritance tax (IHT) purposes the taxable estate amounted to £350,000.00, the legacies to the charities being exempt. IHT amounted to £40,000.00. This has been paid and a certificate of discharge obtained.

The residue has been divided between the beneficiaries (Miss Emily and Miss Amy Thomas) and this is shown in the accounts. Miss Thomas's investments have been divided equally between the beneficiaries. The values stated in the beneficiaries' accounts form the acquisition value for the purposes of capital gains tax.

Part of the contents of Spring Cottage was divided between the Misses Thomas as they agreed, and the remainder was sold. Spring Cottage was sold at the agreed probate value. The estate's liability to income tax was met by deduction of tax at source.

Lowe, Snow & Co.

Capital account

ASSETS	£	£
Spring Cottage, Huxley		
Probate value	£300,000.00	
Net proceeds of sale		290,000.25
Investments per Schedule		
at probate value		39,512.00
Halifax Building Society		
Share A/c – Capital	4,039.64	
– Interest to date of death	60.36	
		4,100.00
Cash – In house		21.00
Bank A/c – NatWest, Hixley		
Current A/c	721.50	
Deposit A/c	5,000.00	
– Interest to date of death	106.50	
		5,828.00
Arrears of retirement pension		42.00
Contents of house and personal effects		
Distribution *in specie* (estimated value)	2,000.00	
Proceeds of sale of rest	442.25	
		2,442.25
GROSS ESTATE		341,846.25
Less		
Debts due at death		
Eastern Electricity Co. – electricity a/c	31.00	
British Gas – gas a/c	52.00	
Inland Revenue – income tax due		
Inland Revenue – at death	295.00	
Funeral expenses		
G. Smith & Co.	525.00	
Administration expenses		
Commissioner's fees	9.00	
Probate Court fees	60.00	
Stockbroker Co. – valuation fees	17.50	
Lowe, Snow & Co. – charges for		
administering the estate	1,650.00	
VAT	288.75	
Inheritance tax	40,000.00	
		42,928.25

NET ESTATE		298,918.00

Less		
LEGACIES		
Cheshire Home of Rest for Horses	1,000.00	
Hixley Dogs Home	250.00	
Cheshire Donkey Sanctuary	250.00	
		1,500.00

RESIDUE		297,418.00

Divisible		
Miss Emily Thomas – one half	148,709.00	
Miss Amy Thomas – one half	148,709.00	
		297,418.00

Estate income account

Income Tax Year 200– to 200–	£	£
Dividends received		
1.9.200–	255.00	
Interest received		
Halifax Building Society		
Interest to close a/c on 26.8.200–	76.02	
NatWest Bank, Hixley		
Interest to close deposit a/c 30.8.200–	45.60	
Refund of income tax	15.55	
		392.17
Less loan interest		
NatWest Bank, Hixley		
Interest on loan to pay IHT		62.20
		329.97
Divisible		
Miss Emily Thomas – one half	164.98	
Miss Amy Thomas – one half	164.99	
		329.97

Beneficiary's account

MISS EMILY THOMAS

	£	£
Share of residue due to you per Capital Account		148,709.00
Share of income due to you per Income Account		164.98
Total due to you		148,873.98
Represented by –		
Transferred to you		
Shares at probate value		
1,650 Marks & Spencer Ord. Shares	3,795.00	
900 Tesco Stores Ord. Shares	1,620.00	
640 Shell T & T Ord. Reg. Shares	8,316.00	
400 Lonrho Ord. Shares	1,125.00	
600 Tate & Lyle £1 Shares	4,850.00	
		19,706.00
Retained by you		
Share of furniture at agreed value		1,000.00
Interim payments to you		
10.7.200–	12,250.00	
13.11.200–	75,000.00	
		87,250.00
BALANCE now due to you		40,917.98
		148,873.98

Beneficiary's account

MISS AMY THOMAS

	£	£
Share of residue due to you per Capital Account		148,709.00
Share of income due to you per Income Account		164.99
Total due to you		148,873.99
Represented by –		
Transferred to you		
Shares at probate value		
1,650 Marks & Spencer Ord. Shares	3,795.00	
900 Tesco Stores Ord. Shares	1,620.00	
640 Shell T & T Ord. Reg. Shares	8,316.00	
400 Lonrho Ord. Shares	1,175.00	
600 Tate & Lyle £1 Shares	4,850.00	
		19,706.00

	£	£
Retained by you		
Share of furniture at agreed value		1,000.00
Interim payments to you		
10.7.200–	12,250.00	
13.11.200–	75,000.00	
		87,250.00
BALANCE now due to you		17,497.74
		125,503.74

Schedule of investments

PROBATE VALUES

Amount	Stock	Probate value £	Miss Emily Thomas No.	Miss Emily Thomas Value £	Miss Amy Thomas No.	Miss Amy Thomas Value £
3,300	Marks & Spencer Ord. Shares	7,590.00	1,650	3,795	1,650	3,795
1,800	Tesco Stores (HIdings) Ord. Shares	3,240.00	900	1,620	900	1,620
1,280	Shell Transport & Trading Ord. Shares	16,632.00	640	8,316	640	8,316
800	Lonrho Ord. Shares	2,350.00	400	1,175	400	1,175
1,200	Tate & Lyle Shares	9,700.00	600	4,850	600	4,850
		39,512.00		19,756		19,756

16.3.2 Notes on the specimen estate accounts

The accounts start with the narrative Introduction, giving details of the grant and explaining the distribution of the estate.

In this estate, apart from three pecuniary legacies, the entire net estate was divided between two beneficiaries. So all that is required is a *capital account*, showing assets and liabilities and the net residue, an *income account* showing income received during the administration, and *beneficiaries' accounts* showing the division of their entitlements and how these were met between the beneficiaries, and a *schedule* showing details of the investments.

16.3.3 Capital account

In preparing the capital account there is a choice: the account can be produced in two parts or in one:

- If the account is in two parts, the first part will mirror exactly the estate as disclosed in the Inland Revenue account (amended by any corrective account). The probate value of all assets, whether or not sold, will be listed together with deductions permitted for IHT purposes, e.g. debts due at death, funeral expenses. The figure produced will therefore be the same as that agreed with the Revenue, but of course it will not be the amount available for distribution to the beneficiaries: for example, administration costs may have been incurred which cannot be deducted for IHT purposes (e.g. IHT itself, solicitors' costs, probate court fees, etc.). These costs will have to be deducted in the second part of a two-part capital account, to produce a sum which does represent the net estate available for the beneficiaries.
- If the account is in one part (as here) it shows the net estate available for the beneficiaries. This method produces a different sum from the one shown in the Inland Revenue account, and shows the amount the beneficiaries are actually receiving after tax and administration expenses. It may be that most beneficiaries would find this more interesting and understandable than a two-stage capital account.

A one-part account is used in this example. Accordingly, for any items sold, e.g. Spring Cottage, the net proceeds of sale are used.

Some or all of the *investments* may have been sold. If so, the probate value of all the holdings will be included, plus or minus the gain or loss on sale as appropriate. (Details of the transactions would be shown in the schedule of investments.)

In this estate, and others where the investments are divided equally between the beneficiaries, the value included in the accounts is the probate value, i.e. value at the deceased's death. This is unlikely to be the same as the market value at the point when the shares are vested in the beneficiaries. However, any increase or decrease in value will be shared equally between the beneficiaries, so this produces no unfairness. The probate value is also the beneficiaries' acquisition value for capital gains tax (CGT) purposes.

All the assets, then, are listed at the probate value or actual realised value.

In relation to *bank and building society accounts*, etc., the probate value includes interest accrued to the date of death. For IHT purposes, this interest forms part of the deceased's estate and so is shown in the capital account. (Interest earned after death and before the closing of the account will be shown in the estate income account.) For income tax purposes, however, the accrued interest before death, and any interest received between death and the closing of the account are regarded as income of the PRs and should be included by them in their income tax return. Accordingly, the income shown in the income account is not the amount of income on which PRs actually pay income tax.

The *contents of the house* have been valued at an estimated £2,500. Some items have been sold and turned into cash. The actual amount received, i.e. the net proceeds of sale, is shown.

Once the gross estate is established, all the *debts and liabilities* are then deducted from the gross estate figure, including debts not permitted as deductions for IHT purposes.

A sum representing the net estate results. In this estate, of course, there are legacies to be paid before the net estate is distributed between the residuary beneficiaries. So, *non-residuary gifts* are deducted from the net estate figure, and then the *division of residue* is shown. These figures are transferred to the individual beneficiaries' accounts.

16.3.4 Income account

This deals with income received during the administration of the estate. In this estate, all the income is received in one tax year. If the administration straddled more than one tax year, two or more separate sets of figures would be shown.

If income is received net of tax, show the net figure. If income is received gross, the PRs will have to pay income tax at basic rate. This payment will be shown as a deduction from income. Also deducted here will be any payments out of income, such as interest on loans, interest on IHT, any solicitors' or accountants' charges related to post-death tax returns.

In this estate, income and capital are received by the same beneficiaries, and no such distinction has been made in the solicitors' charges. If different beneficiaries were entitled to income and capital, e.g. in a life interest, a proportion of the solicitors' charges, referable to income, would be deducted here.

Again, the net entitlement to income is shown, and the balances are taken to the beneficiaries' accounts.

16.3.5 Beneficiaries' accounts

The entitlements have been brought forward and listed. In this estate the beneficiaries are due capital and income.

Once the total due to a beneficiary has been ascertained, the account shows how this has been satisfied. There may be, as with Miss Emily Thomas, three elements:

- assets transferred 'in specie'. Here, the shares were divided equally. As these were entered in the capital account at probate value, again probate values are used. Some furniture was also transferred 'in specie' at values agreed between the beneficiaries;
- assets which were retained by the beneficiaries. This is regarded as an 'advance' of part of their respective entitlements, and brought into account;
- payments of cash on account, or interim distributions.

Balancing the books

The balance after these calculations represents the amount due to the beneficiary and all together should add up to the amount left in the client ledger, after costs and disbursements.

If these figures do not agree, something has gone wrong. It can sometimes be a trying process to find the mistake, but it must be found.

Note: It could happen that a balance appears to be due from a beneficiary to the estate. This will usually mean that interim distributions were too big – interim payments should only be made after considering all future liabilities, such as tax and costs. A situation like this often causes great difficulty, as the beneficiary will, at the very least, be disappointed.

16.3.6   Schedule of investments

Rather than include on the capital account details of the investments, these can be listed in a schedule or annex. As no items have been sold this schedule is simple, giving capital values and showing the division of the shares between the beneficiaries. If numerous dividends had been received these could also have been recorded in a schedule.

If items had been sold, the sale price and any gain or loss could be shown. This information would be included in the capital account.

16.4   CAPITAL GAINS TAX

PRs are chargeable to CGT in respect of gains realised on or after 6 April 1998 at the uniform trusts rate of 34 per cent.

As with individuals an indexation allowance will be given for periods up to 6 April 1998 but not thereafter.

So, for assets held at 6 April 1998 and disposed of after that date an indexation allowance will be calculated for the period from acquisition to 6 April 1998. For assets acquired after that date no indexation allowance will be available.

Taper relief will be available to PRs and trustees who hold assets for an appropriate period (one year for business assets, three years for non-business assets).

PRs continue to receive the same annual exemption as an individual for the tax year of death and the two subsequent tax years.

PRs will be able to treat as allowable acquisition costs a proportion of the costs of obtaining the grant: details are set out in Inland Revenue Statement of Practice SP8/94. Costs of transferring the asset to the beneficiaries are also allowable (see Taxation of Chargeable Gains Act 1992, s.6(1)).

It is advisable to give a specific legatee a note of the value of the asset at the date of the death so that the legatee can calculate liability for CGT without having to refer back to the solicitor, perhaps many years after a file has been closed.

16.4.1 Release for PRs

In this particular estate, the PRs and beneficiaries are one and the same, so there is no need for the beneficiaries to release the PRs from further liability. A note of the beneficiaries' approval of the accounts might, however, be advisable as far as the solicitors are concerned. This could take the form of a simple statement on the accounts indicating their approval.

16.5 INCOME TAX

PRs pay basic or lower rate tax on income of the estate. They will pay the net income to beneficiaries with an appropriate tax credit.

Up until 6 April 1995 beneficiaries were assessed to income tax on income of the estate in the tax year in which it was paid to them but at the end of the administration the total of income paid out was apportioned evenly over the whole administration period on a daily basis. This led to recalculation of the beneficiary's tax liability for each tax year of the administration. In cases where a beneficiary was close to the limit of a tax band the apportioning of income could take the beneficiaries into or out of a particular band.

Since 6 April 1995 income paid to a beneficiary is treated as income of the tax year in which it is paid and there is no apportioning of income at the end of the administration. This can result in a beneficiary paying an unnecessarily high rate of tax. For example, if PRs make no interim income payments and pay out all the income at the end of the administration period to a beneficiary, that beneficiary may be pushed into higher rate tax for that year, whereas had the payments been made in two tax years the beneficiary might have remained a basic rate taxpayer.

PRs are now under an obligation to provide residuary beneficiaries with form R185E.

Administration of the Deceased's Estate. We have set out below a helpful article by Mary Hase, partner in charge of executorship at chartered accountants, Hereward Phillips. This article first appeared in [1997] *Solicitors' Journal*, 20 June and we are most grateful to Mary Hase and to the *Solicitors' Journal* for allowing us to reproduce it.

ADDITIONAL TAX RESPONSIBILITIES FOR SOLICITORS

The introduction of self-assessment puts increased responsibilities on solicitors acting as or advising executors. Tax matters can no longer be left until an estate is fully administered. Put simply, good management of an estate is essential. It saves time, money and – above all – professional reputation.

As a result of self-assessment, solicitors are responsible for ensuring that an estate is administered in a tax efficient manner, with tax returns completed on time and payments made in stages for the current year according to the dates laid down by the new tax regulations.

In the past, it has been common practice for solicitors to leave sorting out the tax on an estate until the estate has been substantially completed. Such practice would now lead to a series of mounting fines for the executor and beneficiaries.

Tax planning

This is the key to success. Consider at the outset when the estate's income is likely to be received and plan the distributions accordingly.

Also consider the financial position of the beneficiaries at the beginning. For wealthy beneficiaries looking to minimise their tax liability it may be best to delay distributions and thereby postpone the impact of higher rate tax until a more convenient time. For those in the middle range the payments might be spread to avoid hitting the higher rate tax threshold. Needy beneficiaries may desire a speedy settlement but again spreading their entitlement over a number of tax years may be more likely to help them utilise allowances and fall beneath tax thresholds.

Remember too that a large income distribution in one year may affect the beneficiaries' tax payments on account in the next.

If in doubt, call in the accountants/tax advisers early to assist with the planning.

The solicitor, acting as executor, must advise the Inland Revenue of the estate's untaxed income and capital gains. The normal deadlines apply – 30 September if the Revenue are to calculate the tax, 31 January if not. However, the Revenue will not work out the income and chargeable gains for you. Beneficiaries who have an absolute interest must also be advised of the income element included in their distributions to enable them to include these figures on their personal tax forms. It is the executor's responsibility to ensure that beneficiaries can meet their deadlines, which may be 30 September if the beneficiaries do not wish to calculate their own tax.

Payments on account

Payments on account underline the importance of good management. Plan the date of cessation and work out how the resulting accounting will be done, so that the beneficiaries are provided with the necessary information in good time to complete their own tax returns and assess their own payments on account.

The basic rule is that a payment on account should be half the previous year's tax liability, excluding capital gains. This is fine when income flow is regular, but distributions from an estate may involve payments over the short term only. It can be particularly difficult for executors and beneficiaries with unreliable income sources to deal with the tax payments. Once assets are realised, and the ensuing untaxed income sources cease, the executor may seek to reduce the payment on account.

Executors should also beware of placing any cash sums received from the estate in investments which pay income gross, such as the money markets, even if this is on a temporary basis. If the liability turns out to be greater than that anticipated when the payment on account was assessed, the executors will be liable for interest and possibly penalties.

For smaller estates it is advisable to avoid these complications by selecting investments which deduct tax at source, even if it means sacrificing one or two interest points and the cash flow advantage of gross income.

For beneficiaries the problem is worse. They may be looking at total income, taxed and untaxed, and can have no idea what their payment on account should be unless the executors give them guidance on how much and when the income distributions are likely to be. Remember that for absolute interest beneficiaries, their distributions will be part income, part capital so merely telling them how much in total to expect is not sufficient.

For life interest beneficiaries, their whole distribution is income so the amounts and dates will suffice for them during the period of administration. Any balance unpaid will be taxable at the date the administration ceases so the date(s) should be planned and made known to the beneficiaries.

Trustees' responsibilities for tax returns start on the death of the person in question, though there may be nothing to report until the estate's assets are vested in them. If a discretionary trust is set up, the payment of income to the trustees or direct to the trust beneficiaries will trigger a liability at the trust rate. So the responsibility for submission of trust returns may start before the closure of the administration.

Even if no formal trust is set up under the will, often it is convenient to leave the estate's assets in the hands of the executors after completion of the administration. This becomes a bare trust and under self-assessment bare trustees are not liable to make returns or to calculate and pay basic rate tax on behalf of the beneficiaries.

Tax liabilities of the deceased

When someone dies, their tax liabilities become the responsibility of the personal representatives, who must then try to keep to the dates above. This may be difficult if the deceased's tax affairs were in arrears, or if there is a delay in obtaining letters of administration.

Problems would occur simply by a death occurring, say, in December. This is because the tax return for the previous year, with up to three tax payments, must all be paid by the following 31 January. These tax payments would be for (a) any outstanding income tax for the previous financial year, (b) capital gains tax for the previous year, and (c) the first tax payment for the current year. As yet, there appears to be no legislation giving the executor more time to assess the tax situation, or to wait until probate is granted, or, indeed for the penalties to be mitigated in these circumstances.

If delay is unavoidable, it would be advisable to write to the Revenue at the earliest opportunity (and before the relevant deadline has passed) explaining the situation, giving an indication of when matters could be dealt with and requesting no penalties.

Delays may be considerable where a will is contested and it may not be clear which beneficiary gets which assets if applications are to be made under the Inheritance (Provision for Family and Dependants) Act 1975. The rigidity of the self-assessment regime cannot cope with such uncertainties.

Early clearance of income and capital gains tax

It has, however, been announced that procedures will be introduced to facilitate the speedy completion of trusts and estates. This will include early issue of tax returns and early written confirmation that the Revenue do not propose to enquire into the return. This will assist both executors and trustees who would otherwise have to wait for a year following the next 31 January to know if the deceased's and the estate's income and capital gains tax liabilities are settled and that they are in the clear.

In summary

It is likely that further legislation will be passed or concessions granted to simplify some of these matters. Until that time, early tax planning for the entire adminis-tration of the estate is the best approach.

16.6   TOP TEN TAX TIPS

In an article in [2000] *Solicitors' Journal*, 21 January, Mary Hase gave her top ten tips for making the preparation of key tax reports relatively straightfor-ward whether solicitors are preparing them themselves or instructing account-ants. We are grateful to *Solicitors' Journal* for allowing us to list the tips.

As a preliminary three general tax planning tips:

If PRs sell assets, they can claim a full CGT exemption for the first 3 tax years of the administration. Any tax payable by PRs will be at 34% rather than the 40% a higher rate beneficiary will pay.

If the beneficiaries have unused CGT exemptions and/or pay tax at the standard rate, PRs may consider transferring assets to them for sale especially if the admin-istration has exceeded three tax years.

If the beneficiaries are non-UK residents or if they have capital losses against which they could offset any gains, transfer assets to them prior to sale in order to avoid a tax liability.

Date the Accounts

Show the starting date (the date of death) and the end date (the date the adminis-tration ends or the date of interim accounts). This will clarify which tax year you are dealing with.

List all assets

It is important to itemise all assets (not just those which are encashed) and what happens to them. This is because assets transferred to a beneficiary count as a distribution to that beneficiary when calculating the amounts to be shown on their tax return.

Keep a note of sub-totals

Make sure that you keep a record of income received each tax year and within each year, work out a sub-total for each income source. Even if you don't show this information directly in the accounts, it will help you to fill in the Statement of Residuary Income Forms 922 and also the tax certificates R185 (Estate Income).

Highlight gross income and the date received

It is the date of receipt which determines the fiscal year for which you complete the tax return. Bear in mind that if you do not receive a return, the onus is on you to ask the Revenue for the relevant tax return under Self Assessment.

If you do not receive a tax return and there are capital gains or untaxed income to report:

– Advise the Revenue before the 5 October after the end of the tax year (eg before 5 October 2000 for the tax year 1999/2000).
– Submit the tax return by 31 January following the end of the tax year in order to avoid the automatic penalty (eg by 31 January 2001 for 1999/2000).

However:

– If you miss the 5 October deadline but subsequently ask for the tax return and submit it with the tax by 31 January, you will avoid any penalties or interest.
– If you don't know which tax office deals with the estate's affairs, contact the tax office which dealt with the deceased during his lifetime and explain the position.

Keep running totals of any capital gains

Calculate the capital gains as they arise and keep running totals for each fiscal year. If the gains exceed the losses at the end of year, a tax return should be submitted. (Also be aware that if the gains exceed the annual exemptions at the end of the first three fiscal years, a tax return should be completed.) The procedure is as above. But do remember to retain enough cash to pay the tax due on the following 31 January.

Record distributions to beneficiaries

Note the date of all distributions to the residuary beneficiaries as they occur. Remember that any transfer of assets counts as a distribution, so list these transfers as well as cash payments. The dates will tell you the tax years for which R185s are needed. Remember the R185s must be given to the beneficiaries in good time for them to meet the deadlines on their personal tax returns ie 30 September or 31 January following the end of the tax year.

General tips

Interest on TESSA or ISA accounts is taxable after the date of death.

PEPS lose their tax exemption on death. Thereafter income and gains are taxable.

The sale of the deceased's main residence may not be exempt from CGT – check to see whether the concession applies.

Income accrued and not paid at the date of death, but which is shown on the IHT 200 should be included as part of the estate income when it is received. Relief from double taxation can be claimed on form 922 by noting the relevant amounts. (However, it is only worth doing this calculation if a beneficiary pays higher rate tax.)

Deduct administration costs for R185 (Estate Income) calculations

When you work out income less deductions for the R185 calculations, you can deduct part of the administration expenses relating to income. Unless bills are rendered separately, you will have to estimate the amount which can be deducted, but it is important to reduce the tax liability for beneficiaries who are higher rate taxpayers. Deductions can be made for the 'management of assets of the estate properly chargeable to income'. This includes the cost of completing the income tax part of the tax return and completion of the Statements of Residuary Income and preparing the relevant figures for forms 922 in addition to the R185s.

Interest on loans for IHT

Record the dates on which you pay interest on any loans taken out to pay IHT. The interest is tax deductible so include it on the tax return. However, if you would not otherwise submit a tax return because there is no untaxed income or capital gain, you can claim a tax repayment against the estate's income which is taxed at source.

Interest on tax

Although interest on a loan to pay IHT can be deducted against estate income, any interest on IHT or other tax is only deductible against the beneficiaries' higher rate tax – and then only if they have limited interests in residue. No relief is given if the beneficiaries have absolute interests. All other income management expenses will reduce the beneficiary's higher rate tax whether limited or absolute interest.

Keep specific legacy income separate

Keep a separate record of income from assets which are specific legacies and advise the relevant legatee so that he can put the appropriate amounts on his annual tax return.

16.7 RECEIPTS FOR LEGACIES

This article first appeared in [1992] *Gazette*, 14 October. It is reproduced here, edited and with a revised draft of the recommended receipt and discharge wording approved by the Law Society's Land Law and Succession

Committee. Mr Richard Oerton revised the original wording of the receipt and discharge for the journal *Clarity*. This version is identical to Mr Oerton's with one minor change.

Receipts for payment of legacies

Periodically the Law Society receives complaints from beneficiaries who have been asked by solicitors administering an estate to sign receipts for their legacies before payment is made. This has been considered by the Land Law and Succession Committee (now the Wills and Equity Committee).

It should now be standard practice for all solicitors to write to legatees and beneficiaries early in the administration of an estate to inform them of their legacies and entitlements and then, when funds are available, to pay legatees and beneficiaries direct by cheque, unless other arrangements have been made.

The Committee (except as stated below) considers that it is no longer reasonable or necessary for legatees and beneficiaries to be asked to sign receipts in advance of payment and that such a practice is bound to generate additional correspondence and thus to add unnecessarily to the cost of the administration of the estate.

Precedents for simple forms of receipt for the payment of pecuniary, specific and residuary legacies are available. However, solicitors may find it more convenient to ask the legatee or beneficiary to acknowledge receipt by signing and returning a duplicate copy of the letter accompanying the cheque. In any case, Cheques Act 1957, s.3 provides that: 'An unindorsed cheque which appears to have been paid by the banker on whom it is drawn is evidence of the receipt by the payee of the sum payable by the cheque.'

Solicitors are also reminded of the protection for cheques which is afforded by the 'account payee' crossing under the Cheques Act 1992.

With regard to residuary beneficiaries, the estate accounts will first have to be approved by the personal representatives. When that has been done, solicitors should then, in most cases, proceed with the final distribution by sending the residuary beneficiaries copies of the approved accounts, and cheques in payment, with a request that the beneficiaries acknowledge payment by signing a receipt either endorsed on the accounts or supplied separately; the receipt to include, if needed, a discharge to the personal representatives.

If difficulties have arisen during the administration, there may be occasions when solicitors, before making final distributions, wish to make sure that the residuary beneficiaries are not going to object to the amounts. In such cases the residuary beneficiaries should be sent, in advance, copies of the approved accounts and be asked to sign a form of receipt and discharge to the personal representatives on the basis that they will be sent a cheque immediately upon the solicitors receiving back the signed form.

It is recommended that the receipt and discharge should be in the following form:

THE LATE_____

The estate accounts show the final sum due to me as £_____

I approve the accounts and will accept that sum in full satisfaction of all my claims against the estate.

Please pay it by a crossed cheque in my favour and send it to me by post.

Finally, it must be remembered that a discharge will only be fully effective if the beneficiaries have been given full details of all the assets and liabilities of and all dealings with the estate.

16.7.1 Problems with legacies to minors

PRs need to consider who can give a good receipt on behalf of a minor. First, look at the will to see whether it authorises parents or guardians to give a good receipt on behalf of the minor or whether it authorises the minor to give a good receipt at a specified age (usually 16).

Even in the absence of such authority PRs do not need to hold the legacy until the minor is 18. If the legacy is contingent, there will usually be trustees appointed who can hold the legacy. If it is absolute, the PRs can appoint trustees under Administration of Estates Act 1925, s.42 to hold the legacy.

There is a further alternative. In an interesting article in (1997) 1 *Private Client Business*, 37, Michael Waterworth of 8 Gray's Inn suggests that there is not (and has not been for some time) any problem with receipts for legacies to minors. As a result of the Children Act 1989 all parents with parental responsibility have the same rights, powers and duties as guardians appointed under Children Act 1989, s.5. These rights are set out in s.3 and include:

> the right to receive or recover in his own name *for the benefit* of the child, property of whatever description and wherever situated, which the child is entitled to receive or recover.

The words in italic indicate that the parent or guardian will hold the property in a fiduciary capacity.

16.8 CHARITABLE BENEFICIARIES

There are a number of special factors to bear in mind if a charity is left a substantial gift. The rest of this chapter highlights the important issues. We are grateful to the Charity Commissioners for their advice, and the help of the Institute of Legacy Management and Brian Walsh of Hempsons in revising those parts of the Handbook covering charities, has been invaluable.

16.8.1 Charities and wills

Charities now work very hard to maximise their legacy income. Because of the importance legacies have for charitable funding, you will find that the larger charities in particular are very knowledgeable about their rights and entitlements and are very experienced beneficiaries. You can expect them to be well organised and efficient. Remember that charities have a responsibility to protect their trustees against any claim that the charity has not sought its full entitlement.

Where a charity is a residuary beneficiary, you are not *obliged* to inform them that they have been named in the will. Harman J reviewed the relevant case law in *Cancer Research Campaign* v. *Earnest Brown & Co.* [1997] STC 1425 and said:

> Until an executor is fully satisfied that there has been a complete payment of all debts, he cannot be under any obligation whatever to pay any legacy or, to my mind, to give notice to legatees of their prospective gain.

However, although there is no obligation to inform a charity (or any other legatee), it is good practice to do so. You will probably find that the charity contacts you anyway as many charities subscribe to a notification service, so it is better to take the initiative. The charity will appreciate being sent a copy of the will and if possible a schedule of assets and liabilities to give an idea of their possible entitlement.

Certain charitable and other residuary beneficiaries are entitled to obtain a remuneration certificate, see Chapter 2.

16.8.2 Checklist: charitable beneficiaries

The following reminders should help avoid problems:

1. *Changed circumstances.* A charity may feel a moral obligation to renounce part of its entitlement under a will (or even make a payment from the estate) if there are grounds for believing that, in the events which have happened, the will does not in fact carry out its maker's intentions. The charity will need full details of the circumstances justifying the payment.

   A charity normally needs authority from the Charity Commissioners to make an ex gratia payment. They have a discretion to refer individual cases to the Attorney-General for a decision. Applicants can have their cases considered afresh by the Attorney-General if the Commissioners refuse authority. The Charity Commission's leaflet CC7 explains the procedure (see Appendix 6). In [2001] *Probate Section Journal*, March, Michael Carpenter, Legal Commissioner at the Charity Commission made three points:

   – The application to the Commissioners must come from the trustees of the charity who must regard themselves as under a moral obligation. The Commissioners will not entertain an application from executors, members of the family, disappointed beneficiaries or their advisers.
   – Where there is a genuine dispute, for example an Inheritance (Provision for Family and Dependants) Act 1975 claim, the ex gratia regime is irrelevant. The charity has a power to compromise claims.
   – A disappointed beneficiary may allege that a solicitor prepared a will negligently. A negligence action against the solicitor would not

involve the charity so the charity would have no power to compromise it. However, *Walker* v. *Medlicott & Son* [1999] 1 WLR 727 determined that in appropriate circumstances a disappointed beneficiary might be expected to bring a rectification action. The charity would be affected by a rectification action and, therefore, might use its power to compromise. It would only consider compromise 'where there is a genuine case which is likely to be successful'. There may be cases where a rectification claim might fail for technical reasons unconnected with the substantive merits. The Commissioners will consider an ex gratia application from the charity in such a case provided the charity considers that it would be morally unacceptable not to carry out the deceased's wishes.

Changes do not always work to a charity's advantage – a gift may be adeemed, for example, and clients should be warned about this possibility when making a will.

2. *Wrong descriptions.* Problems of a different kind are caused by wrongly describing the intended charity in a will.

Responsibility for correctly reproducing the institution's current name rests with the draftsman. Brightman J said in *Re Recher's Will Trust* [1972] Ch 526 that it was his 'elementary duty' not only to get the name right but to ensure that the institution was in existence at the date of the will. It is possible to check registered charities on the Charity Commission's website **www.charity-commission.gov.uk**. If a charity is not registered, check its details with its treasurer.

Where the name is wrong solicitors would expect to have to apply to court for a direction on how to apply the legacy. However, in a very useful article in [2001] *Solicitors' Journal*, 22 June, Victoria Forwood of the Government Legal Service Charities Team explained the procedure for applying to the Attorney-General for a direction under the Royal Sign Manual. Such a Direction identifies the charitable beneficiary whose identity was previously uncertain. The PRs then administer the gift in accordance with the direction. Examples of such gifts are to 'the Cancer Research Trust', 'the association for the preservation of tropical rain forests', the Ethiopa Fund. The procedure is quick (weeks unless there is a dispute) and cheap – the Attorney-General does not charge.

3. *Charity dissolved.* The case of *Re ARMS (Multiple Sclerosis Research) Ltd* [1997] 2 All ER 679 highlights a particular problem in relation to incorporated charities. In that case a charitable company overspent and went into liquidation. The court had to decide whether legacies to the charity taking effect after the date of the winding up order but before dissolution were payable to the liquidator – so as to be available to the company's creditors – or whether, as the Attorney-General argued, the

legacies were given and should be applied for the charity's purposes. The court directed that all the legacies were payable to the liquidator.

This case is significant for the probate practitioner when administering an estate and also when drafting wills including legacies to incorporated charities. The draftsman should consider adapting the standard amalgamation/dissolution clause to create a substitution or to give executors a discretion where a legatee is in liquidation at the date of death but not yet formally dissolved.

This decision also illustrates the clear distinction between incorporated charities, which take legacies beneficially in their own right, as opposed to unincorporated charities which take for their charitable purposes. Gifts to incorporated charities are much more likely to fail if the charity no longer exists at death than gifts to unincorporated charities which are more likely to take effect as gifts for the purposes of the defunct charity. It is, therefore, particularly important when drafting gifts to incorporated charities to include substitutional gifts or to give the executors a power to apply funds to similar charities. It made no difference that one of the legacies in the *ARMS* case was expressed to be 'for the general purposes' of the charity.

4. *Conditional gifts.* If your client wants to give a gift on condition, find out from the charity whether the terms of the gift will be acceptable or feasible; alternatively, provide in the will for what is to happen if the charity declines the gift.

It is also important to make clear what is to happen if it is impossible to carry out the condition at the time of the testator's death (e.g. a gift which is conditional on a charity caring for the testator's pets and at the time of the testator's death there are no pets). Failure to do so will result in uncertainty and possible litigation. (See *Watson* v. *National Children's Home* [2001] WTLR 1375). There is a useful article in [2001] *New Law Journal*, Christmas Appeals Supplement, 3 December by Lucy Hickman summarising points to bear in mind when drafting gifts to charities.

5. *Delayed distribution.* If your client wants to enable the PRs and trustees to be able to distribute a gift over an extended period of time, you need to draft this carefully. The Commissioners' Annual Report for the year 1990 highlights the decision in *Re Muller's Estate* (unreported) which concerns a gift using a precedent in *Williams on Wills* (6th edn) vol. 2, p.1185. It was held that the gift implied that distribution would be made within a reasonable time, and hence this formulation may not be suitable if your client wishes to provide otherwise.

6. *R185E. Form* R185E – annual certificate of tax deduction – is especially important to charities. They need these certificates for each tax year of the administration, as evidence that tax – which they can reclaim – has been deducted. The Institute of Legacy Management reports that firms sometimes say that there is no need for form R185E because their client

account pays gross. However, it is important to remember that charities can reclaim not only tax on income which has arisen during the administration period, but also tax which has accrued prior to the date of death and not been paid (e.g. building society interest) – but not without form R185E. The repayments form a valuable addition to the funds available to charities. The amounts may be small in each individual estate but the total is a significant addition to charities' income.

Solicitors' failure to issue these forms is a complaint frequently made to the Law Society and it is the responsibility of the firm undertaking the administration, and not the bank or building society, to prepare them and send them to beneficiaries. Having to produce these forms is a chore but as the charities will continue to ask for them, producing them early will allow the file to be closed more quickly.

Complete form R185E with the tax district reference number. Without this number, charities cannot reclaim the tax shown on the certificate.

If the deceased was a non-taxpayer, and you do not have the tax district reference number, you can solve the problem by writing to your local tax office. Send a copy of the estate accounts and ask the Inland Revenue to waive the need for tax returns for the administration period. The local tax district reference number can then be quoted on form R185E. (See also at 16.10.4 below.)

7. *Charities Act 1993.* If a will leaves land to a charity, both the charity and the executors must comply with Charities Act 1993, ss.36 and 37. An absolute gift to a charity of a house, for example, means that the charity can require the executors to transfer or assent the property to it: from the date of assent the charity must comply with the Act's provisions in relation to sale.

A gift to a charity, for example, of a house, on condition that it will permit another beneficiary to occupy it for life, means that the executors' freedom to sell the property is curtailed. Because they hold the property on trust for the charity, the executors too are bound by ss.36 and 37 of the Act, even before assent.

8. *Interest.* Interest will be due on legacies not paid at the end of the executors' year and may be due beforehand.

9. *Form of gift.* Discuss with the charity the best way for them to receive the gift: in some cases appropriation in specie may allow the charity to sell an asset and thus save CGT. The charity may customarily use a particular auction house or estate agency, with which they may have a special arrangement relating to fees, which may also be able to assist. Appropriation of assets can be done on paper, that is, without any necessity physically to transfer securities. The sale is then made as bare trustee on behalf of the charity. It is, however, important to have a written record of the appropriation. See point 14 and at 16.9.5 below.

10. *Deeds of variation.* Consider deeds of variation to make the gift in the most effective way (see the points set out at 16.10 below).

11. *Exempt and non-exempt beneficiaries.* If the residuary gift is to both exempt and non-exempt beneficiaries, the problem of how to distribute the estate in the light of Re Benham arises. See at 16.9 below.

12. *Early notice.* Sending a copy of the will at an early stage alerts a charitable residuary beneficiary to its entitlement and enables it to put forward its own wishes for the PRs' consideration. Obtaining the PRs' consent to briefing the charity on progress can also be worthwhile. However, PRs remain, of course, obliged to act in the interests of the estate as a whole, not just those of one particular beneficiary.

13. *Interim distributions.* Consider whether one or more interim distributions can be made. The Institute of Legacy Management comments that some firms only write to charities when the administration is complete, sending their first letter, estate accounts and cheque all together. The justification is that it saves costs. Crispin Ellison of The Institute of Legacy Management says that most charities would agree to a little more in costs in return for more information during the administration and some interim distributions. He also comments that while banks charge more, their level of service in providing regular information and in their accounting is superior.

14. *CGT.* CGT may be more easily reclaimed by the charity if an exchange of letters has taken place between the solicitors acting in the estate and the charity beneficiary, authorising the sale.

15. *VAT.* Charities are no longer able to recover VAT on costs associated with sales made in relation to land or buildings.

16.9 THE PROBLEM OF *RE BENHAM* AND *RE RATCLIFFE*

The case of *Re Benham's Will Trust, Lockhurt* v. *Harker, Reed and the National Life Boat Institution* [1995] STC 210 caused great problems for PRs. To some extent they have been alleviated by the later case of *Re Ratcliffe* [1999] STC 262. [The notes at 16.9.1 *et seq* have been written specially for us by Chris Whitehouse, Barrister of 2 Stone Buildings and we are most grateful to him for doing so.]

As a general rule a testator is free to decide where the burden of inheritance tax is to fall. Specific gifts are, in the absence of any direction to the contrary, tax free with the tax being paid out of residue. To preserve the value of exempt transfers, however, and notably of gifts to spouses and charities, IHTA 1984, s.41 provides that:

Notwithstanding the terms of any disposition:

(a) none of the tax on the value transferred shall fall on any specific gift if or to the extent that the transfer is exempt with respect to the gift; and

(b) none of the tax attributable to the value of the property comprised in residue shall fall on any gift of a share of residue if or to the extent that the transfer is exempt with respect to the gift.

In a simple case where residue is split between chargeable and exempt beneficiaries (for instance, between the testator's son and his wife) any tax attributable to the son's share must be borne out of that share; no part of that tax can come out of the portion of residue passing to the surviving spouse.

16.9.1   When is it necessary to consider *Re Benham* and *Re Ratcliffe*?

In practice, difficulties only arise if residue is split between chargeable and exempt beneficiaries. Commonly this occurs when part of the residue is left to charity with the rest passing to the relatives of the testator. A will leaving a specific legacy to charity with residue to the testator's family does not, therefore, give rise to problems. A second point to bear in mind is that *Benham* is concerned with the calculation of inheritance tax on the chargeable portion of an estate. Accordingly, if that portion falls within the testator's nil rate band, no computational difficulties can arise.

16.9.2   Grossing up a chargeable share of residue

Given that IHTA 1984, s.41 prevents tax on a chargeable share of residue from being borne by an exempt share, how can the wishes of a testator that the net residue after payment of all expenses and IHT is to be divided equally between (say) his wife and daughter be satisfied? Only, it is thought, if the will provides for the chargeable share (in this example the daughter's share) to be grossed up to include the tax which is charged on it.

Illustration

Assume net residue of £100,000 to be divided equally between surviving spouse and daughter, estate rate 40 per cent.

- Option 1: deduct tax on £50,000 and divide balance (£80,000) equally: prohibited by s.41.
- Option 2: divide equally so that spouse gets £50,000 and daughter gets £50,000 but then bears tax so that she ends up with £30,000.
- Option 3: gross up daughter's share (X) so that both end up with the same, i.e.:

$$X + \frac{100X}{60} = £100,000 \quad X = £37,500$$

Both receive £37,500; gross value of daughter's share is £62,500.

	Spouse (£)	Daughter (£)	Tax Man (£)
Option 1	40,000	40,000	20,000
Option 2	50,000	30,000	20,000
Option 3	37,500	37,500	25,000

The facts of Re Benham's Will Trust

In this case, under clause 3 of the will residue was left as follows:

- upon trust to pay debts, funeral and testamentary expenses;
- after such payment 'to pay the same to those beneficiaries as are living at my death and who are listed in List A and List B hereunder written in such proportions as will bring about the result that the aforesaid benefic-iaries named in List A shall receive 3.2 times as much as the aforesaid ben-eficiaries named in List B and in each case for their own absolute and beneficial use and disposal'.

List A contained one charity and a number of non-charitable benefici-aries; and List B contained a number of charities and non-charitable ben-eficiaries. By an originating summons, the executor sought, *inter alia*, the opinion of the court on the following questions:

- whether the wording in clause 3(b) meant that each qualifying beneficiary in List A should receive 3.2 times the sum taken by each beneficiary in List B, or whether the List A beneficiaries should between them receive 3.2 times the total sum taken by the List B beneficiaries;
- whether, in view of IHTA 1984, s.41 and the terms of the will, the non-charitable beneficiaries should receive their shares subject to IHT, or whether their shares should be grossed up; and
- whether the shares of legatees who predeceased the testatrix accrued by survivorship to the other legatees or became applicable for the payment of funeral and testamentary expenses and debts.

The deputy judge agreed that the choice between the two interpretations of clause 3(b) was not so clear that it could be said that there was no real doubt or ambiguity and he admitted extrinsic evidence under Administration of Justice Act 1982, s.21(1)(b). He then concluded that clause 3(b) directed payment of the residue to two groups of beneficiaries and, whilst the persons named in Lists A and B, respectively, took as between themselves in equal shares provided that they survived the testatrix, the part of the residue avail-able to List A beneficiaries to share equally between them was a fund 3.2 times as large as the fund available for the List B beneficiaries.

On the second question, there were three possibilities:

- the non-charitable beneficiaries received their respective shares subject to IHT, which would mean that they would receive less than the charities;
- the non-charitable beneficiaries should have their respective shares grossed up, so that they received the same net sum as the charities; or
- the IHT was paid as part of the testamentary expenses under clause 3(a), and the balance was distributed equally between the non-charitable beneficiaries and the charities.

The deputy judge agreed that the third possibility was precluded by IHTA 1983, s.41. However, he did not agree that the charities should receive more than the non-charitable beneficiaries. The plain intention of the testatrix was that each beneficiary, whether charitable or non-charitable, should receive the same as the other beneficiaries on the relevant list. That result, he concluded, was consistent with the express terms of the will and s.41. Thus, he considered that the non-charitable beneficiaries' shares should be grossed up.

Finally, clause 3(b) made it a condition that any named beneficiary should be living when the testatrix died. Thus, the deputy judge said, the two funds should be divided between the beneficiaries in the two lists, after deleting those who had died.

16.9.3 Difficulties arising from *Re Benham*

The main difficulty posed by *Re Benham* lies not in the actual facts of the case (which were obviously somewhat unusual!), but in the assertion of the judge that 'the plain intention of the testatrix is that at the end of the day each beneficiary, whether charitable or non-charitable, should receive the same as the other beneficiaries'.

This view, if correct, would appear to result in the implication (as a matter of construction) of a grossing up clause in all cases where:

(a) the residue is left to be divided between exempt and non-exempt beneficiaries;
(b) the will provides for them to take in equal shares and there is no evidence that the testator did not intend *Benham* to apply; and
(c) the value of the estate is such that IHT is payable on the chargeable portion of residue.

This approach goes against the existing practice which had been to apply s.41 in such cases.

16.9.4 Attitude of Inland Revenue (Capital Taxes)

The attitude of the Inland Revenue to the *Benham* case and the consequent problems of construing and drafting wills can be gleaned from the following exchange of correspondence.

The British Heart Foundation wrote to Inland Revenue Capital Taxes in the following terms:

Re: Benhams Will Trusts
The British Heart Foundation, like many other charities, is alarmed at the potential threat to its income if, as has been widely propounded in the legal press, the decision in the above case is applied in cases where the will is drawn not in the terms of the *Benham* will but in the very much more common terms usually applied.

The cases I refer to are of course those involving gifts of residue to exempt and non-exempt beneficiaries, where the will directs the executors to pay IHT and legacies and then divide the residue. Our concern is that if the *Re Benham* judgment is applied then non-exempt beneficiaries wrongly benefit from the exempt status of organisations such as ourselves, contrary to s.41(b) of the IHT Act 1984; that is that charities as a whole could lose a great deal of money, part of which will effectively go towards paying the IHT of non-exempt beneficiaries, contrary to our charitable objects.

We at the Foundation believe that *Re Benham* really turns on the rather unusual terms of the will and has no general application to bequests of shares of residue between exempt and non-exempt beneficiaries as expressed in the common cases outlined above. We and other charities are currently considering two cases to be put to the court, but clearly a decision may take some time. Whilst this information may hold off executors from distributing estates along the lines of *Benham*, we would be obliged however if you would confirm the following: that the CTO's view is also that the *Re Benham* decision is inapplicable for this more common type of provision and that in such cases no IHT will arise that will deplete charitable shares of residue as a result of the *Benham* decision.

The CTO's response indicates that they will abide by a proper construction of the will (so that the fact that extra tax is payable if grossing up applies is not a factor to be taken into account):

We consider the decision to be primarily concerned with ascertaining the intention of the testatrix and hence as not directly involving the Inland Revenue. In an attempt to be helpful, however, we would comment as follows.

Like you, our view is that the decision followed from the particular facts of the case with the court deciding that the plain intention of the testatrix was that at the end of the day and therefore after the payment of tax each beneficiary whether charitable or non-charitable on the respective lists should receive the same amount as the other beneficiaries in that list.

Generally speaking the court is concerned in such cases to establish the intention of the testator or testatrix from the wording of the will and admissible extrinsic evidence. If the will is drafted in common form with a direction to ascertain residue after payment of funeral and testamentary expenses and debts followed by a bequest of that residue then it is focusing on the ascertainment and division of disposable residue rather than on what each residuary beneficiary is to receive. Accordingly wills so drafted would not appear to involve *Benham* style grossing up computations. P. Twiddy

16.9.5 *Re Ratcliffe*

The testatrix gave her residuary estate to her trustees (the plaintiffs) on trust, after payment of her debts and funeral and testamentary expenses, to hold one half for the two sons of her cousin ('the cousins') in equal shares absolutely, and the other half for four charities ('the charities') in equal shares.

The charities contended that the two half shares of residue were to be calculated after providing for the debts and funeral and testamentary expenses (and three legacies) but before payment of the IHT due on the cousins' half share. The cousins would thus receive less because of the deduction of tax. The cousins contended that there were to be equal half shares of net residue after payment of the appropriate amount of IHT, which was to be treated as a testamentary expense. They argued that this equality was to be achieved, as in *Benham*, by grossing up their beneficial share of residue to produce an initial unequal division of residue which would leave equal amounts once the tax was paid.

Blackburne J held that it was a question of construing the will to decide what the testatrix had intended. The wording used was a common form trust for sale. Blackburne J found that while the testatrix could have left her residue to be divided unequally as the cousins contended, there was nothing in the wording used to indicate that this was her intention.

Of *Re Benham* he said this:

> The difficulty that I feel about that decision is that, with all due respect to the deputy judge who decided it, it is not at all clear why he came to the conclusion that the testatrix's plain intention was that 'at the end of the day each beneficiary, whether charitable or non-charitable, should receive the same as the other beneficiaries in the relevant list'.

He went on to say that had he thought that *Benham* laid down some principle, then, unless convinced that it was wrong, he would have followed it. However, he did not consider that it did and, accordingly, was not bound to follow it.

16.9.6 Practical advice on the distribution of residue

(a) Whenever an estate which exceeds the nil rate band is to be divided between exempt and non-exempt beneficiaries, it is necessary to consider the wording of the will to determine whether or not the basis of division is clear.

If the will clearly provides for the beneficiaries to receive equal amounts (*Benham* division) or unequal amounts (*Ratcliffe*) division, that is the end of the matter. For practitioners who find themselves in the unenviable position of having to perform a *Benham* calculation there is an interesting article on software available to do the job in [1997] *Private Client Business*, April, 197–202.

(b) If not, everything turns on a correct construction of the document. A relevant exercise is to calculate the IHT that would be payable on the alternative bases of:

(i) applying IHTA 1984,s.41; and

(ii) grossing up.

It will normally be the case that, if grossing up occurs, the tax take is increased; chargeable beneficiaries get a greater slice of the estate and the loser will be the exempt beneficiary (i.e. either spouse or charity).

(c) When the only beneficiaries of the residue are family members (typically therefore the surviving spouse and children) it is often possible to agree an approach which will resolve the difficulties. Commonly the children will be prepared to accept that *Benham* should not apply thereby ensuring that more is received by their mother than would otherwise would be the case (and, of course, that less is received by the Inland Revenue!).

(d) If a 'deal' is not possible then counsel's advice may be taken and the executors may then act in accordance with his opinion. Executors should always be warned that it does not prevent them from being sued by disappointed beneficiaries and in reality the absolutely safe course is to go to the court for directions. (Note, in this connection, that the court's general power to excuse executors and trustees under Trustee Act 1925, s.61 depends on the executors satisfactorily showing that a failure to obtain the court's directions before carrying out the relevant distribution was not culpable.)

(e) If full agreement cannot be reached between the beneficiaries as to what is to be done then the executors may decide to apply s.41 if an indemnity is given either by the charity or by the surviving spouse. Given the uncertain value of such indemnities and the difficulties of enforcement, this approach cannot be wholeheartedly recommended.

Note: When drafting a will where residue is to be divided between exempt and non-exempt beneficiaries, make clear whether the division is to be equal before consideration of IHT (*Ratcliffe* division) or whether the beneficiaries are to receive equal amounts after consideration of IHT (*Benham* division). The following are examples of suitable precedents.

***Benham* division**

I declare that the shares of my estate of any beneficiaries who do not qualify for exemption from inheritance tax shall be deemed to be of amounts such that the amounts received, after payment of inheritance tax due, shall be the same for all the beneficiaries named in clause –.

> **Ratcliffe division**
>
> I declare that if the share in my estate of any beneficiary named in clause –
> does not qualify for exemption from inheritance tax, that share shall bear its
> own tax. so that the amount received by each beneficiary named in that clause
> is the same before the payment of inheritance tax.

16.9.7 Importance of assent or appropriation of assets to charity entitled to residue

Charities benefit from CGT exemption in respect of gains realised on the disposal of assets if the gains are applicable and applied for charitable purposes (see Taxation of Chargeable Gains Act (TCGA) 1992, s.256). However, the exemption will only apply if the relevant property is beneficially owned by the charity. If, during the administration of an estate, an asset, which has increased significantly in value since the date of death, is to be sold, it will be important either for the assets to be vested in the name of the charity prior to the sale, or for the executors to execute an assent declaring that they hold the asset for the charity absolutely. Failure to take these elementary steps will mean that the gain will be realised by the executors and not by the charity and the Inland Revenue may claim CGT on the gain realised, even if the benefit of the sale proceeds will ultimately pass to the charity. The need to consider appropriation before sale is a good reason for consulting charities early in the administration.

A specimen memorandum of appropriation is available on the solicitors section of the ILM website **www.ilmnet.org.uk**.

Many of the major charities have very helpful notes advising executors on the correct procedure. We print by way of example the note issued by the Guide Dogs for the Blind Association:

> May we please draw the attention of the executors and their advisers to the fact
> that as a national charity we are exempt, under the provisions of TCGA 1992,
> s.256(1), from payment of capital gains tax on the sale of any securities made
> on our behalf.
>
> The exemption relates to any sale made on our behalf in respect of the
> residue or shares of the residue of the estate to which we are entitled.
>
> The procedure to be followed to comply with Inland Revenue requirements is
> that the securities should be appropriated to our account by a simple but clear
> designation in your books, or by a memorandum or resolution signed by the personal representatives in your files. Any sales subsequently made by you are
> made as bare trustee on our behalf under TCGA 1992, s.60.

Executors should be careful if they require an indemnity from the charity for the payment of administration expenses in return for the transfer of assets to the charity. The Revenue may argue that such an indemnity is to be construed as a payment for the asset and accordingly a sale by the executors, or alternatively that the gain realised by the charity is not fully applicable and applied for charitable purposes.

16.10 ADMINISTRATION EXPENSES

[The notes below are based on an article originally published in [1991] *Gazette*, 15 February by Alan Jarvis, a partner in Wilde Sapte & Co. We are most grateful to him for allowing us to adapt and update it.]

16.10.1 Administration expenses and IHT

Most administration expenses are not deductible for IHT purposes. Careful planning at the time of the preparation of the will can, however, achieve an additional benefit whereby the administration expenses will, in effect, be deductible for IHT purposes.

For example, a testator leaves an estate of £642,000 with a gift to charity of £200,000 and the balance of the estate passing to a nephew absolutely. The IHT position will be as follows:

	£
Value of estate	650,000
Legacy to charity	200,000
Residue to nephew	450,000
Less	
Inheritance tax on residue	(80,000)
Administration expenses	(6,000)
Net amount received by nephew	364,000

An alternative approach might be to give the nephew a specific legacy which after the payment of IHT, would leave him a net sum of £356,000. The residue of the estate would then pass to the charity. The revised IHT position will be:

	£
Gross legacy to nephew	440,000
Less inheritance tax on legacy	(76,000)
Net legacy sum due to nephew	364,000
Residue	210,000
Less administration expenses	(6,000)
Net residue payable to charity	204,000

Similarly, a benefit can be given to charity where none previously existed at no extra cost to a beneficiary:

Intended disposition	£
Gross estate due to beneficiary	650,000
Less inheritance tax	(160,000)
Net estate	490,000
Less administration expenses	(6,000)
Net amount received by beneficiary	484,000

Alternative disposition	£
Legacy to beneficiary	
(£484,000−£250,000 grossed up at 40%	
+ £250,000)	640,000
Less inheritance tax	(156,000)
Net amount received by beneficiary	484,000
Residue to charity	10,000
Less administration expenses	(6,000)
Net amount received by charity	4,000

16.10.2   Use of discretionary wills

Fine tuning to the degree mentioned in the above examples is not normally possible at the time of preparing the will since the estate is likely to alter in nature or value before death. Consideration might be given to two alternative approaches.

First, the testator may wish to consider the establishment of a two-year discretionary trust established under the will (see IHTA 1984, s.144). If a discretionary trust is established by will, any distributions or appointment from the trust within two years of death will be treated for tax purposes as a disposition under the will occurring on death. The advantage, as demonstrated in either of the above examples, can be achieved with full knowledge of the value of the deceased's estate. The disadvantage of a discretionary trust is particularly that the Inland Revenue will seek to charge inheritance tax in full on the application for the grant of representation, even if subsequent appointments from the trust may invoke spouse or charitable exemptions. This problem may be avoided by the executors exercising their discretionary powers before making the application for the grant since, unlike administrators, executors' powers commence upon death. (Do be careful not to make a distribution from the trust within three months of the death or the advantages of s.144 will be lost. This trap is pretty well known but *Frankland* v. *IRC* [1996] STC. 735 shows that people can still get caught out.)

Secondly, it is still possible to effect a post-death variation of the will of the deceased under IHT 1984, s.142.

16.10.3 Administration expenses and income tax

As most expenses of administration are not deductible for income tax, they will be paid out of the income of the administration which has borne tax at the basic rate. This will reduce the income which is distributed to the charity and, therefore, the scope for a repayment claim as the charity cannot reclaim the tax deducted from the income used to pay income expenses. The fewer expenses which are attributable to income, the greater will be the tax repayment to the charity. However, without specific power to pay income expenses out of capital, the level of expenses which are attributable to income will not be determined according to the executors' discretion but according to the law.

It may be appropriate to include in a will a direction that the executors shall have the power to pay administration expenses out of capital or income at their discretion, thereby enabling the executors to attribute all expenses to capital and allowing the charity to effect a full recovery of all basic rate tax paid.

In the absence of this power, it is important for the executors to ensure that no more than the correct amount of expenses is set against income. The matter should, however, be given careful thought and not merely determined by reference to the usual rough and ready estimate. Certain expenses may, upon a careful analysis, be properly attributable to capital rather than income.

16.10.4 Tax credits and charities

In the 1997 Budget the Chancellor announced changes to the system of tax credits. From April 1999 the rate of tax credits is 10 per cent and tax credits are no longer payable to shareholders with no tax liability. The tax credit continues to satisfy the tax liability of taxpayers in the lower and basic rate tax bands.

To compensate charities for the loss of tax credits the government will make payments to charities equal to a percentage of their dividend income. This was 21 per cent in 1999/2000 falling to 4 per cent by 2003/04.

16.10.5 Inspection of charities' records

The Inland Revenue have produced a helpful booklet entitled CoP5: *Inspection of Charities' Records* giving the Code of Practice in this area (see their website for further information). If you have any complaints relating to the application of this Code of Practice you should contact the Financial Intermediaries and Claims Office (see Appendix 6).

The Charity Commissioners have a useful website **www.charitycommission. gov.uk**.

CHAPTER 17

Probate practice checklist

Solicitors in private practice may adapt or adopt these checklists for the purpose set out on page iv but not for any other purpose.

17.1 PERSONAL REPRESENTATIVES AND PLANNING CHECKLIST

Before you begin to deal with the assets and liabilities have you:

1. Obtained clear instructions from the personal representatives (PRs)?
2. Explained to the PRs:

   - their duties;
   - the nature and extent of the work to be done;
   - what is included in your retainer;
   - costs, charging, expenses;
   - Inheritance (Provision for Family and Dependants) Act 1975, statutory advertisements, deeds of variation, plus time limits – and noted relevant dates in your diary;
   - potential hold-ups: elapse of survival period, Inland Revenue Capital Taxes, etc.;
   - any welfare benefits relevant and how to apply? (See Chapter 9.)

   Sent to PRs:
   - information letter (see Chapter 3);
   - client care letter/leaflet (see Chapter 3);
   - copy will?

3. Obtained your clients' addresses and phone and fax numbers and their availability?
   Agreed reporting frequency and logged dates in your diary?
   Agreed billing frequency and logged dates in your diary?
4. Established an anticipated, realistic, timetable for completion of the administration?
   Confirmed this to PRs?
   Established target dates for completion of each stage?

Logged these into your diary? Plus six-month and 12-month anniversaries of death and other significant dates such as two-month anniversary of statutory advertisements?

Established whether there is any need to obtain the grant urgently? If so, and if inheritance tax (IHT) is payable, checked with the Inland Revenue on possibility of submitting account with estimated valuations.

5. Checked will for validity?

Contacted witnesses if affidavits are necessary?

Checked gifts for ademption, lapse, contingencies, etc.?

Checked form of ownership of assets (sole name, joint tenancy, co-ownership)? In case of assets which appear to have passed to the deceased by survivorship, checked whether there might have been severance by mutual agreement at an earlier stage?

6. Obtained PRs' consent to contact residuary beneficiaries with copy will and estimated timescale?

Obtained PRs' consent to contact legatees with estimated timescale?

7. Confirmed beneficiaries' and next of kin's addresses with PRs?

Taken steps to trace any missing beneficiaries?

Considered whether statutory advertisements are appropriate? The cost may not be justified where the executor is taking the entire estate.

If appropriate, inserted statutory advertisements?

8. Informed:

- deceased's bank or building society;
- other professional advisers;
- insurers;
- others?

Obtained figures for balances of funds held, accrued interest, etc.?

Arranged valuations?

Included balances and valuations on draft accounts?

Obtained details of deceased's tax office and current position?

9. Established whether deceased was a member of Lloyd's?

If so, decided whether:

- it is safe to rely on indemnities or insurance,
- or whether it is necessary to apply to court under *Practice Statement: Chancery Division: Estates of Deceased Lloyd's Names* [2001] 3 All ER 765 for leave to distribute without making provision for contingent liability in the event of Equitas being inadequate?

Made application, if necessary?

10. Begun to prepare the accounts by:

- listing all assets and estimated values;
- deciding whether specialist advice is needed;
- listing all liabilities?

11. Prepared list of asset holders needing to see the grant of representation?
12. Considered with PRs the method of payment of IHT.
    Made the necessary arrangements? (See para. 13.35 for specimen letter to a bank to arrange a 'global' loan facility.)
13. Established the nature of money coming into the office in terms of the Solicitors' Accounts Rules 1998 requirements? (See Chapter 5.)
14. Considered whether variation desirable?

17.2 IMMEDIATE PRACTICAL ACTION CHECKLIST

Items   *For action by Family/Us*

1. Register death.
2. Check for directions re disposal of body in wills, personal assets log, and amongst papers.
3. Arrange funeral/cremation (as directed if appropriate).
4. Notify time, date and place to family.*
5. Deceased's house:

   - remove valuables (if to office, does our insurance cover value? Do any special conditions, e.g. regarding guns, apply?);**
   - arrange maintenance (e.g. drain water system) if appropriate;
   - cancel deliveries, e.g. milk, papers;
   - redirect mail;
   - lodge keys securely, not marked with address;
   - deal with insurers, landlord and council tax as appropriate.

6. Deceased's car:

   - inform insurers;
   - transfer insurance, etc., if to be used by family;
   - arrange for security if not to be used.

7. Livestock and pets:

   - arrange for their immediate welfare;
   - check if prior long-term arrangements have already been made with friends or family (the Law Society personal assets log includes a point on pets);
   - if not, pedigree pets may sometimes be returned to the breeder; otherwise the Kennel Club, Cat Fancy and welfare organisations could help (addresses in Appendix 6).

   * Some firms counsel clients not to announce the death in the local or national paper, nor the funeral, because many families have – almost unbelievably – come back from the funeral to find the house has been burgled.
   ** See the helpful article on firearms in this context by Peter Sarony in [1995] *New Law Journal*, Probate Supplement, 29 September.

17.3 TESTATE ESTATE CHECKLIST

1. Is the will valid and properly signed and dated, with an appropriate attestation clause, and correctly witnessed? If not, list remedial action needed and advise the client.
2. Is this definitely the last will? Are there any codicils?
3. Is there likely to be any dispute about the validity of dispositions included in the will? Did the testator or testatrix marry or divorce after the date of the will? Are any of the presumptions, e.g. capacity, validity, etc., likely to be rebutted? If so, is there any evidence of the circumstances surrounding the execution? Can the witnesses be traced if affidavits have to be obtained? List remedial action, and advise the client.
4. Does the will refer to unexecuted writings, chattels by memo, etc.? Is there a letter explaining why a person has not been provided for in the context of an IPFDA 1975 claim? Is a claim likely? (See Chapter 10.) Advise the client.
5. Is there any evidence of secret or half-secret trusts? If so, have the requirements for validity been met? If the will contains precatory words, can they be complied with?
6. Is there any evidence of an agreement that will should be mutual? If so, where the death is of the first testator make sure that the existence of the trust now binding on the property of the surviving testator is clearly recorded; if the death is of the surviving testator remember that the terms of any will left by the surviving testator cannot overrule the terms of the trust imposed on the death of the first testator.
7. If the will refers to contingencies, have they been satisfied?
8. Is all the property referred to in the will available for beneficiaries, or have any gifts adeemed?
9. Have all beneficiaries been traced? Do any gifts lapse?
10. Have any legacies been adeemed by subsequent lifetime gifts as a result of the doctrine of satisfaction?
11. Is the estate solvent?
12. Is there any evidence of PETs and other transfers?
13. Is a variation appropriate?

17.4 INTESTATE AND PARTIALLY INTESTATE ESTATE CHECKLIST

1. The death: if the deceased and spouse or partner died together in an accident, remember 14-day survivorship period applies to spouses but not to others. Does this affect this estate? Advise client.
2. Has a search for a will been made? (If it is thought a will was made, the 'Wills and Whereabouts' page in the *Gazette*, local solicitors, the deposit facility at the Principal Registry (see Appendix 6) and enquiry of the deceased's bank, friends and relatives may all be of assistance.)

3.   Will the estate be solvent? Does it exceed statutory legacy limits of £125,000/£200,000? How will the existence of any undisposed-of property affect the payment of debts?

4.   List the surviving relatives; in more complex cases drawing up a family tree is usually easier than describing relationship. Can they all be contacted? Will there be any problems establishing identity and relationship? Might there be an IPFDA 1975 claim? (See Chapter 10.)

5.   Establish who will be entitled to the estate; note minor children's ages and the years in which they will attain majority.

6.   Establish who will take the grant. Will two administrators be needed?

7.   How will the statutory trusts apply, if at all?

8.   Does the spouse wish to redeem the life interest and/or appropriate the matrimonial home? Log the 12 months' deadline from the issue of the grant into the diary. Does the value of the matrimonial home exceed the value of the statutory legacy? What arrangements need to be made for equality money?

9.   Is there any evidence of PETs and other transfers?

10. Is a variation appropriate?

17.5   THE OATH AND AFTER CHECKLIST

1.   List assets and liabilities.

2.   Is an Inland Revenue account required? (See paras. 14.3–14.4). Which pages?

3.   Prepare oath and Inland Revenue account.

4.   Send tax cheque to Revenue.
     Lodge papers and receipted D18 at Probate Registry.
     Order plenty of office copies – it is false economy to order too few.
     Does timetable need adjusting? If so, inform PRs.

5.   Prepare for payment of debts. Will assets need to be sold? If so, contact PRs and residuary beneficiaries:

     • Which ones? Arrange valuations if necessary.
     • Consider tax implications – deed of variation?

6.   Update draft accounts.
     Update other lists.
     Review file generally, especially initial letters, and check expiry dates and deadlines – review schedule if necessary and advise client.
     Are charities interested in estate? If so, check whether they wish assets to be appropriated to them to avoid unnecessary CGT
     Check proceeds of sale of shares and land against probate valuations to see if assets qualify for IHT loss on sale relief (IHTA 1984, ss.178–189). If so, claim relief and file corrective account.
     Check proceeds of sale of assets generally against probate valuations to see if there are gains or losses for CGT purposes.

7. Log in diary due dates for IHT interest payments in relation to instalment option property, if appropriate.
8. Interim bill? (Did you agree this with the PRs in advance?)
9. Interim distribution? May be advisable to avoid a beneficiary receiving a large income receipt in one tax year pushing beneficiary into higher rate tax unnecessarily (see Chapter 16).

17.6   OBTAINING THE GRANT CHECKLIST

[This checklist, with reminders, has been specially revised and reformulated by Kevin Donnelly, Chief Clerk at the Probate Registry, Somerset House, and we are most grateful to him for doing so, and for permission to use it.]

YES/NO

Oath form

1. *Extracting solicitors*

    - Has your name, address (including post code), DX number and reference (if required) been included at the heading of the oath?

2. *Name of deceased*

    - Does the name correspond with the will (if any)?
    - If not, or if an alias is necessary for any other reason, has the true name been identified and the reason for the alias been set out in the oath by way of a footnote?
    - Was the deceased known by any other name or was the death registered in any other name? If so, these should be included on the oath (although these names may not appear on the grant).

3. *Address of deceased*

    - Has the last residential address been included? (A short stay in hospital can be ignored for these purposes.) Include post code.

4. *Names of applicants*

    - Are these the true names?
    - Do they correspond with the will (if any)?
    - Is an affidavit of identity required?
    - Has the applicant included any extra initials in his or her signature to the oath? (Any extra initials should be investigated and the oath resworn to show the true name if necessary.)
    - Include address and post code

5. *Survival clause in will*

    - Does the will contain a clause providing that the executor or executrix must survive by a specified period before the appointment becomes effective?
    - If yes, has the period expired?

6. *Date of death*

    - Does the date of death given in the oath agree with that on the death certificate? (If the death certificate does not give a specific date of death, the oath should state when the deceased was last seen or known to be alive and when his or her body was found.)

7. *Codicil*

    - Did the deceased leave any codicils to the will?
    - If yes, has reference been made to them in the oath?
    - If yes, have they been marked in accordance with Rule 10 of the Non-Contentious Probate Rules (NCPR) 1987 by the applicant and swearing Commissioner?

8. *Age of the deceased*

    - Has the age and date of birth of the deceased been included in the oath?

9. *Domicile of the deceased*

    - Has the domicile of the deceased been included in the oath? (If the deceased died domiciled out of England and Wales and different systems of law operate within the country, the state of domicile must be shown, e.g. the State of Victoria, the State of New Jersey.)

10. *Settled land*
    - Has the clause concerning settled land been included/completed? (This clause must be included in every oath.)

11. *Life/minority interest*

    - Did the deceased leave a will?
    - If yes, is the executor or executrix appointed in it applying for the grant?
    - If no, or if the deceased left no will, does a life or minority interest arise out of the estate?
    - Has the appropriate section in the oath been included/completed? (The oath must state, in terms, whether a life or minority interest arises unless an executor or executrix is applying for the grant.)

12. *Title*

   - Have all the persons with a prior entitlement to the applicant been accounted for in the oath?
   - Has the applicant's title been stated in full? (Unless all clearings have been included and the title stated in full the oath is certain to be queried and is likely to require reswearing.)

13. *Value of the estate*: Is the estate an 'excepted estate'? (See para. 14.3.)

   - If yes, have the band figures appropriate to the date of death been included in the oath?
   - Has the net estate been stated to the nearest thousand?
   - Have the words 'and this is not a case in which an Inland Revenue account is required to be lodged' (or similar) been included in the correct clause? (Failure to include this clause will result in the oath having to be resworn.)
   - If not, and the deceased died domiciled in England and Wales, has the total of all the estate passing under the grant been included?
   - Does this total agree with that shown in the Inland Revenue account?
   - If not, has an explanation for the difference been included in the oath?
   - If the deceased died domiciled out of England and Wales, has the relevant clause been amended to refer to estate only in England and Wales? (It is possible to have an 'excepted estate' for a deceased who died domiciled in Scotland.)

14. *Jurat*

   - Has the oath and will/codicil(s) (if any) been signed by (all) the applicant(s) and swearing Commissioner(s)?
   - Has the oath been dated and the place of swearing stated? (Please bear in mind that the oath and any supporting affidavits cannot be sworn before the solicitor extracting the grant or a member of his or her firm.)

Special types of application

1. *Attorney grants*

   - Has the limitation to be recited in the grant been included in the oath? (The usual limitation is 'for the use and benefit of – [*the donor*] and until further representation be granted'.)

2. *Grants for minors*

   - Are there two applicants?

- Is it necessary to lodge a nomination of the second applicant?
- If the application relies upon court orders, are court-certified copies available?
- Does the oath state that a minority interest arises?
- Does the oath have the correct limitation? (The usual limitation in such application is 'for the use and benefit of – [the minor(s)] until he/she/one of them shall attain the age of 18 years'.)

3. *Domicile out of England and Wales*

- Has the domicile of the deceased been described correctly?
- Have those facts upon which the deponent to the affidavit of law (if any) has relied when reaching his or her conclusions been included in the oath or another sworn document? (These facts are usually recited in the affidavit of law following the words 'I am informed and verily believe' or similar. If they are not sworn, the application will be delayed whilst the oath or affidavit is resworn.)
- Have the words 'in England and Wales' been added to the clause dealing with the estate?
- Are any foreign court documents to be used in support of the application copies certified by the court?
- Has the correct form of Inland Revenue account (IHT 201) been completed and controlled by the CTO?
- Has any necessary order under the NCPR 1987 been obtained or approved? (It may not be necessary to have the order drawn before swearing the oath but prior approval of the district judge or district probate registrar must be obtained.)

4. *Lost wills*

- Has the original will been seen since the deceased's date of death?
- Was the will known to have been in the possession of the deceased up to the date of his or her death?
- If the answer to the first question is no and the second yes, does the evidence in support of the application rebut the presumption of revocation of the will by the deceased in his or her lifetime?
- Can the authenticity of the copy will be confirmed?
- Does the affidavit in support of the application exhibit the copy will to be proved?
- Does the oath in support of the application for the grant describe accurately the copy will being proved? (It is suggested that the affidavit(s) in support of the application be prepared in draft form in the first instance to enable any further evidence required by the district judge or registrar to be incorporated.)

Wills and codicils

1. Has the testator or testatrix signed the will?

- Has the will been witnessed by two witnesses?
- Does the will contain a properly worded attestation clause?
- Has the will been dated?

(Although these are obvious points, a large number of wills are rejected by the probate registries each year for these simple defects. The factors also apply to codicils. It may still be possible to prove a will/codicil with any of these defects if validity can be established under the Wills Act 1963.)

2. Does the will/codicil have any unattested alterations or additions?
3. Is there a valid appointment of executrix/executor(s)? (Care should be taken to ensure that the appointment is correctly worded; if there is any doubt, evidence of the testator's or testatrix's intention will be necessary.)
4. Did the deceased leave any codicils to his or her will?

- If yes, are they all available?
- Is the appointment of executors affected by the codicil?
- Does the codicil confirm the will by the correct date? (If the date is not correct, evidence that the right will is being proved may be necessary.)

5. Have the will and codicils (if any) been marked by the applicant(s) and swearing Commissioner(s) in accordance with Rule 10 of the NCPR 1987?

Inland Revenue accounts

1. Has the correct account, appropriate to the date of death and type of application, been used?
2. Has the account been signed and dated by the applicant(s)

- Does the account need to be controlled by the Inland Revenue? (Although any account may be controlled, generally speaking this need be done only in the estates of persons who die domiciled out of England and Wales.)
- Is the date of death of the deceased before 13 March 1975?
- If the answer is yes, has the Inland Revenue account been sworn? (NB This is a requirement.)
- Has the certificate regarding payment of IHT been signed?

Fees

1. Has the correct fee been paid?
2. Does the payment include the fee for any copies ordered?

17.7 COLLECTING THE ASSETS, PAYING THE DEBTS CHECKLIST

1. Cancel/obtain refund/collect/return/pay/check:

   - council tax;
   - social security payments;
   - trade union or professional association subscription – and some death benefit may be payable;
   - club and other memberships such as charities, libraries, pressure groups, voluntary organisations, political parties and consumer and motoring organisations;
   - subscriptions: journals, magazines, book clubs;
   - borrowed items: library books, records, videos, hospital equipment such as wheelchair;
   - payments made in advance by deceased, e.g. gas or electricity account may be in credit;
   - payments due to deceased which may be in arrears, e.g. pension;
   - laundry or dry cleaning, or items sent for valuation or repair;
   - items on hire: TV or washing machine, computer, possibly evening or formal dress;
   - relevant direct debits/standing orders, etc., at bank or building society;
   - milk, papers and other deliveries;
   - passport;
   - credit cards.

2. List all the assets and refunds and include a column for noting what happened to the asset, its value and relevant dates.

3. Is there any property abroad? How will this be dealt with? Do foreign law rules conflict with the will or the intestacy rules? Specialist advice may be needed.

4. Valuation: some items may be more valuable than one might expect.

   Certain charities, such as the PDSA, offer house clearance services (others may advertise in local papers and free sheets) but ensure that nothing possibly of value is overlooked. See specialist valuers address list (Appendix 6) for items needing an expert's opinion.

5. Send office copies of the grant to asset holders – use standard letters on a word processor to save time and get plenty of office copies, too few is a false economy. Include a request in letters to bank, building societies, etc., for all the necessary paperwork for closure of accounts to be sent.

6. Keep standard letters to creditors on a word processor to save time. Send these early so that relatives are not troubled by reminders about bills.

7. Make a list of all the deceased's liabilities, with columns for the dates and amounts of payments. Tick each off as it is dealt with.

8. Ensure that assets in your office are insured and listed, and any special regulations (e.g. re guns, antique or modern) are observed.

9. Pay bills promptly when funds becomes available – if this takes time, does the timetable need adjusting? If so, advise the client.
10. It may be helpful to keep all the paperwork related to paid debts – bills, receipts and correspondence, etc. – in a separate file once they are no longer current matters.

17.8 ACCOUNTING AND DISTRIBUTION CHECKLIST

1. Prepare any corrective account for IHT which has become necessary. For small amounts, correspondence may suffice.
2. Make interim distributions, but reserve enough money for outstanding tax, costs and other contingencies. Consider ensuring that PRs and residuary beneficiaries are satisfied with the draft accounts before making large distributions.
3. Ensure arrangements for payment of tax by beneficiaries have been made, where necessary.
4. Offer beneficiaries receiving substantial legacies your firm's investment advice if you are authorised. See also Chapter 4 on undertaking investment business.
5. Do any beneficiaries need:

   - wills?
   - codicils?
   - tax advice?
   - enduring powers of attorney?

6. Have all beneficiaries received forms R185E where appropriate? This is particularly important for charities who will need to obtain refunds of income tax.
7. If problems in obtaining a discharge arise consider insurance, payment into court under Trustee Act 1925, s.63, etc.
8. Have the important dates for protecting PRs passed – two months for statutory advertisements, six months from date of grant for IPFDA 1975 claims? (See Chapter 8 on probate time limits.)
9. Prepare accounts (or have them prepared for you).
10. Obtain receipts and discharges from beneficiaries (see para. 15.25).

17.9 CLOSING YOUR FILE CHECKLIST

1. Is your file closure letter satisfactory?
   It is an important document as it should stand proof that you have completed your work satisfactorily. To perform this function it shoud incorporate the following points:

261

- It should explain why the file has been closed. This is usually because the matter has been completed. However, the client may have changed solicitors or decided to deal with the matter in person. This needs to be fully explained so that the client cannot allege later that you were still instructed. It is particularly important where you were retained to deal with only certain aspects of the administration.
- It should explain exactly what work your firm has done and what the outcome was. There may be a misunderstanding between what you have done and what the client thinks you have done. It is better for the client to realise this at a time when further instructions can be given easily.
- It should set out clearly any tasks which the client has to perform (for example, the payment of instalments of inheritance tax) with, if necessary, exact timings and the consequences of failing to adhere to those timings.
- Consider sending two copies of the letter to your client asking for one to be signed and returned.

2. Which documents belong to the client?
   See *The Guide to the Professional Conduct of Solicitors 1999* ('the Guide'), Principle 12.11 and 12.12, and Annex 12A, 'Guidance: ownership, storage and destruction of documents'.
3. How long must the file be kept? See the Guide, Annex 12A para. 4 'How long should I retain old files?'.
4. Which documents should be preserved? This list is not exhaustive:

- documents belonging to the client;
- documents of title;
- significant correspondence with the Inland Revenue, returns, accounts, etc.;
- court orders;
- valuations (it may be advisable to supply probate valuations to non-residuary legatees – otherwise they will contact you in the future if CGT becomes an issue for them).

5. Consider asking the client if any old, but non-essential, documents could be of interest to a local history society or museum.
6. Could any of the letters or documents you prepared form the basis of stock letters for future use by you or within the office? If so, consider keeping these in a separate, indexed, precedent file.

17.10   EVALUATING CHECKLIST

Ten things I know now I wish I'd known then:

1.

2.

3.

4.

5.

6.

7.

8.

9.

10.

PART IV

Profitable Probate

Much of this Handbook is intended to help with cost-effective case and file management. This Part of the book looks more widely at practice management and the organisation of work in the office both generally and individually, so it is hoped it will be of interest whether or not you have management responsibilities.

CHAPTER 18

Computing and technology issues

Charles Christian

Charles Christian is a former practising barrister turned independent writer and commentator who has been following developments in legal technology and online legal services since the late 1970s. He is the publisher of the industry newsletter *Legal Technology Insider* and an adviser to the Law Society on its 'Software Solutions' scheme. This chapter was specially written for us by Charles Christian and we are most grateful to him for doing so.

18.1   INTRODUCTION

Thanks to the high profile coverage computer systems and information technology (IT) related matters now enjoy in the legal press, there is a growing belief among solicitors' practices that computerisation is the universal panacea for all problems. However, while it might be nice to think that if you are not making enough money out of probate practice, the easiest solution is to install a new 'probate case management software' application, not only is this a far too simplistic approach – but it could also prove to be commercially disastrous.

Leaving aside the cost and inevitable disruption (including the time taken up with administration matters that would otherwise be devoted to fee earning) associated with all computerisation projects, you risk running foul of the old computer industry adage – GIGO, garbage in, garbage out. In other words, if your practice has problems, installing a computer will not fix them, it will merely computerise them.

That's the bad news. The good news is that a properly implemented law office computerisation project will yield positive benefits. And in the case of probate practitioners, at the very least this should include reducing the time and overheads associated with individual probate matters, so you can both increase the volume of work you can handle and increase the profitability of that work.

This chapter will therefore be looking at: (1) putting technology in its proper context in terms of practice development and return on investment; (2) the type of IT systems available; (3) how IT can help probate practitioners; (4) how probate practitioners should approach the purchasing of IT systems (the principles of IT procurement); and (5) suppliers of probate systems.

18.2   TECHNOLOGY IN CONTEXT

The starting point for any discussion about legal technology must be with the premise that technology is not an end in itself but merely a tool to help implement a law firm's overall business and practice development plans. In other words the emphasis is upon the creation of a joined-up, rather than a semi-detached, strategy.

Unfortunately too many firms still approach computerisation projects from the wrong direction, putting the proverbial cart before the horse, and make the decision to invest in technology without fully thinking through its longer term implications. Just because the firm down the road has bought a new probate system is not a good enough reason for your firm also to buy one, you need to look at the bigger picture. For example, where is your firm planning to go over the next five years? Will you still be doing private client work? Do you plan to expand or contract your probate practice? Are there any obvious problems with the way you currently process probate work that could benefit from technology? And what benefits do you envisage technology delivering?

The answers to all these questions will help determine your priorities, however particular emphasis should be paid to the issue of the anticipated benefits of technology – or the 'return on investment' (ROI). Solicitors' practices are notorious for fudging the answer to this question and despite the fact that a firm can currently expect to spend about 5 per cent of its annual turnover each year on IT, the method of measuring the ROI is, to put it charitably, naive and unscientific. I have lost count of the number of times I have heard a firm justify some huge expenditure solely on the grounds that 'it will help us to provide a better service to our clients'. This is stating the obvious – of course you hope it is going to help provide a better service, otherwise you would not buy the system. But warm, cosy, touchy-feely sentiments like that will not pay your bills – nor generate the fee income to keep the partnership happy. When assessing ROI the questions a firm should be asking are: 'How much money is this new system going to save us?', for example, will you be able to cut down on the number of staff in the probate department? And: 'How much in extra fees is this system going to help us earn?', for example, will the system enable you to handle more matters with the same staff resources?

Firms should also ensure that any ROI calculations focus upon profitability, as distinct from mere increases in turnover because you are able to generate more billable hours. If this increase in turnover has only been achieved by also increasing your overheads, the slightest downturn in the economy will put pressure on your profit margins, which once again will not please the rest of the partnership. Lecture over, now let's start looking at the technology options available.

18.3 PROBATE SYSTEMS

Probate systems are a confusing area of law office automation in that the same term is often loosely applied by suppliers to a broad range of applications covering everything from will writing software through to investment trust accounting and portfolio management systems. For the sake of convenience I have broken these down into the following seven categories, although for the purposes of this Handbook we will be focusing upon just the last two.

18.3.1 Will writing software

Most of the packages commercially available have been designed for the DIY market or will writing businesses and so are probably unsuitable for probate solicitors in private practice.

18.3.2 Electronic forms and precedents

Arguably a more useful tool for practitioners are the type of systems that contain legal precedents in an electronic format (typically on CD-Rom or via a download from the Internet) so clauses can be selected and automatically incorporated within a will without the need to retype any wording. Some of these products will also incorporate a 'document assembly' or 'document automation' system (the most widely used is currently 'HotDocs') to streamline the process further. However, many firms manage perfectly adequately relying solely on their own word processing precedents.

18.3.3 Wills and deeds registers

This is really just another name for a computerised index of all the wills your firm holds copies of and where they are physically located. Back in the days of stand-alone technology, specific software packages were sold to handle this type of application. Today, with the emphasis in law firm IT on central databases, this type of information will usually be stored within an overall practice management system or else be one of the elements of a probate case management system.

18.3.4 Trusts and portfolio management systems

This area of legal work sees the practitioner moving beyond the conventional bounds of probate practice and into the broader private client/investment/financial services arena which is outside the scope of this Handbook. It is, however, worth bearing in mind that a number of suppliers of probate systems also supply trust accounting and management systems.

18.3.5 Internet systems

At the time of the last edition of this Handbook, when we were just starting to move into the 'dot.com' boom era, there was a lot of excitement about the possibility of law firms selling wills and related services online via the Internet. Events subsequently revealed that this market was illusory, with firms finding there was simply not a commercially viable volume of demand for online wills services. Indeed firms that did go this route have discovered that the fees generated failed even to recoup the cost of the systems needed to deliver such services.

It is also worth noting that online legal services raise the prospect of some potentially truly awful professional indemnity risks. For example, do you really know who the client is, is there impersonation going on and how do you guard against the person making the will, at the other end of the modem link, being subject to duress and undue influence? With the benefit of hindsight we can now see that online services may have a role to play in complementing the delivery of conventional legal services but they will never replace them.

18.3.6 Probate case or workflow management systems

These systems introduce an element of automation to probate work by building a workflow routine that effectively controls the way the work is processed. These can be very useful where work is being handled by a department and the partner in charge needs not only to be able to review and manage the progress of matters but also to ensure that tasks delegated to non-legally qualified staff take place within a sufficiently rigid framework, so there is no room for mistakes to be made.

For prospective purchasers there are a number of issues to consider here. The first is whether they have the volume of work or organisational structure (if your lawyers are not prepared to delegate probate work to more junior staff the introduction of computerisation will merely turn fee-earners into very expensive keyboard operators) to justify the workflow management approach? Firms that do not have the probate business volume may find an accounts system offers a better return on their investment.

Another issue is whether the software is being sold on a stand-alone or integrated basis? For example, some suppliers sell software on a stand-alone basis, so you can buy a probate workflow application and run it out of the box, with or without links to your firm's accounts or practice management software. (This is also sometimes called the 'best of breed' approach.) However a lot of software sold into the UK legal systems market consists of integrated products, so you cannot use one supplier's probate system unless you also install that supplier's accounts system. If you are happy with your existing accounts/practice management system, you will therefore usually find that the cheapest and most hassle-free option is to install that supplier's probate system. It is also worth noting that while some suppliers offer ready-to-go packaged probate workflow applications, most modern general purpose case and workflow management software can be used to form the basis of a probate system.

18.3.7   Probate accounts software

This is used to help practitioners compile estate accounts, print interim statements for beneficiaries and prepare completed IHT returns. Most of these systems also contain some form of workflow management-style diary reminders and checklists. Bearing in mind that the preparation of estate accounts can be one of the most time-consuming features of probate work, this is a system many practitioners would benefit from using. However, do be certain when talking to software sales staff that they do not fudge this issue. Can it really handle all aspects of probate accounts – for example can it produce IHT forms? And do not be fobbed off with promises that although the system currently only offers workflow facilities 'an accounts module is under development'. That is no good, you need to know what it can do for you now, not what it might be able to do at some dim and possibly very distant date in the future. (Some of these systems also handle trust accounting although this is outside the scope of this chapter.)

18.4   HOW PROBATE SYSTEMS CAN HELP PRACTITIONERS

This is a potentially contentious topic, for it does not matter how good a computer system may be in theory, unless a practice is prepared to invest adequately in training – so its members really know how to operate the computers on their desks – the full benefits of the system will never be realised. Whatever else you do, do not skimp on training. Leaving aside this important qualification, there are five potential areas of benefit.

18.4.1   Achieving immediate objectives

There are a number of situations that can arise where computerisation is successfully undertaken to achieve immediate, relatively limited, short-term objectives.

For example, suppose an experienced probate practitioner is heading for retirement and planning to work on a part-time consultancy basis. If the firm still has a healthy probate practice then investing in a probate accounts system that can act as an *aide-mémoire* to another less experienced lawyer and take over some of the donkey work on the estate accounts preparation work may be a cost-effective alternative to replacement of the consultant.

Similarly, if the firm were to win a major commercial client, such as a financial institution, and with it the prospect of a major increase in the volume of its probate work, then installing IT would be a cost-effective alternative to recruiting additional probate department staff. This also meets one of our measurements for ROI, namely how much will this system help us save? (See at 18.2 above.)

18.4.2   Better information

In discussing computerisation most people tend to focus on the 'technology' aspect of 'information technology'. However, we should also remember the 'information' aspect.

Although computers have earned a poor reputation in the past for generating impenetrable reports of monumental length, modern systems are excellent tools for extracting valuable business information from large volumes of data – information that would be almost impossible to obtain (or at least take a long time and prevent staff from getting on with their normal work) using manual methods.

For example, access to detailed information about clients and work types allows firms to be more precise in their marketing and cross-selling efforts, which in the past probably involved little more than sending Christmas cards to every client name on the books, regardless of whether anyone had seen them in the last decade. (This aspect of legal software is increasingly referred to as 'client relationship management' or CRM.)

For firms who anticipate that most of their probate work will be generated from the results of earlier wills campaigns (such as the annual Law Society 'Wills Week') a good information system also allows the firm to become proactive rather than reactive, so clients can be periodically contacted to see if they need to review and update their wills. After all, this year's happily married shopkeeper could be next year's lottery winner with a younger spouse, new family and an increasingly complex network of commercial interests.

18.4.3   Greater efficiency and productivity

One of the more obvious benefits of computerisation is that IT is very good at doing relatively dull repetitive tasks very quickly and accurately, such as adding up long columns of figures. In the probate department this means error-free estate accounts can be prepared within hours whereas previously staff could have been tied up for days. This in turn means the firm now has the capacity to handle more work with the same or fewer resources, so there is no need to recruit extra staff and/or existing staff may be allocated to other tasks. Once again this meets the ROI criteria for saving money and/or helping the firm earn more money.

It is also true that while workflow and case management systems primarily come into their own in the context of helping manage the delegation of routine aspects of work to more junior staff – a particular boon for firms handling high volumes of work – even in those firms where probate work is handled by just one highly skilled solicitor, there can still be productivity gains. For example, there is always a degree of routine work associated with any matter, such as sending out client care letters, replying to correspondence and to enquiries about the progress of a matter, cheque requisitions for official fees, plus associated diary entries and updates to files and archives. This has led to a suggestion that if a workflow system can automate just some of these tasks, perhaps only saving a fee-earner five or 10 minutes a day, in the long term this can add up to a substantial saving in time. (Ten minutes a week is the equivalent of 50 hours a year, the equivalent of £5,000 to £7,500 in fees.)

18.4.4   Better service

Having an IT system also opens up the possibility of offering services to clients which previously firms would have been reluctant to offer because of the additional workload it would have involved. For example, producing interim accounts for the beneficiaries of an estate becomes an automated click-of-a-button operation. Leaving aside the potential for generating extra fees, or taking less time to earn the same amount of fees, the ability to offer additional services is a plus point in terms of establishing a longer-term professional relationship with a client and helping to differentiate your firm from the competition.

18.4.5   Increased profitability

If an IT system can help increase productivity among secretarial, clerical and fee-earning staff, so that the same people can get through more work in the same or less time, then this will clearly have an impact upon the firm's profitability in that it frees staff for additional fee-earning activities. However, computerisation can also bring about an increase in profitability by its potential for reducing overheads.

For example, it is not uncommon to find that smaller firms have an administrative 'tail' with a ratio of 1:2, in other words, for every fee-earner in the firm, there are two back office staff (including secretaries). However, if IT is introduced, so fee-earners can start doing jobs that would have previously involved dictating instructions to secretaries and waiting for them to effect them, it becomes possible to reduce the size of this tail. A 1:1 ratio is the minimum to aim for (typically by sharing secretaries between fee-earners, assigning some secretaries to quasi-fee earning activities and reducing the reliance on 'temps') but many firms have already achieved 2:1 or greater.

Less reliance on support staff does in turn have a number of other benefits. For example, it means it is possible to recruit more fee-earners without also having to recruit a corresponding number of secretaries, which in turn means an expanding firm is likely to outgrow its existing office space less quickly than it would otherwise do.

Clearly having proportionally fewer staff means less is being spent on overheads, which in turns means increased profits. However, bearing in mind the competitive market in which solicitors operate, carrying smaller overheads means firms can also afford to compete on price – for example against banks and other financial institutions – by cutting their margins yet still managing to make some profit on a matter.

18.5 PRINCIPLES OF IT PROCUREMENT

Along with salaries, accommodation and professional indemnity insurance, for many solicitors' practices their investment in a new computer system, or some related form of IT, will be one of the single largest financial commitments they ever take on. Current research suggest firms spend between 2 per cent and 7 per cent of their total fee income each year on IT: small firms average 4 per cent, larger firms just over 5 per cent.

Furthermore, unlike buying conventional office equipment, such as a new photocopier, an investment in IT is potentially going to alter the way a whole firm operates. Book-keepers, secretaries, receptionists, fee-earners, partners and clients will all find that the new technology has some impact upon them and the legal services they either supply or receive. It is, therefore, essential that the IT procurement process is as efficient and problem-free as possible, for if you get it wrong, not only will a lot of time, money and effort have been wasted but the firm's commercial viability and professional reputation may have been irreparably compromised.

18.5.1   Strategy

Most solicitors probably know of 'computing disasters' that have occurred within other firms. However, what is not always appreciated is that the bulk of these disasters stem not from choosing inappropriate hardware or software but from attempts to implement fundamentally flawed IT strategies. The key element to bear in mind here (and I make no apology for repeating part of the message that appeared at the outset of this chapter because it is important) is that IT – even a stand-alone probate system – is not a self-contained entity but is instead merely an enabling technology or tool that should be regarded as an integral part of the practice's overall business development plan. If you want to get your IT strategy right, a firm must first have (or devise) an appropriate general business strategy.

To give a simple example, there is no point worrying about choosing a supplier of probate software, if the firm's only probate practitioner is considering retiring. In addition, any strategy should also take into account the firm's medium-term requirements and longer-term aspirations, for example opening branch offices or diversifying into new areas of practice, such as trust and portfolio management. In other words, do not buy a system that meets your immediate needs, buy one that will also meet your anticipated needs.

The first stage in devising an IT strategy therefore has nothing to do with computers but rather involves drawing up a business or practice development plan. Only once this is in place should partners begin considering how IT can be used to help implement that plan over the next few years.

Next comes the process of drawing up more detailed specifications and requirements – in effect a computerisation shopping list – that will help realise the IT strategy. For example, is the proposed system only going to be used by one fee-earner as a productivity tool? In this case you will typically be looking for a stand-alone software application that will run on a personal computer. Or is probate work to be handled by a department, with different tasks delegated between fee-earning and secretarial staff? In this case a networked case management product is going to be more appropriate.

Whether or not you need to draw up a formal 'Invitation to Tender' (ITT) document is a matter of policy, but you must certainly have a clear understanding of your requirements, if you are to be able to brief prospective suppliers properly and evaluate their responses on a like-for-like basis.

18.5.2   Budgets

It is essential at this stage to consider budgets and the availability of finance to support the proposed investment in IT (whether from cash reserves, leasing, bank loans, etc.). An important factor to bear in mind here is that calculating the overall IT spend is a lot more complicated than adding the cost of PC hardware and a single user software licence together and multiplying it by the total number of users.

Along with hardware and software, there is the cost of installing the supporting network cabling, which in older premises may mean major rewiring and redecorating exercises. There is also the cost of training – and it cannot be stressed strongly enough that it is essential to train everyone who is intended to use computers properly. Then there are the ongoing running costs, including insurance, annual maintenance contracts, renewable software licences (where applicable), hardware and software upgrades, additional training for additional or replacement staff and computer 'consumables' such as replacement laser printer toner cartridges and pre-printed 'continuous' stationery.

As a rule of thumb today, in terms of capital costs, for a probate accounts software package, plus a PC to run it on and training, budget on between £3,000 and £5,000 per user plus a further one-third of this capital cost for each subsequent year by way of ongoing running costs.

18.5.3   Finding a supplier

Having decided what you want to buy and how much you are prepared to pay for it, you are now in a position to look for a suitable supplier. This may seem a daunting task, particularly when you consider the total number of suppliers. However, when broken down into logical stages, it becomes more manageable:

- First of all thin down the number of contenders – if you are not interested in trust accounts, the case management approach or will writing software, drop them from the list.
- Then contact the remaining suppliers for further information, such as brochures and promotional literature containing details of their track records and installations; visit their stands at exhibitions; attend any of the sales presentations they will inevitably invite you to, once they realise you are a prospective buyer; talk to contacts within the profession; reference sites given by the supplier and anyone else who has experience of dealing with them.
- Given the size of the probate systems market, this process will help whittle down the total number of possibles to a shortlist of three or four suppliers. (In fact your choice may be even more restricted if you are looking for software that is compatible with your firm's existing practice management system.) Send these shortlisted companies copies of your ITT document (if you have one) so you can evaluate their responses on a like-for-like basis.
- Visit their premises (or user reference sites) for detailed system demonstrations and discussions about how they would propose to handle the implementation of your project, including training. (Incidentally, do

ensure the staff who will actually be using the proposed new system attend these demonstrations.)

- Follow up any user references that are given and start exploring the contractual terms that are being offered, as this is frequently a protracted stage of the negotiations, not least because you are lawyers and will inevitably find aspects of their contractual wording you disagree with!
- Do take notice of your own business instincts. Your relationship with the supplier does not end the day the new computer goes 'live': you will be dealing with them for at least the next three to five years, so be certain these are people you feel you can trust and work with on a longer term basis.
- Do not be blinded by science. A lot of suppliers are now claiming their respective products are better than those of their competition because they have been developed using 'better' software development tools. This is all 'under the bonnet' stuff. What really matters is the functionality of the software – does it do the job you want it to do, in the way you want it done?
- Be clear what you are getting for your money. For example, how does the supplier of a probate accounts package deal with the fact that inheritance tax rules change at least once a year and this may require both amendments to the way the software calculates returns and the incorporation of new forms to be submitted to the Inland Revenue. So, will you get an automatic update as part of your ongoing software maintenance contract or is this a chargeable extra?
- Finally, do take into account that price should not be the key factor (in fact in many firms it still appears to be the only factor) in the selection process. Along with the ROI issues mentioned earlier, for those firms that lack their own in-house IT resources (and most firms with 30 or fewer staff fall into this category) the availability of what is sometimes called a 'trusted supplier' (someone who can be relied on to help you out in a crisis) is essential. You rarely get this kind of service from suppliers who have been selected purely on the basis of price. It is also arguable that 'implementation' (see below) – including installation, training (especially of lawyers) and ongoing support – is a more important stage than selection.

18.5.4 Implementation

Now you are in a position to place an order. And is that it? Well actually no, for you now enter one of the most sensitive stages – and one where problems can frequently arise because law firms do not devote sufficient management resources to this aspect of the project. At the very least a partner should have responsibility for overseeing the project management side of system installation and implementation.

There is a co-ordination job to ensure that the installation of the network cabling, the delivery of the hardware, the loading of the software and the training of staff to use the new system is properly scheduled and takes place satisfactorily according to a mutually convenient and pre-agreed timetable – for example, you will probably want to avoid the holiday season and the end of your financial year – not least because you will normally be expected to pay for substantial chunks of the system on the completion of each of these stages.

18.6 SUPPLIERS OF PROBATE SYSTEMS

The following list gives details of suppliers (in alphabetical order, with contact details) of probate accounts and workflow software applications. Systems with accounts functionality are marked ▨ , while those that will operate in a stand-alone capacity are marked ▱ . Please note that software applications are regularly upgraded and a number of suppliers are also talking about adding probate accounts functionality to their workflow systems. Suppliers of trust accounting systems have not been included in this list. As also mentioned previously, although your existing legal software supplier may not have a dedicated probate workflow application, it may be relatively straightforward to develop one based on their generic care management system

▨ AIM Professional: 'Evolution Probate' (replaces previous 'TrustCharter' system); estate accounts are produced via Microsoft, 'Word'
Tel: 01482 326971; **www.aimlegal.com**

Axxia Systems: 'Case Manager' (probate workflow templates available)
Tel: 0118 960 2602; **www.axxia.com**

▨ + ▱ Cognito Software: 'Custodiens' (handles trusts as well as probate accounts)
Tel: 01363 775582

▱ DPS Software: 'DPS Probate'
Tel: 020 8804 1022; **www.dps-net.co.uk**

▨ + ▱ Excelsior LawDesk: 'ProbateDesk' (Microsoft 'Excel' add-on. Also 'FormDesk' applications for IHT 200 and residuary income R185 calculations.)
Tel: 01273 494978

▨ + ▱ Isokon Systems: 'Isokon 2' (top of the range system. One of the newer products available, attracting a lot of interest among larger firms)
Tel: 020 7482 6555; **www.isokon.com**

+ Laserform International: 'Probate CaseControl' (product sits mid-way between 'ProbatePlus' and 'Isokon')
Tel: 01925 750020; **www.laserform.co.uk**

+ Lawbase Legal Systems: 'Lawbase Probate Accounts & Case Management'
Tel: 020 7242 1454; **www.lawbase.co.uk**

Linetime: 'Liberate Probate' module (has 'Excel' integration)
Tel: 0113 250 0020; **www.linetime.co.uk**

Mountain Software: 'Probate Accounts & Support System'
Tel: 01476 573718; **www.mountainsoftware.co.uk**

Oyez Legal Software: 'Probate CaseLite' (based on the Pracctice system)
Tel: 020 7556 3200; **www.oyezstraker.co.uk**

+ Paula for Probate: 'Paula for Probate' (PAULA = Professional Accounting User LAnguage) (another new system from the same team behind the Laserform system. Based on Microsoft 'Word' and also sold in conjunction with the Amicus 'Attorney' case and file management system)
Tel: 020 8940 3798; **www.paula-accounts.co.uk**

Peapod Solutions: 'Probate Workflow'
Tel: 020 8574 8288; **www.peapod.co.uk/legal**

Pracctice: 'Osprey Probate' (an accounts module is planned)
Tel: 01432 372100; **www.pracctice.com**

Sanderson IT Systems: 'Galaxy Probate' (also includes workflows for wills and trust administration)
Tel: 0121 359 4861; **www.sanderson.com**

+ Sweet & Maxwell: 'Probate Plus' (developed and originally sold by Law Systems but now exclusively distributed and supported by Sweet & Maxwell. Low cost system popular with small firms)
Tel: 020 7449 1111; **www.sweetandmaxwell.co.uk**

+ Solicitec Legal Systems: 'SolCase Probate' (new system, launched spring 2002, featuring workflow and accounts)
Tel: 0113 226 2000; **www.solicitec.com**

Videss: 'Legal Office Probate'
Tel: 01274 851577; **www.videss.co.uk**

CHAPTER 19

Managing private client business for profit

Gill Steel

19.1 OVERVIEW

- Why plan at all?
- Obtaining commitment – stemming the decrease in profits
- Reviewing existing services and the competition
- Tactics, action plan and review
- Structure of department and staffing issues
- Knowledge management and IT
- Risk assessment and quality management systems
- Marketing

19.2 WHY PLAN AT ALL?

Pressure on the management of law firms is increasing day by day. Within recent memory, the legal profession has undergone many major reforms and faces continued criticism over self-regulation. This is coupled, in the wider business world, with the development and introduction of sophisticated information technology packages which streamline and improve performance, and the introduction of quality management procedures.

In broad terms, the impact of these (and other) radical reforms have to a large extent passed probate practitioners by. The move towards the introduction of quality management procedures was largely driven by the Legal Aid Board's Franchise Specification, which mostly impacted on contentious departments. Until recently, there has been little investment within probate departments in integrated case management systems. Overt promotional activity has been more directed at will making than at probate work.

As a result, most probate departments, in management terms, have not had to cope with significant change. Probate practitioners have been a steady, reliable but unchanging group producing constant, profitable fees in reasonable volume.

This perception and situation should change – indeed, must change in the light of pressures affecting the profession as a whole. The profession is faced with an unpalatable economic scenario in which both traditional sources of core income are under threat: e-conveyancing and the growth of the large property transaction offices and the lack of profit and increased bureaucracy in the provision of publicly funded court work. The major reviews in government within the public sector including the introduction of e-conveyancing, and major reviews of the work of the Probate Service and the Inland Revenue Capital Taxes Office (CTO) also mean that the way in which probate is delivered and the way in which the probate practitioner operates must change.

Margins throughout the firm are becoming tighter. As a result, partnerships are seeking to develop other remunerative areas of practice. The attention of the managing partner is inevitably turning towards the ever-reliable probate department as a source of significant levels of fee income and profit – and probate practitioners need to respond to this challenge by providing not only an efficient and friendly service for the client, but also an increasingly profitable income stream for the practice.

Such a situation demands a reconsideration of the way in which probate is delivered. Without in any sense compromising on the quality of work delivered or the relationship with the client, efficiency must be sought, revenue must be maximised and systems must be streamlined.

Probate practitioners need to look to their management systems to improve efficiency and enhance performance.

19.3   OBTAINING COMMITMENT: STEMMING DECREASING PROFITABILITY

Some firms do not have an overall business plan. Hopefully, these may be few in number. Even with an overarching firm plan some probate lawyers may not be familiar with the idea of a departmental plan. However, without a business plan it is impossible to stretch or challenge existing perceptions of what is reasonable and difficult to evaluate progress and performance. A departmental plan will identify the strategy, set the objectives to be achieved and provide that yardstick against which to measure successful performance.

Having a business plan for your department is not a foolish notion. It does not matter how small or large your department is, the need to know what you are trying to achieve and whether you have done so is just plain common sense. How else will you know whether investments made were cost effective? How else will you choose appropriate staff in the future?

Sometimes it helps to get started if you pose for yourself and your colleagues a really wild question just to get the creative juices flowing. For example, if you could invest £500,000 in the next year (over and above your firm's current available funds) with the goal of achieving a thriving, more competitive and secure practice:

- What would you spend it on?
- Why would you choose those particular things/actions?
- How would you set about it?
- Who would be responsible for actioning it?
- When would you expect to achieve it?
- How would you know you had achieved it?

Once you have done some freewheeling with those questions for a large sum ask yourself why were those your priorities and can any of those ideas actually become reality. Gain your partners' agreement that there is a balance to be had between the short-term issues of maintaining cash flow and profitability now whilst at the same time investing resources in the future success of the practice by developing new ways of meeting the clients' needs in the future. This includes finding enough time for managing the practice and the department. You will need time to reflect, plan and implement any changes effectively.

Concentrate on setting up a strategy for your core business: if private client work is at the centre of your firm then it is important that you have a strategy for it to improve the overall profitability of the firm. Be creative about considering new ways of doing things! Do you have a culture of 'but this is the way we do things around here'? Why? Trying to improve competitiveness requires changing habits – your habits and those of your partners. Change can be a painful process. Managing change needs new skills, management skills, not just professional skills.

Sveiby and Lloyd in their book *Managing Know-How* (see Appendix 5) identified 10 success factors for a professional organisation. How does your firm match up?

- *Day to day leadership.* This is not just the technical ability to conduct the work but rather possessing the basic skills and attributes of the successful leader, which include: the ability to help others succeed, not just strive for your own success; the need to have a set of principles and to enthuse and motivate colleagues to achieve their roles; the requirement to have constructive new ideas on how to improve the practice and productivity of the team and the ability to act as the team's coach, both collectively and individually nurturing and challenging everyone to achieve the identified goals.
- *Quality control.* The need has never been greater to identify the client's real requirements and at the same time acknowledge the standards of professionalism required to meet those requirements and those of the regulators. The more people in your team or conducting work of this type the more important it is to have control over the outputs to minimise disappointing the client, reduce negligent errors and to enhance reputation.

  It is widely accepted that clients do not take into account technical competence when evaluating the 'quality' of the service they experienced –

unless they are lawyers themselves how can they know whether they have been given the 'right' advice? Instead they rely on how the service was delivered. Was it:

- reliable?
- responsive to their needs?
- accessible?
- courteous?
- a process of communication: information provision and active listening?
- credible?
- secure?
- tailored to the specific client?
- performed in satisfactory offices, by appropriately dressed staff using effective equipment?

- *Respect for know-how.* Know-how is value-added information, the sort of information that arises out of complex problem solving. Law firms must therefore be know-how businesses since you sell your ability to produce solutions to often complex problems. In the probate team you are often dealing with technical details over taxation and sometimes difficult family problems based on solid experience from having tackled similar problems in the past. A firm needs to respect the building and sharing of know-how as it is the main asset it is selling.
- *Combination of professional and managerial know-how.* It is important not just to identify, develop and share know-how about technical matters but also about the management of the department and firm. The successful Head of Department will not just have basic knowledge and information about the probate system and law but needs the skills and attributes of the manager such as analytical, problem-solving, decision-making skills; social skills and abilities; emotional resilience to cope with difficult situations; the ability to respond proactively to events; creativity; mental agility; balanced learning habits and skills (an independent learner with a 'helicopter mind' which can move between the theoretical and the practical) and plenty of self-knowledge so that s/he can identify when personal factors are influencing the decision-making process.
- *A strong, well-defined culture.* So often it is the culture of a firm that is either enabling or inhibiting to successful change. Every firm has a culture whether it has been explicitly identified or not. Effective managers need awareness of and understanding of the power dynamics within their firm. To get things changed will require the ability to identify where a particular source of power is in play and whether there is a particularly under-used source of power that can be brought into play.
- *Focus on core know-how.* Firms that know what their clients actually want, as opposed to what the firm thinks they want, are on the right track to identifying what know-how is required to produce what the client wants.

Firms that have focused on the main know-how to achieve what their client base wants have proved to be the most successful in terms of repeat business and recommendation.

- *Know-how preservation.* Since know-how is hard to come by, as it is as much about experience and practice as it is about technical knowledge, capturing and preserving it when key staff leave is difficult to do but some firms are led by people who have identified that it is a key success factor for the future of their firm.
- *Developing the people.* As we cannot do everything ourselves and remain sane it is vital that any professional service firm employs people who it recognises need to be continually developed to attain the changing skills relevant to the job in hand. More needs to be done by firms to help people find out what it is to serve a client, and about how to work with people, whether they are your juniors, your seniors or your colleagues.
- *Changing key people.* The marketing adage that 'people buy people' is certainly true of private client practice in law firms. A successful firm will properly ensure succession planning so that when people change a client is kept informed and retained rather than left floundering.
- *Stable structures.* If you want to achieve or maintain a successful firm then you need to create or preserve stability. Looking only at the short term does not help you to develop policies for long-term stability.

The above ideas should have got your creative juices flowing. It will be apparent that if you have not got a commitment from all the equity partners (the owners of the business) to spend some of your time on planning, managing and implementing the plan (non-chargeable work), then if your firm focuses only on personal billing levels you will find yourself being criticised. Far better to explain what you propose doing so as to ensure your sanity and your partners' equilibrium. Also, if all the partners decided independently to re-organise their area of work or department at the same time then the firm's cash flow would take a nose-dive!

If you are to spend time thinking, planning and coming up with ideas to develop your area of practice then you are going to need to *delegate* some of your fee-earning work to other people: junior people. Why do you not do this already?

- Great emphasis is placed on personal billing; in a recession there is a danger that senior people hoard what work there is to maintain their personal level of billing.
- The practice does not hold the individual partners responsible for finding ways of reducing the costs of the way the firm delivers the particular legal service; partners are usually only responsible for finding and doing the work.
- There is a reluctance to 'invest' time in coaching and supervising staff and yet people are the key resource in know-how businesses.

- *Fear*: that if you delegate you will have to find other work of a more complex nature to do and may feel out of your depth.

If you are going to succeed in planning for change not only do you need the support of the owners of the firm but also of the staff in your department, office or firm – your team. You must work hard to ensure that you have a well-integrated, effective and supportive team in place. This requires talking to all in the team, both individually and as a group, about their concerns, views and ideas. Do not use this as an opportunity to criticise but rather to listen and learn. Research and practice shows that a well balanced team will outperform any other team.

A group of people become a team if they have:

- a strong leader;
- respect for one another;
- a clear idea of what is expected of them and why;
- an incentive to share resources for the benefit of each other;
- an ability to resolve conflict between themselves;
- an interest in their own future.

19.4 IDENTIFYING YOUR BEST OPPORTUNITIES: REVIEW EXISTING SERVICES AND THE COMPETITION

As a team you should review everything:

- Consider what is going on in the world at large: the demographic changes making it an ageing population; Government policy making the provision of care for the elderly a major area of concern; the social structure making it less likely for families to care for their old folk; the technological revolution making it easier to work from home and more important to harness its power to remain competitive; the state of the economy which affects the 'feel good factor' of not just potential clients but also the partners and staff.
- Examine what services are currently offered by the firm in this area, e.g. wills, probate, enduring powers of attorney (EPAs), living wills, tax advice, help with care in the community decisions.
- Identify current and future potential competition in the area from all sources for these services, e.g. other law firms now (rivalry amongst existing firms), but also will-writing companies and individuals making their own wills (substitutes for your service) and accountants looking to expand into probate services in the future (threats from new entrants to the field).
- Review which of the services are profitable (and why) and which are not (and why). What determines profitability?

285

- How much does it cost to deliver the service, e.g. overheads, staff salaries?
- How much are buyers prepared to pay for the service? If they can do it themselves and see no perceived valued in what you can do, then will they really pay?
- Can you minimise the costs and maximise the price?

- Consider which agencies and bodies provide services and information to the elderly locally and tap into them.
- Decide what resources you already have available or are prepared to commit to this project, e.g. money, time, people (with their particular strengths and weaknesses) and technology.
- Examine what services are often needed but which you do not provide, e.g. independent financial advice, something solicitors are well placed to offer. It is not something to be undertaken lightly but you will succeed with preparation, careful recruitment of the right people and everyone in the firm supporting it. The feedback from clients will be excellent, particularly the elderly who want financial advice from someone they trust.

One way of examining the level of competition for the type of services you already offer or for what you propose to offer is to use the 'Five Forces of Competition' framework designed by Michael Porter in his book, *Competitive Strategy* (see Appendix 5). This review helps to focus the mind on the difficult questions of how the service you are currently offering or the one you propose is or will succeed against the competition for those services. It helps you to identify the strengths and weaknesses in your own services and those of your competitors.

(1) Think about who are your suppliers and how dependent you are on their services, e.g. your staff, any organisation to which you outsource work.
(2) Which organisations are your direct competitors for these services: name them and examine your strengths and weaknesses relative to them.
(3) Are there any potential competitors who might be able to offer these services in the future? For example, other professionals might be able to extract a grant if the restrictions are ever removed.
(4) Which organisations or people can offer substitute services? There may be local charities that offer advisory services; more retired people have the time to extract a personal grant.
(5) Who are the types of clients who want or need your services?

19.5 TACTICS, ACTION PLAN AND REVIEW

19.5.1 Defining aspirations

At the outset of the planning process, management needs to set acceptable standards of financial performance. Questions which need to be resolved include:

- What are acceptable billing figures?
- What are acceptable profit levels?
- What are the required levels of growth?

These targets will be affected by the factors which motivate the practice as a whole. Different firms are driven by different motivations and the business plan must reflect these differences. Motivation will generally be composed of a balance between:

- money;
- power;
- material gain;
- promotion;
- status;
- improving the environment;
- job satisfaction;
- helping others.

19.5.2 Content of the business plan

Having defined departmental aspirations, an analysis of how to meet those aspirations must be undertaken. There are two simple but effective tools which assist with this task.

PESTE analysis

A PESTE analysis is a review of the external influences and factors operating on the department. It covers the following issues:

P: Political
E: Economic
S: Sociological
T: Technological
E: Environmental

A PESTE analysis within a probate department might consider the following:

(1) *Political*

    (a) Structural reforms, recent political decisions that have made an impact:

(i)   abolishing the professional prohibition on 'touting' for work;

(ii)   abolishing monopolies in probate;

(iii) authorised probate practitioners;

(iv) taxation issues.

(b) Financial changes with political origins, e.g. reductions in fee rates.

(c) Legislative changes, changes in the law you advise on, and changes in how you practise.

(2) *Economic*: general economic forces impacting on:

(a) property;

(b) increasing wealth;

(c) declining estate values.

(3) *Sociological*

(a) Social attitude influencing demand, e.g.

(i)   towards home ownership;

(ii)   towards cohabitation, marriage, divorce and the family.

(b) Consumer awareness affecting client expectations, e.g.

(i)   price awareness;

(ii)   heightened consumer awareness of legal rights;

(iii) greater service standard expectations.

(c) Demographic trends, e.g.

(i)   population trends;

(ii)   age structures, nationally and regionally.

(4) *Technological*: office equipment:

(a) computers have revolutionised production and management techniques;

(b) methods of doing business, e.g. online banking facilities, telegraphic transfers, email, video-links and others.

(5) *Environmental*

(a) office location;

(b) use of 'green' products such as recycled paper.

SWOT analysis

A SWOT analysis is a review of the internal influences and factors operating on the department. It covers the following issues:

S: Strengths
W: Weaknesses
O: Opportunities
T: Threats

Consider the internal strengths and weaknesses of your department or team, and then seek to address your planning so that you:

- maximise opportunities (capitalising upon strengths); and
- minimise threats (in order to eliminate weaknesses).

A SWOT analysis is often carried out by examining the department's strengths, weaknesses, opportunities and threats in the context of:

- structure;
- administration;
- finance;
- services;
- partners;
- staff;
- clients;
- know-how and information technology (IT);
- marketing.

A SWOT analysis carried out against these management disciplines within a probate department might consider the following:

(1) *Structure*

(a) Does the department have a suitable shape? What are the partner/fee-earner/support staff ratios?

(b) Is the department's management structure appropriate?

(2) *Administration*

(a) Who is responsible for administration?

(b) Does the quality of your administration meet client and staff needs?

(c) Do your systems have their intended effects? What are their intended effects? Could you streamline your systems to make them more efficient?

Be ruthless with office procedures. Question everything. Are there any gaps in what you perceive your clients want and what the individual client expects of your service because of his or her:

(i) past experience of your firm?

(ii) own needs?

(iii) view of your competitors' services?

  (iv)   knowledge through word of mouth recommendation?
  (v)   knowledge of any promotional information you have supplied?

Probate is a process that lends itself to standardisation. Wills are tailor made for the client but are built up from a set of tried and tested precedents. There are well known steps for the mitigation of inheritance tax (IHT). Where you can, develop uniform procedures within your team. Retain only those steps in the process that are essential and will deliver a quality service in the way the type of clients your firm serves will recognise as 'quality'.

(3) *Finance*

  (a)   Are you charging enough?
  (b)   What are your profit/billing expectations?
  (c)   Is your credit control effective?
  (d)   Are you effective at recovering all your chargeable time?

(4) *Partners*

  (a)   Do the partners have the necessary management skills to develop the department?
  (b)   What is the partnership's attitude towards delegation, teamwork and communication?

(5) *Staff*

  (a)   Do you have the right calibre of staff? Do they understand their jobs?
  (b)   Are your staff properly trained? Do they have skills which are different and more valuable than the competition, e.g. bereavement counselling skills, the ability to communicate well with the deaf and blind?
  (c)   Are they motivated?
  (d)   Are you over/under staffed?
  (e)   How do you monitor staff performance?

(6) *Clients*

  (a)   Who are your clients?
  (b)   Where are your clients?
  (c)   What do they want of you?
  (d)   Are your clients satisfied with your performance?
  (e)   Do you converse and write in plain English and in such a way as to get the best out of every interaction with your clients?
  (f)   Ask yourself why do clients ask a law firm to undertake probate work?

(i)   they do not know how to do it themselves;

(ii)   they do not have the time to do it;

(iii)   it would not be an effective use of their time;

(iv)   the particular case is too complicated;

(v)   there is a dispute and someone independent is required to deal with it;

(vi)   they have no choice, the testator appointed partners in the firm as executors.

There are many more reasons but whichever reason applies in a particular case will have an effect on how that client perceives the quality of the service you are providing. If the case is complicated the client may be looking to you because your firm is regarded as having an acknowledged expert and the client may only want to deal with him or her. The 'client' may have no choice as the firm are the executors. This may be resented, e.g. where the 'client' has acted in an estate personally before and the process holds no mystique. He or she may well focus on how quickly you finish the job and how cheaply you do so.

(7) *Know-how and IT*

(a)   What will the future impact of technology be?

(b)   Can you use IT more effectively?

(c)   Can you make better use of existing equipment?

(d)   Consider how technology can serve you and provide meaningful systems that manual methods could not. Do not just seek to computerise what you already do. Try to see if there is a better way of delivering the service that can be computerised. Often manual systems have grown up over the years in a piecemeal fashion and have become 'the way it has to be done'. Yet the only reason the existing way was developed was because it was not possible to organise it manually any other way; whereas now you are not limited to doing it manually – computers are there to help!

(e)   The client expects you to do things in the most cost-effective way. Why should the client pay for your time to do something manually when the job could be done at a fraction of the price and more efficiently if a computer system was used?

(f)   Can you make it easy to share skills and experience learnt by one person with others in the team and keep those skills and knowledge even if that person chooses to leave? It is no good buying computers and finding out that only one person knows how to use the system/package just as that person goes on maternity leave!

(8) *Marketing*

    (a)   Have you thought through an effective marketing strategy?

    (b)   Are you providing the right services? Can you keep in touch with the developments in this area to such an extent that you know before your competitors about any changes to rules, services (such as social service delivery in your area) law?

    (c)   Is your marketing spend sufficient to meet your strategic goals?

19.5.3 Strategic plan

Having carried out the PESTE and SWOT analyses in the light of the department's aspirations, the strategic goals of the department will become clear. Strategic goals will often be very simply expressed. Examples might include:

- to increase the number of wills written per month by – per cent by 31 December 200–; or
- to implement the use of an estate accounts software package before 1 August 200–.

In today's volatile trading conditions, an appropriate 'strategic window' for planning purposes is perhaps two to three years. Anything longer is unrealistic, as the PESTE and SWOT factors affecting the department are likely to change radically over such a length of time.

    Developing a strategy and implementing it is about wanting to succeed. It is hard work! Features of a strategy that contributes to success are:

- it comprises goals that are simple, consistent and long term;
- it displays a profound understanding of the competitive environment;
- it contains an objective review of resources available;
- it is effectively implemented.

19.5.4 Operational plan

Once you have established your strategic goals, you must consider the implementation issues and develop an operational plan. The operational plan defines the activities the department must undertake in order to achieve its strategic goals. This is often the main body of the overall plan and it is generally short or medium term in character, covering a one to two year period.

    The team's commitment to any plans is essential. Without it the plans will never get off the drawing board. Developing a workable strategy needs the people at the 'bottom' to contribute. After all it is the team who will have to carry it out.

Consult people; encourage ideas; develop suggestions; assess skills

This is where involving your team is essential. Play to their strengths and minimise their weaknesses. Do you know what are their personal career goals? Do you know how you might involve the attainment of those in the delivery of the firm's goals? Do you encourage an environment where people will freely express their areas of weakness without fear of criticism? Why not agree with your partners that the team has a combined fee target whilst agreeing with the team a division that allows you development time, as team leader?

Do you have sufficient management information to review fee income at least monthly against the team target? To check how and where the fees were generated? (Always thank introducers of business.) Can you review overheads and identify the cost of supplying the services offered in the way you do?

Structure actions; allocate jobs; delegate; set targets

Why not draw up a separate sheet of paper for each goal you want to achieve as a team and draw up a table to be completed of:

- what needs to be done to achieve it;
- who is to take responsibility for each of these actions;
- how much time will be needed or is available to spend on each action;
- what is the deadline for completion of the action;
- how the team will know that the action has been achieved;
- what budgets have been set for the activity.

Give people a few weeks to consider what actions they are prepared to commit to and then arrange a follow up meeting to discuss it. For example, the strategic goal of increasing the volume of wills written demands consideration of a wide range of issues – research into the market place, promotional activity, allocation of additional work, and so on. As the team leader, ensure that you end up with a workable and practical set of actions which different members of the team have taken responsibility for implementing. Ensure you agree a fixed date in the future to conduct an evaluation.

Budgeting is vital but often poorly thought through. Unless there is a strategic reason which justifies it, there is little point in undertaking a promotional campaign if the expenditure involved will be greater than the level of profit that the promotion is anticipated to yield. The budget should therefore include profit and loss and cash flow projections for the period under consideration.

19.5.5   Goals

At all stages of the planning process goals need to be SMART:

- *Specific*: stated in such a way as to aid verification. What evidence would be required to establish success?
- *Measurable*, so that specific data can be collated to identify achievement or otherwise.
- *Achievable*, to stretch but not over-challenge the individual and the team.
- *Realistic*: avoid arbitrary quantifications such as stipulating a 20 per cent reduction when there are no grounds for thinking this is any more or less attainable than a 50 per cent or 100 per cent reduction.
- *Timed*: how far ahead is it necessary or sensible to set certain objectives – one month/one year? Without imposed deadlines the plan will lose impetus as short-term priorities intervene.

19.5.6   Evaluation and review

If you have not documented what you are trying to achieve, by whom and by when, then the chances are you will not achieve your goals. If you have not considered what 'success' will look like then how will you know whether or not you have achieved it?

Periodically examine how you are doing, what worked and what did not. Were the actions identified successfully completed within budget and on time? If not, why not? What did you learn as a result of trying to achieve the goals you set? How can this experience inform your next lot of planning? Then continue with the next lot of action planning.

Ensure your strategies keep up with the market place in which you operate by ongoing review and action. If you do then you are certain to succeed.

Continually ask yourself the question: how can we get better at what we do?

19.6   STRUCTURE OF DEPARTMENT AND STAFFING ISSUES

The single largest overhead incurred in any probate department is likely to be the payroll and its associated costs. Given the very high ratio of payroll costs to income generated, it is vital to ensure that the best possible value is obtained from the firm's investment in staff.

As a simple example, a significant impact of poor personnel management is often high staff turnover. This not only subjects the department to the disruption encountered when a key member of staff moves on, there are also the significant costs incurred in replacing that member of staff and a learning curve to be overcome when a new member of staff begins work.

Good personnel management practices will ensure that staff are properly motivated, committed to the practice, properly trained and resourced and dedicated to meeting the needs of clients.

Within the department, however small, various roles will be performed:

- *Head of Department* holds principal responsibility for the effective and profitable operation of the department. The role encompasses:

  - the development and implementation of departmental operating plans geared to meeting targets established by the firm;
  - the establishment and achievement of departmental budgets and targets;
  - the provision of coherent leadership and management support;
  - the supervision, training and development of departmental staff;
  - marketing and the development of the department's client base.

- *Fee earners* hold principal responsibility for the delivery of prompt, effective and accurate advice and services. The role encompasses:

  - provision of legal advice and assistance to the firm's clients;
  - development of excellent working relationships with clients and referring agencies alike;
  - familiarisation with and use of the department's IT systems;
  - familiarisation with and adherence to the department's prescribed operating systems and procedures;
  - maintenance and development of relevant technical legal knowledge and skills;
  - direction of support staff to maximise the performance of the department;
  - resolution of client/referrer enquiries which cannot be dealt with by the support staff.

- *Support staff* hold principal responsibility for providing secretarial and administrative support to the collective fee-earning staff. The role encompasses:

  - provision of word-processing services and the completion of forms as directed by the fee-earners;
  - attendance of clients on the telephone and the accurate taking of messages;
  - establishment and maintenance of accurate filing facilities on behalf of the fee-earners and Head of Department;
  - data input of time records;
  - maintenance of fee-earners' diaries and appointments;
  - provision of photocopying services to the department;
  - preparation and sorting of incoming and outgoing mail;

- familiarisation with and adherence to the firm's prescribed operating systems and procedures;
- answering routine enquiries relating to progress.

It may be that one person fulfils all the roles or that there are several people fulfilling the same roles. When reviewing the structure of the department and its ability to deliver the operational and strategic plans which have been devised, a review of the functions which have to be performed, the roles of the team members in conducting each of the functions and the relevant competencies of personnel to conduct them, is essential.

Some practitioners battle on with unrealistic caseloads believing the firm will not agree to any further staff assistance because overall fee income is low, without looking at why the income is low. If the same person is responsible for organising the way work is done, for attracting the work as well as doing it, it is inevitable that too much emphasis will be placed by that person on doing the work rather than on the significant area of how the work could be achieved in a more cost effective way.

A cheaper member of staff can justify their salary and contribute to the profits much quicker than a senior member of the firm. The workload of the senior manager could be made more realistic and real improvements to the bottom line achieved just by changing the staffing mix.

The larger the team the more essential it is that the department head is relieved of day-to-day fee-earning and allowed to concentrate on the management of the team and its development in line with the strategic goals it has to achieve. This is always hard for professional people who have undoubtedly been chosen to head up the department or team because of their seniority or technical legal know-how. Whilst their experience will still be called into use and their knowledge of particular clients will inevitably involve them in client contact the effective manager will try to delegate most of the routine matters to free up valuable planning and implementing time.

Gaining commitment from others in the team to take on some of these more routine matters and caseload will only be achieved if promises to deliver on matters only a partner or manager can implement are kept. This means setting an exemplary example of being a person who can manage their time and their work to beneficial effect. There are only 24 hours in the day and seven days in the week for each and every one of us. The Prime Minister has no more time each day than the head of a department in a law firm. So it is not about having more time, it is about how we use the time available. Achievement is about being focused, organised and effective.

There are plenty of courses, books and programmes to help people re-think how they manage themselves but the big hurdle is to recognise this may be a weakness; arrange to do something about it and keep an open mind as to what you may need to alter in your life to change what are essentially bad habits. Remember, it is easy to make New Year's resolutions but so much harder to achieve them.

When you have explored the services you are to offer the clients and the ways in which you are going to deliver these services it will be apparent what legal skills are needed in the team. However, also work through the processes that are necessary to have in place to deliver these services and the non-legal skills required in order to operate the processes that are just as essential to the fulfilment of the plan. Map out these primary and secondary functions and processes so that you can then be clear what competencies are needed within the team to ensure it functions in the way that you, and more importantly the client, want.

For example in marketing terms the aim of a business is to deliver more to the client than the client believes it cost him to do business with you:

$$\text{Superior delivered value (SDV)} = \frac{\text{Total value offered to a client} - \text{Total}}{\text{cost to the client}}$$

Total client value comes from:

- services value: how the client values what you are selling;
- product value: how the customer values what the producer is selling;
- people value: how the customer rates the people s/he is doing business with;
- image value: how the customer views the firm's overall image.

Total client cost comes from:

- monetary price: the actual price paid or payable;
- time cost: the client's time used in connection with using your service and how the client values that time;
- energy cost: the amount of effort required by the client both to ensure that you do the job s/he has bought and that you require of the client to contribute to the process;
- psychic cost: the mental anguish of dealing with you or with difficult matters!

Buying decisions by clients as to whether or not to use your service are therefore made on an acceptable balance between cost, value and quality. If you apply this idea to a will-making service, some clients you might want to target might only be interested in the cost in which case our services have to focus on cost type ideas; whereas you might want to attract clients who are more interested in services which offer them value for money rather than cheapness, in which case you might focus on the scope and depth of the value added components. For example:

297

Cost components	Value added components	Quality components
Reasonable fee	Home visits	High standard of client care
Special promotion	Accessibility of office	Optimum office environment
Loyalty bonus	Flexible opening hours	Experienced and skilled
	Duty of care	practitioners
	Record keeping systems	
	Easy to understand service	

One way of considering the SDV of your service is to use a tool called a 'value chain': this is a means of identifying ways to create differentiation through value enhancement. Value chain activities are categorized into two types:

- primary activities, such as legal work categories; marketing, analysis and advice;
- support activities; a firm's infrastructure; personnel, IT, Library etc.

For a law firm generally these might be described as:

Support	Primary
Law firm infrastructure	Services offered
Human resources: the knowledge, attributes and skills of your staff; the management of people and their development	Marketing services, including client care
	Data collection and management
IT, used and developed by the firm	Legal analysis, interpretation and recommendations
Physical assets owned by the firm, e.g. offices, library and other equipment	Reporting and communication
	Outcome evaluation and after sales service, including complaints handling

For a will-drafting service, the primary activities will include:

- marketing the service, including providing cost information;
- collection of information about the client, his/her assets, dependants and needs in a way which is easy to manage and verify;
- legal analysis of the information against current law and taxation with recommendations of how to approach will drafting;
- reporting to the client with a draft will and an explanation of the clauses;
- finalising the will and checking, providing copy, secure storage of the original, invoicing in line with information provided.

For each primary and secondary activity a firm can use a SWOT analysis to determine how effectively it is currently attending to the delivery of the particular component. It can then concentrate on and invest in improving any weaknesses in the delivery system.

If you use this same idea to help you decide what primary and secondary functions are needed within the team and in the wider firm to help you deliver your probate service it becomes easier to then identify what competencies are needed to perform these functions and therefore what mix of staff skills, behaviours and attitudes will be required.

The more you can involve the team in identifying these competencies the easier it will be to develop a job role guide comprising the critical success factors needed for each person to perform their role and to identify any gaps in knowledge and skills which need to be filled either by the recruitment of suitable additional staff or by the utilisation of appropriate IT or by the development of existing staff.

The more everyone in the team is involved in this exercise the more likely it is that you will build a successful team where each member knows what is expected of them and the others in the team, how the individual skills fit together and who is responsible for what activities. It also helps when it comes to setting a pay structure where salaries can be set for the combination of factors within a person's job role for which they are accountable. The critical success factors for which that person is accountable also provide the yardstick against which their own personal performance can be measured both on the job and when implementing regular appraisals to update training and development plans.

19.7   KNOWLEDGE MANAGEMENT AND IT

There are three kinds of knowledge:

- improvement of a process or service;
- exploitation of existing knowledge to develop new processes and services;
- innovation by applying existing knowledge to produce new knowledge.

19.7.1   Developing knowledge

Managing information successfully means getting the right information, in the right form, to the right person at the right time to add value. The use of IT in the workplace has substantially reduced the turn-around time for communications and this of itself can increase pressure on us all. Sometimes the demands of the client are unreasonable and it is necessary to be assertive in order to enjoy sufficient time to reflect on the problem in hand in order to give appropriate advice.

The huge increase in the use of specialist software applications in law firms and departments is changing staffing levels so that you are being asked to do more with fewer people. Clients want the ability to have 24-hour a day, seven days a week access to the progress of their matters. Without harnessing the use of IT how can you realistically do this? Case management systems accessed via a web-based product and secured by codes and encryption are already well used by some firms and those who have yet to address these issues and make the investment required are already behind the game.

If you do not allow management development time to address these issues and training time to use the equipment and software properly you will still have to perform to your clients' chosen standards – which may mean working until you drop – or you will eventually lose those clients to those organisations who are prepared to invest and learn.

So to work smarter you need to be able to:

- distinguish between useful information and data;
- to sort, order and display information in the most communicative way;
- to identify innovative ways of using the information to add value.

Hugh Garai in *Managing Information* (Gower Publishing, 1997) identified four principles of information management which he argued can turn worthless data into powerful intelligence, which, when applied, will generate effective change:

(1) Data + Relevance + Purpose = Information
(2) Information + Insight = Understanding
(3) Understanding + Communication = Intelligence
(4) Intelligence + Action = Effectiveness

If you simply hoard data and never get rid of anything then how big will your office have to be by the time you die or retire? We all need to become organised or we will be swamped. How long does it take you or your helpers to find things? Think how much time you could save if you simply organised your files on the computer, or tidied your desk, or implemented an effective filing system, or destroyed 'bumph'?

19.7.2 Knowledge from resources such as books, lectures, cases, conferences, precedents

In our search for profit one of the ways of boosting the bottom line is to reduce the overhead costs, so advocating expenditure on sources of knowledge may not be popular. Actually, what would make both common sense and economic sense would be if the business made a better return on its expenditure on gaining knowledge. Instead of individuals being trained or seeing training as gathering continuing professional development points, the firm should want to see more focus in the choice of training and more use by all relevant practitioners in the firm of the information gained by the individual.

Basically, lawyers are selling knowledge based on their experience and skill. It therefore makes sense for a firm to take the explicit knowledge gained from these sources and have the ability to enable all who need to, to be able to access this knowledge freely at any time, e.g. having access to the firm's precedents via laptop and portable printer when visiting a terminally ill client to prepare an emergency will.

19.7.3   Knowledge from people such as experience, practical observation

A powerful selling point for any organisation is the experience and skill of its people. It is often the most difficult source of knowledge to capture but as any firm will know whose senior lawyer dies suddenly or leaves early or retires without some succession planning having been done, once a source of tacit knowledge about individual clients or tried and tested schemes or just plain human psychology which comes from a lifetime of dealing with people disappears, it can take years to recover, if at all.

Trying to identify this kind of experience as knowledge, is the first step to being able to design systems to capture it.

If the firm treats profit sharing as 'eat what you kill' rather than the traditional 'lockstep approach', where rewards reflect long-term contribution to the firm not just personal profitability at the expense of developing 'firm' clients rather than 'my' clients, then it is harder to change the culture to one where individual knowledge and experience needs to be captured for the long-term good of the firm, whether or not that individual is there.

19.7.4   Sharing knowledge

Of systems

It is not just legal knowledge that needs to be shared but experience of the use of any systems in place in the firm, such as file management systems, accounting procedures, how the firm likes to set out its estate accounts, etc.

Understanding why a particular procedure is undertaken helps newcomers contribute to how the systems might be improved or streamlined. Systems that ossify are an impediment to progress but equally checks and safeguards, recognised as such, will more likely be honoured if people obliged to follow them understand the reason for them.

Of access to information

We need to recognise the old adage 'knowledge is power'. If people are rewarded for keeping information to themselves then the power is held by individuals and stops people from being open and willing to share. Shared knowledge is greater power in the market place for your firm and that means encouraging understanding of the means of access to as much information as possible within your firm, e.g. enabling fee-earners and administrative staff to obtain billing guides and client account balances rather than this being done only in the accounts department.

Availability

Sharing personal knowledge and experience requires senior people to be available to the more junior. This can be expensive in the short term but over time the more you can develop the younger individuals you will be securing the succession to your firm for the future. People may want increasing salaries but they also want to develop and see a career path. Talking to them and helping them to understand why you approach a problem a particular way can really smooth the transition for clients. This is no good if the culture of your firm generally is not positively disposed to this kind of approach, as who will carry it forward and so keep these people you have invested in within the firm, when you retire?

Rewarding the creation of 'firm's knowledge' not just personal knowledge

People often do need incentives to change their behaviour. If you want people to share what they know you will need to make it positively pointless to hoard knowledge and make it much more financially rewarding to share it. For example, promotion may depend on how well someone acts for the benefit of the team by entering course summaries into your own knowledge bank for sharing internally.

19.7.5 Training

In developing systems

To what extent does your firm encourage people to learn how to solve a problem? Do you ever attend courses on large changes such as the Financial Services and Markets Act 2000 and then never develop the systems needed in the firm to address the changes?

Training in technical matters tends to dominate the training budgets of many firms and yet some training on how to go about designing and implementing a system for use in the firm or how to manage a project like the selection and installation of a new IT system are often going to be that much more useful to senior people. A large organisation may have specialist people to organise this sort of thing but unless they also have input from you as the probate practitioner, what you will end up with may have severe shortcomings that you and your team have to deal with on a daily basis.

In use of systems

It is a common complaint of staff that partners produce a new system, particularly IT systems, and simply say 'there you are, now get on with it'. This type of 'sink or swim' approach is far from cost effective. Work output plummets, stress levels soar and everyone is unhappy. If only the installation and training budget for new IT were at the top of the list of items when purchasing a new system then some of the 'hidden' costs of change would be properly identified and dealt with in a positive way.

How can a member of staff show a new employee how to use something that they have only learnt by trial and error, which often means half of what the system has to offer is never used? It is human nature to learn enough to get your daily work done and not spend time on learning what else the system can do, even if this might mean you learn useful shortcuts or safety procedures.

In technical aspects

Achieving strength and depth in the wider areas of law within the probate department helps once more to sell the services of the firm. There is the need to have the ability to undertake estate planning, living wills, financial services, community care planning, as well as the core services of will drafting, EPA preparation and administration, probate and intestate succession and trust drafting and administration.

19.7.6 Using software and the Internet

Estate accounts packages

There are a number of companies offering estate account packages for probate and trusts. The Probate Section of the Law Society published a software guide in 1999, which was updated by Computer Counsel Ltd in 2000. This is a useful summary of what is available as a stand-alone piece of software for a particularly tedious part of the job.

Some companies do offer integrated systems which include probate as part of a suite of software but this is often not as good as the stand-alone systems, several of which have originally been the brainchild of probate practitioners who have developed the program to help themselves with their day-to-day work.

Case management software

This is where the system acts as a comprehensive supporter of the workflow in the probate field, supplying as it does templates, databases of contacts, probate registries, local authorities, standard letters and the forms used in the process. The idea is that you enter the details once about the deceased and his/her estate and those databases are interrogated by the system as required to complete the IHT 200, the oath, letters to institutions, beneficiaries, executors etc.

The main thing is that it enables para-legals to help with the work and reminds the practitioner what to do next, often through the use of task lists or diary reminders.

Forms: data entry only, self-calculating, integrated

Whether or not case management systems are necessary (most firms will have a series of good manual systems which can deal with most of the probate process adequately) the use of technology to complete forms, particularly tax forms, is a must.

There are simple forms on screen where you type in the details yourself every time. Apart from saving the storage of hard copy stationery and ensuring, through a maintenance package with the supplier, that you always have the most up-to-date form, this data entry type of form does not provide you with very much more.

Some tax forms are integrated with the production of estate accounts. There are estate accounts packages which include e.g. IHT 200, as the information needed for the one activity is clearly needed for the other, and this might be set up to take the data when input once and then utilise it for the other use. It is important to ensure that the government department concerned has formally approved any official form that might be included.

Some types of tax form are self-calculating. The Inland Revenue itself has now put on its website the IHT 200 in a version which enables you to download it from the website, enter your data offline, save it and have the program calculate the tax due. Once you are satisfied you have all the information entered, you can then print it off and submit it in the usual way. This software is free and all that is needed for saving and printing is an additional piece of low-priced software from Adobe.

As with all software, it takes time to become familiar with it, but once you have it can save so much time and therefore money. It can also mean that the quality of your service to the client improves, as you can produce a set of accounts at the push of a button rather than pore over the file for half a day!

Library information

The excellent *Internet Newsletter for Lawyers* produced by Delia Venables (contact her to subscribe at **delia@venables.co.uk**) has debated the pros and cons of developing an electronic library in comparison with a print library. Electronic libraries are useful research tools and avoid 'losing' books and periodicals within an office just when they are needed. It is easier to keep them up to date – simply by loading the update CD – rather than having to file paper updates, an important but time-consuming job.

However, lawyers are often working not on current law but on the law that applied some time earlier when the cause of action arose, for example, and therefore still need access to paper versions that may contain the relevant information rather than the 'current' information provided electronically.

Practically too, there is no industry standard as to how systems are updated. Whilst it is easy to update stand-alone PCs with update CDs, it can be impossible to do so over a network and may require individual machines to be loaded with relevant CDs, a logistical nightmare and hard to police in order to comply with user licence conditions.

Websites

We live in an age of information overload and certainly within the law there is a plethora of ways that we can access information over the Internet. A series of web portals has grown up to help find a simple way through to the most useful sites and two favourites are **www.venables.co.uk** and **www.infolaw.co.uk**, the latter of which is run by Nick Holmes.

As many commentators have noted, the law on the Internet is not comprehensive nor is it easily accessible for research purposes. This is because the approach taken by each website is independent of each other. Government-supplied statutes are available going back to around 1988 but not statutes still current which date before then. Some case reports are available on the Internet for free but only since around 1996 and for some areas such as Employment Appeal Tribunals only from 2000. Alongside the freely available information are the subscription-only sites and these are often set up so that the user can indicate his/her chosen area of interest and have delivered to their computer each day an email of developments and articles upon any of those selected subjects.

The daily update is a wonderful tool but how many people actually read them and then save what they need and delete the rest? Are you one of those people who print them all out and add the paper to the growing heaps of reading which is the lawyer's lot! New means of acquiring knowledge need new skills in harnessing it and making it work for you.

19.8 RISK ASSESSMENT AND QUALITY MANAGEMENT SYSTEMS

19.8.1 Risk assessment

To ensure our professional indemnity insurance premiums are kept at manageable levels, risk assessments need to be undertaken. If the firm is committed to the provision of quality services then file management will be at the heart of the office's systems and procedures. The two are linked as those firms that have gained the Lexcel Quality Mark promoted by the Law Society have found that the premiums quoted for indemnity insurance are reduced by between 10 and 25 per cent.

It is acknowledged that implementing a file management system will inevitably incur administrative time but at some stage it is likely that this will become a professional standard, so as always it is better to experiment with it whilst it is not compulsory rather than be faced with having to instigate systems under pressure. There are many firms and individuals who will testify to the advantage of having to implement similar approaches in the litigation areas of practice to continue to offer publicly funded work.

One way of checking whether your systems and procedures are safe and reliable is to identify the possible risks that can arise in the probate process and check if you have robust safety systems in place.

A few common risks are identified below with their obvious risk management actions alongside:

Risks	Actions
Delay	File management system for keeping files under review and moving
Failure to attend to tax matters	Software to help complete forms; training to understand compliance during the administration; checklist/diary to recognise due dates
Missed deadlines	Central diary system
Over-distribution to beneficiaries	Estate account package should minimise risk of paying out before IHT paid but still need file management system review before distribution
Sending money to wrong person/address	Accurate database, properly trained staff, file management system to review
Deeds of variation	Knowledge and skill as to whether relevant and how to conduct it; diary system to record by when it should be done
Failure actively to manage investments	Training to obtain knowledge and skill over asset management and realisation to deal promptly to best effect

19.8.2   Quality management systems

There are a number of quality management standards which are appropriate for incorporation within law offices and probate departments. They are:

- ISO 9001;
- Investors in People;
- Lexcel, the Law Society's Practice Management Standards.

ISO 9001

ISO 9001 is an externally audited management standard with its roots in the American defence industry. It is a self-defined standard: users establish their own management and file systems against the framework requirements of the standard itself, and are then audited against their own written systems. The standard is not specific to the legal profession but can be interpreted within a legal context. ISO 9001 tends to enjoy higher popularity within larger firms with commercial practices.

Investors in People

Investors in People (IIP) is a management standard developed within the United Kingdom and applied and audited in England and Wales through the national network of Learning and Skills Councils. IIP is based upon the premise that a business will be successful if:

- it has a clear set of objectives which are communicated to all staff;
- all staff understand their contribution to those objectives;
- all staff are properly trained and equipped to fulfil their responsibilities;
- performance is continually evaluated and reviewed.

As with ISO 9001, IIP is not specific to the legal profession, but fits very well within it.

Lexcel

The Law Society's Practice Management Standards (PMS) represent Law Society guidance on good management practice. Specific to the legal profession, the Lexcel system covers:

- management structure;
- services and forward planning;
- financial management;
- managing people;
- office administration;
- case management;
- file management.

307

The Law Society arranges external accreditation and audit of the standard under the brand name of 'Lexcel'. Accredited practices are able to make use of the Lexcel logo and take part in Lexcel promotional initiatives. The audit process is simplified for those firms which are already accredited under other quality management standards.

There are several shared characteristics between these standards:

- all require external assessment and audit of the firm seeking accreditation;
- all measure the quality of the management systems in place within the practice, and not the quality of the legal advice and experience on offer;
- all require a measure of strategic planning to have been carried out;
- all require defined systems to be in place for the delivery of the product or service on offer;
- all require effective mechanisms for personnel management, training and development to be in place.

The quality management standards provide a framework within which efficient management practices can be developed and implemented. In particular, systems for the efficient running of client files, incorporating safeguards to minimise the possibility of error or client dissatisfaction, are a key feature of quality management systems within the legal environment.

The need for such systems is clear. When the Solicitors' Indemnity Fund (SIF) was the profession's main insurer 5 per cent of claims by number and 4 per cent by settlement amount were attributable to wills and probate matters. Penalty deductibles (effectively, an additional deductible of 50 per cent) arose from failure to:

- execute a deed of variation within two years (Inheritance Tax Act (IHTA) 1984, s.142(1));
- give written notice to the Inland Revenue within the six months permitted under IHTA, s.142(2).

The main problems encountered by SIF within the probate arena include:

- wills:
  - delay in preparing wills – disappointed beneficiaries;
  - failure to comply with formalities for attestation;
  - failure to consider tax implications;
  - invalid gifts (e.g. severance of joint tenancy);

- administration:
  - delay – loss of value in assets;
  - failure to submit tax returns as trustees;
  - failure to review fund investments;
  - failure to act promptly in sale of shares/stocks/currency;

- shares sold at loss within 12 months of death – failure to substitute lower value for value of shares at time of death;

• deeds of arrangement:

- failure to consider tax consequences;
- failure to meet time limits – deeds of variation;
- failure to give notice of election within six months;

• beneficiaries:

- failure to verify IHT liability prior to payment of beneficiaries;
- failure to verify correct beneficiaries/address;
- duty to disappointed beneficiaries;

• trusts:

- failure to ensure trust drafted to make favourable tax treatment available.

19.8.3   File management systems

The checks and balances inherent in an efficient file management system can be broken down into a series of key areas:

• response to enquiry and collection of marketing information;
• providing costs information and follow up;
• allocation of work;
• opening a file;
• use of checklists;
• undertakings;
• arrangement of file contents;
• file supervision to include fee-earner review; file review and the legal process;
• updating the client;
• file closure;
• complaint handling systems.

19.8.4   Response to enquiries

The provision of telephone quotations is often seen as a mere irritant. Many probate practitioners, when asked to give a quotation over the phone, will do so briefly and without any attempt at 'selling' the service or the department. It is important to:

• give responsibility for responding to enquiries to the person who is best equipped to do it – not necessarily a partner but ideally someone with:

- a good telephone manner;
- sales experience;
- an outgoing personality;

- prepare a checklist of all the information that must be provided to the client;
- take a positive approach: not a defensive attitude to competitive pricing;
- cross-sell: ensure that the client is well aware of all the issues and services attached to his initial enquiry. You may, for example, encourage clients to consider an enduring power of attorney whilst discussing wills (see Chapter 21 on marketing);
- capture information: it is vital to keep a record of the enquiry and to find out from the client what prompted the enquiry in the first place. Knowing the source of the enquiry will enable you to monitor and plan your marketing strategy for the future.

19.8.5 Information on costs and follow-up

This is a major source of client dissatisfaction and complaint. It is compulsory under Practice Rule 15 to address how costs will be calculated at the outset and in particular to provide terms of business setting out whether the 'value' element will be used in calculating the bill in a probate matter.

Even if it was not compulsory it is certainly true that the full and adequate provision of information about the likely costs of the matter, at the start and during its progress, will assist the client by providing a clear expectation. Failure to provide this information inevitably leads to shock at the size of the final bill. One of the most frequent complaints in probate matters is the unexpected nature of the bill.

It is important to agree the funding arrangements and payment terms. To help convert an enquiry into firm instructions, it is essential to follow up initial enquiries with a personalised letter. Ensure that the response is made on the day of receipt of the initial enquiry, unless this is patently unreasonable, and that it is accompanied by appropriate sales or promotional literature, particularly that concerning related services.

The details of the quotation, the client and the source of the enquiry should be recorded for future follow-up and in order to monitor sources of work and conversion rates.

19.8.6 Allocation of work

The successful probate department will be efficient in confirming instructions in writing to the client and obtaining the necessary data from the client to progress the matter.

Upon receipt of the confirmed instructions, allocate the work to the most appropriate fee-earner. This means achieving a balance between:

- experience;
- workloads;
- nature of the instructions;
- value of the work.

Failure to control the workload being handled by an individual fee-earner spells potential disaster, particularly if file management/supervision procedures are absent.

At the same time, undertake a case planning exercise to try to identify problem areas as the matter progresses. In a probate matter, such a planning exercise might cover:

- difficult interpretations of law;
- beneficiaries lacking capacity;
- insolvent estate;
- all assets in possession of deceased;
- outstanding tax or other liabilities;
- whether deed of variation necessary/appropriate;
- IHT implications;
- whether statutory advertisement for creditors required;
- whether charities properly identified.

The case planning exercise might also seek to establish targets and key dates relating to:

- assets collected;
- liabilities settled;
- time limits (variation, etc.);
- interim billing;
- grant of probate;
- distribution, interim and final.

19.8.7   Opening a file

By now, the vast majority of the information required in order to carry out this function should be available. Client details are available and must be transferred on to the file and on to any electronic database or case management software, if in place.

19.8.8   Use of checklists

Fee-earners should complete professional checklists at key stages in the conduct of the matter. The purpose of a checklist is to act as an *aide-mémoire* to ensure that all relevant professional issues have been properly addressed prior to moving forward to the next stage in the matter.

If all is as it should be, the checklist will act as evidence on the file to confirm this: if the checklist throws up an omission, no matter how major or minor, the fee-earner will be prompted to go back into the file to rectify the identified problem.

19.8.9 Undertakings

Strict control is required over the granting of undertakings, which bind the firm and its partners. Any undertakings, other than standard wording undertakings (e.g. those recommended by the Law Society in a conveyancing transaction), should receive a partner's prior authority.

A central register of undertakings granted should be established in addition to a clear record being placed on the file. Many firms now use a system of synopsis sheets on the front covers of files, which summarise key data relating to the file: it is sensible to include space on the synopsis sheet to show when an undertaking has been granted. Verbal undertakings should always be confirmed in writing.

19.8.10 Arrangement of file contents

Case files should be laid out neatly to ensure easy accessibility to all information by all fee-earners and support staff and to enable supervisors regularly to review work. Working papers should be arranged so that:

- all correspondence is in sequence on a filing clip;
- all file notes/attendance notes are stored in sequence on the correspondence clip;
- a synopsis sheet is prominently attached to all files;
- deeds and other documents of title are stored in secure filing facilities, properly cross-referred to the file;
- any other papers are neatly arranged on the file, if necessary in a plastic wallet.

19.8.11 File supervision

Supervision of the management of the matter breaks down into two areas:

- fee-earner supervision; and
- file review.

Fee-earner supervision

Supervision equates to effective support of the fee-earner. The objective of supervision is to ensure that:

- all fee-earners know who is supervising them;
- arrangements to ensure supervision of the conduct of case work are in place and understood within the department;
- arrangements are in place for a regular independent review of case files in terms of procedural and legal content; and
- arrangements are in place to supervise the conduct of work carried out by non-fee-earning staff.

The supervision process tends to be divided into three areas:

- checking of incoming post;
- checking (but not necessarily signing) of all outgoing post;
- regular supervision meetings.

The level of supervision required will depend upon the experience of the fee-earner concerned. Fee-earners who are considered to be of sufficient experience should be granted the ability to supervise their own post, but they should still be subject to regular supervision meetings by their supervisor.

Base the frequency of supervision meetings on the fee-earner's experience. Meetings should include coverage of issues such as:

- new cases taken on;
- existing workloads;
- progress on current cases;
- problem clients;
- the outcome of cases;
- training needs;
- undertakings granted or given;
- any other problems encountered.

The purpose of the meeting is for the supervisor to guide and assist the fee-earner in the delivery of legal services.

File review

All files should be subject to independent periodic review. The review should cover both procedural matters and substantive legal issues. A supervisor who is independent from the day-to-day conduct of the matter should carry out the review.

The frequency of reviews is dependent upon the experience of the fee-earner involved: five files per quarter will give an accurate, cross-sectional overview of the workload of most fee-earners. The file review should be evidenced by means of a file review sheet which should be signed off and agreed by both parties to the review process. The review should check at least the following issues:

- substantive legal issues properly addressed;
- papers referenced;
- file notes used consistently;
- undertakings recorded;
- conflict of interest check conducted;
- requirements or instructions of the client recorded;
- advice given recorded;
- action to be taken recorded;
- costs arrangements recorded;
- terms of business despatched;
- key dates recorded and backed up;
- client properly updated;
- changes in costs notified.

Any poor levels of compliance should be drawn to the fee-earner's attention and rectified within an agreed period of time.

19.8.12 Updating the client

Fee-earners should ensure that clients are appropriately updated throughout the matter and this includes ensuring that:

- information about action taken in a case, or its handling, is given to the client promptly;
- information relating to delays are passed on to the client immediately.

Both of the above points should be evidenced on file, either by attendance notes or by means of a copy letter to the client.

19.8.13 At the end of the matter

Proper procedures need to be put in place to ensure that any outstanding points are properly dealt with before the file is closed formally within the firm. This is best achieved by means of a file closure checklist. Issues addressed on the checklist should include:

- that the client has been informed of the outcome of the matter;
- that the client (or beneficiary in a probate) has been accounted to for any outstanding money;
- that interest on the client account has been calculated (where applicable);
- that original documents have been returned to the client unless storage arrangements have been agreed;
- that, where appropriate, the client has been informed about arrangements for storage and retrieval of papers;
- that the client has been advised whether the matter should be reviewed in the future, and if so, when;

- that final bills have been received and settled and that account balances are zero;
- that a future review date (if applicable) has been diaried forward and that a file destruction date has been allocated.

19.8.14   Complaint systems

Complaint systems are not simply to provide clients with the ability to whinge. Complaint systems are a part of the process of assessing client satisfaction. They are a means of identifying problems, resolving those problems and ensuring that the resulting benefit is passed on to the client base.

Complaint systems should include a means not only of resolving the initial client complaint, but also of planning to ensure that the problem which gave rise to it never recurs.

In probate matters it is possible that complaints are received from residuary beneficiaries, particularly in cases where the firm is the sole executor, and solicitors' rules dictate that the residuary beneficiaries would have to approve the costs in any event.

19.9   MARKETING

19.9.1   New customers versus existing clients

Profitable organisations recognise that the best source of profit and sustainable revenue is gained by focusing on existing clients. It costs far more to convert a prospective into an actual client than to sell your services to an existing client.

This assumes, however, that the client is a potential repeat buyer of the services offered and that the segment of the market you are targeting will generate good and profitable business. If the type of client and the type of service are not in a profitable segment of the market no amount of selling to them will generate good business.

The current emphasis stresses customer relationship management (CRM), i.e. that you should develop close alignment with your clients, being able to customise your messages and activities to the different needs and values of your clients.

19.9.2   Customer relationship management (CRM)

The smaller firm has probably been practising CRM for years: it offers a service that is personal to each client. This works for as long as only one person deals with that client, but as the firm grows and as the personnel changes it is inevitable that the 'closeness' of the service offered originally is weakened and this is when clients often do not stay but choose to take the opportunity to move to another practice.

To learn enough to differentiate between clients you need to have a system for capturing each individual's contact with the client (particularly if you want to cross-sell your probate services to clients who have only used your litigation team or conveyancing colleagues) so that you can keep track of the dialogues and interactions which will help with your side of the work the firm proposes to do for the client.

Clients find it much more difficult to start over with another firm so you need to help them to create their own barrier to leaving your firm behind. You are trying to build and keep their trust. To keep them biased towards your firm you need to find out what the client values from the way your firm delivers its services and then make sure that is what you deliver to them.

Clients are always going to value things that make their life easier – the challenge is to find out what this might be for the probate service. Can you avoid them having to call into the office and so save them time by giving them regular reports, or allowing them access to basic information over the Internet? The more your marketing can identify what the individual client is doing (behaviour) and thinking (feelings) the more emotional attachment there will be to your firm if you address these behaviours and feelings, and the more likely it is they will stick with you.

Everyone in the team needs to be able to adapt his or her delivery to suit the level of sophistication of the particular client. Do be clear about:

- what the service you are offering actually entails;
- how much this service is actually going to cost;
- how you justify the level of cost for the type of service provided;
- how you will deal with any problems.

Make contact with the bodies who are providing services to the elderly locally: provide free advice, join the local committee, discover what they are looking for from the lawyer. In this way you raise the profile of the firm to undertake work in this field in your area and encourage referral of work.

Market the team's services by undertaking seminars to local groups, to clients, with the local care agencies, and write editorials for publications. You cannot market successfully until you are clear about what it is you are marketing.

When the firm has developed its own specific value chain to its satisfaction it can promote this value to its clients, e.g. by having better IT and systems than rival firms to collect all information necessary both accurately and ef-ficiently (lower cost advantage), or by performing activities in a unique way such as producing the will at the person's place of work or home to increase greater perceived value to the client (differentiation advantage).

In the will drafting sector, solicitors are not the only people offering the service, so it is important to benchmark not just other solicitors' value chains (which is difficult outside groups such as LawNet or outside local areas) but other organisations or firms that might see this as a service to offer.

The Law Society commissioned a benchmarking study of other professions and commercial companies in relation to client care. The result of this was that solicitors are advised to:

- manage expectations and communications;
- provide customer charters;
- manage dissatisfaction before it becomes a complaint;
- set up an Interprofessional Benchmarking Group to exchange information about issues such as service and conduct improvement goals, best and worst practice.

The simplest of these guidelines for individual firms to address is the first: manage expectations and communications. The report recommends that:

- You are specific and clear in all communications:
    - use of plain English – have you ever appraised the competence of the practitioners in your firm in this respect?
    - use of guidance notes and leaflets – does your firm have clear terms and conditions of business or client care guide? Do you use explanatory leaflets that you have tried and tested for understanding by lay people?

- You know the concerns of your audience, i.e. the different needs of different types of client:
    - scenario 1: you are invited to speak at an Age Concern lunch club about what is involved in making a will; you are permitted to promote your own firm's will-making service. What would you say?
    - scenario 2: the Excess Bank plc invites you to a seminar they are holding for some of their high net worth clients. The Bank does not have its own will-drafting service. It is recognised as being expert at putting its customers first. Do you offer to make a presentation? What would you say?
    - scenario 3: the local branch of the Institute of Directors is holding a trade fair. Do you take part? How would you present the firm's will-writing service?

- You match content and style to your market, i.e. if you only act for scenario 1 clients, it is no good offering a scenario 3 service.
- You never commit without being able to deliver: it is a marketing adage that you should always under-promise and over-deliver, i.e. promise to produce a new will in two weeks time and produce it in one week.
- You make rules and guidelines accessible to all:

    –   internally, involve staff in designing and monitoring;
    –   externally, ensure lay people can understand what is intended.

Interestingly, the Fact Sheet produced by the Law Society's Research and Policy Planning Unit identifies that firms can strengthen and expand their client bases through good client care. The Fact Sheet points out:

- Private clients and smaller businesses usually choose solicitors on the basis of past experience or recommendation. Existing clients are more likely to be retained and new clients attracted if clients are satisfied with the service purchased.
- The public is demanding higher levels of service from all professionals. Firms which demonstrate first class client care will gain a competitive edge in the market place.
- There is a strong correlation between good colleague care and good client care. Developing good client care is likely to lead to improved relationships between members of the firm whereas poor client care can seriously damage internal relationships.
- The Legal Services Ombudsman has called for solicitors to adopt a more 'consumerist' mentality to complaints from clients about processes and service, rather than negligent professional service.
- Effective client-centred complaint handling may increase client loyalty. Research has shown that where a complaint is satisfactorily resolved, 75 per cent of consumers were likely to go back.
- There is also evidence that excellent complaint handling can lead to even higher customer loyalty than amongst those clients who experience no problems at all.
- If clients are not adequately cared for the reputation of the profession as a whole suffers.

The Fact Sheet goes on to identify the areas that comprise good client care as:

(1)   developing appropriate interpersonal and organisational skills such as effective interviewing, communication and managerial skills;
(2)   the setting up of efficient management systems;
(3)   the gathering of clients' opinions about completed work;
(4)   the provision of 'client friendly' office accommodation and information;
(5)   a regime of regulation which reinforces good client care practice, through training, appraisal, monitoring and compliance mechanisms;
(6)   appropriate mechanisms for the swift handling and resolution of clients' complaints at the right level;
(7)   the development in law firms of a culture of client care which values complaints and reports of clients' dissatisfaction as crucial feedback which can be used to improve the legal services offered.

CHAPTER 20

Avoiding complaints and claims

Mike Frith

20.1 INTRODUCTION

> Central to a civilised society are informed citizens who know and are able to access
> their rights: Ann Abraham, Chief Executive, *National Association of Citizens
> Advice Bureaux 1995/96 Annual Report*

Since Ann Abraham wrote the above words she has become the Legal
Services Ombudsman who reviews the work of OSS and therefore of complaints against solicitors. These few words illustrate graphically the demands
of consumers ('complainants') in their dealings with solicitors and with OSS.

20.1.1 Anticipation

Probate work depends on having a system and sticking to it. This requires
proper supervision from a qualified and experienced fee-earner, good individual organisation and systematic work methods – and not taking on more
work than the firm can handle. Probate questionnaires, standard letters and
standard forms greatly assist this process.

This advice will also apply in future to the developing areas of private
client work such as contentious probate, enduring powers of attorney and, as
OSS is increasingly discovering, matters relating to financial services.

20.1.2 Beneficiaries

> As a layman I must say that I find it surprising that solicitors administering estates
> do not have a greater obligation to beneficiaries: Michael Barnes, Legal Services
> Ombudsman, *1994 Annual Report*

A substantial number of complaints in probate matters are made by beneficiaries, particularly residuary beneficiaries. Are these complaints that a
solicitor is obliged to deal with under the firm's internal complaints
procedure?

The answer depends on who are the executors. The normal rule is that a
solicitor only has to deal with service complaints from his own client.

Unfortunately, probate matters supply the one possible exception to this rule. In probate, the solicitor's clients are always the executors. It is to the executors that he owes his duties under Practice Rule 15.

In cases where the executors are all laymen, it is simple. They are the clients; they must be given the information required under Practice Rule 15 and they are the ones who are entitled to raise complaints about the service provided. If a complaint is received from a residuary beneficiary, it can be explained to them that they are not the client and the solicitor is unable to deal with their complaint because to do so would involve him in a breach of his duty of confidentiality to the client. They should be advised to take their complaints up with the executors, who, in turn, can raise them with the solicitor if they wish to do so.

In instances where the executors are the solicitors who are dealing with the estate, this could cause undue hardship to residuary beneficiaries because, if the solicitors refused to contemplate complaints from them, they would have no alternative than to embark on potentially expensive litigation. Therefore, if there are no lay executors, solicitor/executors will be expected to accept, and deal with, complaints from residuary beneficiaries.

However, in the event of a justified service complaint reaching the OSS under these circumstances, because a compensatory award can only be made in favour of a client, the only sanction that can be imposed is a reduction of costs.

What happens where there is a solicitor-executor acting with a lay executor? Unfortunately, there is no hard and fast answer. It all depends on the direct personal interest that the lay executor has in the efficient administration of the estate. If the lay executor is also a residuary beneficiary he obviously has a substantial interest, and, in such cases, other beneficiaries can be asked to channel their complaints through him.

On the other hand, if the lay executor is not even a beneficiary, or is only entitled to a small pecuniary legacy, he has very little personal interest in the efficient administration of the estate. In such instances the solicitor should accept complaints from residuary beneficiaries, as in the circumstances described above.

There will be cases that fall into the middle ground. In such instances, it is a question of making a judgement about the standing of the lay executor.

Notwithstanding the above, solicitors might well consider treating residuary beneficiaries as if they were actually clients, even if, strictly speaking, they are not. It might well be worthwhile, if there are not too many of them, giving them costs information and keeping them informed of progress as a matter of course.

If they are so numerous that to do so would be unduly expensive to the extent that the cost could not be justified as an expense of the estate, consider circulating the residuary beneficiaries, explaining the situation and offering to keep individuals informed at their own expense – in which case do not forget to give them information about how much it will cost them!

However, there could not be a finding of inadequacy of service in favour of anyone who was not actually a client unless in the circumstances dealt with above.

Do not forget that, if there are no lay executors, residuary beneficiaries have the right to require a remuneration certificate to be obtained.

20.2. THE DEADLY SINS

20.2.1 Failure to communicate

It is essential to keep clients regularly informed as to how the administration is progressing. It is also sensible to consider doing so in the case of residuary beneficiaries who are not also executors and, therefore, clients. Failure to keep clients informed is a frequent head of complaint.

If there are likely to be circumstances that will cause delay in progressing the administration, e.g. Inland Revenue queries or a claim made under the Inheritance (Provision for Family and Dependants) Act 1975, remember to inform the clients, with a full explanation, as soon as the circumstances are known, and, if it is possible to do so, give an estimate of the likely delay.

20.2.2 Delay

This is, in fact, the most common head of complaint in probate matters – and one that is most commonly found to be justified. The usual causes are failing to give explanations of potential, and actual, periods of delay and failing to manage clients' expectations. Laymen have a tendency to think that matters are much simpler, and consequently capable of being dealt with much quicker, than is really the case. Unless they are told the reality of the situation *at the outset of the retainer*, a later complaint is likely.

20.2.3 Costs information

Remember that lay executors should always be given costs information at the outset of the retainer. Complaints do also arise when solicitors simply deduct interim costs without informing lay executors, or, if there are none, the residuary beneficiaries, or even rendering an interim bill. If a costs estimate has been given and it is realised this is likely to be exceeded, inform the executors/residuary beneficiaries as soon as it is known this is the case.

Remember that all costs information should be confirmed in writing.

20.2.4 Failure to follow instructions

This is usually caused by a breakdown in communications between solicitors and client. It can arise because of the solicitor's failure to explain his reasons for taking a particular course of action.

Remember that complaints about the service provided must relate to what is done in the capacity of a solicitor and not, for example, decisions taken as an executor. For example, a decision taken to delay the sale of an asset because it is thought it might increase in value is a decision taken as an executor and is not open to challenge by way of a service complaint. On the other hand, delay in the disposal of the asset, once the decision has been made to dispose of it, is a complaint about the service provided.

20.2.5 Investment advice

Investment business complaints often do not come to light until some years after the investment business itself took place, but they do, nevertheless, still need to be dealt with at that time.

If the investment business activity happened before 1 December 2001, the OSS handles it. However, a new regime was brought into effect on 1 December 2001 by the Financial Services and Markets Act 2000. The Law Society, as a Designated Professional Body, regulates all firms of solicitors except those directly authorised by the Financial Services Authority (FSA). All firms conducting mainstream investment business, namely advising on and arranging investments, require FSA authorisation. They may otherwise be committing a criminal offence if they undertake regulated activities.

If the investment business activity took place after 30 November 2001, an investment business complaint may be dealt with by either the Financial Services Ombudsman (FOS) or the OSS depending on the type of business involved. Complaints involving mainstream investment business are dealt with by the FOS. This only arises with firms that are FSA-authorised, as FSA authorisation is required for mainstream business. Complaints arising from non-mainstream business are dealt with by the OSS, even if the firm is FSA authorised. With FSA-authorised firms it is possible that complaints could arise involving both mainstream and non-mainstream business.

A great deal more help is available in the Information Pack on the new scheme for the regulation of financial services, which can be obtained from The Professional Ethics Division (see Appendix 6).

20.2.6 Loss of property

Any property handed over in connection with an estate should *immediately* be listed and a receipt given. Any valuables, cash and personal effects should be kept in a safe or strongroom. It is an inadequacy of service for a solicitor to lose anything left with him for safe-keeping.

20.2.7   Failure to pay adequate interest

Failure to obtain a reasonable rate of interest on monies held on a designated client account or to pay a fair sum in lieu of interest on money held on a general client account constitutes a breach of the Solicitors' Accounts Rules 1998 (Rule 25) and also constitutes inadequate professional service.

20.2.8   Failure to make appropriate interim distributions

Accurate and prompt distributions of estate funds should be made as soon as the extent of any estate liabilities becomes clear. Legacies should be paid as soon as funds are available and residuary beneficiaries' wishes (particularly those of charity beneficiaries, or others having special tax considerations) should be ascertained and discussed with the executors.

Care should be taken to ensure that final accounts are not delayed (a common cause of complaint) and that the accounts are correct, with all liabilities being cleared. Another common cause of complaint is overpayments to residuary beneficiaries, who then have to be asked to repay some of the money sent to them. This is treated as an inadequacy of service and it is no excuse to say the beneficiary must have known he was getting more than he expected or that he did not check the accounts himself.

20.2.9   Failure to provide tax deduction certificates

These should be provided promptly as a matter of course and without charge.

20.2.10   Late production of estate accounts

As indicated above, delay in producing final accounts is a constant source of complaint. Final accounts should provide full details of assets, payments, receipts and must distinguish between capital and income (see also the comments on tax deduction certificates and deposit interest above).

20.2.11   Conflict of interest/instructions from third parties

Solicitors should not accept instructions from third parties, who may be the source of referral work or who may be residuary beneficiaries, without obtaining the approval of the real client. Solicitors should also be alert to possible conflict of interest and, in such cases, ensure that independent professional advice is obtained by all parties.

20.2.12 Errors

If an error or mistake is made, which does not give rise to issues of negligence, admit it and correct it as soon as possible. Attempts to cover up errors are counter-productive, usually get discovered and then compound the problem, and the redress, when the complaint reaches the OSS.

20.2.13 Excuses

It may be salutary for practitioners to be aware of a number of the most common excuses given to OSS when a complaint is raised:

- I have never made a mistake in – years of practice.
- I have mislaid the file.
- Someone else is dealing with this matter.
- We have had an office re-arrangement.
- I have been in court all day/all week/all month and have not had time to deal with this matter.
- Funny you rang. I was just planning to write to you.
- I do not reply to letters; why don't you telephone me?
- I do answer telephone calls but only on a weekly/monthly basis.
- There is/will be a letter/fax on the way to you today.

20.3 ADVICE FROM THE OSS

The OSS confirms that delay and failure to keep clients (and, where appropriate, residuary beneficiaries) informed result in the majority of complaints made to it. It points out that good estate administration is greatly assisted by proper supervision by qualified and experienced fee-earners, good individual organisation and systematic work methods – and not taking on more work than the firm can handle. It agrees that the majority of complaints about ordinary probate work originate in an unsystematic approach and poor client communication, rather than lack of knowledge of the law.

Interestingly, the OSS adds that contentious probate is a growing field and one with which more and more practitioners are likely to have to deal.

20.3.1 OSS's ten reminders

Ten reminders from the OSS:

(1) Inform executors (and residuary beneficiaries where appropriate) of progress and of costs incurred at the agreed stages of a probate matter. Too much information is better than too little.

(2) Assess at the first interview the time likely to be needed to complete the administration, and settle at what stages the clients will be informed of progress and about costs. Tell them promptly and in writing about any adjustments which have to be made. Use a client care letter to record and follow up initial discussions – examples of information for clients are in Chapter 3. (Solicitors in private practice may adapt or adopt these specimens for the purpose set out on page iv but not for any other purpose.)

(3) Develop a system and stick to it: keep lists of assets and debts, and note what happens to each asset and when it is dealt with or received, to avoid any possibility that assets or debts get overlooked.

(4) It is essential not to take interim costs from estate funds until the executors have been advised and have given their approval.

(5) Estate accounts should be simple enough for lay people to follow but need to give full details of assets, payments and receipts. (For example, in relation to the sale of stocks and shares, the sale prices and net proceeds per holding should be listed.) See the clients in person to explain the accounts, if necessary. (Chapter 15 includes advice from the College of Law about estate accounts.)

(6) Place estate money on deposit at the best practicable rate of interest.

(7) Always make attendance notes, and send letters to confirm oral instructions as a matter of course.

(8) If clients hand in cash, valuables or papers, detailed lists should be prepared and receipts should be given; estate valuables, cash items and personal effects should be kept in a safe or strongroom (and remember that if the estate includes items such as guns, antique or modern, there may be additional rules).

(9) Make accurate, and prompt, distributions of estate funds once the extent of the liabilities is clear. Pay legacies as soon as funds become available and make interim distributions where possible. Residuary beneficiaries' wishes should be ascertained and the matter discussed with the executors if their views cannot be carried out.

(10) If an error or mistake has been made, admit this to the clients and correct the matter as soon as possible – attempts to conceal an error are, the OSS says, inevitably counter-productive and very likely to result in a complaint.

20.3.2   Issues for the insurers

Do not forget the issues that could cause difficulty with professional indemnity insurers, for example:

- time limits:

    - check the time limits for execution of deeds of arrangement and deeds of variation;
    - check the time limits for giving notice to the Inland Revenue;

- extent of retainer:

    - clarify at the outset with the client and confirm in writing;
    - clarify the areas of responsibility between departments if the conduct of the file is divided;

- drafting:

    - ensure that the draft documentation is checked against original instructions;
    - ensure that engrossments are checked against the final draft with someone else;

- delay:

    - ensure that wills are drafted and executed quickly – those for elderly and infirm clients and those in dangerous occupations or going abroad very soon may need urgent attention;
    - beware of rushing after a delay, e.g. to distribute the estate – it might result in paying out to the wrong beneficiaries;

- record of wills:

    - ensure that a proper record is kept of wills held by the firm. The estate might be distributed only to discover a later will.

20.4 COMMUNICATIONS: MEETING CLIENTS' NEEDS

20.4.1 Clients in distress

The debate over Rule 15 of the Solicitors' Practice Rules (see Chapters 2 and 3) highlighted the issue of client care in general. Probate clients may have special needs. Bereaved clients may be going through a lot of emotional difficulties and while it is not a solicitor's role to act as a counsellor, in probate, as in divorce and other work, it is important for firms to be aware of and to cope sensitively with clients' feelings. Could you refer clients to local sources of help if necessary? For counselling and support organisations see Appendix 6.

20.4.2 Plain English

Do not forget that clients need to be able to understand the legal work being done for them and the advice which is given. If they cannot do so, the information might as well not be given in the first place. Always bear in mind that words that have a particular legal meaning are capable of being jargon as far as a layman is concerned, even if it is a word in common, everyday use.

Clarity (see below) say that research has shown that clients may think they understand a lawyer's letter when in fact they seriously misunderstand it. Clients are not always willing to ask for explanations, nor to complain directly to the firm about perceived difficulties, unless they are aware that this is acceptable – which is why the client care provisions cover these issues fully.

Communications in plain English are usually very much appreciated by clients and can avoid misunderstandings. Some points about plain English are included in the following paragraphs.

Sources of information

Clarity (address in Appendix 6), is the lawyers' movement to simplify legal English. It produces a journal and runs seminars. Relevant books are shown in Appendix 5, including the Law Society's own publication, *Clarity for Lawyers* by Mark Adler. Some computer programs are available: more information can be obtained from the Law Society's IT adviser (see **www.lawsociety.org.uk**).

Using plain English

One of the unjustified criticisms levelled at plain English is that it is 'not accurate' and so is not appropriate for legal use. This is entirely wrong. Plain English can certainly be accurate English – more accurate than 'legalese', which, because of its obscurity, may easily be misunderstood and cause confusion.

A commitment to using plain English may mean rethinking your approach, but it does not mean abandoning legal precision, technical accuracy, established legal usage, elegance of expression or useful, familiar legal terms when these will be understood by the reader; nor does it mean being undignified or patronising, nor that all your letters and documents must be written in words of one syllable.

Legal concepts are sometimes difficult, but nothing is gained by further binding them up in impenetrable language. A picture saves a thousand words, so use a chart, diagram or sketch if it would help.

A legal term can be the equivalent of a sketch, shorthand between people who know all that is implied by it. Effective plain English involves considering your readers, and if you know they will all understand a phrase such as *per stirpes* there is no reason to avoid it – as long as you bear in mind all the risks of taking a shortcut. Sometimes setting everything out in full, even just in your mind, highlights questions which would have been overlooked if the shortcut had been taken. When using expressions like *per stirpes* always ensure that its meaning is explained to the client, together with the reason why it is being used, and that the client understands.

Writing to clients

Few clients will object to easy-to-use letters, which set out in straightforward terms what is meant and what they have to do. Most will have pressure on their time, and at best, other things on their minds; at worst, some clients will be acutely worried and distressed and not thinking clearly. Under those circumstances they need you to help as much as possible by assisting them to identify what is important, in letters and papers you send them, virtually at a glance. Good organisation and layout help immensely. Have the confidence to be unassuming and clear rather than impressive but incomprehensible!

Bear in mind constantly that if a client does not understand what you have written to him, he is less likely to tell you, because he either has to sit down and write to you, which many people are not comfortable with, or they have to telephone you. Either way, it means the client being pro-active in contacting you to say he does not understand and people are sometimes diffident about admitting they do not understand because they think it might make them look stupid.

Clarity's suggestions are not carved in stone, and have probably been transgressed (inadvertently) many times in this volume, but are intended to give an idea of where to start and to act as a reminder.

20.4.3   Document planning

The following points will help with document planning, the first step in clear communication:

- As you are putting pen to paper, or picking up your dictaphone, picture your reader(s) and ask yourself:
  - what is this document for?
  - who is going to read it? Are their interests in its content all the same? If not, whose take priority? What do I need to do about the others?
  - what will its reader(s) want to get out of it?
  - what do I *really* want to say?
- Consider how the answers to those questions will affect the way your message needs to be formulated and set out.
- Identify the kinds of things you will be doing in the document: summarising the relevant facts, asking somebody to do something, reviewing

the options open to your client, explaining the law, recording an agreement, reassuring, warning, advising; decide how those should be arranged to make your points clear to your reader(s).

- Work out the headings which will summarise the points you have to make; decide the order in which you are going to put those points.
- Plan how layout, headings, paragraph numbering and so on can help make the document easy to read and how these can make the most important points stand out:

  - use bullet points;
  - number paragraphs or sections to make cross-referring easier;
  - use sub-headings.

- Put important points at the beginning (of letters or paragraphs) and if need be mention them again at the end. Do not lose them in the middle where they may be overlooked.
- If you have to use expressions which are likely to be unfamiliar or even slightly threatening ('an order of the court'), explain.
- Use lists for series of items.
- Underline the most significant part.
- Add a summary at the end, referring to the relevant paragraphs for detail.
- Read the finished document critically to check that you actually said what you intended – and if you didn't, start again (or at least make a note for next time).
- To paraphrase a famous saying, avoid being unintentionally pompous, ambiguous, vague or rude!

Your client will appreciate this kind of forward planning and, when you check your file to see that everything has been done, so will you.

Picturing your readers

Picturing your readers will highlight the differences and similarities between you and them, and how your document needs to reflect these. Readers may well come from a completely different professional, educational or cultural background from writers: what seems commonplace to one side may be entirely new to the other. Documents may have multiple uses, and some readers may not be aware of all of them. Accordingly your readers may well not share your assumptions about what is clear and what is not, nor about what is implicit and what is not.

Common shortcuts, such as 'where the context so admits', 'the singular includes the plural' and 'the masculine includes the feminine' can be traps. People may disagree about whether the context admits or not; one trustee's powers are not always the same as those of two; and many people do not automatically assume that the word 'he' is sometimes intended to mean 'he and/or she'. At least one Canadian jurisdiction is using 'gender neutral' language in all official publications, including statutes, because of this social change. (The old usage, and un-thought out questions like, 'What is your Christian name?' may also upset clients unnecessarily.)

Some shortcuts and habitual formulations shift what is properly the writer's burden – clarifying meaning – to the reader. Problems can then arise. It is better to be plain about exactly what you mean at the outset and ensure your document expresses it without ambiguity. After all, there is no point in saying, 'Well, it is obvious what I meant' when a glance at the law reports shows that virtually nothing is beyond dispute.

Not using plain English

Although some firms are actively changing to plain English for all work, others remains dubious. Lawyers who are comfortable using it in letters and informal documents may balk at using it in wills because of fears that plain English documents will not 'work' if tested in court. This is not the place to cover all the arguments; these are issues firms and individuals have to consider carefully if they share these concerns. If the verdict is against plain English, this means being extra-conscientious about explanations, in letters and meetings; and good layout and sensible document organisation can do a lot to clarify meaning.

Do not underestimate the amount of explanation that may be needed. Clients who have never been involved in estate administration may need an outline of the whole process, including what a grant is, why one is needed and what their duties are as PRs. The Law Society has a range of publications which may be of help (see Appendix 5). Specimen letters and leaflets are included throughout this book (which solicitors in private practice may adapt or adopt for the purpose set out on page iv but not for any other purpose). Use of these materials and careful explanations should help prevent another person being in the position of the client who telephoned the Law Society to ask, 'What is probate?'.

CHAPTER 21

Marketing wills and probate

Kim Tasso

21.1 INTRODUCTION

This chapter aims to achieve the following:

- to dispel the myths about marketing and to explain the core concepts of marketing to prepare you, the probate practitioner, for effective marketing;
- to provide an analysis and planning framework to help probate practitioners understand their present position, articulate what they want their marketing to achieve and to develop a plan of attack;
- to provide some practical guidance on selecting which of the many marketing tools are appropriate to the marketing tasks practitioners face;
- to help the probate practitioner develop and implement effective marketing action plans.

21.2 UNDERSTANDING THE BASIC PRINCIPLES OF MARKETING

21.2.1 What is marketing?

'Marketing is the management process responsible for anticipating and meeting client needs profitably' is the official definition of marketing and one that few professionals would argue with – after all, isn't every lawyer there to meet the needs of their clients whilst making a modest profit? But the definition is of little value on its own.

Marketing operates at three levels. First, there is a marketing function. Someone within your practice needs to take overall responsibility for marketing to ensure that the appropriate resources are available, that all the different marketing activities throughout the firm happen in a co-ordinated and effective way and to manage the various marketing information systems that you need to draw upon. It is also helpful to have a source of marketing expertise on which all members of the firm can draw to ensure that marketing mistakes do not occur.

Second, marketing is a philosophy that focuses – at every point in the firm – on the needs of the client. This is apparent when we consider the importance of internal marketing. From a cross-selling perspective we must ensure everyone knows what the probate team has to offer, its particular strengths and weaknesses and how to introduce clients to the services available. From a service delivery perspective, every member of the firm who has contact with the client (whether as a receptionist, switchboard operator, secretary, trainee etc.) creates an impression about the firm and either supports or undermines the firm's overall brand or service promise.

Third, marketing is a series of tools and techniques (for example, advertising, direct mail, publications, selling, etc.) designed to do different marketing tasks and these are described further below.

Marketing typically comprises a number of elements that are blended together into what is called 'the marketing mix'. The elements are:

- product (the legal advice and the way in which that advice is processed and delivered);
- place (the market where the services are promoted and delivered or the channels involved, e.g. web-based services);
- price (ensuring clients perceive value for money);
- promotion (all those activities designed to alert clients and potential clients to the services and benefits available);
- people (the lawyers and their support staff who are the marketers, sellers, producers and deliverers of the services).

These different elements are explored further in the remainder of this chapter but it is important that all elements are considered together – a promotional campaign alone is unlikely to succeed.

There is often some confusion within the legal profession about the terms 'marketing', 'selling' and 'business development'. They are distinct activities aimed at different parts of an ongoing and integrated cycle.

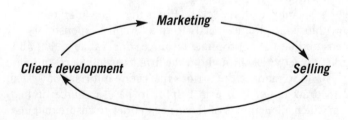

Figure 21.1 The business development cycle

21.2.2 What is selling?

Marketing is concerned with identifying needs in the market (therefore research and analysis are important), identifying or developing the services that meet those needs (e.g. service or market development) and communicating the appropriate messages to the market. It is where the firm 'broadcasts' a message to many members of a market (for example, a market might be all the wealthy people within a 10-mile radius or it might be all accountancy practices with between one and eight partners). Marketing would also be concerned with developing the reputation or brand of the organisation, service or individual. Typically, marketing is conducted by those who have some training in marketing, for example, professional marketing staff, designers, copywriters, PR experts and so on. If marketing is successful enquiries will be generated.

When you move from communicating with a market to communicating with a particular organisation or individual you have moved into the selling phase. Here the focus is on the specific needs of that one organisation or individual rather than the generalised needs of the whole market. Some argue that selling is more orientated to 'pushing' the product or service you want to sell, although in the legal market the most successful selling is driven by the needs of the buyer. Typically in a law firm, selling is the preserve of the most senior lawyers: they have the experience and knowledge to promote their own and the firm's benefits. Sometimes, there is a formal tendering process (or 'beauty parade') involved if there is a large volume of work or a legal panel at the client organisation.

Converting a prospect through successful selling results in a client. However, one set of instructions does not a client make. The continued marketing and selling to that client (within the framework of client relationship management (CRM)) ensures further instructions are received for additional or new services. This is a vital activity in every law firm as usually around 80 per cent of a firm's annual income is from existing clients. Typically, this area of client or account development is where the majority of lawyers focus their efforts. In the past it was common to say 'The only marketing we need do is a really good job for our existing clients'.

This view of marketing should dispel the myth that it is only about new business: a major component of law firm marketing is about developing the existing client and referrer base through relationship marketing.

21.2.3 Consumer versus business-to-business marketing

Before you embark on a practical framework to get you marketing your probate and wills practice, you need to appreciate that marketing techniques vary depending on the nature of your target client. You will also need to consider the importance of segmenting the market into smaller, more manageable segments with common characteristics or needs. Clever segmentation can result in a highly profitable niche practice, which makes achieving a premium fee for specialist work much easier.

When you are promoting wills, you are typically targeting private individuals or families. There are over 58 million people in the United Kingdom and they can be grouped by socio-economic group, by age, by location, by household, by lifestyle and in various other ways. Even though you have focused on a particular group, it would be difficult and not very cost effective to try to mail all members of that group or to spend hours in one-to-one meetings with them. So, more indirect methods of marketing might be adopted, such as advertising or media relations. The members of each group or segment will have common interests or needs that you can address within a marketing campaign. The smaller and more focused your segment the easier it will be to reach the members with a suitable marketing tool and the easier it will be to tailor your message to address their specific needs.

Some elements of the private client market are keen to use the Internet, and there are a number of examples of successful websites that provide an efficient online solution to simple wills and probate matters. Similarly, other elements of the private client market might appreciate a much greater level of face-to-face interaction when dealing with legal matters, perhaps even in their own home environment. By segmenting the market we can tailor the service, the price and the promotional activity more precisely to their needs.

However, you might adopt a radically different approach and decide to target businesses in your area, offering a will-writing service to their employees. There are significantly fewer businesses than individuals in the country and there is a great wealth of information about them in various public directories and publications. Business people are less likely to be reached effectively through advertising so you might adopt a more direct approach to marketing to this group: by direct mail, through seminars or perhaps by having a lawyer make visits to employers' premises. Their needs will be different too: whereas individuals might need a will for peace of mind, to provide for their children, to minimise their tax liabilities on death, etc., a business will have different needs. If it offers a will-writing service to its employees it might be because it is genuinely concerned with staff welfare, it might be more concerned with minimising time away from the place of employment to sort such matters out, or it might wish to minimise difficulties in the event of death in service for the company's pension scheme. Therefore, the way of reaching the business audience will be different and the message you communicate needs to be different.

A further alternative might be that you decide to reach referrer organisations to generate will or probate business. You might look at retirement homes, hospices, doctors, accountants, advice centres, charities or even banks. Here you are targeting organisations so the business-to-business techniques are more likely to be effective.

In marketing terms, this is the difference between consumer (private client) and business-to-business (commercial client or referrer) marketing. Often, lawyers do not make the distinction and use the wrong technique. As a rule of thumb (there are always exceptions!), if you are marketing to consumers you use indirect methods, while for businesses you use more direct approaches. The following are the various techniques that could perform these tasks:

Indirect methods	*Direct methods*
advertising	networking
signs/posters	selling (presentations and visits)
media relations	tenders
sponsorship	direct marketing
literature (left on display)	literature (mailed)
websites	seminars/briefings
word of mouth	hospitality
	telemarketing

21.2.4 A marketing framework for probate practitioners

Having reviewed the main marketing ideas, what follows now is a framework to guide you through the various steps you should take to prepare yourself and your firm for effective marketing and to prepare a marketing plan to focus on your marketing, selling and client development activities. It may seem that a lot of analysis, thinking and planning has to take place before you get to any real 'action'. However, most solicitors' marketing fails because insufficient attention is paid to precisely these issues.

21.3 ANALYSING YOUR PRESENT SITUATION

21.3.1 Analysing your current work, clients and sources

Let us start by looking at the sorts of sources of work and clients you might have:

Those inside your firm	*Those outside your firm*
private clients	private individuals
matrimonial	low income
personal	people with ageing parents
residential conveyancing	high net worth/rich clients
financial services	company directors

Commercial clients
corporate/commercial: directors,
senior employees, shareholders
employment: senior employees

Referring individuals
existing/past clients
those who know you

Other staff
friends and family

Referring organisations
accountants
surveyors/agents
advice centres/bureaux
banks
carers
hospitals/homes
funeral directors
other law firms

This illustrates the great variety of clients and prospective clients (both private and commercial), sources of referral or work and needs with which wills and probate practitioners must get to grips. Prepare a similar diagram for your own firm, ensuring that you check the various information sources in your firm to get an accurate feel for the amount of work coming from each source. If your firm does not have the information then an early priority is to ensure that systems (usually a client and contact database and a work referral or lead tracking system) are established to collect this information in the future. Marketing without sound information is rather like building on sand – it is without foundation and liable to crumble away.

Understanding your major sources of work will help you develop a strategy to focus your marketing efforts in those areas where they are most likely to bear fruit. You cannot possibly market to all sources and markets effectively so you will need to make choices. Your choices should be based on information as accurate and as up-to-date as possible. You need to know the amount of fee income, the type of work, the profitability and the importance to the firm (e.g. to other departments) of each type of work.

This analysis should provide you with three or four areas on which you need to concentrate. Or it may show you that your marketing challenge is to alter radically the nature of clients and work you are generating. Once you have identified the types of clients or referrers you want to target, you should start collecting information about them. This should include their names and addresses, their needs and concerns, any links within your firm, background information about them and ideas on how you might approach them or build the relationship if they are existing clients.

If you have the time available, you will find talking to a number of existing clients and referrers an invaluable aid to future marketing. It will help you to identify why people come to your firm, what they like (and do not like) about the service, what additional help or advice they would like and what it

is about your firm that is different from others. Time and e
gating the perceptions and satisfaction of existing clients is
It is important to ensure that when talking to clients and
not concentrate alone on the wills and probate service. You
client's point of view, as very often the reason they will valu
be more than your expertise in one particular legal specialism

21.3.2 Reviewing your skills, staff and services

The next thing is to review the skills and abilities of the staff
moting, doing and servicing the wills and probate work. Do t
specialist expertise, for example, in complicated tax issues, in co
in situations with cohabiting couples, with overseas assets? If y
some expertise that is unlikely to be found in comparable firms t
on your way to finding a key point of difference which will mak
and marketing much easier.

Are there any gaps in your expertise? It is important to be clear ii
any areas where your advice is likely to be less than optimal: eithe
or skills development is required or you need to steer your market
from these areas and onto other stronger offerings.

Are your staff able and motivated to sell? Perhaps you need to c
some interpersonal skills training to develop their enthusiasm and con
for generating new business. Perhaps you need to review the rewards
so that they are encouraged to invest time and energy in winning new
ness. Even if you decide to take on the major share of marketing yoursel
will still need to ensure that all those have contact with clients under
what you are trying to achieve, deliver the services in the way you
promised and achieve a high level of client satisfaction.

21.3.3 Looking at the market

Now you understand where your work comes from, and the resources yo
have to develop and deliver work in the future, you must look outside yo
firm to the local market.

You should start by assessing local demands and needs. The demand ir
your area may be different to that in other parts of the country depending on,
for example, the demographic socio-economic spread of the local population,
the prevailing attitudes towards planning and professional advice of the local
people, the extent of nursing and private care homes and facilities and the
nature of the competition in the area. You can obtain this information either
by researching at local reference libraries or by seeking help from your local
Training and Enterprise Council who often have concise overviews of areas
and the main economic and social trends. Networking at local events will also
enable you to learn about the dynamics within your market place and will

ovide vital marketing intelligence. It will have the added benefit of raising
our firm's profile for all its services.

It is important to remember that effective marketing requires you to iden-
fy and anticipate needs. Without a need it will be impossible to sell any-
hing. Be objective when researching and considering local needs. You may
ave to rethink the nature and packaging of the services you are providing,
e.g. living wills being more important than traditional wills, DIY probate
packages for lower income families rather than high value services for
wealthier clients or employee support packages for local employers with large
workforces.

A key issue to consider will obviously be the strengths and weaknesses,
strategies and activities of your competitors. These may not all be solicitors.
You will also need to consider banks, accountants (especially those with tax
and trust departments), financial advisers and independent will writers. In
any market you will face a variety of competitors. The key will be to identify
the main ones and develop your strategies accordingly. Information about
your competitors is not sufficient. You must use this information to modify
your approach and activities in order to find a different marketing position
offering different benefits.

21.3.4 Pulling your research together

You may find that an analysis of your internal strengths and weaknesses and
how these translate into external opportunities and threats helps identify the
key issues on which you need to act.

As you consider each opportunity and threat, think what you need to do
– as a specific action – to resolve or grasp the situation. The more time you
spend on synthesising the key findings of your internal and external research,
the easier it will be to develop a marketing strategy and action plan that
works for you.

21.4 DECIDING WHAT WORKS FOR YOU

21.4.1 Setting objectives

The first action will be to determine what your firm's overall objectives are,
both in terms of financial targets (what fee income and profit contribution is
expected from the wills and probate team?) and in terms of the perception
and impression the firm wishes to create in the market and the nature of the
key clients it wishes to target. It is at this stage that many wills and probate
practitioners find a difficulty, especially if the firm is focusing on developing
commercial clients and work rather than private client work. It may also be
difficult if there are other practice groups targeting similar client and referrer

groups to those targeted by the probate and wills team. You will need to work together carefully in this case to produce an integrated plan for marketing to private clients (see the comments in the case studies section below).

Once you have identified the firm-wide objectives and the short-term (usually one year forward and based on utilisation, fee income and profit) objectives set for the wills and probate team, you can start to draft some more specific long- and short-term objectives for your team. Setting objectives that are measurable and realistic (see the discussion of SMART at 19.5.5 above) is hard but without them it will be difficult to focus your marketing efforts appropriately and impossible to measure the success of your marketing.

21.4.2　Selecting your targets

With clear objectives set, it will help considerably if you can be as specific as possible about the amount and type of work you hope to obtain from existing clients and contacts (in the short term) and from new clients in the longer term.

Producing lists of referrer organisations, the names of existing clients and other detailed information at this stage will save much time later. Again, such lists will focus the mind and help you assess whether your marketing is working effectively. You can produce these lists as a department but it will also be useful to work up by asking each lawyer or para-legal to produce their own lists.

21.5　AGREEING A STRATEGY

21.5.1　Position in the market

From previous studies into lawyer marketing, a common mistake is to try to be all things to all people. For example, lawyers often try to provide a high quality, high added-value service at the lowest possible price. Not only is this a recipe for working 24 hours a day with no return but also for financial disaster.

You need to decide what position you want to achieve in the market. If all the other wills and probate service providers are pushing the low cost, pre-packaged wills 'product' then look at whether there are opportunities for firms offering a higher priced, more tailored 'service'. If others are targeting the low income families, consider targeting the wealthy. If others are focusing on reaching the 'man in the street', why not consider reaching the executive in the boardroom or local employers?

A key element of your positioning will be trying to identify what it is that you offer that others do not – it may be expertise in a particular area, it may be your accessibility, it may be your client care philosophy, it may be your level of computerisation (e.g. Internet delivery) or the degree of integration with other legal and financial services. Unless you are pursuing a 'cost leadership' strategy, you will need to identify a suitable differentiation strategy.

If you are unable to differentiate your firm across the whole market, then you may need to identify and select a particular niche in the market. For example, a suitable 'segment' might be accounting firms over a certain size with no tax planning capabilities, or agricultural estates.

It is important that your strategy takes a slightly longer-term view as well. You already have financial targets for the next year so use the positioning stage to identify where you want your wills and probate practice to be in, say, three of four years' time. It will take this long for the market to learn and understand a new positioning statement.

21.5.2   Packaging the product and the people

An integral part of deciding your strategy and positioning will be agreeing what it is you are selling in the market. Some firms have differentiated the services of their wills and probate team by packaging together a range of services such as wills, living wills, enduring powers of attorney and advice on financing long-term care either in an 'elderly citizens' package or as a 'families with ageing relatives' package. Some firms 'package in' tax, financial, trust and conveyancing services in different combinations to suit the particular needs of slightly different audiences.

The actual legal 'product' is similar in all such packages, what differs is the particular needs of the particular target audience being addressed and the emphasis. The packaging can shift the emphasis away from things people are reluctant to consider (the lack of a will when they die) to more positive issues such as financing the education of their grandchildren.

Another approach might be to package the way you offer or deliver the advice, e.g. there are some highly innovative websites which offer a fixed price procedure for straightforward grants of probate in low value estates or will drafting.

In addition to packaging what you are actually offering, you need to consider the way in which you deliver the advice and this involves taking a long and hard look at everyone (lawyers, para-legals, secretaries and switchboard staff) involved in client communications for wills and probate services. Clients are unlikely to be able to tell whether they are getting good or bad advice from their solicitors, so they will infer your 'quality' through the impressions that are generated by the way in which you answer the telephone, the speed with which their queries are answered, the accuracy and layout of the letters and documents they receive, the friendliness of the legal and support staff they meet and the tidiness and comfort of the reception areas and office they visit.

Getting everyone to be a valued and integral part of your service promise will require training, communication and involvement in the marketing, planning and implementation process, so if you have not involved them so far, do so now. This can be achieved through team meetings where you explain what you are trying to achieve and ask those present to discuss the barriers they perceive and the help they require in delivering the promise. An alternative approach would be to appoint people to specialist roles, such as handling telephone enquiries, explaining the service or first meeting management.

21.5.3 Pricing

Clients will choose on price alone if they perceive no other differences in what is being offered by different suppliers. Therefore, if there is no perceived difference in the will writing or probate service offered by your firm or any other provider, then price will dominate the decision. Remember the need to make a decision between trying to offer 'cost leadership' service in the market (i.e. the cheapest) and providing something different or better. The above section on strategy will assist.

A key element of marketing is to move clients away from thinking about the price to thinking about the benefits of the service and other factors, such as speed, accessibility, ease of use, friendliness, personal service, etc.

The price must equate to the value of the service as perceived by clients. They are not interested in the cost of providing that service (i.e. how much time you take to produce a perfect document). Therefore, you must think of price in both strategic terms (what are my broad hourly or fixed fee rates and what level of profitability do I wish to achieve) and in tactical terms (how much for this particular piece of work). Some firms are becoming more creative in pricing, moving away from hourly rates to fixed price deals, value billing, retainer arrangements or shared risk arrangements and bonus arrangements. This gives clients the benefits of certainty.

21.5.4 Promotion and internal marketing

At last we get to the phase with which most lawyers will be more familiar – the marketing and selling of the services they provide. The objectives and earlier analysis should reveal where your efforts are to be focused and should have indicated the types of marketing tool that are going to be most effective in achieving them.

The following section identifies some of the key issues to consider when planning to use some of the most common marketing tools. You might seek further information and advice from marketing books; there are plenty written for the specific needs of solicitors.

21.5.5 Advertising

Advertising is where you pay a media owner (e.g. a directory, a newspaper, a magazine, a radio station, a poster site operator, a TV channel) to reproduce your message exactly as you require. There are two elements to the cost: the cost of designing and producing the advert and the cost of the space.

Advertising is a tool to get a simple message to a large audience that is perhaps difficult to reach by other means. It is generally more suited to winning legal aid or private client work. Common places where probate practitioners advertise for private client work include telephone directories, local newspapers and poster sites near advice centres. There are a growing number of magazines targeted at the older generation which may prove useful to will and probate practitioners, especially if they have produced a package of advice and service tailored to the needs of the older client.

There are over 1,400 trade and technical journals which are targeted at specific business, professional or trade audiences. For example, there are magazines aimed at funeral directors, nursing home staff, those who care for the elderly and accountants.

One-off adverts are rarely effective so if advertising is your chosen tool then make sure adverts will appear on more than one occasion over a suitable period of time. You must be clear of the following before you attempt any advertising:

- Who is my target audience and what media might reach them efficiently?
- What message am I trying to convey?
  - Is it simple and clear?
  - Does it focus on a specific need and mention benefits?
  - Is it sufficiently different from other solicitors' advertisements?
- What action does it prompt the reader/viewer to take?

With all marketing activities, you should be sure you can respond to any enquiries that are generated (have your switchboard and reception staff been briefed?) and that you can measure the response from any specific activity to assess its effectiveness.

Most solicitors focus on display adverts. Other types to explore include: inserts in printed media; messages on appointment cards; posters; give-aways; leaflets in counter top dispensers; door-to-door leaflets; cable television (considerably cheaper than national or terrestrial television and much more focused on particular areas or audiences); local radio and the promotional materials of non-competing organisations targeting the same audience. The Internet is another important advertising medium.

21.5.6 Direct mail

Direct mail is a cost-effective method of reaching commercial clients and referring organisations, as opposed to advertising which is probably best for reaching private clients. The starting point is some form of database which contains, as well as the name of the individual, their position, the organisation name, the address and telephone number. Other useful information would be specific areas of interest (e.g. tax advice), other relationships or services used within the firm, a list of past contacts and any other information that helps with analysis and segmentation.

Short, simple letters following the AIDA rule (Attention, Interest, Desire and Action) are often effective, especially when the follow-up action is low commitment (e.g. sending in for an information pack, requesting a copy of a helpful checklist) rather than high commitment (e.g. a meeting). A covering letter will increase the chances of any brochure or newsletters being read. You should also look at ways to facilitate an easy response such as reply-paid envelopes, freephone telephone numbers or pro forma fax sheets. Many firms now offer websites with further information and some have invested in setting up modest call centres to manage enquiries.

Be creative in thinking what you might send to people that will be of value – items should be focused on specific messages or issues. Copies of articles or of speeches you have delivered, feedback or testimonials from clients facing similar situations, invitations to informal briefings or receptions, notification of books or speeches your lawyers will be preparing, could all be used.

Although there has been a tendency for law firms to produce high quality, glossy promotional materials, direct mail will work just as well (sometimes even better) if the materials are produced smartly and inexpensively in-house. Such items can often feel more immediate and personal than their glossy counterparts. They can also be tailored to specific needs, topical issues or special audiences with ease.

Direct mail can be used to communicate on a regular basis with existing clients and referrers as well – helping to build relationships, provide added-value service and keep your firm's name 'front of mind'. This is particularly cost-effective and easy to do if you employ an email alert system.

21.5.7 Public relations (including media relations)

Public relations is a broad term which covers a whole range of activities involving the firm in two-way communications with the various publics it serves. Relevant publics for probate practitioners might include existing wills/probate clients, other clients of the firm, potential clients, local referrers, the local media, existing staff, potential staff, the legal profession and government officials:

343

- *Media relations* is one of the most useful tools for probate practitioners, i.e. communications with the printed and broadcast media. Timely press releases about topical issues, offering the expert views of your leading tax, probate or private client experts, short articles providing practical advice, articles containing checklists to help readers assess their situation and 'legal problem pages' are all inexpensive (but time intensive) ways of getting your message across. You might scan the main newspapers and be ready to provide comments and advice when a high profile will or probate case hits the headlines. However, unlike advertising, the editor will always have the final say on whether your items are used and the manner in which the material is used, so you have much less control. Unless you have some experience of dealing with the media it is often useful to employ the services of someone who does – freelance press officers can be used on an occasional basis and their rates are often very reasonable. If you choose wisely you will find a public relations officer with good knowledge of and contacts within the media you have targeted.
- *Publications* are another aspect of marketing that fall broadly into public relations. You might have a firm brochure, a private client brochure or leaflets describing the services offered by your wills/probate team. Again, the key words here are 'focus' and 'benefits'. Too many solicitors' publications focus on 'we' the firm rather than 'you' the client and contain features rather than benefits. Truly client-facing publications will be written from the clients' point of view (e.g. problems, needs, questions, concerns, issues, etc.) rather than the firm's point of view (location, departments, services, etc.). Newsletters will serve a number of purposes. Whether they are general and aimed at all clients or focused on the needs of particular groups (such as private client, elderly clients, professional carers, etc.) they will:

   – alert readers to changes in the law;
   – educate them on possible needs they might have;
   – provide simple advice so that they can help themselves;
   – explain difficult legal issues in simple terms;
   – remind them that the firm is proactive and able to assist;
   – cross-sell services of the firm;
   – secure the loyalty and memory of existing or dormant clients.

- *Events* for existing or potential clients or referrers would also fall under the public relations umbrella. Some firms take exhibition or stand space at local county or town shows – an opportunity to meet, face-to-face, local people who might be clients or potential clients. Stands at trade exhibitions (e.g. for professional careers or home operators) can also be useful if targeted properly.
- *Speakers*. You might also provide 'expert' speakers to address the audiences of local business, trade or social groups. Organisations such as the

Institute of Directors, the Chambers of Commerce and Business Links are often heavily targeted by other solicitors, so seek out more unusual organisations. Similarly, you might send representatives of the firm out to network at these events, the aim being both to develop contacts that might generate or refer business in the future and also to gather vital information or market intelligence about local needs and competitors and to ensure that the firm's name appears regularly at local events.

Seminars are covered separately below.

21.5.8   Internal marketing

This area of public relations – communicating with those within your firm – is vitally important to will and probate practitioners because often other members of the firm will be an important source of referrals for you and because sometimes you may be targeting similar audiences to others in your firm.

In smaller firms it is easier to talk informally to the partners, assistants, trainees and secretaries within other departments without having to arrange special meetings or prepare lists of the services provided, the clients served and ways in which you can help each other develop business.

Internal marketing is important because you have limited resources within the wills and probate team. However, the marketing and communication load can be significantly spread if all members of your firm understand what you are offering, to whom, the relative benefits and how to 'pass across' clients or referrers with the sorts of questions or problems that the probate and wills team can deal with.

21.5.9   Organising events and networking

These again are aspects of public relations. You might consider planning your marketing on the basis of events that your firm will organise and those that others will organise but your firm will attend.

Organising events can take a huge amount of time and preparation. You will need to call upon your support staff to assist with preparing invitation lists, monitoring the response and the myriad of logistical arrangements (e.g. room preparations, catering, cloakrooms, handouts, audio-visual materials, etc.).

At the most informal level, you might invite a selection of clients, potential clients or referrers to your office for lunch or a glass of wine. This provides them with an opportunity to network with other people.

However, many people are invited to 'plain' cocktail parties and receptions so it will help considerably if you can think of something that will make your event different, for example, by having an external guest of honour or by theming the event in some way. Better still, provide a business rationale for the event: so, for example, invite a group of staff involved in residential and nursing homes to an informal round table discussion where issues of common concern (with a legal flavour but not entirely legally focused) can be discussed.

The events taking most effort are where you are presenting or showcasing your legal expertise – a briefing for small firms of accountants on inheritance tax planning, a seminar for high net worth people on future changes in estate planning. It is often better with high net worth clients to package any wills, tax and probate topics with other private client topics such as property trans-actions, trust creation and maintenance, overseas funds, etc. Inviting external speakers to your events will both increase the attractiveness to your invitees and reduce the burden on your staff of preparing materials.

Networking can be used to achieve a number of purposes and can be done at your own and other people's events. For example, you can raise the profile of the firm in the local business community or amongst a particular audience (e.g. local social services people or local GPs). You can effect introductions and start to establish personal relationships with referrers or potential clients. Networking may also be used to help develop your understanding of the needs, interests and motivations of your target audience.

Talking to people (and listening carefully to what they say) – especially potential clients – is one of the best ways to gather market intelligence. Regular attendance at the same organisation's meetings or events will increase your chances of being recognised and establishing ongoing contacts. Offering to present topical subjects or to explain complicated legal issues with a wide appeal in a simple way, and getting yourself on their speaker's platforms, will help to raise your profile. People at the events will then feel a little easier about approaching you.

21.5.10 Presentations

Typically, probate practitioners are not marketing to the end user (private clients) of their services but to other intermediaries such as doctors, social services people, professional carers, banks, accountants, surveyors, bereave-ment counsellors, etc.

After establishing contact (or, indeed, to create an opportunity to establish contact) a short presentation about a topical issue alongside some informa-tion about the credentials and experience of your firm, your team and your services will ensure the relevant information is conveyed efficiently and accurately.

Yet not everyone is comfortable making presentations and some lawyers have little experience. It is helpful to prepare audio-visual materials (whether these be pre-written sheets to talk against, overhead projector slides or PC-based presentations) to guide the speaker and provide additional interest for the audience. Advance planning and rehearsals are vitally important if the quality of your talk is not to undermine your professional skills. Summaries of talks should always be distributed, with your name, the firm's name and contact details marked discreetly but clearly on each separate sheet.

21.5.11   Process and physical appearance

These are two aspects of the service you provide that will have an impact on your marketing effectiveness.

Physical evidence covers a number of things including the appearance of your offices and meeting rooms, the appearance of your legal and support staff, the style and layout of your marketing materials and correspondence and even the type of cups you use to serve tea and coffee. As mentioned above, clients are rarely able to determine the quality of the legal advice they receive and will therefore make assumptions about the quality of advice on the basis of those more tangible things that they can observe.

Process brings us back to the product element of the marketing mix. Here you need to be concerned with aspects of case management, project control, efficiency and the use of computer systems to assist in the production and management of legal work. We know that price is often driven by costs in law firms (how many hours to do this or do that) rather than by the value perceived by the client. Reducing the time and level of skilled staff involved in processing the work will reduce the cost and increase the profitability margin.

But process is not simply a 'behind the scenes' production issue. Your process should be designed to maximise client perception and value, through regular communication, keeping them up-to-date with progress, showing exactly what legal work has been completed, and providing copies of key documents. Too often, clients are unhappy with bills because either they were not informed of progress or they were unaware of just how much work the solicitor had undertaken for them.

21.6   IMPLEMENTING YOUR PLAN

21.6.1   Developing an action plan

You have established your objectives and overall marketing strategy and the sections above should have provided you with a number of ideas about how to implement a strategy. You now need to prepare a short, clear, task-orientated action plan, assigning the names of the responsible individuals and the target dates by which the tasks will be completed.

The action plan will achieve a number of things – it will:

- ensure you select those activities which will help you achieve your objectives;

- ensure you assign priorities to those actions;
- ensure you are realistic about what can be achieved with the human and financial resources you have available;
- communicate to everyone in the probate team (and in the wider firm) exactly what is planned and their role and responsibilities;
- help you monitor progress.

An example of a suitable action plan for a solicitor in a probate department is shown below:

1 Jan.	Analyse past information about sources of work
1 Jan.	Analyse past information about nature/types of client
2 Jan.	Talk to 10 intermediaries to ask them for their views on the services provided by the team
3 Jan.	Attend two meetings with other private client practice groups in the firm to identify ways in which joint marketing can be conducted
1 Feb.	Research a list of 30 local financial advisers
2 Feb.	Research a list of the 20 nearest small accounting firms
3 Feb.	Attend a meeting of the corporate and commercial group to identify 10 high net worth directors who may be interested in estate planning
4 Feb.	Identify the main local business and consumer media and read some back copies to identify opportunities for placing articles
1 Mar.	Prepare a checklist of the sorts of legal questions most likely to be asked by old/nursing home residents and their families
2 Mar.	Prepare a short article for the local hospital about the issues surrounding relatives and enduring powers of attorney
3 Mar.	Visit the three main referrers of past work
3 Mar.	Identify two local organisations that should be targeted for networking

21.6.2 Agreeing a budget

In the view of the author of this chapter, the main cost in marketing probate services will be the time of the solicitors involved in the marketing. Firms often budget out-of-pocket marketing expenditure very carefully but fail even to think about how much time will be used and whether sufficient return on that time investment will be achieved.

Therefore, you need to prepare your budget in two parts. The first is the out-of-pocket expenditure and should cover items such as advertising (especially directory entries), postage for mailings, catering for events, membership and attendance of local events, the cost of entertaining people at lunches and dinners, the production of marketing materials such as leaflets and presentation aids (although many of these can be produced in-house at no cost by using advanced word-processing or desktop publishing facilities) and sponsorships.

As a rule of thumb, professional firms should spend between 1 and 2 per cent of their gross annual fee income on marketing and business development. Consider the overall fee income of the probate team and think about what proportion you should spend on marketing. Remember that if you have done little or no marketing in the past, you will probably need a little more cash to get you started in the first year than in subsequent years.

The second and more important part of your budget is agreeing how much time each fee-earner and support person will spend on marketing each week or each month. The action list, having broken the various marketing activities down into their component tasks, might help with the estimating.

Alternatively, you can allocate a specific amount of time each week or month for each fee-earner to spend marketing and selling. You may need to adjust your time recording system to capture and report on non-chargeable time spent on marketing. One of the main reasons why solicitors (particularly non-partners) do not do marketing is because they feel they only receive recognition and reward for chargeable time.

21.6.3 Monitoring the results

After an initial burst of enthusiasm, many law firm marketing initiatives flounder and fade away. This is often because there are no mechanisms for:

- monitoring what is happening (and taking action to ensure that it does); and
- feeding back the results and success stories to keep motivation high.

You need to monitor two parts of your marketing, the process and the results. In the early days there may be few results (it is likely to take a few months before any results materialise) so you must monitor the process. You can use the action plan to tick off what actions have been completed. You can review the amount of non-chargeable time being spent by various solicitors. You can count how many events are attended, how many mailings are issued, how many press releases or articles are produced, and so on.

Monitoring the results may require some changes to your internal systems. You need to be able to monitor additional work from existing clients or referrers and to pinpoint enquiries and work as a direct result of each marketing activity. Logging calls, enquiries, meetings, instructions, income or the amount of press coverage are all valid ways to measure the success of marketing.

However, at the end of the day the only true measure will be whether the marketing activity delivers the objectives which you set at the beginning of your planning process. That is why it is so important that you spend time ensuring that the objectives are clear and measurable at the outset.

The marketing planning process is summarised below:

- *Step 1: analysing your present situation:*

  - current work, clients and sources;
  - skills, staff and services;
  - the market;
  - pulling your analysis together;

- *Step 2: deciding what you want to achieve:*

  - setting objectives;
  - selecting targets;

- *Step 3: agreeing a strategy:*

  - position in the market;
  - packaging the product and the people;
  - pricing;
  - promotions and internal marketing;
  - process and physical evidence;

- *Step 4: implementing your plan:*

  - developing an action plan;
  - agreeing a budget;
  - monitoring the results.

21.7   SOME CASE STUDIES

The following case studies originally appeared in an article by the author of this chapter in [1997] *Gazette*, 11 June, 21.

21.7.1   Cole & Cole (now Morgan Cole)

Cole & Cole was a 30-partner Thames Valley firm with offices in Oxford and Reading. Heather Redman was the senior solicitor in charge of the four-strong probate team within the private client department. She said:

> The safe full of wills is no longer a guarantee of probate work. The increasing mobility of people means that if they have moved away they will simply request the will to be transferred. This means that initiatives such as Make a Will Week and WillAid, in which we have participated in the past, need to be very carefully assessed.

However, she was keen to point out that having analysed the source of probate work over the years it mostly comes from the firm's existing clients. An interesting discovery was that work from intermediaries was mostly from accountants, despite concerns about accountants trying to lure this work away from the legal profession.

An early marketing exercise for Heather was in segmenting her market – looking at the different types of clients and referrers and building marketing programmes that suited the needs of each segment specifically. Separating out the high net work individuals (e.g. directors at commercial clients, agricultural clients, etc.) with high value estates and more complicated will, tax and trust requirements from the lower value clients was an important breakthrough. A close liaison between those doing lifetime tax planning and others concentrating on probate matters was necessary.

Another important distinction was between marketing to existing clients and to those without prior contact with the firm. Developing programmes to reach existing clients of the firm – through articles in the firm's tax and commercial newsletters, preparing a number of plain English packages to help clients when considering enduring powers of attorney, etc., using the databases in the residential conveyancing and family departments, raising awareness internally of the services available and 'cross-selling' – is the cornerstone of her marketing success. Heather also recalls an exercise aimed at one of the intermediary segments:

> We invited the senior staff from local residential and nursing homes to attend an informal seminar designed to brief them on the range of questions, wills, enduring powers of attorney, living wills, etc., that their residents were likely to ask.

As well as establishing important referrer relationships the seminars helped Heather's team to learn more about their client's needs and perceptions – market research is a vitally important aspect of any marketing programme.

21.7.2 Mundays

The experience of Mehboob Dharasmi, private client partner at the 14-partner practice Mundays in Esher, supports Heather's views. He says:

> We used an innovative advertising campaign immediately after the election to raise awareness of possible IHT changes and we have presented talks to nursing homes and elderly clubs. We have developed inserts for newsletters of similar organisations and have produced a range of comprehensive guides helping people to understand their duties and responsibilities as personal representatives and trustees . . .
>
> But by far the most successful marketing we do is as the private client team overall which is aimed at establishing and developing relationships with a large range of intermediaries – accountants, banks, agents, and financial advisers – for whom we do a substantial amount of probate related work such as sales, etc. We do have a regular programme of informal and social events where we get together. We are also running workshops for intermediaries looking at case studies. But the main source of work remains others within the private client department, whether it is conveyancing, family or tax work.

Mehoob's firm took segmentation one stage further than Cole & Cole:

> We decided to concentrate on the higher value and more complex wills and probate work which enables us to provide a higher level of personal service – visiting clients at locations and times that suit them and taking time to explore and explain different options and opportunities. These are the clients that value a quality service, a high degree of specialisation and the back-up that a firm of this size can provide.

21.7.3 Kaye, Tesler & Co.

Michael Kaye, of two-partner High Street practice Kaye Tesler & Co., uses an innovative website to target a very different segment:

> We are targeting those in the 35–50 year age group with parents who have smaller estates – there is rarely any inheritance tax. They don't want advice – they know how to gather and distribute the estate – they want a finished product in applying for the relevant grant. [He offers a grant of probate for £185 plus VAT.] The interactive website makes them read through some explanatory material and prompts them for the information we require. This information then goes direct into our computer system so the relevant forms and documentation are produced. We state the relevant warnings and disclaimers for those with more complicated needs.

He goes on to talk about how the market will change in the future:

> People my age ask each other for recommendations. Those at university and the younger generation think nothing of getting online and seeking the information they need that way. It is a fundamental attitude and buying shift. Our site has generated enquiries and probate work. More surprisingly, it has generated a lot of enquiries from the United States (which of course we cannot service). However, the USA is a little ahead of the UK in terms of Internet use so we will be ready when the UK catches up. Technology means we can provide an efficient, interactive service that meets the specific needs of our target clients. The Internet environment means that the small firms like mine are on an even playing field with the largest firms in the country.

21.7.4 Other examples of innovative marketing approaches

Theatre sponsorship

A small practice in the West Country places a range of inexpensively produced but attractive leaflets on all its services in dispensers at a local theatre. A wills leaflet states that it has members of the Society of Trust and Estate Practitioners and that it also offers an investment management service. This is an example of integrated marketing, where the firm's sponsorship of a popular local arts venue provides: (a) an excellent opportunity to entertain clients and intermediaries in a location where there is a clear link to the firm; (b) publicity and awareness raising from the strong branding in the signage supporting the sponsorship; (c) advertisements in event programmes and (d) marketing materials on display in a location where they know members of their target audience – better off people of a slightly older generation – will see and read them.

Educational video

Kevin Ludgate, a partner at Sugdens solicitors in Huddersfield, has produced a short video called 'Making a Will – Explained' which comes complete with a glossary which explains terms such as executor, intestate, residue, trust and witness in the video case cover. He has also produced a short colour flier that he mails out to promote the video. The video is rated 18 with an explanatory statement saying 'Essential viewing for all adults in England and Wales!'. The video explains very simply why you need a will and the likely contents through some realistic examples – a young couple, a middle-aged couple and an older single woman. The feedback he has received has been excellent and he is providing the leaflets and video to intermediaries, building societies, accountants and the like.

Kevin's rationale for this exercise was that he had found from research that although people were interested in learning more about wills they were rather put off by the prospect of meeting a solicitor and the possible cost that might be incurred. A video that they could watch in their own homes at their leisure (the promotional flier says that the video is shorter than the average soap opera episode) would overcome both potential problems. He also considered that if a potential client spends 30 minutes watching a video – rather than asking him questions for an hour on general background and common issues – it would make his life easier too: a win-win situation!

APPENDIX 1

Warnings

PINK CARD: WARNINGS ABOUT UNDERTAKINGS

This is the slightly edited text of the Pink Card produced by the Law Society's Professional Ethics Division and the Solicitors' Indemnity Fund (SIF) in May 1993 to remind practitioners of the pitfalls involved in giving undertakings and to encourage good practice. If undertakings go wrong, it can cost the profession money through claims to SIF, as well as causing difficulties to the individuals involved. Most undertakings in probate work will probably relate to sales of estate property, but avoid being trapped by loose wording or otherwise into giving an undertaking, for example, to a bank, to repay PR clients' loans for the payment of IHT.

WARNING ON UNDERTAKINGS

Cost to the profession

The giving of sloppy or negligent undertakings is a considerable drain on the Solicitors' Indemnity Fund and the Compensation Fund. SIF estimate that such undertakings cost in excess of £5 million per annum. However, many undertakings may result in a liability within the deductible (i.e. excess) – exposing solicitors to considerable personal liability. Your work is made easier because people know they can rely on a solicitor's undertaking. However, it can be a two-edged sword. The wide and routine use of undertakings can result in a lack of care. The profession can no longer afford to underwrite the bill!

Remember – there is no obligation on a solicitor to give an undertaking, even to assist the progress of a client's matter.

Financial guarantees

Think twice before standing guarantor for a client – you could be personally liable for a substantial sum. There can be cases where SIF provides no cover if an undertaking is given which amounts to a bare guarantee of the financial obligations of a client or third party. Moreover, you would have no cover from SIF if you give an undertaking to a lender to repay money which you have borrowed and which you then re-lend to a client who subsequently defaults.

Be **SMART** when giving undertakings – make sure they are:

• **S Specific**

Undertakings should refer to a particular task or action which has been clearly identified and defined. Do not give general or open-ended undertakings, such as

354

an undertaking to discharge 'all outstanding mortgages on a property' or the 'usual undertaking'. Make sure that any undertaking to pay monies out of a fund is qualified by the proviso that the fund comes into your hands, and that it is sufficient.

- **M Measurable**

Undertakings should include agreed measures or steps which are understood by both parties and can easily be monitored or checked, so that there can be no dispute as to whether an undertaking has been fully discharged. If an undertaking involves the payment of a sum of money, make sure the amount is clear or that it is easy to calculate. Ambiguous undertakings will be construed in favour of the recipient.

- **A Agreed**

Undertakings should be expressly agreed by both the person giving and the person receiving them and should be confirmed in writing. They may be given orally or in writing and *need not necessarily include the word 'undertake'* – beware of inadvertent undertakings.

- **R Realistic**

Undertakings should be achievable. Before giving an undertaking consider carefully whether you will be able to implement it. If any events must happen before you will be able to implement your undertaking, it is good practice to spell out those events on the face of the undertaking. An undertaking is still binding even if it is to do something outside your control. As you give the undertaking – you can stay in control.

- **T Timed**

Undertakings should indicate when, or on the happening of which event, they will be implemented. In the absence of an express term, there is an implied term that an undertaking will be performed within a reasonable time, having regard to its nature.

General points

Costs

- Don't ask other solicitors to provide an undertaking in terms you wouldn't give yourself. This applies particularly to undertakings as to costs: it is unfair to expect another solicitor to give an open-ended undertaking to pay your costs. Be prepared to give an upper limit or agree a basis of charging.
- An undertaking to pay another party's costs is generally discharged if the matter does not proceed to completion. If you intend some other arrangement, make this clear.

Conveyancing, property and succession

- The Law Society's formula for exchange of contracts and its Code for Completion by Post contain certain undertakings. Are you sure that you and your staff really know what undertakings they are giving in a normal conveyancing transaction?

- Make sure that each of your replies to requisitions on title concerning mortgages specifies exactly which mortgages or charges you intend to discharge. Vague replies will probably result in you being liable to discharge all charges – whether you know of them or not.
- Do not give unconditional undertakings without sufficient enquiry into the amount owed on prior charges – don't rely on what your client tells you.
- If your ability to comply with an undertaking depends upon action to be taken by another solicitor, make sure that he or she will be able to comply, e.g. by obtaining an undertaking to a similar effect.
- Beware of bank 'standard form' undertakings – they sometimes go beyond what is in your control – it may be necessary to amend them.

Good management

- Principals are responsible for undertakings given by staff. Clear guidance should be given to staff, specifying those permitted to give undertakings and prescribing the manner in which they can be given. Find out how safe you are by doing an 'undertaking audit' – ask staff to check files for undischarged undertakings. Note how many have been given in a sloppy or negligent manner and calculate the size of the potential claims if things go wrong. Then introduce a system to put things right. This might be to:
  - draw up standard undertakings for use, where possible, by all fee earners, with any deviation from the norm to be authorised by a partner;
  - have all undertakings checked by another fee earner prior to being given;
  - confirm all telephone undertakings (given or received) in writing;
  - make sure that undertakings are not overlooked by:
    - (i) copying undertakings and attaching them to the file;
    - (ii) indicating on the file cover, using coloured labels, that an undertaking has been given and its date.

The Guide to the Professional Conduct of Solicitors 1999 has a chapter about undertakings (Chapter 18) which contains useful guidance – please read it!

BE SMART!

GREEN CARD: WARNINGS ABOUT PROPERTY FRAUD

The text of the Green Card is now included in *The Guide to the Professional Conduct of Solicitors 1999* as Annex 25G. It is designed to help practitioners spot and avoid involvement in fraud. Although the warning is primarily directed to conveyancing transactions, it is important for probate practitioners to be familiar with the content since many estates involve the sale of properties.

Warning signs of property fraud include:

- **Fraudulent buyer or fictitious solicitors** – especially if the buyer is introduced to your practice by a third party (for example a broker or estate agent) who is not well known to you. Beware of clients whom you never meet and solicitors not known to you.
- **Unusual instructions** – for example a solicitor being instructed by the seller to remit the net proceeds of sale to anyone other than the seller.
- **Misrepresentation of the purchase price** – ensure that the true cash price actually to be paid is stated as the consideration in the contract and transfer and is identical

to the price shown in the mortgage instructions and in the report on title to the lender.

- **A deposit or any part of the purchase price paid direct** – a deposit, or the difference between the mortgage advance and the price, paid direct, or said to be paid direct, to the seller.
- **Incomplete contract documentation** – contract documents not fully completed by the seller's representative, i.e. dates missing or the identity of the parties not fully described or financial details not fully stated.
- **Changes in the purchase price** – adjustments to the purchase price, particularly in high percentage mortgage cases, or allowances off the purchase price, for example, for works to be carried out.
- **Unusual transactions** – transactions which do not follow the normal course or the usual pattern of events:
  - client with current mortgage on two or more properties;
  - client using alias;
  - client buying several properties from the same person or two or more persons using the same solicitor;
  - client reselling property at a substantial profit, for which no explanation has been provided.

If you have any suspicions that a transaction is fraudulent, take the steps set out on the Green Card (e.g. question your client, check that the true price is included on all documentation).

Remember that, even where investigations result in a solicitor ceasing to act for a client, the solicitor will still owe a duty of confidentiality which would prevent the solicitor passing on information to the lender. It is only where the solicitor is satisfied that there is a strong *prima facie* case that the client was using the solicitor to further a fraud or other criminal purpose that the duty of confidentiality would not apply.

> **Any failure to observe the signs and to take the appropriate steps may be used in court as evidence against you if you and your client are prosecuted, or if you are sued for negligence.**

Further guidance can be obtained from the Law Society's Practice Advice Service.

BLUE CARD: WARNING ON MONEY LAUNDERING

The text of the Blue Card Warning on Money Laundering was included in *The Guide to the Professional Conduct of Solicitors 1999* as Annex 16D. In rare cases, funds in an estate or funds from the deceased's investments may be the product of money laundering. As with property fraud, the issue is more likely to arise in conveyancing work, but again it is important that probate practitioners are familiar with the content. More information about money laundering can be obtained from the address given at the end of this chapter. (See also Chapter 6.)

Signs to watch out for include:

- unusual settlement requests, e.g. cash or third party cheque;
- unusual instructions, e.g. a client with no discernible reason for using the firm's services;
- large sums of cash;
- a secretive client;
- suspect territory, i.e. an introduction from a third party based in a country where drug trafficking is prevalent.

Other training and reference materials can be obtained from:

The Joint Money Laundering Steering Group [British Bankers' Association]
Pinners Hall,
105–108 Old Broad Street,
London
EC2N 1EX
Tel: 020 7216 8800
Fax: 020 7216 8811

High street banks' charges for estate administration

This appendix gives a summary of what are understood to be the major high street banks' 2002 charges for estate administration. Practitioners are advised to confirm details and obtain fuller information from the bank concerned where necessary. Leaflets advertising banks' executorship services are available and these usually give details of definitions, conditions and any right reserved to make additional charge over and above the standard fees.

BARCLAYS BANK PLC

Setting up and responsibility fee (based on the gross capital value of the estate):
£750 plus:

on the first £250,000	3.5% plus
on the next £750,000	1.5% plus
on the remaining value	1%

Activity fee:
£265 for every relevant beneficiary
£50 for every asset

HSBC

Administration fee (based on the gross value of the estate):
For a simple case:

on the first £250,000	4%
on the excess over £250,000	1%

For an intermediary case:

on the first £250,000	5%
on the excess over £250,000	1%

For a complex case:

on the first £250,000	6%
on the excess over £250,000	1%

LLOYDS TSB

Acceptance and responsibility fee (based on the gross value of the estate, excluding joint property):

on the first £500,000	4%
on the next £500,000 up to £1M	3%
on the excess over £1M	1.5%

There is a **minimum charge** of £2,000.

NATWEST

Administration fee (charged on the gross value of the estate and normally payable on issue of a grant of representation):

on the first £250,000	4%
on the next £750,000 up to £1M	2%
on the excess over £1M	1%

There is a **minimum charge** of £1,500.

ROYAL BANK OF SCOTLAND

Administration fee (charged on the gross value of the estate and normally payable on issue of a grant of representation):

on the first £250,000	4%
on the next £750,000 up to £1M	2%
on the excess over £1M	1%

There is a **minimum charge** of £1,500.

CREST

Since July 1996 the CREST system has provided electronic settlement in shares and other corporate securities in the United Kingdom and Ireland. The system maintains electronic records of holdings and the credit available to make payments. It receives and validates electronic instructions for making securities transfers or payments. It checks that the buyer and seller have given the same instructions for the settlement of the transaction and on the settlement date CREST checks that the seller has sufficient stock and the buyer sufficient credit available to cover the transaction. Thereupon simultaneous instructions to transfer legal ownership of the security and to make payment are issued through the system to effect the transaction.

The institution of CREST has coincided with increased speed of settlement. At present trades are settled on the London Stock Exchange on T+3, that is settlement must be transacted within three days of the trade. Moreover the pressure for investors to dematerialise their holdings is growing.

The CREST system itself does not create difficulties for solicitors: the shorter settlement periods do. In particular it may be difficult to meet the deadline if a client's assets are held as physical share certificates. It is possible to reach arrangements with brokers for longer settlement but increasingly that entails higher charges.

As a result solicitors are being encouraged by brokers to dematerialise securities and to transfer them to their nominee companies to facilitate transactions. Solicitors will need to consider the advantages and disadvantages for their client and themselves of following that advice.

General guidance on various aspects of CREST appears regularly in the *Gazette*.

APPENDIX 4

The future: the work of the Probate Section

The Probate Section was launched in 1997 by the Law Society and now has 2,300 members. Since many probate solicitors also deal with other work, the Probate Section embraces a number of related areas of legal practice. It is a service aimed at all practitioners working in the areas of:

- wills and trusts;
- tax planning;
- financial planning;
- Court of Protection;
- elderly client/care planning;
- estate administration.

The Probate Section intends to give practical help to solicitors, with member benefits including a regular newsletter, low-cost local seminars, information on marketing and information technology, and a website. The Section gives individual solicitors the opportunity to have a direct say in deciding the nature of services provided to them. Members run the Section and set its agenda. Membership is open to all those holding a current practising certificate, who pay an annual fee. Recently, associate membership has been extended to legal executives and solicitors who do not have a practising certificate, but who remain on the Roll.

Historically, those members of the profession practising in probate and allied areas have been quite isolated. This, coupled with the fact that probate-related practice is still profitable, is why the area was chosen to test trial the idea of sections. Generally lawyers in this field do not meet their fellow professionals to exchange ideas and information about law and practice. This lack of contact between solicitors can in part be ascribed to the nature of the work which, unlike litigation or conveyancing, presents very limited opportunities for contact with fellow professionals from different firms and in different parts of the country. Relative isolation may have also resulted in part from the perception of other solicitors as competitors. The Law Society is keen to alert solicitors to the wider picture, having undertaken research which found that most solicitors have not fully considered the threat of competition coming from outside the profession, whether from accountants, banks or unqualified legal advisers – a threat that may in fact prove to be the greatest challenge to the profession undertaking probate-related work over the next few years.

One of the most important functions of the Probate Section is to ensure that all members are made aware of new developments in law and practice, through the provision of accessible information, thus helping to equip practitioners to meet future challenges.

If you want to join the Probate Section or make enquiries about the services it offers to members please write to the Probate Section Administrator at the Law Society, 113 Chancery Lane, London WC2A 1PL or DX 56 London/Chancery Lane or look at the Probate Section's website at **www.probatesection.org.uk**.

APPENDIX 5

Further reading

1 PROBATE AND ESTATE ADMINISTRATION

Adams, T. (1996) *Probate Practice Manual*, Sweet & Maxwell (looseleaf).
Barlow, J. *et al*. (1997) *Wills, Administration and Taxation: A Practical Guide*, Sweet & Maxwell.
Carmichael, K. S. (1996) *Ranking, Spicer and Pegler's Executorship Law, Trusts and Accounts*, Butterworths.
D'Costa, Roland (2001) *Executorship and Administration*, Cavendish Publishing.
Goodman, D. and Hall, B. (1997) *Probate Disputes and Remedies*, Sweet & Maxwell.
Halliwell, Mark (1996) *Distribution on Intestacy*, Sweet & Maxwell.
Oughton, R.D. (1997) *Tyler's Family Provision*, Butterworths.
Ross, Sidney (2000) *Inheritance Act Claims: Law and Practice*, Sweet & Maxwell.
Sherrin *et al*. (eds.) (2002) *Williams on Wills*, Butterworths.
Sunnocks *et al*. (2000) *Williams, Mortimer and Sunnucks: Executors, Administrators and Probate*, Sweet & Maxwell.
Whitehouse, C. (Gen. Ed.) (2000), *Administration of Estates*, Tolleys (looseleaf).
Winegarton, D'Costa and Synak (2001) *Tristram and Coote's Probate Practice*, Butterworths.
Wright, Cherry E. (Gen. Ed.) (1996) *et al., Butterworths Wills, Probate and Administration Service*, Butterworths (looseleaf).

2 INHERITANCE TAX

Golding, J. (2002) *Tolley's Inheritance Tax 2002–2003*, Tolley.
Greenfield, R., (2001) *Dymond's Capital Taxes*, Sweet & Maxwell (looseleaf).
Hutton, M. and Ferrier, I. (2002) *Tolley's UK Taxation of Trusts*, Tolley.
McKie, S. and Antsey, S. (2002) *Tolley's Estate Planning 2002–2003*, Tolley.
Mellows (1996) *Taxation for Executors and Trustees*, Butterworths (looseleaf, updated by Julie Anderson).
Ray, Ralph P. (2001) *Ray's Practical Inheritance Tax Planning*, Butterworths.
Wallington, R.A. (Gen. Ed.) et al. (1991) *Foster's Inheritance Tax*, Butterworths (looseleaf).

3 WILLS AND WILL PRECEDENTS

Endicott, D. (1997) *Brighouse's Precedents of Wills*, Sweet & Maxwell.
Martyn, J.R., Bridge, S. and Oldham, M. (2001) *Theobald on Wills*, Sweet & Maxwell.
Sweet & Maxwell's Express Wills (1997) Sweet & Maxwell (CD-Rom).
Taylor, E. (1996) *Parker's Modern Wills Precedents*, Butterworths.
Withers (1987) *Practical Will Precedents*, Sweet & Maxwell (looseleaf).

4 TRUSTS AND TRUST PRECEDENTS

Kessler, J. (2002) *Drafting Trusts and Will Trusts: A Modern Approach*, Sweet & Maxwell (hardback and CD-Rom).

Oakley, A.J. (1998) *Parker and Mellows: The Modern Law of Trusts*, Sweet & Maxwell.

Pettit, P. (2001) *Equity and the Law of Trusts*, Butterworths.

Withers, *Practical Trust Precedents* (1986) Sweet & Maxwell (looseleaf).

Riddall, J.G. (2002) *The Law of Trusts*, Butterworths.

Hayton, D.J. (2002) *Underhill and Hayton: Law Relating to Trustees*, Butterworths.

5 OTHER RELEVANT READING

General

Ashton, G. (2000) *Elderly Client Handbook*, Law Society.

Berry C., Bailey, E. and Schaw-Miller, S. (2001) *Personal Insolvency: Law and Practice*, Butterworths.

BMA (1995) *Assessment of Mental Capacity*, BMA/Law Society.

Camp, P. (2002) *Solicitors and Financial Services*, Law Society.

Cretney, S. and Lush, D. (2001) *Enduring Powers of Attorney*, Jordans.

Practice management, costs, client care, etc.

Boutall, T. and Blackburn, B. (2001) *Solicitors' Guide to Good Management*, Law Society.

Charlton, S. (ed.) et al. (1988) *Encyclopedia of Data Protection*, Sweet & Maxwell (looseleaf).

Garai, H. and Cochrane, P. (1997) *Managing Information*, Gower Publishing.

Frith, M. (2001) *A Solicitor's Guide to Complaints Avoidance and Handling*, EMIS Professional Publishing.

Holland, J.A. (Gen. Ed.) (1996) *Cordery on Solicitors*, Butterworths (looseleaf).

Klafter, C. and Walker, G. (1995) *Legal Practice Management and Quality Standards*, Blackstone.

Law Society, *Lexcel Practice Excellence Kit* (2000), Law Society. (All books in the kit are available separately: *The Lexcel Office Procedures Manual*, *The Lexcel Assessment Guide*).

Legal Aid Board, *Legal Aid Handbook 1998/1999*, Sweet & Maxwell.

Moore, M. (2001) *Quality Management for Law Firms*, Law Society.

Otterburn, A. (2002) *Profitability and Law Firm Management*, Law Society.

Pannett, A. (1995) *Managing the Law Firm*, Blackstone.

Porter, M. (1998) *Competitive Strategy: Techniques for Analyzing Industries and Competitors*, Simon & Schuster.

Smith, M. (2002) *Setting Up and Managing a Small Practice*, Law Society.

Stewart, H. (2003) *Excellent Client Service*, Law Society.

Sveiby and Lloyd (1987) *Managing Know-How*, Bloomsbury Publishing.

Media and marketing

Adam, L. (2001) *Marketing Your Law Firm*, Law Society.

Bown-Wilson, D. and Courtney, G. (2002) *Marketing, Management and Motivation*, Law Society.

Stapely, S. (1994) *Media Relations for Lawyers*, Law Society.

Legal writing and research

Adler, M. (1990) *Clarity for Lawyers: The Use of Plain English in Legal Writing*, Law Society.
Blake, S. (2002) *A Practical Approach to Legal Advice and Drafting*, Blackstone.
Clinch, P. (2001) *Using a Law Library*, Blackstone.
Ellinport, J.M. (1997) *Tools of the Trade: Practical Legal Writing*, Austin & Winfield.
Holborn, G. (2001) *Butterworth's Legal Research Guide*, Butterworths.
Stott, D. (1998) *Legal Research*, Cavendish.

6 JOURNALS AND NEWSLETTERS

British Tax Review, Sweet & Maxwell.
Capital Tax Planning, Sweet & Maxwell.
Personal Tax Planning, Review, Key Haven.
Private Client Business, Sweet & Maxwell.
PS: The Probate Section Newsletter, Law Society.
Tax Journal, Butterworths.
Tolley's Insovency Law and Practice, Tolley.
Taxation, Tolley.
Tolley's Practical Tax, Tolley.
Trusts and Estates, Legal Studies and Services.

7 ONLINE SERVICES

Insolvency Law Direct, Butterworths.
Trusts and Estates Direct, Tolley.
Tax Direct, Tolley.

8 LAW SOCIETY MATERIALS

Making a Will Won't Kill You. (Client information booklet.)
Personal Assets Log. (Checklist for clients.)
Questionnaire for Personal Representative Clients.
Your Will: Client Questionnaire.

The above packs and other books published by the Law Society can be ordered from good bookshops or direct from Marston Book Services, tel. 01235 465 656, email **law.society@marston.co.uk** (please check price including carriage when ordering). Free publications are available from individual Law Society departments or the website: check Appendix 6 for details and references in the text.

APPENDIX 6

Useful addresses

PROBATE REGISTRIES

Principal registry

First Avenue House
42–49 High Holborn
London WC1V 6NP
Tel: 020 7947 7000
Fax: 020 7947 6946
DX: 941 Lond/Chancery Ln

District registries

Birmingham

The Priory Courts
33 Bull Street
Birmingham B4 6DU
Tel: 0121 681 3414
Fax: 0121 236 2465
DX: 701990 Birmingham-7

Brighton

William Street
Brighton
East Sussex BN2 2LG
Tel: 01273 684 071
Fax: 01273 625 845
DX: 98073 Brighton-3

Bristol

The Crescent Centre
Temple Back
Bristol BS1 6EP
Tel: 0117 927 3915/926 4619
Fax: 0117 925 3549
DX: 94400 Bristol-5

Ipswich

Level 3, Haven House
17 Lower Brook Street
Ipswich IP4 1DN
Tel: 01473 253 724/259 261

Leeds

3rd Floor, Coronet House
Queen Street
Leeds LS1 2BA
Tel: 0113 243 1505
Fax: 0113 247 1893
DX: 26451 Leeds Park Sq

Liverpool

The Queen Elizabeth II Law Courts
Derby Square
Liverpool L2 1XA
Tel: 0151 236 8264
Fax: 0151 227 4634
DX: 14246 Liverpool-1

Manchester

9th Floor, Astley House
23 Quay Street
Manchester M3 4AT
Tel: 0161 834 4319
Fax: 0161 832 2690
DX: 14387 Manchester-1

Newcastle upon Tyne

2nd Floor, Plummer House
Croft Street
Newcastle upon Tyne NE1 6NP
Tel: 0191 261 8383
Fax: 0191 230 4868
DX: 61081 Newcastle 14

Oxford

St Aldates
Oxford OX1 1LY
Tel: 01865 793 050
Fax: 01865 793 090
DX: 96454 Oxford-4

Winchester

4th Floor, Cromwell House
Andover Road
Winchester
Hants SO23 7EW
Tel: 01962 863 771
Fax: 01962 840 796
DX: 96900 Winchester-2

Probate Registry of Wales

PO Box 474
2 Park Street
Cardiff CF10 1TB
Tel: 029 2037 6479
Fax: 029 2037 6466
DX: 122782 Cardiff-13

Sub-Registries

Bangor

Council Offices
Ffordd Gwynedd
Bangor LL57 1DT
Tel: 01248 362 410
Fax: 01248 364 423
DX: 23186 Bangor–2

Bodmin

Market Street
Bodmin
Cornwall PL31 2JW
Tel: 01208 72279
DX: 81858 Bodmin

Carlisle

Courts of Justice
Earl Street
Carlisle CA1 1DJ
Tel: 01228 521 751
Fax: 01228 590 588
DX: 63034 Carlisle

Carmarthen

14 King Street
Carmarthen SA31 1BL
Tel: 01267 236 238
Fax: 01267 229 067
DX: 51420 Carmarthen

Chester

5th Floor, Hamilton House
Hamilton Place
Chester CH1 2DA
Tel: 01244 345 082
Fax: 01244 346 243
DX: 22162 Chester (Northgate)

Exeter

Finance House
Barnfield Road
Exeter
Devon EX1 1QR
Tel: 01392 274 515
DX: 8380 Exeter-1

Gloucester

2nd Floor, Combined Courts Building
Kimbrose Way
Gloucester GL1 2DG
Tel: 01452 522 585
Fax: 01452 421 849
DX: 98663 Gloucester-5

Lancaster

Mitre House
Church Street
Lancaster LA1 1HE
Tel: 01524 36625
Fax: 01524 35561
DX: 63509 Lancaster

Leicester

90 Wellington Street
Leicester LE1 6HG
Tel: 0116 285 3380
Fax: 0116 285 3382
DX: 17403 Leicester-3

Lincoln

360 High Street
Lincoln LN5 7PS
Tel: 01522 523 648
DX: 11048 Lincoln-1

Maidstone

Law Courts
Barker Road
Maidstone
Kent ME16 8EQ
Tel: 01622 202 048
DX: 130065 Maidstone-7

Middlesbrough

Teesside Combined Court Centre
Russell Street
Middlesbrough
Cleveland TS1 2AE
Tel: 01642 340 001
DX: 60536 Middlesbrough

Norwich

Norwich Combined Court Centre
The Law Courts
Bishopgate
Norwich NR3 1UR
Tel: 01603 728 267
Fax: 01603 760 863
DX: 97385 Norwich-5

Nottingham

Buttdyke House
33 Park Row
Nottingham NG1 6GR
Tel: 0115 941 4288
Fax: 0115 950 3383
DX: 10055 Nottingham

Peterborough

1st Floor, Crown Building
Rivergate
Peterborough PE1 1EJ
Tel: 01733 562 802
Fax: 01733 313 016
DX: 12327 Peterborough-1

Sheffield

PO Box 832
The Law Courts
50 West Bar
Sheffield S3 8YR
Tel: 0114 281 2596
Fax: 0114 281 2598
DX: 26054 Sheffield-2

Stoke on Trent

Combined Court Centre
Bethesda Street
Hanley
Stoke on Trent ST1 3BP
Tel: 01782 854 065
Fax: 01782 274 916
DX: 20736 Hanley-1

York

Duncombe Place
York YO1 7EA
Tel: 01904 624 210
Fax: 01904 671 782
DX: 61543 York

OTHER USEFUL ADDRESSES

ANIMAL WELFARE CHARITIES

The Blue Cross
Shilton Road
Burford
Oxon OX18 4PF
Tel: 01993 825 500
Fax: 01993 823 083
www.thebluecross.org.uk

Cats Protection League
17 Kings Road
Horsham
West Sussex RH13 5PN
Tel: 01403 221 900
Fax: 01403 218 414
E mail: cpl@cats.org.uk

Governing Council of the Cat Fancy
4–6 Penel Orlieu
Bridgwater
Somerset TA6 3PG
Tel: 01278 427 575
Fax: 01278 446 627
E mail: GCCF_CATS@compuserve.com

Kennel Club
1 Clarges Street
London W1J 8AB
Tel: 0870 606 6750
Fax: 020 7518 1058
E mail: info@the-kennel-club.org.uk
www.the-kennel-club.org.uk

**National Canine Defence League
(NCDL)**
17 Wakley Street
London EC1V 7RQ
Tel: 020 7837 0006
Fax: 020 7689 0482
E mail: info@ncdl.org.uk
www.ncdl.org.uk

**People's Dispensary for Sick Animals
(PDSA)**
Whitechapel Way
Priorslee,
Telford
Shropshire TF2 9PQ
Tel: 01952 290999
Fax: 01952 291035
www.pdsa.org.uk

RSPCA
Wilberforce Way
Southwater
Horsham
West Sussex RH13 9RS
Tel: 0870 010 1181
Fax: 0870 753 0048
E mail: webmail@rspca.org.uk
www.rspca.org.uk

COUNSELLING AND SUPPORT

Age Concern England
Astral House
1268 London Road
London SW16 4ER
Tel: 020 8765 7200
E mail: ace@ace.org.uk
www.ace.org.uk

Age Concern Wales
4th Floor, 1 Cathedral Road
Cardiff CF11 9SD
Tel: 029 2037 1566
E mail: enquiries@accymru.org.uk

British Association for Counselling
1 Regent Place
Rugby
Warwickshire CV21 2PJ
Tel: 0870 443 5252
Fax: 0870 443 5160
E mail: bac@bac.co.uk
www.bac.co.uk

Child Poverty Action Group (CPAG)
94 White Lion Street
London N1 9PF
Tel: 020 7837 7979
Fax: 020 7837 6414
E mail: staff@cpag.demon.co.uk
www.cpag.org.uk

Counsel and Care
Twyman House
16 Bonny Sreet
London
NW1 9PG
Advice Line: 0845 300 7585
Admin Line: 020 7241 8555
Fax: 020 7267 6877
www.counselandcare.org.uk

CRUSE Bereavement Care
126 Sheen Road
Richmond
Surrey TW9 1UR
Tel: 020 939 9530
Fax: 020 8940 7638

EXIT (formerly Scottish Voluntary Euthanasia Society (VESS)
17 Hart Street
Edinburgh EH1 3RN

Gingerbread
7 Sovereign Close
Sovereign Court
London E1W 3HW
Tel: 020 7488 9300
Fax: 020 7488 9333
E mail: office@gingerbread.org.uk
www.gingerbread.org.uk

Mind
Granta House
15–19 Broadway
London E15 4BQ
Mind*info*Line: 0845 766 0163
Legacy Officer (for publications): 020 8215 2241
Email: info@mind.org.uk
www.mind.org.uk

National Association of Widows
National Office
48 Queens Road
Coventry
CV1 3EH
Tel: 024 7663 4848

Terrence Higgins Trust
52–54 Gray's Inn Road
London WC1X 8JU
Tel: 020 7831 0330
Fax: 020 7242 0121
E mail: info@tht.org.uk
www.tht.org.uk

Voluntary Euthanasia Society
13 Prince of Wales Terrace
London W8 5PG
Tel: 020 7937 7770
Fax: 020 7376 2648
E mail: info@ves.org.uk
www.ves.org.uk

COURTS

Court of Protection
Public Guardianship Office
Archway Tower
2 Junction Road
London N19 5SZ
Tel: 020 7664 7000
Fax: 020 7664 7168
DX: 114750 Archway 2 London

Principal Registry of the Family Division
First Avenue House
42–49 High Holborn
London WC1V 6NP
Tel: 020 7947 6000
Fax: 020 7947 6995
DX: 396 Lond/Chancery Ln

Royal Courts of Justice
The Strand
London WC2A 2LL
Tel: 020 7947 6000 (general)
Tel: 020 7947 6945 (probate)
Fax: 020 7947 6946 (probate)
DX: 44450 Strand WC2

GOVERNMENT

Department for Work and Pensions
Room 450, The Adelphi
1–11 John Adam Street
London WC2N 6HT
Tel: 020 7712 2171

DTI
1 Victoria Street
London SW1H 0ET
Tel: 020 7215 5000
www.dti.gov.uk

Inland Revenue (Capital Taxes)
Ferrers House
PO Box 38
Castle Meadow Road
Nottingham NG2 1BB
Tel: 0115 974 2400
Fax: 0115 974 2432
DX: 701201 Nottingham-4
www.inlandrevenue.gov.uk

You can also use the following national rate telephone numbers for the enquiry services listed below.

General enquiries about Inheritance Tax: 0115 974 2400
Share Valuation (SV) enquiries: 0115 974 2222
Customer services: 0115 974 2424
Stationery: 0845 234 1000
Forms adviser: 0115 974 2706
Heritage section Helpline: 0115 974 2488

Inland Revenue Financial Intermediaries and Claims Office Repayments (Charities)
Unit 361
St John's House
Merton Road
Bootle
Merseyside L69 9BB
Tel: 0151 472 6038

Lord Chancellor's Department
Selborne House
54–60 Victoria Street
London SW1E 6QW
Tel: 020 7210 8500
Fax: 020 7210 8549
Email: general.queries@lcdhq.gsi.gov.uk
www.lcd.gov.uk

Legal Services Commission
85 Gray's Inn Road
London WC1X 8TX
Tel: 020 7759 0000
Fax: 020 7759 1798
DX: 328 Lon/Ch'ry Ln WC2
www.legalservices.gov.uk

Official Solicitor and Public Trustee
81 Chancery Lane
London WC2A 1DD
Tel: 020 7911 7127
Fax: 020 7911 7105
DX: 0012 Lond/Chancery Ln

Treasury Solicitor's Department
Queen Anne's Chambers
28 Broadway
London SW1H 9JS
Tel: 020 7210 3000
Fax: 020 7210 3397
DX: 123242 St James Park

THE LAW SOCIETY
The Law Society's Hall
113 Chancery Lane
London WC2A 1PL
Tel: 020 7242 1222
Fax: 020 7831 0344
DX: 56 Lond/Chancery Lane
www.lawsociety.org.uk

Ipsley Court
Berrington Close
Redditch
Worcestershire B98 0TD
Tel: 020 7242 1222
Fax: 01527 510 213
DX: 19114 Redditch

Office for the Supervision of Solicitors
Victoria Court
8 Dormer Place
Royal Leamington Spa
Warwickshire CV32 5AE
Tel: 01926 820082
Helpline for clients: 0870 606 6565
Fax: 01926 431435
DX: 292320 Leamington Spa-4

Practice Standards Unit
Tel: 01527 883264

Professional Indemnity Section
Tel: 020 7320 5871
www.indemnity.lawsociety.org.uk

Probate Section
Policy Adviser: Sonia Purser
Tel: 020 7320 5691

Sole Practitioners' Group
Permanent secretary: Juliet Heasman
Tel: 020 7320 5801

You can also use the following national rate telephone numbers for the enquiry services listed below.

Central Switchboard: 0870 606 2500
Lawyer Line: 0870 606 2588
Library Enquiries: 0870 606 2511
Practice Advice: 0870 606 2522
Professional Ethics: 0870 606 2577
Public Enquiries: 0870 606 6575

REGULATORY ORGANISATIONS

Adjudicator's Office (Inland Revenue, Customs & Excise and Contributions Agency)
Haymarket House
28 Haymarket
London SW1Y 4SP
Tel: 020 7930 2292
Fax: 020 7930 2298
E mail: adjudicators@gtnet.gov.uk
www.adjudicatorsoffice.gov.uk

Advertising Standards Authority
2 Torrington Place
London WC1E 7HW
Tel: 020 7580 5555
Fax: 020 7631 3051
E mail: inquiries@asa.org.uk
www.asa.org.uk

The Charity Commission (London office)
Harmsworth House
13–15 Bouverie Street
London
EC4Y 8DP
Tel: 0870 333 0123
Fax: 020 7674 2300
www.charity-commission.gov.uk

Financial Ombudsman Service
South Quay Plaza
183 Marsh Wall
London E14 9SR
Tel: 0845 080 1800
Switchboard: 020 7964 1000
Fax: 020 7964 1001
E mail: enquiries@financial-ombudsman.org.uk
www.financial-ombudsman.org.uk

Financial Services Authority
25 The North Colonnade
Canary Wharf
London E14 5HS
Tel: 020 7676 1000
Fax: 020 7676 1099
www.fsa.gov.uk

SOLICITOR'S ASSOCIATIONS

Association of Contentious Trust and Probate Specialists (ACTAPS)
c/o Henry Frydenson
ACTAPS
Berwin Leighton Paisner
Bouverie House
154 Fleet Street
London EC4A 2DQ

Law Society Probate Section
113 Chancery Lane
London WC2A 1PL
Tel: 020 7242 1222
Fax: 020 7831 0344
DX: 56 Lond/Chancery Ln
www.probatesection.org.uk

Society for Computers and Law
Administrative Secretary
10 Hurle Crescent
Clifton
Bristol BS8 2TA
Tel: 01179 237 393
Fax: 01179 239 305
E mail: ruth.baker@scl.org
www.scl.org

Society of Trust and Estate Practitioners (STEP)
26 Dover Street
London W1S 4LY
Tel: 020 7763 7152
Fax: 020 7763 7252
www.step.org

Solicitors Benevolent Association
1 Jaggard Way
London SW12 8SG
Tel: 020 8675 6440
Fax: 020 8675 6441
DX: 41608 Balham
E mail: solben@btclick.com
www.sba.org.uk

Solicitors Indemnity Fund Ltd
100 St John Street
London EC1M 4LR
Tel: 020 7566 6000
Fax: 020 7566 6006
DX: 46601 Barbican EC1

SPECIALIST VALUERS

Central Association of Agricultural Valuers
Market Chambers
35 Market Place
Coleford
Gloucestershire GL16 8AA
Tel: 01594 832 979
Fax: 01594 810 701
E mail: CAAVAgVal@aol.com

Fleurets
Chartered Surveyors – Hotel and Licensed Property Valuers
18 Bloomsbury Square
London WC1A 2NS
Tel: 020 7636 8992
Fax: 020 7636 7490
E mail: ldn@fleuretsltd.demon.co.uk
For auctioneers, surveyors and valuers whose sole or main business is concerned with the sale and valuation of hotels, public houses and licensed property generally.

Institute of Revenues, Rating and Valuation
41 Doughty Street
London WC1N 2LF
Tel: 020 7831 3505
Fax: 020 7831 2048
E mail: enquiries@irrv.org.uk
Rating and local revenues administration; valuation for rating and general purposes; valuation appeals.

LAPADA, The Association of Art and Antique Dealers
Suite 214
535 Kings Road
Chelsea
London SW10 0SZ
Tel: 020 7823 3511
Fax: 020 7823 3522
E mail: lapada@lapada.co.uk
For established antiques and fine art dealers and related ancillary trades – fine art packers/shippers, restorers, valuers.

National Association of Goldsmiths
78a Luke Street
London EC2A 4XG
Tel: 020 7613 4445
Fax: 020 7613 4450
E mail: nag@easynet.co.uk

Society of Fine Art Auctioneers (SOFAA)
London Road
Send
Woking
Surrey GU23 7LN
Tel: 01483 225 891
Fax: 01483 222 171
Fine art auctioneers, antiques and chattels auctioneers.

Stanley Gibbons Ltd
399 Strand
London WC2R 0LX
Tel: 020 7836 8444
Fax: 020 7836 7342
E mail: info@stanleygibbons.co.uk
Valuation of postage stamps and postal history. Philatelic auctioneers.

Wildy & Sons Ltd
Lincoln's Inn Archway
Carey Street
London WC2A 2JD
Tel: 020 7242 5778
Fax: 020 7430 0897
E mail: info@wildy.com
Valuation of legal books for probate matters.

MISCELLANEOUS

British Bankers' Association,
Joint Money Laundering Steering Group
Pinners Hall
105–108 Old Broad Street
London
EC2N 1EX
Tel: 020 7216 8800
Fax: 020 7216 8811
www.jmlsg.org.uk

British Medical Association
BMA House
Tavistock Square
London WC1H 9JP
Tel: 020 7387 4499
Fax: 020 7383 6400
www.bma.org.uk

British Red Cross
9 Grosvenor Crescent
London SW1X 7EJ
Tel: 020 7235 5454
Fax: 020 7245 6315
www.redcross.org.uk

Charity Commissioners for England and Wales
Harmsworth House
13–15 Bouverie Street
London EC4Y 8DP
Tel: 0870 333 0123
Fax: 020 7674 2300
www.charity-commission.gov.uk

Clarity
c/o Mark Adler
Adler & Adler
74 South Street
Dorking
Surrey RH4 2HD
Tel: 01306 741 055
Fax: 01306 741 066
E mail: adler@adler.demon.co.uk
www.adler.demon.co.uk

Companies House
Crown Way
Cardiff CF14 3UZ
Tel: 029 2038 8588
Fax: 029 2038 0900
DX: 33050 Cardiff-1
www.companies-house.gov.uk

EAGLE (Exchange on Ageing, Law, and Ethics)
Astral House
1268 London Road
London SW16 4ER
Tel: 020 8765 7377
Fax: 020 8765 7218
E mail: moorec@ace.org.uk

Ergonomics Society
Devonshire House
Devonshire Square
Loughborough
Leicestershire LE11 3DW
Tel: 01509 234 904
Fax: 01509 235 666
E mail: ergsoc@ergonomics.org.uk
www.ergonomics.org.uk

Ergonomics and Safety Research Institute
Holywell Building
Holywell Way
Loughborough
Leicestershire LE11 3UZ
Tel: 01509 283300

General Council of the Bar
3 Bedford Row
London WC1R 4DB
DX: 240 LDE
Tel: 020 7242 0082
Fax: 020 7831 9217
E mail: GeneralOffice@Barcouncil.org.uk
www.barcouncil.org.uk

Insolvency Service
Bankruptcy Search Room
Ladywood House
45 Stephenson Street
Birmingham B2 4UP
Tel: 0121 698 4000
Fax: 0121 698 4406

Institute of Advanced Legal Studies
University of London
Charles Clore House
17 Russell Square
London WC1B 5DR
Tel: 020 7862 5800
Fax: 020 7862 5770 (Library)
     020 7862 5850 (Other departments)
E mail: ials@sas.ac.uk
www.sas.ac.uk\ials

Public Record Office
Ruskin Avenue
Kew
Richmond
Surrey TW9 4DU
Tel: 020 8876 3444
Fax: 020 8392 5286

Traceline (Office for National Statistics)
P.O. Box 106
Southport
PR8 2WA
Traceline team: 0151 471 4811

Index